St. Teresa of Avila

THE BOOK OF HER FOUNDATIONS

Marc Foley, O.C.D.

A STUDY GUIDE

St. Teresa of Avila

THE BOOK OF HER FOUNDATIONS

Marc Foley, O.C.D.

A STUDY GUIDE

ICS Publications
Institute of Carmelite Studies
Washington, DC

2011

ICS Publications
2131 Lincoln Road, NE
Washington, DC 20002-1199
www.icspublications.org

The text for *The Book of Her Foundations* is taken from the *Collected Works of Saint Teresa of Avila*, volume 3, translated by Kieran Kavanaugh, O.C.D., and Otilio Rodriguez, O.C.D. ICS Publications.

Library of Congress Cataloging-in-Publication Data

Foley, Marc, 1949–
  The book of her foundations by St. Teresa of Avila: a study guide / Marc Foley.
    p. cm.
  Includes bibliographical references and index.
  ISBN 978-0-935216-82-0
  1. Teresa, of Avila, Saint, 1515-1582. 2. Discalced Carmelite Nuns—Spain—History—16th century. 3. Convents—Spain—History—16th century. I. Teresa, of Avila, Saint, 1515–1582. a Libro de las fundaciones. English. II. Title.
  BX4700.T4F65 2011
  282.092—dc22
  [B]
                                         2010043406

Appreciation
To my dear friend Sandra Gettings,
for the many hours that she spent
helping me write this book.

Contents

Translations and Abbreviations

All passages of St. Teresa's writings are quoted from *The Collected Works of St. Teresa of Avila*, trans. Kieran Kavanaugh, O.C.D., and Otilio Rodriguez, O.C.D., 3 vols. (Washington, D.C.: ICS Publications, 1976–1985) and *The Collected Letters of St. Teresa*, trans. Kieran Kavanaugh, O.C.D., 2 vols. (Washington, D.C.: ICS Publications, 2001–2007). The following abbreviations will be used in referring to Teresa's works:

L   *The Book of Her Life* (vol. 1)

ST   *Spiritual Testimonies* (vol. 1)

S   *Soliloquies* (vol. 1)

W   *The Way of Perfection* (vol. 2)

M   *Meditations on the Song of Songs* (vol. 2)

IC   *The Interior Castle* (vol. 2)

F   *The Book of Her Foundations* (vol. 3)

LE   *The Collected Letters of St. Teresa of Avila* (vol. 1 and vol. 2)

Regarding *The Way*, *The Life*, and *The Foundations*, the first number refers to the chapter and the second number to the paragraph. Thus, (W. 3. 4.) refers to chapter three, paragraph four of *The Way of Perfection*. Regarding the letters, the first number refers to the volume of the collected letters the second number refers to the number of the letter, and the third number refers to the paragraph. Thus, (LE. 1. 15. 4.) refers to volume one, letter fifteen, paragraph four of the collected letters. Regarding *The Interior Castle*, the first number refers to the specific dwelling place, the second number refers to the chapter, and the third refers to the paragraph. Thus, (IC. 2. 4. 3.) is a reference to the second dwelling place, chapter four, paragraph three.

Introduction

Of St. Teresa of Avila's four major works, *The Book of Her Life*, *The Way of Perfection*, *The Interior Castle*, and *The Book of Her Foundations*, the last is the least read, the least quoted, the least known. Why this is so is open to speculation. Maybe it is because Teresa's teaching on prayer and the spiritual life is more systematically and fully set forth in her first three works. Perhaps, it is because readers of the *Foundations* become bored as they get bogged down with numerous names and historical details. I know that this was true for me. Consequently, I questioned whether it would be possible to write a reflective commentary on the *Foundations*. I wondered whether I would be able to find enough "spiritual" material to comment upon.

However, my misgivings began to vanish as I delved into the text. What I first thought would be immaterial for reflection became the raw material for reflection. St. Teresa grew in holiness not *in spite* of obstacles such as being entangled in lawsuits, mired down in disputes over dowries, tied up in interminable bureaucratic red tape, involved in the political infighting of the Church, and having to deal with unscrupulous businessmen, but *because* of these difficulties. All of these challenges set up roadblocks to the establishment of Teresa's foundations, but none of them impeded her spiritual growth. Quite the contrary, they were the trials through which she triumphed.

The *Foundations* is much more than a chronicle of the establishment of convents. It is a record of how Teresa *practiced* the virtues that she wrote of in her other works—charity, detachment, humility, and, most notably, patience. St. Paul

3

rightly ranks patience as the foremost characteristic of love, for authentic love requires perseverance and a firm resolution to embrace the cross with a "determined determination" (W. 21. 2.).

The *Foundations* could be subtitled "The Spirituality of the Long Haul." It chronicles fifteen long, grueling years from 1567 to 1582, during which time Teresa endured numerous trials in the process of founding seventeen convents (fifteen, which she founded personally, and two others that were founded under her direction). Teresa finished writing the *Foundations* toward the end of June 1582. And almost as if she knew that she had completed all the work that the Lord had assigned to her, she died four months later on October 4, 1582.

The *Foundations* can be read from two perspectives. It can be read as a historical account of the establishment of her convents or as a spiritual narrative. Since the purpose of this book is to make connections between Teresa's life and our own, the latter is more germane to our consideration. Teresa grew in holiness in the marketplace as much as in the cloister, perhaps even more so. *None* of us have ever been called to found a convent, but *all* of us are called to practice virtue within the fray of daily life.

This book is designed for both private reflection and group discussion. Each chapter is divided into three parts. Part one is titled Summary and Background. It is a summary of the chapter, supplemented by historical information derived from various sources. Part two contains reflections on either passages found in the chapter under consideration or on the background material referred to in the summary. Part three consists of questions for reflection.

Context

At the time that Teresa entered the Incarnation in 1535, the community consisted of approximately one hundred nuns. By 1552, the number had swelled to one hundred and eighty, and by 1565, it had increased to nearly two hundred nuns (Teresa left the Incarnation in 1562).

The women who entered the Incarnation came from every strata of society, from the very poor to the very rich. Those from poor backgrounds slept in common dormitories. Those from aristocratic families were provided with a suite of rooms, including a kitchen and often a private oratory. They also brought with them maids and cooks. One of these more privileged nuns was Doña Teresa de Cepeda y Ahumanda — St. Teresa.

The cloister of the monastery, though prescribed, was rarely observed. Frequently, the nuns visited family and friends, sometimes for lengthy periods. Also, relatives and friends could enter the cloister, some of whom even took up residence in the monastery. For example, after their father died, Teresa's sister, Doña Juana de Ahumanda, lived in Teresa's cell for nine years. Visiting in the monastery's front parlor was a daily occurrence, a pastime to which Teresa became very attached. The keeping of silence, though valued by the nuns, was difficult to maintain because of the size of the community and the constant traffic of laypeople.

The prayer life of the community consisted of reciting the Divine Office and daily Eucharist. However, there was no designated time set aside for mental prayer in the monastery's daily schedule. There are also indications that novices were not given any instruction in mental prayer. Teresa attests to this fact. She says that until she had read Osuna's *The Third Spiritual Alphabet*, she "did now know how to proceed in prayer or how to be recollected" (L. 4. 7.). The impact of Osuna's book on Teresa was immeasurable. It was as if she had found the spiritual master whom she needed. "I began to take time out for solitude, to confess frequently, and to follow that path, taking the book for my master" (L. 4. 7.).

Teresa lived in the Incarnation for twenty-seven years, which constituted sixty percent of her religious life. During this time, she grew in virtue, and God awakened within her a deep desire to live a life marked by silence, solitude, and contemplative prayer. However, Teresa's gregarious temperament was also drawn to wasting time in the front parlor, visiting friends and relatives. "I began to go from pastime to pastime . . . and I began to lose joy in virtuous things and my taste for them" (L. 7. 1.).

Teresa was torn. "On the one hand God was calling me; on the other hand I was following the world . . . It seems I desired to harmonize these two contraries" (L. 7. 17.). This struggle lasted for years. "Thus I passed many years, for now I am surprised how I could have put up with both and not abandon either the one or the other" (L. 7. 17.).

Finally, Teresa accepted the fact that she could not live the life that God was calling her to in the Incarnation. She needed a different environment, a different structure of life in which she would not be sorely tempted. "I was a nun, there was no vow of enclosure" (L. 4. 5.). "That's why it seems to me it did me great harm not to be in an enclosed monastery. For the freedom that those who were good were able to enjoy in good conscience . . . would have certainly brought me to hell, if the Lord . . . had not drawn me out of this danger" (L. 7. 3.). It is important to note that Teresa was not disparaging the nuns of the Incarnation. She was simply accepting the fact that *she* could not live the life that God was calling her to if she remained in the Incarnation. "What was a danger for me was not so much for others" (L. 7. 6.).

Consequently, in 1562, Teresa left the Incarnation where she had lived for twenty-seven years. She founded St. Joseph's convent in Avila so that she could live the life that God had called her to. It was neither Teresa's intention nor desire to found a new religious order. However, God had different plans for her. The *Book of Her Life* ends with the founding of St. Joseph's. The *Foundations* takes up the narrative of Teresa's life five years later.

The Origin of The Book of Her Foundations

In 1571, after founding eight monasteries of nuns—St. Joseph's in Avila (1562), Medina del Campo (1567), Malagón (1568), Valladolid (1568), Toledo (1569), Pastrana (1569), Salamanca (1570), Alba de Tormes (1571)—St. Teresa was ordered by her religious superiors to return to the convent of the Incarnation in Avila to be prioress. The stated reason for this decision was that the Incarnation was on the brink of financial and spiritual collapse, and someone of Teresa's caliber was needed to rescue the convent from utter ruin. While it is true that the Incarnation was experiencing financial and spiritual difficulties, it has been questioned whether they were of such a critical nature to warrant that someone should be sent there to rectify the situation. It has been speculated that Angel de Salazar, the Carmelite provincial, ordered Teresa to return to the Incarnation to further his own ends.

On May 7, 1571, Angel de Salazar made a pastoral visitation to the Incarnation. He declared that the conditions of the convent were acceptable, though there was evidence of laxity. This was also the evaluation of Pedro Fernández, O.P., the apostolic visitator from Rome, who inspected the convent the following month. So, why was there such an abrupt turnabout regarding the evaluation of the condition of the Incarnation from acceptable to critical only two months later (Teresa was appointed prioress in July 1571).

Salazar had backed Teresa's reform at its inception but wavered in his support as her foundations began to multiply.

He felt that Teresa's venture was spinning out of control. An opportunity to rein in this "restless gadabout nun" as Philip Sega, the papal nuncio of Spain, called Teresa, presented itself in 1571, during the election of the prioress of the Carmelite convent at Medina del Campo.

Because Sr. Inés of Jesus had proven to be a competent prioress, her reelection was assured. However, without consulting the community, Salazar appointed as prioress Sr. Teresa de Quesada, a nun from the Incarnation who lacked administrative skills. In protest of Salazar's appointment, the community of Medina del Campo, with St. Teresa's approval, reelected Inés of Jesus.

Salazar was so infuriated that he ordered St. Teresa and Inés of Jesus to leave Medina del Campo and return to St. Joseph's in Avila. They obeyed. However, when Pedro Fernández visited the monastery of Medina del Campo and saw that the community was depressed and disgruntled due to Salazar's appointment, he removed Teresa de Quesada from office, sent her back to the Incarnation, and appointed St. Teresa in her stead.

Salazar had been thwarted but not defeated.

Salazar had nursed a long-standing grudge against the Incarnation because years before, they had disregarded his recommendation for the appointment of a prioress. Now, he was resentful toward the community of Medina del Campo for disregarding his authority. So, how could he reek revenge upon both communities and, in the process, stop Teresa from founding more convents? His plan was ingenious.

He convinced Pedro Fernández that the financial and spiritual condition of the Incarnation was worse than they had previously thought. In fact, Salazar convinced Fernández that the Incarnation was in such a dire state that only a person like Teresa could rectify the situation. Thus, Teresa was ordered to serve as prioress of the Incarnation.

By this one appointment, Salazar deprived Medina del Campo of Teresa's presence, forced Teresa upon the nuns of the Incarnation, and put an end to Teresa's travels. So he thought. He had no idea with whom he was dealing.

Teresa was installed as prioress of the Incarnation on October 14, 1571, but not without opposition. At first, the nuns barred the door and would not allow Teresa to enter. After Teresa's installation, she asked Salazar's permission to temporarily leave the Incarnation in order to attend to her fledgling foundations that were in need of help. Salazar flatly refused.

Undaunted, and one step ahead of her foes as usual, Teresa wrote to King Philip and obtained the desired permission. With royal approbation in hand, Teresa was on the road again. She first traveled to Alba de Tormes, then to Salamanca. The year was 1573. This is where our story begins.

Teresa went to Salamanca to procure a more suitable house where her community could live because the house they were living in was damp and unhealthy. While she was there, Jerónimo Ripalda, S.J., her confessor, commanded Teresa to write a history of her foundations. He had read Teresa's *Life*, with an affixed account of the founding of St. Joseph's, and felt that it would be a great service to God if Teresa would write about the founding of her other seven monasteries. Teresa, obedient to her confessor, set to work writing the book that we are about to consider.

Prologue
JHS

1. Apart from what I have read in many places, I have seen through experience the great good that comes to a soul when it does not turn aside from obedience. It is through this practice that I think one advances in virtue and gains humility. In obedience lies security against that dread (which for us as mortals living in this life is a good thing) that we might stray from the path to heaven. Here one finds the quietude that is so precious in souls desiring to please God. For if they have truly resigned themselves through the practice of this holy obedience and surrendered the intellect to it, not desiring any other opinion than their confessor's (or, if they are religious, their superior's), the devil will cease attacking with his continual disturbances. He will have seen that he is losing rather than gaining. Also, those restless stirrings within us, which make us fond of doing our own will and which even subdue reason in matters concerning our own satisfaction, come to a stop. Those who practice obedience remember that they resolutely surrendered their own will to God's will, using submission to the one who stands in God's place as a means to this surrender.

Because His Majesty, in His goodness, has given me light to know the rich treasure contained in this precious virtue, I have striven—although weakly and imperfectly—to obtain it. Yet, often the small amount of virtue I see in myself contradicts what I just said. For with some things they command me to do I realize that such striving doesn't suffice. May the divine Majesty provide what is lacking for the accomplishment of this present task.

2. While in St. Joseph's in Avila in the year 1562, the same year in which the monastery was founded, I was ordered by Fr. García de Toledo, a Dominican, who at the time was my confessor, to write of that monastery's foundation, along with many other things; whoever sees that work, if it is published, will learn there of those events.[1] Now here in Salamanca, in the year 1573, eleven years later, my confessor, a Father Rector from the Society, whose name is Maestro Ripalda,[2] having seen this book of the first foundation, thought it would be of service to our Lord if I wrote about the other seven monasteries[3] that were since founded through the goodness of the Lord, and also about the first monastery of the discalced Fathers of this ancient order.[4] And so he commanded me to write this. It seemed impossible for me to do so because I was so busy, both with correspondence and with other necessary occupations ordered by my superiors. I was recommending myself to God and somewhat distressed for being so useless and in such poor health. Even without this feeling of being useless, it often seemed to me because of my poor health and my lowly natural inclinations that I wouldn't be able to bear doing this work. While I was in this prayer, the Lord said to me: "Daughter, obedience gives strength."

3. May it please His Majesty that this be so, and may He grant me the grace to be able to recount for His glory the favors that through these foundations He has granted this order. One can be certain that this account will be given in all truthfulness, without any exaggeration, in so far as possible, but in conformity with what has taken place. For even in something

of very little importance I wouldn't tell a lie for anything in the world. In this work that is being written for the praise of our Lord, any untruthfulness would cause me great scrupulosity. I believe that such a thing would involve not only a waste of time but deception concerning the works of God, and instead of being praised for them He would be offended. It would be a great betrayal. So that I might accomplish this task, may it please His Majesty not to let me out of His hand.

Each foundation will be expressly mentioned. And I will try to be brief, for my style is so heavy that although I may want to be brief, I fear that I will become tiresome and tire even myself. But because of the love my daughters have for me, they who will possess this work after my days are done will be able to put up with the style.

4. I do not seek my own benefit in anything, nor do I have any reason to do so, but only His glory and praise, for many things will be seen for which glory and praise should be given Him. Thus may it please our Lord that anyone who reads this will not think of attributing praise to me, since to do so would be against the truth. Rather, let readers ask His Majesty to pardon me for the poor way in which I have benefited from all these favors. There is much greater reason for my daughters to complain about this defect than to thank me for what has been done through these favors. Let us, my daughters, give all our thanks to the divine goodness for the many favors He has granted us. I ask the reader to recite a Hail Mary out of love for Him that it may help me to leave purgatory and reach the vision of Jesus Christ our Lord, who lives and reigns with the Father and the Holy Spirit, forever and ever, amen.

5. Since I have a poor memory, I believe that many very important things will be left unsaid and that other things will be said that could be omitted. In sum, the work will be in accord with my lack of intelligence and culture and my lack also of the quiet necessary for writing. They also are ordering me, if the occasion offers itself, to deal with some things about prayer and how, by being deceived, those who practice it could be kept from making progress.

6. In all things I submit to what the holy Roman Church holds, with the resolve that before this work reaches your hands, my Sisters and daughters, learned and spiritual persons will see it. I begin in the name of the Lord, taking for my help His glorious Mother, whose habit I wear, although unworthily, and also my glorious father and lord, St. Joseph, in whose house I am, for he is the patron of this monastery of discalced nuns,[5] through whose prayer I have been continually helped.

7. In the year 1573, feastday of St. Louis, king of France, which is August 24.[6] May God be praised!

SUMMARY AND BACKGROUND

The year is 1573. The place is Salamanca. Fr. Jerónimo Ripalda, S.J., Teresa's confessor, has ordered her to put in writing an account of the seven monasteries that she has founded, subsequent to the establishment of St. Joseph's convent in Avila. Teresa is bone-weary and has a deep resistance to writing. She feels that the task is too much for her. "It seems impossible for me to do so because I was so busy, both with correspondence and with other necessary occupations ordered by my superiors. I . . . was distressed for being useless and in such poor health" (F. Pro. 2.). In addition, when Teresa arrives in Salamanca, she becomes entangled in negotiations involving the purchase of a house for her community. These negotiations dragged on for years. The owner of the house was Pedro de la Banda, a slippery shyster of a nobleman, who caused Teresa a great deal of grief. "This business with Pedro de la Banda is never-ending" (LE. 1. 58. 5.). In spite of all her problems, Teresa decides to write the *Foundations*.

Reflection. Teresa's confessor was not the first person to order her to put into writing an account of her foundations. Three years previous (1570), Teresa received an imaginative vision in which God told her to make more foundations and to *write* a history of them.

> [The Lord] told me that now was not the time for rest, but that I should hurry to establish these houses . . . [He also

15

told me] that I should write about the foundation of these houses. I thought of how in regard to the house at Medina I never understood anything in a way I could write of its foundation. He told me that was all the more reason to write of it since He wanted it to be seen that the Medina foundation had been miraculous. He meant that he also founded that house, since it had seemed absolutely impossible to fund. As a result, I decided to write about the founding of these houses. (ST. 6.)

It was three years between the time that Teresa *decided* to write about her foundations and actually put pen to paper. Why did she wait so long, considering that *God* had told her to do so? Why was she procrastinating? Most likely, Teresa's situation was much like our own. She had many irons in the fire and she was overworked. At the end of the day, she was exhausted.

We all can identify with Teresa's situation. Picture yourself coming home at the end of a long, hard day at work. You plop yourself down at your desk to check your e-mail and on your desk, staring you in the face, are notes that you have written to yourself. "Make an appointment for a yearly checkup." "Buy birthday cards for Phil and Mary." "Visit grandma in the nursing home." "Give Connie a call regarding the study group." As you see these notes, you heave a sigh. You feel guilty for not attending to what you know you should do, but you just can't summon up the energy to begin. In fact, just thinking of the tasks makes you tired. So, where do you find the necessary energy at these times? Teresa gives us an answer. "While I was at prayer, the Lord said to me; 'Daughter, obedience gives strength' " (F. Pro. 2.). Once Teresa said *yes*, the energy was given.

Question. For three years, Teresa lived in limbo between a decision made and a decision acted upon. She said *yes* to God but told herself that she would begin *tomorrow*. And tomorrow turned into a week, and a week turned into a month, and a month turned into a year. The task before her was gathering dust not because it was *unimportant* but because it wasn't *urgent*. All of us are familiar with Teresa's situation. Our lives are busy. We let some things slide. The immediate duty places other important responsibilities on the back burner. We often neglect to attend to the important things and people in our lives because "we don't have enough time." In what ways can you simplify your life so that you will have more time and energy for what is truly important?

Begins with the Foundation of the
Carmel of St. Joseph in Medina del Campo

Chapter 1

On the circumstances surrounding the beginning of both this foundation and the others.

1. From what I can understand now, the five years I spent in St. Joseph's in Avila after its foundation[1] seem to me to have been the most restful of my life, and my soul often misses that calm and quiet. During those years some young religious women entered, whom the world, apparently, had already held in its grasp as was manifested in their display of its elegant and fashionable dress. Drawing them quickly away from those vanities, the Lord brought them to His house, endowing them with so much perfection that it was to my embarrassment. He did this until the number reached thirteen, which had been set as the maximum number.[2]

2. It was a delight for me to be among souls so holy and pure, whose only concern was to serve and praise our Lord. His Majesty sent us what was necessary without our asking for it; and when we were in want, which was seldom, their joy was greater. I praised our Lord to see so many lofty virtues, especially the detachment they had from everything but serving Him. I, who was the superior there, never remember worrying about the necessities of life. I was convinced that the Lord would not fail those who had no other concern than to please Him. And if at times there wasn't enough food for everyone and I said that what there was should go to those

most in need, each one thought that she could do without, and so the food remained until God sent enough for everyone.

3. With respect to the virtue of obedience, to which I am very devoted (although I didn't know how to practice it until those servants of God so taught me that I couldn't be ignorant as to whether or not I possessed it), I could mention many things that I saw there. One thing comes to mind now, and the incident came about in the refectory one day when they served us helpings of cucumbers. My portion consisted of one that was very thin and rotten inside. Secretly, I called a Sister, one of those with greater intelligence and talents, to test her obedience and told her to go and plant the cucumber in a little vegetable garden we had. She asked me if she should plant it upright or sideways. I told her sideways. She went out and planted it, without the thought entering her mind that the cucumber would only dry up. Rather, since she planted it out of obedience, she blinded natural reason so as to believe that what she did was very appropriate.[3]

4. It occurred to me to charge one of them with six or seven contradictory duties. She undertook them, remaining silent, thinking it would be possible for her to do them all. There was a well with very bad water according to those who tried it, and it seemed impossible for the water to flow since the well was very deep. When I called some workmen to dig a new one, they laughed at me as though I were wanting to throw money away. I asked the Sisters what they thought. One said that it should be tried, that since our Lord would have to provide someone to bring us water as well as food, it would be cheaper for His Majesty to give us the well on the grounds of the house and that thus He would not fail to do so. Observing

the great faith and determination with which she said it, I became certain. And, contrary to the opinion of the one who understood all about founts and water, I went ahead. And the Lord was pleased that we were able to put in a conduit which provided enough water for our needs, and for drinking, and which we now have.[4]

5. I do not present this as a miracle, for there are other things I could tell, but to show the faith these Sisters had since the things did happen in the way I tell them. Nor is it my first intention to praise the nuns of these monasteries, for through the goodness of the Lord, all of them act in this way. And of these things and many others one could write at length, and with benefit, for at times those who follow will be inspired to imitate these Sisters. But if the Lord should desire this to be known, the superiors will command the prioresses that they write of it.

6. Well now, this wretched one was among these angelic souls. They didn't seem to me to be anything else, for there was no fault they hid from me, even if interior. And the favors, and ardent desires, and detachment the Lord gave them were great. Their consolation was their solitude. They assured me that they never tired of being alone, and thus they felt it a torment when others came to visit them, even if these were their brothers. The one who had the greater opportunity to remain in a hermitage considered herself the luckiest. In considering the real value of these souls and the courage God gave them to serve and suffer for Him, certainly not a characteristic of women, I often thought that the riches God placed in them were meant for some great purpose. What was later to come about never passed through my mind, because it didn't seem

then to be something possible. There was no basis for even being able to imagine it, although my desires to be of some help to some soul as time went on had grown much greater. And I often felt like one who has a great treasure stored up and desires that all enjoy it, but whose hands are bound and unable to distribute it. So it seemed my soul was bound because the favors the Lord was granting it during those years were very great, and I thought that I was not putting them to good use. I tried to please the Lord with my poor prayers and always endeavored that the Sisters would do the same and dedicate themselves to the good of souls and the increase of His Church. Whoever conversed with them was always edified. And these were the things with which my great desires were fully taken up.

7. Four years later, or, I think, a little more than that, a Franciscan friar happened to come to see me, whose name was Fray Alonso Maldonado,[5] a great servant of God, who had the same desires for the good of souls as I, but he was able to transfer them into deeds for which I envied him greatly. He had recently come back from the Indies. He began to tell me about the many millions of souls that were being lost there for want of Christian instruction, and before leaving he gave us a sermon, or conference, encouraging us to do penance. I was so grief-stricken over the loss of so many souls that I couldn't contain myself. I went to a hermitage[6] with many tears. I cried out to the Lord, begging him that he give me the means to be able to do something to win some souls to His service, since the devil was carrying away so many, and that my prayer would do some good since I wasn't able to do anything else. I was very envious of those who for love of our Lord were

able to be engaged in winning souls, though they might suffer a thousand deaths. And thus it happens to me that when we read in the lives of the saints that they converted souls, I feel much greater devotion, tenderness, and envy than over all the martyrdoms they suffered. This is the inclination the Lord has given me, for it seems to me that He prizes a soul that through our diligence and prayer we gain for Him, through His mercy, more than all the services we can render Him.

8. Well, going about with such great affliction, while I was in prayer one night, our Lord represented Himself to me in His usual way. He showed me much love, manifesting His desire to comfort me, and said: "Wait a little, daughter, and you will see great things."

These words remained so fixed in my heart that I could not forget them. No matter how much I thought about this promise I couldn't figure out how it would be possible, nor was there a way of even imagining how it could come about. Nevertheless, I remained very much consoled and certain that these words would prove true. But the means by which they eventually did never entered my mind. Thus another half year, I think, passed, and afterward there took place what I shall now describe.

THE AWAKENING OF DESIRE

Summary and Background: Chapter 1

As Teresa begins to write her account of the six grueling years of her life (1567–1573) during which time she founded seven monasteries, she does so on a note of nostalgia, as she remembers the peaceful years that she had lived in St. Joseph's in Avila. "From what I can understand now, the five years [1562–1567] I spent in St. Joseph's in Avila after its foundation seem to me to have been the most restful of my life, and my soul often misses that calm and quiet" (F. 1. 1.).

These years of calm and quiet were a time of spiritual gestation. Because Teresa was faithful to her calling, her desires to serve God grew. "[M]y desires to be of some help to some soul as time went on had grown much greater. And I often felt like one who has a great treasure stored up and desires that all enjoy it, but whose hands are bound and unable to distribute it" (F. 1. 6.).

These desires filled her with a holy envy toward those who were able "to transfer [their desires] into deeds" (F. 1. 7.). This was especially true of missionaries who were preaching the Gospel in the New World. "I was very envious of those who for love of our Lord were able to be engaged in winning souls, though they may suffer a thousand deaths . . . This is the inclination the Lord has given me" (F. 1. 7.). One day, Teresa's desire to save souls and her holy envy turned into grief when she had an unexpected visitor.

Fray Alonso Maldonado, a Franciscan friar, who had recently returned from Mexico (1566), told Teresa "about the millions of souls that were being lost there for want of Christian instruction." Teresa said, "I was so grief-stricken . . . that I couldn't contain myself . . . I cried out to the Lord, begging Him that He give me the means to be able to do something to win souls to His service" (F. 1. 7.).

Chapter one ends with an exhortation from God to *wait*. One night as Teresa prayed, she heard a voice say to her, "Wait a little, daughter, and you will see great things" (F. 1. 8.).

Reflection. One of the great sufferings of the spiritual life is to have a desire to serve God in a particular way but to lack the means to fulfill it. "[M]y desires to be of some help to some soul as time went on had grown much greater. And I often felt like one who has a great treasure stored up and desires that all enjoy it, but whose hands are bound and unable to distribute it" (F. 1. 6.). This was also the case with St. Thérèse of Lisieux. She writes:

> Ah! my Jesus, pardon me if I am unreasonable in wishing to express my desires and longings which reach even unto infinity. Pardon me and heal my soul by giving her what she longs for so much! To be Your *Spouse*, to be a *Carmelite*, and by my union with You to be the *Mother* of souls, should not this suffice me? And yet it is not so. No doubt, these three privileges sum up my true *vocation: Carmelite, Spouse, Mother*, and yet I feel within me

other *vocations*. I feel the *vocation* of the WARRIOR, THE PRIEST, THE APOSTLE, THE DOCTOR, THE MARTYR. Finally, I feel the need and the desire of carrying out the most heroic deeds for *you, O Jesus*. I feel within my soul the courage of the *Crusader*, the *Papal Guard*, and I would want to die on the field of battle in defense of the Church.[7]

Thérèse and Teresa both had missionary zeal but were unable to be missionaries because they were cloistered nuns. Thérèse never became a priest, an apostle, a crusader, or papal guard. Yet, her desires were realized as she continued to live her day-to-day convent life. Similarly, Teresa never became a missionary like Alonso Maldonado, but her desire to save souls was realized by founding more monasteries. In short, for both Thérèse and Teresa, their desire to serve God more faithfully was fulfilled but *not in the way* that they had expected. But it was fulfilled in the way that God intended—by their *continuing* to do the work that God had begun in them.

Questions. Like Thérèse and Teresa, have you ever experienced a deep longing to serve God in a *particular way* but felt frustrated because you lacked the means to do so? Have you ever considered that you have misinterpreted *how* God wants this longing to be fulfilled? Have you considered that God is not asking you to serve him by performing heroic deeds, but rather by deepening your commitment to the life that he *has* called you to?

Chapter 2

How our Father General came to Avila and what followed from his visit.

1. Our generals always reside in Rome and none ever came to Spain.[1] So it seemed impossible that one should come now. But since nothing is impossible when our Lord wants it, His Majesty ordained that what had never happened before should come about now. When I came to know of it, I felt grieved. For as was already mentioned concerning the foundation of St. Joseph's, that house was not subject to the friars for the reason given.[2] I feared two things: one, that our Father General would be displeased with me (and rightly so since he was unaware of how the things had come to pass); the other, that he would order me to return to the monastery of the Incarnation, where the mitigated rule is observed, which for me would have been an affliction for many reasons—there would be no point in going into them. One reason should be enough: that in the Incarnation I wouldn't be able to observe the austerity of the primitive rule, that the community numbers more than 150,[3] and that where there are few there is more harmony and quiet. Our Lord did better than I had imagined. For the general is such a servant of the Lord, and so discreet and learned, that he regarded the work as good; moreover he showed no displeasure toward me. His name is Fray Juan Bautista Rubeo de Ravenna, a person very distinguished in the order, and rightly so.[4]

2. Well then, when he arrived in Avila, I arranged that he come to St. Joseph's. And the bishop[5] thought it well that he be

27

given all the welcome that the bishop himself would receive. I gave our Father General an account in all truth and openness, for it is my inclination to speak thus with my superiors, whatever might happen, since they stand in the place of God—and with confessors, the same. If I didn't do this, it wouldn't seem to me that my soul was secure. And so I gave him an account of my soul and of almost my whole life, although it is very wretched. He consoled me much and assured me that he wouldn't order me to leave St. Joseph's.

3. He rejoiced to see our manner of life, a portrait, although an imperfect one, of the beginnings of our order, and how the primitive rule was being kept in all its rigor, for it wasn't being observed in any monastery in the entire order; only the mitigated rule was observed.[6] And with the desire he had that this beginning go forward, he gave me very extensive patent letters, so that more monasteries could be founded, along with censures to prevent any provincial from restraining me.[7] I did not ask for these, but he understood from my way of prayer that my desires to help some soul come closer to God were great.

4. I was not seeking these means; rather the thought seemed to me foolish because a useless little woman as helpless as I well understood that she couldn't do anything. But when these desires come to a soul, it is not in its power to put them aside. Faith and the love of pleasing God make possible what to natural reason is not possible. And thus in seeing the strong desire of our Most Reverend General that more monasteries be founded, it seemed to me I saw them founded. Remembering the words our Lord had spoken to me,[8] I now perceived some beginning to what before I could not

understand. I was very sad to see our Father General return to Rome. I had grown to love him very much, and it seemed to me I was left helpless. He showed me the greatest kindness, and during the times that he was free from his duties he came to speak about spiritual things as one to whom the Lord must grant great favors. In this house it was a consolation for us to hear him. Moreover, before he went away, the bishop, Don Alvaro de Mendoza, very devoted to favoring those who aim after serving God with greater perfection, asked him permission for the foundation in his diocese of some monasteries of discalced friars of the primitive rule. Other persons also asked for this. Our Father General wanted to do so, but he found disagreement within the order. And thus, so as not to disturb the province, he let the matter go for then.

5. After some days passed, I was thinking about how necessary it would be if monasteries of nuns were to be founded that there be friars observing the same rule. Seeing how few friars there were in this province, making me even wonder whether or not they were going to die out, I prayed to the Lord over the matter very much and wrote to Father General. In the letter, I begged him for this permission as best I knew how, giving him the reasons why it would be a great service to God. I pointed out how the difficulties that could arise were not sufficient to set aside so good a work, and suggested to him what service it would render to our Lady, to whom he was very devoted. She must have been the one who arranged it. This letter reached him while he was in Valencia, and from there he sent me the permission for the foundation of two monasteries because he desired the best religious observance for the order.[9] So that there wouldn't be any opposition, he made

his permission subject to the approval, difficult to obtain, of both the present and the former provincial. But since I saw that the main thing was accomplished, I had special hope the Lord would do the rest. And so it happened that through the kindness of the bishop, who took up this matter as his own, both provincials gave their permission.[10]

6. Well then, being consoled in having the permissions, my concern grew in that there was no friar in the province that I knew of who could begin this work, nor any layman who desired to make such a start. I didn't do anything but beg our Lord that he would awaken at least one person. Neither did I have a house or the means to get one. Here I was, a poor discalced nun, without help from anywhere—only from the Lord—weighed down with patent letters and good desires, and without there being any possibility of my getting the work started. Neither courage nor hope failed, for since the Lord had given the one thing, He would give the other. Everything now seemed very possible, and so I set to work.

7. O greatness of God! How You manifest Your power in giving courage to an ant! How true, my Lord, that it is not because of You that those who love You fail to do great works but because of our own cowardice and pusillanimity. Since we are never determined, but full of human prudence and a thousand fears, You, consequently, my God, do not do your marvelous and great works. Who is more fond than You of giving, or of serving even at a cost to Yourself, when there is someone open to receive? May it please Your Majesty that I render You some service and that I not have to render an accounting for all that I have received, amen.

THE PASSING MOMENT

Summary and Background: Chapter 2

The *little* time that God told Teresa she would have to wait turned into months. Alonso Maldonado visited Teresa in August 1566, but it was not until February 1567 that Teresa received a faint glimmer of how her desire would be fulfilled. Fr. Juan Bautista Rossi, the General of the Carmelites (known in Spain as Rubeo), visited Avila from February 16–18, 1567.

Rossi had come to Spain for the purpose of reforming the Carmelite Order according to the decrees laid down by the Council of Trent (1545–1563). His visitation of the houses of the Carmelite Order began in Andalusia, where laxity in chastity and poverty was widespread. Rossi met with fierce opposition. The ringleaders among the friars in Andalusia were Melchor Nieto and his two brothers Baltasar and Gaspar. They and their cronies held influential positions in the Order throughout Andalusia. Melchor was a man who did not take kindly to reform. For example, when he was prior of the monastery of Ecija, he physically assaulted a friar who had been sent to the monastery to investigate abuses. What intensified the opposition of the Nieto brothers was Rossi's heavy-handed approach to reform. His actions so inflamed the situation that a riot almost broke out among the friars.

It is therefore understandable that when Rossi came to Avila, he was both relieved and edified to see Teresa's new way of life.

> He rejoiced to see our manner of life, a portrait, although
> an imperfect one, of the beginnings of our order, and
> how the primitive rule was being kept in all its rigor, for
> it wasn't being observed in any monastery in the entire
> order; only the mitigated rule was observed. And with
> the desire he had that this beginning go forward, he gave
> me very extensive patent letters, so that more monaster-
> ies could be founded, along with censures to prevent any
> provincial from restraining me. I did not ask for these, but
> he understood from my way of prayer that my desires to
> help some soul come closer to God were great. (F. 2. 3.)

These letters restricted the founding of the convents to
the province of Castile. Because of recent experiences,
Rossi felt that extending the permission to Andalusia
would be unwise.

While Rossi was in Avila, he was approached by the
local bishop, Don Alvaro de Mendoza. He asked Rossi for
permission to found in his diocese monasteries of Carmelite friars who followed the primitive rule of Carmel. Aware
of how much the friars of Castile resented his reform
measures, Rossi refused.

However, after Rossi left Avila, Teresa thought about
Mendoza's request. "After some days passed I was
thinking about how necessary it would be if monasteries
of nuns were to be founded that there be friars observing
the same rule" (F. 2. 5.). In consequence, Teresa wrote to
Rossi, asking him to reconsider Mendoza's request. This
time, Rossi acquiesced. He gave his permission that two

monasteries of friars be founded, with the stipulation that they be founded within Castile. Why the change of heart? We don't know. Perhaps it was due to the fact that he was on his way back to Rome and would not have to deal with the possible opposition of the friars.

Now that Teresa had permission, she began to wonder about the feasibility of her project. "Being consoled in having the permissions, my concern grew in that there was no friar in the province that I knew of who could begin this work, nor any layman who desired to make such a start. Here I was, a poor discalced nun, without help from anywhere—only from the Lord—weighed down with patent letters and good desires, and without there being any possibility of my getting the work started" (F. 2. 6.).

Reflection. Rossi had come to Avila to attend a meeting of the Carmelite friars and, as far as we know, had no intention of visiting Teresa's convent. Teresa was apprehensive about inviting him to St. Joseph's since her new foundation was not under the jurisdiction of the Order but that of the local bishop. Teresa was afraid that Rossi would "order [her] to return to the monastery of the Incarnation" (F. 2. 1.). Human prudence would dictate that Teresa should play it safe. However, she took an incredible risk and invited Rossi to St. Joseph's.

What if she had listened to her fears? It is possible that Teresa could have remained in St. Joseph's for the rest of her life without founding any more monasteries of nuns or friars. How different the Church would have been if she had given in to her fears.

Teresa ends chapter two with the following prayer. "O greatness of God! How you manifest Your power in giving courage to an ant! How true, my Lord, that it is not because of You that those who love You fail to do great works but because of our own cowardice and pusillanimity. Since we are never determined, but full of human prudence and a thousand fears, You, consequently, my God, do not do your marvelous and great works" (F. 2. 7.).

This prayer was written from a distance of seven years and seven foundations of nuns and one foundation of friars *after* she took the risk of talking to Rossi. In light of this fact, we may consider it a backward glance upon a major crossroad in her life. One can imagine Teresa musing upon what her life would have been, if she had given in to her fears.

There are certain opportunities in life that will never come again. Rossi's presence in Avila was one of them. He stayed in Avila for only two days. What if Teresa had hesitated too long? Yes, she would have continued to live a holy life in St. Joseph's but possibly with bitter regret. What if her fear had prevented her from taking advantage of Rossi's presence which was "the *means* to be able to do something to win souls" (F. 1. 7.) for which she had prayed? How true are the words of the poet, "For all sad words of tongue or pen, The saddest are these, It might have been."[11]

St. Thomas Aquinas writes that pusillanimity "can be considered in reference to its *effect*, which is to shrink from the great things of which one is worthy" (II. II. q. 133. a. 2.) (italics added). The emotional effect of shrinking from making certain life choices is regret. Regret is the searing juxtaposition between *what is* and *what might have been.*

Many of us have regretted taking wrong turns in life or have mourned roads not taken. The reasons for our choices vary—fear, laziness, carelessness, procrastination. However, the effect is the same—our lives are different than they might have been.

Questions. One day as Jesus was "leaving Jericho," two blind beggars, who were sitting on the roadside, "heard that Jesus was passing by." They were scolded by the crowd to keep quiet. However, they shouted all the louder, "Lord, Son of David, have pity on us" (Mt 20:29). Jesus stopped and cured their blindness.

What if the blind men had allowed themselves to be intimidated by the crowd and had hesitated, even for a moment? Jesus was *passing by*; he was *leaving* Jericho. He would soon be out of earshot, never to return.

Opportunities can be lost forever. Have you ever regretted a missed opportunity? Have you ever mourned what might have been? At this time in your life, is fear preventing you from recognizing and seizing an opportunity to do the will of God? Are you going to let Jesus pass by *again*?

Chapter 3

The circumstances surrounding the foundation of the monastery of St. Joseph in Medina del Campo.

1. While I was having all these concerns, the thought came to me to ask help from the Fathers of the Society, for they were well accepted in that place, that is, in Medina. As I have written in my account of the first foundation, they guided my soul for many years. I always feel especially devoted to them because of the great good they did for it.[1] I wrote to the rector in Medina about what our Father General had ordered me to do. The rector happened to be the one who had been my confessor for many years, whom I mentioned, although I did not give his name. His name is Baltasar Alvarez, and at present he is provincial.[2] He and the others said they would do what they could about the matter. They thus did a great deal to secure permission from the people and the bishop,[3] for since the monastery is to be founded in poverty, permission is everywhere difficult to obtain. So there was a delay of several days in the negotiations.

2. A priest went there to attend to these negotiations. He was a good servant of God, very detached from all worldly things and much dedicated to prayer. He was the chaplain in the monastery where I lived. The Lord gave him the same desires that He gave me, and so I was helped very much by him, as will be seen further on. His name is Julián de Avila.[4]

Well, now that I had the permission, I didn't have a house or a penny to buy one with. Furthermore, how could a poor wanderer like myself get credit for a loan unless the Lord would give it? The Lord provided that a very virtuous young lady, who because of lack of room could not enter St. Joseph's, heard that another house was being founded and came to ask if I would accept her in the new one. She had some money which was very little and not enough to buy a house but enough to rent one and to help with the travel expenses.[5] And so we found one to rent. Without any more support than this and with our Father Chaplain, Julián de Avila, we left Avila. Besides myself, there were two nuns from St. Joseph's and four from the Incarnation, the monastery of the mitigated rule where I stayed before St. Joseph's was founded.[6]

3. When our intention became known in the city, there was much criticism. Some were saying I was crazy; others were hoping for an end to that nonsense. To the bishop — according to what he told me later — the idea seemed very foolish. But he didn't then let me know this; neither did he hinder me, for he loved me much and didn't want to hurt me. My friends said a great deal against the project. But I didn't pay much attention to them. For that which to them seemed doubtful, to me seemed so easy that I couldn't persuade myself that it would fail to be a true success.

Before we left Avila, I wrote to a Father of our order, Fray Antonio de Heredia,[7] asking him to buy me a house, for he was then prior at St. Anne's, the monastery of friars of our order in Medina. He spoke of the matter to a lady who was devoted to him,[8] for she had a house that had completely collapsed except for one room. The house was situated in a fine location. She was so good she promised to sell the house and so they came to an agreement without her asking for any surety or binding force other than his word. If she had asked for any, we would have had no resources. The Lord was arranging everything. This house was so tumble-down that we had rented another to live in while it was being repaired, for there was much to do on it.

4. Well, on the first day, as nightfall was approaching and we were entering Arévalo and tired because of our bad provisions for traveling, a priest friend of ours who had lodging for us in the home of some devout women came to out to meet us. He told me in secret that we didn't have a house because the one rented was near a monastery of Augustinian friars who resisted our coming and that a lawsuit would be unavoidable.[9] Oh, God help me! When You, Lord, want to give courage, how little do all contradictions matter! Rather, it seems I am encouraged by them, thinking that since the devil is beginning to be disturbed the Lord will be served in that monastery. Nonetheless, I told the priest to be quiet about it so as not to disturb my companions; especially two of them from the Incarnation, for the others would suffer any trial for me. One of these two was then subprioress there,[10] and the two did much to impede the departure. They were both from good families and were coming against their will because what we were doing seemed absurd to everyone. Afterward I saw that they were more than right. For when the Lord is pleased that I found one of these houses, it seems that until after the foundation is made my mind doesn't admit any reason that would seem sufficient to set the work aside. After the deed is done, all the difficulties come before me together, as will be seen later.

5. When we reached our lodging place, I learned that in the town was a Dominican friar, a very great servant of God, to whom I had confessed during the time that I was

in St. Joseph's. Because in writing of that foundation I spoke much about his virtue, I will mention here no more than his name. Fray Maestro Domingo Báñez.[11] He is very learned and discreet. By his opinion I was guided, and in his opinion the foundation was not as troublesome as it seemed to others. The person who knows God better does God's work more easily. And from some of the favors that he knew His Majesty granted me and from what he had seen in the foundation of St. Joseph's, everything seemed to him to be very possible. It was a great consolation to me when I saw him, for with his favorable opinion it seemed to me everything would turn out all right. Well, when he came to see me, I told him in strict secrecy of my plan. To him it seemed that we could bring the matter with the Augustinians to a quick conclusion. But any delay was hard for me to bear because I didn't know what to do with so many nuns. And thus, because inside the lodging place the nuns had been told of the situation, we all passed the night with much apprehension.

6. The first thing in the morning the prior of our order, Fray Antonio, arrived and said that the house he had made an agreement to buy was adequate and had an entrance way which if adorned with some hangings could be made into a little church. We decided to move into that house. At least to me the idea seemed very good, for whatever could be done more quickly is what suited us best since we were outside our monasteries. And also I feared some opposition, since I learned through experience from the first foundation. Thus I desired that we take possession of the house before our intentions be made known, and so we determined to do this at once. Our Father Master Fray Domingo, agreed.

7. We arrived in Medina del Campo on the eve of our Lady's feast in August at twelve midnight. We dismounted at the monastery of St. Anne's so as not to make noise and proceeded to the house on foot. It was by the great mercy of God that we were not struck by any of the bulls being corralled at that hour for the next day's run. We were so engrossed in what we were doing that we didn't pay any attention. However, the Lord, who always takes care of those who seek to serve Him (and indeed, that's what we were trying to do), kept us from being harmed.

8. When we arrived at the house, we entered the courtyard. The walls looked to me to be quite dilapidated, but not as dilapidated as they looked when daylight came. It seems the Lord wanted that blessed Father to be blinded and thus unable to see that the place was not suitable for the Blessed Sacrament. When we saw the entrance way, it was necessary to clear away the dirt since overhead was nothing but a rustic roof of bare tile. Because the walls were not plastered, the night almost over, and all we had were some blankets—I believe there were three—which for the whole length of the entrance way were nothing, I didn't know what to do. For I saw that the place wasn't suitable for an altar. It pleased the Lord, who wanted the place to be prepared immediately, that the butler of that lady who was the owner had at her house many tapestries belonging to her and a blue damask bed-hanging; and the lady had told him to give us whatever we wanted, for she was very good.

9. When I saw such nice furnishings, I praised the Lord, and so did the others—although we didn't know what to do for nails, nor was it the hour for buying them. We began to

look in the walls. Finally, through much effort, a supply was found. With some of the men hanging the tapestries, and we cleaning the floor, we worked so quickly that when dawn came the altar was set up, and the little bell placed in a corridor; and immediately Mass was said. Having Mass was sufficient in order to take possession. But not knowing this, we reserved the Blessed Sacrament,[12] and through some cracks in the door that was in front of us, we attended the Mass, for there was no place else for us to do so.

10. Up to this point I was very happy because for me it is the greatest consolation to see one church more where the Blessed Sacrament is preserved. But my happiness did not last long. For when Mass was finished I went to look a little bit through a window at the courtyard, and I saw that all the walls in some places had fallen to the ground and that many days would be required to repair them. Oh, God help me! When I saw His Majesty placed in the street, at a time so dangerous, on account of those Lutherans,[13] as this time in which we now live, what anguish came to my heart!

11. To this anguish were joined all the difficulties that those who had strongly criticized the project could bring up. I understood clearly that those persons were right. It seemed impossible for me to go ahead with what had been begun. Just as previously everything seemed easy to me when I reflected that I was doing it for God, so now my temptation constricted the Lord's power to such an extent that it didn't seem I had received any favor from Him. Only my lowliness and my powerlessness did I have before me. Well now, supported by something so miserable, what success could I hope for? Had I been alone, I think I could have suffered the situation. But

to think that my companions, after the opposition with which they had left, had to return to their houses was a painful thing to bear. Also, it seemed to me that since this first attempt had gone wrong, everything that I had understood I must do for the Lord in the future would not come about. Then, in addition, came the fear concerning whether or not what I understood in prayer was an illusion. This latter was not the least suffering but the greatest, for I had the strongest fear of being deceived by the devil.

O my God, what a thing it is to see a soul when You desire to abandon it to suffering! Indeed, when I recall this affliction and some others that I have had in the course of making these foundations, it doesn't seem to me that bodily trials, even though great, are anything in comparison.

12. With all this anguish that kept me truly depressed, I didn't let my companions know anything because I didn't want to cause them more distress than they already had. I suffered with this trial until evening, for then the rector of the Society sent a Father to see me who greatly encouraged and comforted me. I didn't tell him all my sufferings but only those which I felt at seeing us on the street. I began to speak of his finding us a house to rent, cost what it would cost, so that we could move to another one while this one was being repaired. And I began to console myself in seeing the many people who came, and that none of them had any thought that what we did was foolish, which was mercy from God, for it would have been very right if the Blessed Sacrament had been taken away from us. Now I think back on my foolishness and how no one thought of consuming the Eucharist, though it seemed to me that if it had been consumed, everything would have been undone.

13. Despite our great efforts, no house for rent was found in the whole area. This made me suffer through very painful nights and days. Even though I put some men in charge of always keeping watch over the Blessed Sacrament, I was worried that they might fall asleep. So I rose during the night to watch it through a window, for the moon was very bright and I could easily see it. Many people came during all those days, and not only did they fail to perceive this as wrong but they were stirred to devotion to see our Lord once again in the stable. And His Majesty, as one who never tires of humiliating Himself for us, didn't seem to want to leave it.

14. After eight days had passed, a merchant who lived in a very nice house,[14] told us when he saw our need that we could live on the upper floor of his house and stay there as though in our own. It had a large gilded room that he gave us for a church. And a lady who lived next to the house that we bought, whose name was Doña Elena de Quiroga, a great servant of God, told me she would help so that construction of a chapel for the Blessed Sacrament could be immediately started, and also accommodations made so that we could observe the rule of enclosure. Others gave us many alms for food, but this lady was the one who aided me most.[15]

15. Now with this I began to calm down because we were able to keep strict enclosure, and we began to recite the Hours. The good prior hurried very much with the repair of the house, and he suffered many trials. Nonetheless, the work took two months. But the house was repaired in such a way that we were able to live there in a reasonably good manner for several years. Afterward, our Lord continued bringing about improvements for it.

16. While in Medina, I was still concerned about the monasteries for friars, and since I didn't have any, as I said,[16] I didn't know what to do. So I decided to speak about the matter very confidentially with the prior there[17] to see what he would counsel me, and this I did. He was happy to know of it and promised me he would be the first. I took it that he was joking with me and told him so. For although he was always a good friar, recollected, very studious, and fond of his cell—in fact, he was a learned man—it didn't seem to me he was the one for a beginning like this. Neither would he have the courage or promote the austerity that was necessary, since he was fragile and not given to austerity. He assured me very much and asserted that for many days the Lord had been calling him to a stricter life. Thus he had already decided to go to the Carthusians, and they had already told him they would accept him. Despite all this, I was not completely satisfied. Although I was happy to hear what he said, I asked that we put it off for a while and that he prepare by putting into practice the things he would be promising. And this he did, for a year passed and during that year so many trials and persecutions from many false accusations came upon him that it seems the Lord wanted to test him. He bore it all so well and was making such progress that I praised our Lord, and it seemed to me His Majesty was preparing him for the new foundation.

17. A little later it happened that a young Father came there who was studying at Salamanca. He came along with another, as his companion, who told me great things about the life this Father was leading. The young Father's name was Fray John of the Cross.[18] I praised our Lord. And when I spoke with this young friar, he pleased me very much. I learned from him

how he also wanted to go to the Carthusians. Telling him what I was attempting to do, I begged him to wait until the Lord would give us a monastery and pointed out the great good that would be accomplished if in his desire to improve he were to remain in his own order and that much greater service would be rendered to the Lord. He promised me he would remain as long as he wouldn't have to wait long. When I saw that I already had two friars to begin with, it seemed to me the matter was taken care of; although I still wasn't so satisfied with the prior, and thus I waited a while, and waited also for the sake of finding a place where they could begin.

18. The nuns were gaining esteem in the town and receiving much affection. In my opinion, rightly so, for they were not interested in anything else than how each one could serve our Lord more. In all matter they lived the same way as at St. Joseph's in Avila since the rule and constitutions were the same.

The Lord began to call some women to receive the habit, and the favors He gave them were so great that I was amazed. May He be ever blessed, amen. In order to love, it doesn't seem that He waits for anything else than to be loved.

MEDINA DEL CAMPO (1567)

Summary and Background: Chapter 3

"Here I was, a poor discalced nun, without help from anywhere—only from the Lord—weighed down with patent letters and good desires, and without there being any possibility of my getting the work started" (F. 2. 6.). These words reflect Teresa's dread of founding a new monastery. Memories of the great obstacles and fierce opposition that she had encountered in founding St. Joseph's in Avila must have overwhelmed her as she thought of undertaking a similar venture. However, after she overcame her initial reaction, Teresa wasted no time getting down to work.

First, she decided that her new monastery would be founded in poverty; that is, it would not accept a benefice from a rich benefactor as the means of ensuring its livelihood. Rather, it would live on alms and money procured through the labor of the nuns. In short, it would rely upon Divine Providence. This was Teresa's ideal. However, if this ideal was to become a reality, practical considerations had to be taken into account.

First, the monastery had to be founded in a locale where the populace could support the community. This was probably the reason why Teresa decided upon the city of Medina del Campo, an affluent center of commerce, with a population of 16,000. Second, Teresa knew that she could not undertake this venture alone. In this regard,

Teresa had connections in Medina del Campo. Or as we say, "She had people."

First, there was Fr. Antonio de Heredia, the former prior of the Carmelite monastery in Avila, who had been instrumental in founding St. Joseph's convent. He was now the prior of the monastery in Medina del Campo. Second, Fr. Baltasar Alvarez, S.J., Teresa's former confessor, was stationed in Medina as novice master of the Jesuits. Both played an active role in obtaining the necessary permissions from the local authorities for the monastery to be established. This proved to be no easy task, "for since the monastery is to be founded in poverty, permission is everywhere difficult to obtain" (F. 3. 1.).

The source of the difficulty lay in the fact that a monastery founded in poverty would place a financial strain on the city. Medina del Campo was overflowing with monasteries and convents, and the last thing that it wanted was a community of nuns begging for alms. In consequence, there was much opposition to Teresa's venture among the populace. This opposition was shared by the Augustinian friars.

Fr. Antonio arranged to rent temporary lodgings for the nuns until the house he had purchased could be renovated. However, the owner of the rented lodgings reneged on his agreement, because the Augustinians, whose monastery was adjacent to his house, had threatened to bring a lawsuit against the owner. The last thing that the Augustinians wanted was a group of nuns competing for their alms.

News of the threat of the lawsuit reached Teresa in Arévalo, as she was traveling from Avila to Medina. She and her six companions, accompanied by Fr. Julián, the chaplain of St. Joseph's, had left Avila the previous day. Teresa felt that she could not return to Avila. Fr. Julián recounted similar fears. "When I heard this and remembered the fanfare with which we left Avila, I thought of the laughter and mockery that would greet her on her return."[19] However, where would Teresa and her companions stay if they went forward to Medina del Campo?

That night, after prayer and at the prompting of Domingo Bañez, her former Dominican confessor, Teresa decided to go forward to Medina del Campo and to stay in the house that had been purchased by Fr. Antonio. Antonio told Teresa that the house needed a *few minor repairs* but that these could be taken care of after they had settled in. However, Antonio's optimistic presentation of the house did not correspond to objective reality. The house was in shambles.

Teresa and her companions arrived on the outskirts of town in the dead of night. They dismounted from their creaky wagons, and laden down with what looked like the spoils of a church—candlesticks, vestments, and sacred vessels—they proceeded on foot, lest they awaken the townsfolk and rouse their ire. Fr. Julián chronicled, "We looked like gypsies who had been robbing some church, and certainly, if the police had come upon us, they would have had to take us to the jail until they ascertained where priests, friars, and nuns were going at that hour. What a picture!"[20]

Having safely arrived at their destination, the wearied band immediately cleared away the rubbish that cluttered the floor of their dilapidated dwelling, erected an altar, celebrated the Eucharist, and reserved the Blessed Sacrament. The reason for such haste was Teresa's erroneous belief in what might be termed canonical "squatter's rights." Teresa thought that a foundation was made secure only after the Blessed Sacrament had been reserved. It was years later that she discovered her error.

Reflection. In Arévalo, when Teresa was informed about the opposition of the Augustinians, she decided to keep the information to herself. "I told the priest to be quiet about it so as not to disturb my companions; especially two of them [Isabel Arias and Teresa de Quesada] from the Incarnation, [who] did much to impede the departure. They were both from good families and were coming against their will because what we were doing seemed absurd to everyone" (F. 3. 4.). Teresa believed that sharing the news of the opposition would only deepen Isabel Arias's and Teresa de Quesada's resistance. She did not want to provide them with information that they could use to influence the group to abandon the plan to found a community in Medina del Campo.

Not Adding Fuel to the Fire. In the Book of Numbers, the Israelites stand at a crucial crossroads of their journey. The Promised Land of Canaan is before them. Moses sends out scouts to reconnoiter the land. The scouts return and tell the people that Canaan is indeed a land flowing with milk and honey. However, the majority of the scouts also tell the Israelites that the people who inhabit Canaan are fierce and that they live in fortified cities. "So they spread discouraging reports among the Israelites . . . At this the whole community broke out with loud cries, and even in the night the people wailed" (Nm 13:32). However, two of the scouts, Caleb and Joshua, voiced a different opinion. They also saw the obstacles that stood in the way of conquering the land of Canaan; nevertheless, they encouraged the people to go forward, putting their trust in God.

The success or failure of a great enterprise often hinges upon our perception of the road that lies ahead. If the prospects of success are discouraging, depressing, or frightening, we are likely to turn back. The Israelites might never have entered the Promised Land if they had acted upon their fears.

Isabel Arias and Teresa de Quesada most likely would have spread discouraging reports among their companions if they had gotten wind of what had happened in regard to the Augustinians in Medina del Campo because they "did much to impede the departure" (F. 3. 4.).

What was the form of their opposition? How did they try to obstruct or impede the new venture? We do not know. However, we do have a clue. Teresa writes, "They were both from good families and were coming against their will because what we were doing seemed absurd to everyone" (F. 3. 4.). It is not hard to imagine both Isabel and Teresa predicting disaster at every turn. "It just won't work. How are we going to finance the project? Even the bishop thinks that this is crazy. Remember the uproar when St. Joseph's was founded?" Negative attitudes are contagious; prophecies of doom can fill people with fear and dread. The last thing that St. Teresa needed was to provide her two naysayers with ammunition.

However, there was another reason why Teresa withheld the threat of the possible lawsuit from her companions—*Charity.*

Charity. Currently, I am the prior of our monastery in Washington, D.C. About a year ago, Br. Bryan Paquette, the community's procurator, told me that a computer mishap had occurred and that the monastery's entire mailing list had been deleted. Since this list is used for mailing our newsletter, which is a major source of donations, losing the list would have resulted in a great financial loss.

Bryan called "Geeks on Wheels" to the rescue, and within a couple of days, our mailing list was retrieved. However, it was only *after* the list had been retrieved that Br. Bryan told me what had happened. He said, "I didn't want to tell you until things were fixed because you could have done nothing about the situation except worry." Informing me about a situation over which I was powerless would have accomplished nothing. Yes, I would have worried, and to what purpose? I was very thankful for Bryan's charity.

We see this form of charity in the second reason why Teresa withheld the information about the possible lawsuit.

Teresa was concerned about increasing the fears of two other companions who were easily frightened. What good would it have done to inform them about the opposition of the Augustinians? To do so would have only robbed them of a good night's sleep. "I told the priest to be quiet about it so as not to disturb my companions" (F. 3. 4.).

There are several important questions that we should consider in a choice whether to reveal or conceal information. What will be the effect of this information on others? What purpose will it serve? Why am I sharing it? Do I have the capacity to keep information to myself? Do I have an ulterior motive for sharing information? Let us consider this last question.

Imagine yourself being a member of Teresa's band. You have inadvertently become aware of the situation in Medina del Campo. You are also aware of the opposition of Isabel Arias and Teresa de Quesada. Furthermore, you know that two other traveling companions are fearful by nature. What do you do with the information? Do you keep it to yourself or do you tell your companions? And *why* do you tell them? What issues are involved? Let's explore a couple of possible scenarios.

Let us say that what you have just discovered about the situation in Medina del Campo makes you very anxious. You feel in conflict with yourself. You believe that founding this new monastery is part of God's plan, but you are afraid to go forward. All you want to do is to go back home to St. Joseph's in Avila, but you would feel guilty if by voicing your fears you might persuade St. Teresa to do so. Would you not be tempted to tell Isabel Arias and Teresa de Quesada what you have discovered in the *hope* that *they* would cause such a commotion that St. Teresa would decide to return to Avila?

Let us consider another scenario involving the two fearful nuns. Because these nuns are fearful and timid by nature, you have noticed that many people try to shield them from the harshness of life. This behavior has engendered a secret resentment in you. In consequence, you harbor a grudge against these two nuns. Why should they be protected from their fears? Why should they get a good night's sleep, while I will be tossing and turning all night, worrying about whether or not we will be going to Medina del Campo the next day? It's about time that they grew up and faced reality.

Such are your thoughts and feelings. Now, you have to make a decision. Do you keep the information to yourself or do you share it with these two nuns?

Questions. When we live and work with people long enough, we come to know what makes them afraid. Have you ever shared information with someone *knowing* that it will frighten them? What are the spiritual consequences to your soul for doing so? Have you ever shared information with the ulterior motive of having other people do your "dirty work"?

Chapter 4

Treats of some favors the Lord grants to the nuns of these monasteries and gives counsel to the prioresses about the attitude one should have toward these nuns.[1]

1. Since I do no know how much time on this earth the Lord will still give me, or how much opportunity to write, and since now it seems I have a little time, I thought that before I go further I should give some counsels to prioresses. Through these, the prioresses will learn both to understand themselves and to guide their subjects so that the souls of these latter will receive greater benefit, even though with less satisfaction.

It should be noted that, when they ordered me to write about these foundations, seven monasteries (leaving aside the first one, St. Joseph's in Avila, of which I wrote at that time) had been founded by the Lord's favor. This takes us up to the foundation of Alba de Tormes, which is the last of them. The reason that more have not been established is that my superiors have tied me down to something else, as will be seen later.[2]

2. Well, in observing what has been happening spiritually during these years in these monasteries, I have seen the need for what I want to say. May it please our Lord that I may manage to do so in accordance with what I see is necessary. If the spiritual experiences are not counterfeit, it's necessary that souls not be frightened. For as I have mentioned in other places, in some little things I've written for the Sisters,[3] if we proceed with a pure conscience and obediently, the Lord will never permit the devil to have enough influence to deceive

harmfully our souls; on the contrary, the devil himself is the one who is left deceived. And since he knows this, I don't believe he does as much harm as our imagination and bad humors do, especially if there is melancholy; for the nature of women is weak, and the self-love that reigns in us is very subtle. Thus many persons have come to me, both men and women, together with the nuns of these houses, who I have clearly discerned were often deceiving themselves without wanting to do so. I really believe that the devil must be meddling so as to trick us. But I have seen very many, as I say, whom the Lord in His goodness has not let out of His hand. Perhaps He wants to exercise them through these deceptions they undergo so that they might gain experience.

3. Things pertaining to prayer and perfection are, because of our own sins, so discredited in the world that it's necessary for me to explain myself the way I do. If even without seeing danger people fear to walk this path of prayer, what would happen if we mentioned some of the danger? Although, truthfully, there is danger in everything, and, while we live, we have to proceed with fear and ask the Lord to teach us and not abandon us. But, as I believe I once said,[4] if some danger can be lacking, there is much less of it for those who turn their thoughts more to God and strive for perfection in their lives.

4. Since, my Lord, we see that You often free us from the dangers in which we place ourselves, even in opposition to You, how can one believe that You will fail to free us when we aim after nothing more than to please You and delight in You? Never can I believe this! It could be that because of other secret judgments God might permit some things that must happen anyway. But good never brought about evil. Thus, may what

I have said help us strive to walk better along the road so as to please our Spouse more and find Him sooner, but not make us abandon it; and encourage us to walk with fortitude along a road that has such rugged mountain passes, as does that of this life, but not intimidate us from walking through them. For, in the final analysis, by proceeding with humility, through the mercy of God, we will reach that city of Jerusalem, where all that has been suffered will be little, or nothing, in comparison with what is enjoyed.

5. Well, as these little dovecotes of the Virgin, our Lady, were beginning to be inhabited, the divine Majesty began to show His greatness in these weak little women, who were strong though in their desires and their detachment from every creature. When practiced with a pure conscience, such detachment must be what most joins the soul to God. There is no need to point this out because if the detachment is true it seems to me impossible that one offend the Lord. Since in all their dealings and conversations these nuns are concerned with Him. His Majesty doesn't seem to want to leave them. This is what I see now and in truth can say. Let those fear who are to come and who will read this. And if they do not see what is now seen, let them not blame the times, for it is always a suitable time for God to grant great favors to the one who truly serves Him. And let them strive to discern whether there is some failure in this detachment and correct it.

6. I sometimes hear it said about the first members of religious orders that since they were the foundation the Lord granted them greater favors as He did to our holy forebears; and this is true. But we must always observe that they are the foundation for those who are to come. If we who live now

had not fallen from where our forebears were, and those who come after us would live as they did, the edifice would always be firm. What does it profit me that our forebears had been so holy if I afterward am so wretched that I leave the edifice damaged through bad customs? For it is clear that those who come will not so much remember those who lived many years ago as those they see before them. It would be rather amusing were I to make the excuse that I am not one of the first members and at the same time fail to recognize the difference lying between my life and virtue and that of those to whom God granted such great favors.

7. Oh, God help me! What twisted excuses and what obvious deceit! I regret, my God, to be so wretched and so useless in your service; but I know well that the fault lies within me that You do not grant me the favors You did to my forebears. I grieve over my life, Lord, when I compare it with theirs, and I cannot say this without tears. I see that I have lost what they have worked for and that I can in no way blame You. Nor is it in any way good for persons to complain if they see their order in some decline; rather, they should strive to be the kind of rock on which the edifice may again be raised, for the Lord will help toward that.[5]

8. Well to return to what I was saying,[6] for I have digressed a great deal, the favors the Lord grants in these houses are so many that if there are one or two in each that God leads now by meditation all the rest reach perfect contemplation. Some are so advanced that they attain to rapture. To others the Lord grants a favor of another kind, giving them, along with rapture, revelations and visions that one clearly understands to be from God. There is no house now that does not have one,

two, or three who receive this latter favor. Well do I understand that sanctity does not lie in these favors, nor is it my intention to praise only them but to make it understood that the counsels I want to give have a purpose.

COUNSELS TO PRIORESSES

Summary and Background: Chapter 4

Chapter four was written in the latter months of 1573 in Salamanca, toward the end of Teresa's three-year term as prioress of the Incarnation, an office that had been imposed upon her by obedience. She begins by giving a little dig to her superiors for having burdened her with both the office of prioress and the task of writing an account of her foundations. "It should be noted that, when *they ordered me to write* about these foundations, seven monasteries had been founded by the Lord's favor. This takes us up to the foundation of Alba de Tormes, which is the last of them. *The reason that more have not been established is that my superiors have tied me down to something else*" (F. 4. 1.) (italics added).

Teresa always felt strapped for time, and the last thing that she needed was to be saddled with the task of writing. Writing was a wearisome task that was imposed upon her by others, an irksome duty of which she frequently voiced her complaints. For example, *The Way of Perfection* was the result of Teresa's community at St. Joseph's badgering her to write about the spiritual life. "The Sisters have urged me so persistently to tell them something about it that I have decided to obey them" (W. Prologue. 1.). Yes, Teresa bowed to their wishes but not without expressing her protest.

But what disorder in the way I write! Really, it's as through the work were done by one who doesn't know what she's doing. The fault is yours, Sisters, because you are the ones who ordered me to write this. Read it as best you can, for I am writing it as best I can. And if you find that it is all wrong, burn it. Time is necessary to do the work well, and I have so little as you can see. (W. 15. 1.)

Teresa begins chapter four wondering how much more time she has left to live and how many more opportunities she will have to write. This is perhaps the reason Teresa breaks off the narrative of the establishment of her foundations and begins to write on subjects that she considers more urgent.

Since I do not know how much time on this earth the Lord will still give me, or how much opportunity to write, and since now it seems I have a little time, I thought that before I go further I should give some counsels to prioresses. Through these, the prioresses will learn both to understand themselves and to guide their subjects so that the souls of these latter will receive greater benefit, even though with less satisfaction. (F. 4. 1.)

For the next five chapters, Teresa gives advice to prioresses on subjects ranging from prayer to how to deal with melancholic nuns. Chapter four does not contain any specific advice but rather functions as an overture to an opera, sounding the main themes that she will develop in later chapters—the deceptions of our imagination, extraordinary graces granted to members of her community and melancholic nuns.

However, as is often the case with Teresa, she wanders off on a tangent. As Teresa is writing about detachment as the condition that disposes us to receive favors from God, she begins to reflect upon the importance of being faithful to one's vocation. "If we who live now had not fallen from where our forebears were, and those who come after us would live as they did, the edifice would always be firm. What does it profit me that our forebears had been so holy if I afterward am so wretched that I leave the edifice damaged through bad customs" (F. 4. 6.)?

Teresa ends this chapter with a question. If you find yourself living in a religious order that is in decline, what should you do? Teresa's answer is simple. It is "no good to complain . . . rather strive to be the kind of rock on which the edifice may again be raised" (F. 4. 7.). In short, keep your focus on being as faithful in living your life the best way you can.

Reflection. Ruminating over a situation is an exercise in futility. We have an example of this in the life of Céline Martin, the blood sister of St. Thérèse. One day, Céline told Thérèse that just thinking about religious orders that submitted to the unjust laws against the Church, promulgated by the current anti-Catholic government in France, filled her with indignation. "My entire being rises up in rebellion when I witness such a spirit of cowardice. I would be cut into a thousand pieces rather than belong to any of these communities or assist them in any way."[7] Thérèse responded:

We should not be concerned about such matters at all. It is true that I would be of your opinion and act perhaps in the same way had I any responsibility in the matter. But I have no obligation whatsoever. Moreover, *our only duty is to become united to God.* Even if we were members of those communities, which are being publicly criticized for their defections, we would be greatly at fault in becoming disquieted on that account.[8]

It is as if Thérèse is saying to Céline, "If God is asking you to *do* something about a situation, then you should *do* it. If not, then what good does it do to inwardly fret and fume?" Not only is it an exercise in futility, but it actually does harm; it only distracts one from attending to the presence of God. Becoming emotionally distraught over a situation accomplishes nothing. To emphasize this point, Thérèse tells Céline that if she were a member of one of these communities that she despises, to become "disquieted on that account" would do no good. In such a situation, Céline should try not to *think* about the condition of her order but to *live* her vocation as faithfully as possible. This is what she should *do*. Such is St. Teresa's perspective. It is "no good to complain . . . rather strive to be the kind of rock on which the edifice may again be raised" (F. 4. 7.).

Questions. All of us are like Céline. There are situations in life, many of which we are powerless to change, that trigger frustration, anger, and complaints. Is there a situation in your life that you are powerless to rectify? Given this fact, what is God asking you *to do*?

Chapter 5

Gives some counsels on matters concerning prayer. This chapter is very beneficial for those engaged in active works.

1. It is not my intention or thought that what I say here be taken for certain and as an infallible rule, for that would be foolish in things so difficult. Since there are many paths along this way of the spirit, it could be that I will manage to say certain useful things about some of them. If those who do not walk along the path of which I'm speaking do not understand what I'm saying, it will be because they are walking by another. And if I do not help anyone, the Lord will accept my desire. He knows that even though I have not experienced all of which I speak, I have seen it in other souls.

2. First, I want to treat, according to my poor understanding, of the substance of perfect prayer. For I have run into some for whom it seems the whole business lies in thinking. If they can keep their minds much occupied in God, even though great effort is exerted, they at once think they are spiritual. If, on the contrary, without being able to avoid it, they become distracted, even if for the sake of good things, they then become disconsolate and think they are lost. Learned men will not fall victim to these misconceptions, although I have already met learned men who have had some of them. But it is fitting that we women receive advice with regard to all these misunderstandings. I do not deny that it is a favor from the Lord if someone is able to be always meditating on His works, and it is good that one strive to do so. However, it must be understood that not all imaginations are by their

nature capable of this meditating, but all souls are capable of loving. I have already at another time written about the causes of this restlessness of our imagination, I think;[1] not all the causes—that would be impossible—but some. And so I am not treating of this now. But I should like to explain that the soul is not the mind, nor is the will directed by thinking, for this would be very unfortunate. Hence, the soul's progress does not lie in thinking much but in loving much.

3. How does one acquire this love? By being determined to work and to suffer, and to do so when the occasion arises. It is indeed true that by thinking of what we owe the Lord, of who He is, and what we are, a soul's determination grows, and that this thinking is very meritorious and appropriate for beginners. But it must be understood that this is true provided that nothing interferes with obedience or benefit to one's neighbor. When either of these two things presents itself, time is demanded, and also the abandonment of what we so much desire to give God, which, in our opinion, is to be alone thinking of Him and delighting in the delights that He give us. To leave aside these delights for either of these other two things is to give delight to Him and do the work for Him, as He Himself said: What you did for one of these little ones you did for Me.[2] And in matters touching on obedience He doesn't want the soul who truly loves Him to take any other path than the one He did: obediens usque ad mortem.[3]

4. Well if this is true, from where does the displeasure proceed which for the greater part is felt when one has not spent a large part of the day very much withdrawn and absorbed in God, even though we are occupied with these other things? In my opinion, there are two reasons for this displeasure: The

first and main one[4] is the very subtle self-love that is mixed in here. This self-love does not allow one to understand what it is to want to please ourselves rather than God. For, clearly, after a soul begins to taste how sweet the Lord is,[5] it is more pleasing for the body to be resting without work and for the soul to be receiving delight.

5. O charity of those who truly love this Lord and know their own nature! How little rest they can have if they see they may play a little part in getting even one soul to make progress and to love God more, or in consoling it, or in taking away some danger from it. How poorly would it then rest with this particular rest of its own! And when it cannot help with deeds, it will do so with prayer, begging the Lord for the many souls that it is sad to see being lost. The soul loses its delight and counts the loss as gain, for it doesn't think about its own satisfaction but rather about how it can best do the Lord's will, and this it does through obedience. It would be a distressing thing if God were clearly telling us to go after something that matters to Him and we would not want to do so but want to remain looking at Him because that is more pleasing to us. What an amusing kind of progress in the love of God it is, to tie His hands by thinking that He cannot help us except by one path!

6. I know personally some individuals (leaving aside, as I have said,[6] what I have experienced) who brought me to understand this truth when I was greatly distressed to see myself with so little time. And I thus was sorry for them to see they were so occupied with so many business matters and things that obedience commanded them. I was thinking to myself, and even said so, that it wasn't possible in the midst of such

commotion for the spirit to grow, for at that time they didn't have much spirit. O Lord, how different are your paths from our clumsy imaginings! And how from a soul that is already determined to love You and is abandoned into Your hands, You do not want anything but that it obey, that it inquire well into what is for Your greater service, and that it desire this! There's no need for it to be seeking out paths or choosing them, for its will is Yours. You, my Lord, take up this care of guiding it to where it receives the most benefit. The prelate who is the superior may not be concerned for what benefits the soul but concerned only that the business he thinks is fitting for the community be attended to. Yet, You, my God, do have concern and go about disposing the soul and the things with which it is dealing in such a way that, without understanding how, we find in ourselves spiritual improvement, so great that we are afterward left amazed.

7. There was a person to whom I spoke a few days ago who for about fifteen years was kept so busy through obedience with work in occupations and government that in all those years he didn't remember having had one day for himself, although he tried the best he could to keep a pure conscience and have some periods each day for prayer. His soul in its inclination is one of the most obedient I have seen, and so he communicates this spirit of obedience to all those with whom he deals. The Lord has repaid him well; for he has found that he has, without knowing how, that same precious and desirable liberty of spirit that the perfect have. In it, they find all the happiness that could be wanted in this life, for in desiring nothing they possess all. Nothing on earth do they fear or desire, neither do trials disturb them, nor do consolations move them. In sum,

nothing can take away their peace because these souls depend only on God. And since no one can take Him away from them, only the fear of losing Him can cause them pain. Everything else in this world, in their opinion, is as though it were not; it neither contributes anything nor removes anything from their happiness. Oh, happy obedience and happy the resulting distraction that could obtain so much!

8. This is not the only person, for I have known others of the same sort, whom I had not seen for some, or many, years. In asking them about how they had spent these years, I learned that the years were all spent in the fulfillment of the duties of obedience and charity. On the other hand, I saw such improvement in spiritual things that I was amazed. Well, come now, my daughters, don't be sad when obedience draws you to involvement in exterior matters. Know that if it is in the kitchen, the Lord walks among the pots and pans helping you both interiorly and exteriorly.

9. I remember that I met a religious who had resolved and become very determined never to say "no" to anything his superior commanded no matter how much labor it would cost him. One day he was completely worn out from work; and when it was already late and he could no longer stay on his feet and went to sit down and rest a little, the superior met him and told him to take the hoe and go dig in the garden. He remained silent; although in his human nature he was indeed afflicted, for he couldn't help it. He took his hoe and when he was about to enter a passageway into the garden (I saw the spot many years after he told me of this, for I managed to found a house in that place), our Lord appeared to him weighed down with the cross, so tired and worn that this religious understood

clearly that what he himself was enduring was nothing when compared with what the Lord endured.

10. I believe that, since the devil sees there is no path that leads more quickly to the highest perfection than obedience, he sets up many annoyances and difficulties under the color of good. Note this well and you will see clearly that I am speaking the truth. The highest perfection obviously does not consist in interior delights or in great raptures or in visions or in the spirit of prophecy but in having our will so much in conformity with God's will that there is nothing we know He wills that we do not want with all our desire, and in accepting the bitter as happily as we do the delightful when we know that His Majesty desires it. This seems most difficult (not the doing of it, but this being content with what completely contradicts our nature); and indeed it truly is difficult. But love has this strength if it is perfect, for we forget about pleasing ourselves in order to please the one we love. And truly this is so; for even though the trials may be very great, they become sweet when we know we are pleasing God. And this is the way by which those who have reached this stage love persecutions, dishonor, and offenses. This is so certain, so well known, and so plain that there is no reason for me to delay over the matter.

11. What I intend to explain is why obedience, in my opinion, is the quickest or best means for reaching this most happy state. The reason is that since we are by no means lords of our own will in such a way that we can employ it purely and simply in God, obedience is the true path for subjecting it to reason. For this subjection is not accomplished by means of good reasons; human nature and self-love can find so many of them that we would never arrive at the goal. And

often the most reasonable thing seems to us foolish if it is not to our advantage.

12. So much could be said here that we would never finish dealing with this interior battle and all that the devil, the world, and our own sensuality do to make us twist reason.

Well, what is the remedy? That in obedience, just as in a very dubious litigation, a judge is accepted and both sides place the matter in his hands. Tired of arguing, our soul accepts one who may be either the superior or the confessor with the determination not to have any more argument or to think any more of its own case but to trust the words of the Lord who says, Whoever hears you hears Me,[7] and it disregards its own will. The Lord esteems this surrender very much, and rightly so, because it means making Him Lord over the free will He has given us. By exercising ourselves in this surrender, sometimes denying ourselves, at other times waging a thousand battles since the judgment made in our case seems to us absurd, we come to be conformed with what they command us. It can be painful exercise, but with or without the pain we in the end do what is commanded, and the Lord helps so much on His part that for the same reason that we subject our will and reason to Him He makes us lords over our will. Then, being lords of ourselves, we can with perfection be occupied with God, giving Him a pure will that He may join it with His, asking Him to send fire from heaven so that His love may burn this sacrifice[8] and take away everything that could displease him. We have done what we can by placing the sacrifice on the altar, although through much hardship. And, insofar as is in our power, the sacrifice remains on the altar and does not touch the ground.

13. Clearly, no one can give what he does not have; he must have it first. Well, believe me that in order to acquire this treasure there is no better way than to dig and toil in order to excavate from this mine of obedience. The more we dig the more we shall find; and the more we submit to men, having no other will than that of our superiors, the more we shall be lords over our will so as to bring it into conformity with God's will.

Observe, Sisters, whether leaving the pleasure of solitude is not well repaid. I tell you that it is not because of a lack of solitude that you will fail to dispose yourselves to reach this true union that was mentioned, that is, to make your will one with God's. This is the union that I desire and would want for all of you, and not some absorptions, however delightful they may be, that have been given the name "union." The absorption will be genuine union if afterward there is present the union just explained. But if after this suspension not much obedience remains, and self-will is present, it seems to me the soul will be united with its self-love rather than with the will of God. May His Majesty be pleased that I act in accordance with what I understand.

14. The second reason,[9] it seems to me, for this displeasure is that since in solitude there are fewer occasions to offend the Lord (for some cannot be lacking because the devils and we ourselves are present everywhere), it seems the soul in its journey is freer from stain. For if it is fearful of offending Him, it finds the greatest consolation in not having anything to make it stumble. And certainly this seems to me reason enough for desiring not to have conversation with anyone unless it's about God's great favors and delights.

15. Here, my daughters, is where love will be seen: not hidden in corners but in the midst of the occasions of falling.[10] And believe me that even though there may be more faults, and even some slight losses, our gain will be incomparably greater. Note that I am always presupposing that these things are done out of obedience or charity. For if these latter are not factors, I always repeat that solitude is better, and even that we must desire it. We must desire solitude even when involved in the things I'm speaking of; indeed, this desire is continually present in souls that truly love God. As for my saying that leaving solitude is a gain, I say this because doing so makes us realize who we are and the degree of virtue we have. For people who are always recollected in solitude, however holy in their own opinion they may be, don't know whether they are patient or humble, nor do they have the means of knowing this. How could it be known whether a man were valiant if he were not seen in battle? St. Peter thought he was very courageous; see how he acted when the occasion presented itself.[11] But he came through that experience not trusting at all in himself, and as a result he trusted in God and subsequently suffered the martyrdom about which we know.[12]

16. Oh, God help me, if only we understood how great our misery is! In everything there is danger if we do not understand this misery. For that reason it is a great good for us if we are ordered to do things that show us our own lowliness. I consider one day of humble self-knowledge a greater favor from the Lord, even though the day may have cost us numerous afflictions and trials, than many days of prayer. Moreover, the true lover loves everywhere and is always thinking of the Beloved! It would be a thing hard to bear if we were able to

pray only when off in some corner. I do realize that prayer in the midst of occupations cannot last many hours; but, O my Lord, what power over You a sigh of sorrow has that comes from the depths of our hearts on seeing that it isn't enough that we are in this exile but that we are not even given the chance to be alone enjoying You.

17. Here we see clearly that we are His slaves, our wills being sold, out of love for Him, through the virtue of obedience, since through obedience we in some way give up enjoying God Himself. And yet, this is nothing if we consider that He came from the bosom of His Father out of obedience to become our slave. Well, how can one repay this favor or what service render for it? It's necessary to be on one's guard and careful in the performance of good works by having frequent interior recourse to God, even though these works are done in obedience and charity. And let souls believe me that it is not the length of time spent in prayer that benefits one; when the time is spent as well in good works, it is a help in preparing the soul for the enkindling of love. The soul may thereby be better prepared in a very short time than through many hours of reflection. All must come from His hand. May He be blessed forever.

COUNSELS ON PRAYER

Summary and Background: Chapter 5

Teresa begins this chapter with a discussion about an erroneous concept regarding the nature of holiness, namely, that the measure of holiness is one's capacity to keep one's mind focused on God. "If they can keep their mind occupied in God, even though great effort is exerted, they at once think they are spiritual" (F. 5. 2.). One of the consequences of this belief is that these souls become rigidly attached to their set times for prayer and become upset if they are interrupted. Teresa, while emphasizing the importance of being faithful to regular periods of prayer, teaches that every good thing, even prayer, must be regulated by obedience and the demands of charity.

> When either of these two things presents itself, [obedience or benefit to one's neighbor] time is demanded, and also the abandonment of what we so much desire to give God, which, in our opinion, is to be alone thinking of Him and delighting in the delights that He gives us. To leave aside these delights for either of these other two things is to give delight to Him and do the work for Him, as He Himself said: *What you did for one of these little ones you did for Me.* (F. 5. 3.)

Teresa says that there are two reasons why souls feel a "displeasure" (F. 5. 4.) when their time of prayer is interrupted. The first is a "very subtle self-love" (F. 5. 4.) that blinds them to the fact that they are seeking their own pleasure rather than the will of God. The source of this blindness is that these souls think that the delight that they experience during prayer is *spiritual*, whereas, in fact, it is *sensual*. "For, clearly, after a soul begins to taste how sweet the Lord is, it is more pleasing for the body to be resting without work and for the soul to be receiving delight" (F. 5. 4.). In short, these souls have become so attached to the consolation that they experience in prayer that they do not want to be disturbed.

The second reason for this "displeasure" is the fear of offending God if one gives up one's solitude, "since in solitude there are fewer occasions to offend the Lord" (F. 5. 13.). Teresa says that although these souls have good intentions, they fail to understand that true virtue can only be acquired by struggling with temptation. "Here, my daughters, is where love will be seen: not hidden in corners but in the midst of the occasions of falling. And believe me that even though there may be more faults, and even some slight losses, our gain will be incomparably greater" (F. 5. 15.).

Reflection. How do we determine what gift we will give to a friend? Thomas Green offers the following reflection.

Suppose Christmas is approaching, and a friend wishes to give me a gift. There are two ways she can go about it. She can, first, try to decide what I would like—and what she would like to give—and then shop for the gift of her choice. Or, she can ask me what I would like and then give me what I request, provided she can afford it. Suppose she does it the second way; and suppose when she asks me what I would most like, I say "blue cheese . . . But for my Filipino friend [Green teaches in Manila] it does present some problems: Blue cheese is scarce, it has a "fragrance" which Filipinos find repugnant, and those who have tried it generally don't like it! So my friend might reply, " Ugh! blue cheese! I could never give that to *anyone* as a gift!" So she finds herself with a problem: She knows what I would like, but she has no desire to give it to me. What will she do? It all depends on whether she really wants to give me a gift of *her* choice or to give me whatever *I* would like, however repugnant it might be to her.[13]

Green uses this example as an analogy to our relationship with God. What regulates how we live our spiritual life, our preferences or what God asks of us? For example, when prayer becomes dry and tedious and God is calling us to be faithful to prayer, do we throw ourselves into work because *we* have decided that "good works" is the best way to serve God? Conversely, as we begin to experience consolation in prayer, we can become so attached to our time of prayer that we fail to respond to the demands of charity. "It would be a distressing thing if God were clearly telling us to go after something that matters to Him and we would not want to do so but want to remain looking at Him because that is more pleasing to us" (F. 5. 5.).

Teresa tells us that this attachment to our set times for prayer is such a "very subtle self-love" (F. 5. 4.) that we are *blind to* the fact that we are seeking our will instead of God's will. Teresa does not give us an explicit reason for this blindness; however, it seems to be the result of two factors. The first reason is obvious. These souls are "begin[ning] to taste how sweet the Lord is" (F 5. 4.). They are attached to consolation and do not want to be disturbed. The second reason is rooted in a misconception about the nature of spiritual growth, an error that Teresa herself had once believed. She believed "it wasn't possible in the midst of such commotion for the spirit to grow" (F. 5. 6.). This misconception is rooted in the belief that since prayer is more "interior" than external works, it must be more spiritual.

This misconception, common among fledging souls on the spiritual path, makes a strict dichotomy between activities that are "interior" and "exterior" and between behaviors that are explicitly spiritual and those that are secular. The underlying issue that Teresa is dealing with is one of the most important in the spiritual life—how do we image holiness?

Our concept of holiness is in large part formed by our image of the saints, which is derived from various sources—what we are taught by parents and teachers, biographies and the hagiography of the saints, sermons and stained-glass windows. Many of these sources bathe the saints in an ethereal, other-worldly light. For example, look at the depiction of the saints in stained-glass windows. They are men and women wearing flowing robes of a bygone era, caught up in ecstasy, scarcely conscious of the world about them. Such an image of holiness, which operates both consciously and unconsciously, has a powerful impact upon our spiritual quest. It shapes our ideas about what is spiritual and what is not. However, holiness does not correspond to the images that are in our minds. As Teresa puts it, "Lord, how different are your paths from our clumsy imaginings" (F. 5. 6.)! What Teresa puts before us in this chapter is that holiness consists in being obedient to the will of God. "[Lord] you do not want anything but that [we] obey" (F. 5. 6.).

Teresa shatters our stereotypical images of holiness by placing before us people whom she has known, who, because of their fidelity to their obligations in life, rarely had time for prayer, solitude, or spiritual reading. Yet, they grew in "that same precious and desirable liberty of spirit that the perfect have . . . for in desiring nothing they possess all" (F. 5. 7.). Teresa is implying that these people grew in holiness precisely because they did not cling to behaviors that were explicitly "spiritual." This is because they sacrificed *their* preferences for the common good.

For Teresa, there is only one absolute in the spiritual life and that is doing the will of God, which often entails setting aside our own will. "You [Lord] do not want anything but that [we] obey, that [we] inquire well into what is for Your greater service, and that [we] desire this. There's no need for [us] to be seeking out paths or choosing them, for [our] will is Yours. You, my Lord, take up this care of guiding it to where [we will] receive the most benefit" (F. 5. 6.). But wherever God calls us, Teresa assures us that God will be present. "Well, come now, my daughters, don't be sad when obedience draws you to involvement in exterior matters. Know that if it is in the kitchen, the Lord walks among the pots and pans helping you both interiorly and exteriorly" (F. 5. 8.).

Questions. Each of us prefers to serve God in our own particular way. Some of us are of a more contemplative nature, while others are more inclined to apostolic work. Some of us prefer the quiet of church, while others prefer involvement in ministry. In either case, a sign of true holiness is detachment from our preferred way of serving God. Are you the type of person who finds it very difficult when your prayer is interrupted because of the demands of charity? Conversely, are you the type of person who rarely prays because you become agitated or bored when you are quiet? Have you ever considered that doing what is contrary to your preference *is* that which is most pleasing to God? It all depends on whether you really want to give God a gift of *your* choice or to give God what is pleasing to him.

Reflection. Teresa says that the second reason why certain people feel a "displeasure" for giving up their solitude is fear. "Since in solitude there are fewer occasions to offend the Lord" (F. 5. 13.). She counters this reasoning by telling her nuns that true virtue is only obtained in our interaction with one another. "Here, my daughters, is where love will be seen: not hidden in corners but in the midst of the occasions of falling. And believe me that even though there may be more faults, and even some slight losses, our gain will be incomparably greater" (F. 5. 15.). While Teresa does not tell us what specific faults she is writing about, it is easy to imagine that she is referring to the sins common to communal living: gossip, backbiting, pettiness, snide remarks, idle chatter, and the forming of cliques. Teresa's perspective is this. While community life provides occasions for falling into these temptations, there is no other way to grow in charity except by struggling with them. St. Thérèse says as much by the following image. "Keep in mind the method used to make copper objects shine. You smear them with mud after which they will shine like gold. Temptations are like mud for the soul. They serve to make the virtues, which are opposed to these temptations, to shine forth."[14]

Furthermore, Teresa tells us that solitude poses its own pitfalls—pride and an ignorance of one's true spiritual condition. "For people who are always recollected in solitude, however holy *in their own opinion they may be*, don't know whether they are patient or humble, nor do they have the means of knowing this. How could it be known whether a man was valiant if he were not seen in battle" (F. 5. 15.) (italics added)?

In spite of Teresa's insistence that we should neither isolate ourselves from community nor use solitude as a rationalization to escape from the aggravations of daily life, she also seems to be aware of the opposite danger, namely, socializing as a rationalization for an inability to be alone. Teresa writes, "Note that I am always presupposing that these things are done out of obedience or charity. For if these latter are not factors, I always repeat that solitude is better, and even that we must desire it" (F. 5. 15.).

Questions. Teresa's communities, like any group, were composed of both introverts who gravitated toward solitude and extroverts who had a proclivity to make beelines to the front parlor. She also knew that we all tend to justify our natural bent. However, to do God's will, sometimes demands that we go against the grain of our personalities. In what ways does God frequently ask you to do things that go against your temperament?

Chapter 6

Warns about the harm that can be done to spiritual people if they do not understand when the spirit must be resisted. Treats of the soul's desires to receive Communion and of the delusion that can be present in such desires. There are important things here for those who govern these houses.[1]

1. I have diligently tried to understand the origin of a great absorption I have seen in some persons whom the Lord favors much in prayer and who do their best to prepare themselves to receive these gifts. I am not dealing now with the soul's suspension or rapture given by His Majesty, for I have written much about this in other places.[2] In a matter like rapture there is nothing to speak of because if it is genuine we cannot do anything ourselves to prevent it, however much we try. It must be noted that in rapture the power that takes away our power to be in control of ourselves lasts but a short while. But frequently it happens that there begins a kind of prayer of quiet, something that resembles spiritual sleep, that so absorbs the soul that if we do not understand how one is to proceed therein much time could be lost and our strength diminished through our own fault and with little merit.

2. I would like to know how to explain myself here; it is so difficult that I don't know if I'll succeed. But I do know well that, if they want to believe me, souls who may be proceeding under this misconception will understand. I know some souls of great virtue who remained for seven or eight hours in absorption; everything seemed to them to be rapture. Any virtuous exercise so laid hold of them that they soon

abandoned themselves to the absorption,[3] thinking it was not good to resist the Lord. Little by little such persons can die or become fools if they do not seek a remedy. What I understand about this occurrence is that since the Lord begins to give delight, and our nature is very fond of delight, the soul becomes so occupied in the pleasure that it does not want to stir or lose that experience for anything. Indeed, the pleasure is greater than any of the world's pleasures. And when the experience takes place in a weak nature, or comes from one's own natural inventiveness (or better, imagination), nature will make souls know a thousand delightful lies. In this absorption the imagination does not wander but in apprehending one thing concentrates on it without distraction. Many persons when they begin to think about something, even though the matters may not concern God, are left absorbed or looking at it without adverting to what they are gazing on. They are like people who are slow and who seem, through indolence, to forget what they are about to say. This is what happens in these cases in conformity with the person's nature, or bodily humors, or weakness, or if the individual suffers melancholy; these people end up believing a thousand pleasant lies.

3. A little further on I shall speak of melancholy,[4] but even if this humor is not present, that which I have mentioned[5] happens. And it also happens to persons who are worn out through penance. As I have said,[6] when love begins to give pleasure to the senses these persons allow themselves to be carried away by it. In my opinion their love would be much better if they did not allow themselves to remain in stupefaction, for in this condition of prayer one can easily resist. For just as a person will faint from weakness and be unable

to speak or stir, so this is what happens here; for the strength of the spirit lays hold of nature, when this latter is weak, and subjects it.

4. You could ask me what difference there is between this absorption and rapture since the two are the same, at least in appearance—and you would be right as regards appearance but not as regards reality. For in rapture, or union of all the faculties, as I say, the duration is short, and great effects, interior light, and many other benefits are given, and the intellect doesn't work; it is the Lord who works in the will. In the absorption, things are very different, for although the body is captive, the will is not, nor is the memory or the intellect. But these faculties carry on their delirious activity, and if they rest in something they will perhaps go back and forth over it with ifs and buts.

5. I find no benefit in this bodily weakness—for it is nothing else—except that it arises from a good source. It would be a greater help to use this time well than to remain in this absorption so long. Much more can be merited by making an act of love and by often awakening the will to greater love of God than by leaving it listless. So I counsel the prioresses to make every possible effort to prevent the nuns from spending long periods in this daze. For to remain in such an absorption is nothing else, in my opinion, than to allow the faculties and senses to become crippled and not carry out what the soul commands them. Thus they deprive the soul of the gain that they usually get for it by proceeding carefully. If the absorption is understood to be caused by weakness, take away the fasts and disciplines (I mean those that are not obligatory, and in time it could happen that all of them in good conscience

may be taken away), and give these persons duties that will distract them.

6. And even if one does not experience these swoons, this course of action is necessary if the imagination is greatly occupied, even if with very sublime things of prayer. For it happens sometimes that these persons are not in control of themselves. If they have received some extraordinary favor form the Lord or seen some vision, then, especially, will their souls be left in such a condition that they will think they are continuing to see the vision; but this is not so, for the vision was seen no more than once. Whoever finds herself in this absorption for many days should strive to change the subject she is meditating on, for if a subject pertains to the things of God there is no difficulty in dwelling on one more than another since the faculties will be occupied in God. And sometimes one rejoices as much in considering God's creatures and the power He had in creating them as in thinking of the Creator Himself.

7. O hapless human misery that was left in this condition through sin, for even in good things we need rule and measure so as not to ruin our health and become incapable of enjoying them. And indeed what was said is fitting for many persons, especially those with weak heads or imaginations. If one follows this advice one serves our Lord more, and it is very necessary that what I said be understood. If a nun sees that one of the mysteries of the Passion or of the glory of heaven or of any other similar thing comes into her imagination and remains many days and that, although she wants to, she cannot think of something else or take away this absorption, let her understand that it is fitting for her to distract herself insofar as she can. Otherwise, she will in time come to know the

harm that will be done and that this absorption stems from what I mentioned: either from great bodily weakness or from the imagination, which is worse. A madman, when he goes into some frenzy, is not the master of himself, cannot divert his attention, or think of anything else, nor are there reasons that can move him to do this because he is not in control of his reasoning power. The same thing could happen here; even though the absorption is a delightful madness—or if she has the humor of melancholy—it can do her very great harm. I don't see how it could be good, for the soul is capable of enjoying God Himself. Well, even if the subject matter is not one of the mysteries that I mentioned,[7] since God is infinite, why must the soul be held captive by just one of His mysteries or grandeurs, for there is so much in which we can be occupied? And the more of His mysteries we might want to consider the more His grandeurs will be revealed.

8. I do not mean that in the course of an hour or a day they should think on many things, for this would perhaps amount to enjoying none of them properly. Since these matters are so delicate, I would not want others to think I'm saying what it doesn't enter my mind to say, or to understand one thing for another. Certainly, it is so important to understand this chapter well that even though writing about such a matter may be a tiresome thing to do, it doesn't tire me. Nor would I want whoever does not at first understand this to grow tired in reading it many times, especially the prioresses and the mistresses of novices who must guide the Sisters in prayer. For the Sisters will see that if they do not walk carefully in the beginning, much time will be required afterward to remedy similar weaknesses.

9. If I were to write all that has come to my attention concerning this harm, they would see that I am right to insist so much on the matter. I want to mention only one instance, and from this one they will be able to deduce everything else. There are in one of these monasteries two Sisters, one a choir nun and the other a lay Sister,[8] both of whom are most prayerful, mortified, humble and virtuous, much favored by the Lord, to whom He communicates His great marvels. They are especially so detached and taken up with His love that it doesn't seem, however much we desire to catch up with them, that they fail to respond, in conformity with our lowliness, to the favors our Lord grants them. I have dwelt so much on their virtues in order that those who do not have so much virtue will fear more. When they began to experience some great impulses of desire for the Lord that they could not resist, it seemed to them the desire was mitigated when they received Communion. As a result, they obtained from their confessors permission to receive frequently. Their affliction increased so much that if they did not receive Communion each day, it seemed to them they would die. The confessors, since they saw souls like these with such great desires, thought daily Communion was a suitable remedy for the complaint; and the one confessor was a very spiritual man.

10. The matter didn't stop here. In the case of one of the nuns, her longings were so great that she found it necessary to receive Communion early in the morning so as to be able to live; that was her opinion, for the two were not souls that would feign anything, nor for anything in the world would they tell a lie. I was not there, but the prioress wrote to me of what was going on,[9] saying that she could not get anywhere

with them and that competent persons held that since nothing else could be done this remedy should be used. I at once, by the grace of God, understood the situation. Nonetheless, I remained silent until I could be present there, for I feared lest I be mistaken; and it would not have been right to contradict the one who approved, until giving him my reasons.

11. He was so humble that as soon as I went there and spoke to him he agreed with me. The other one was not so spiritual, hardly at all in comparison. There was no argument that could persuade him. But I cared little about persuading this one because I was not so obliged to him. I began to speak to the nuns and give many reasons in my opinion sufficient to make them understand that it was their imagination that made them think they would die without this remedy. They had their minds so fixed on receiving Communion as a remedy that nothing sufficed, nor was it enough to bring forth reasons. Now I saw that they were to be excused, and I told them that I too had such desires and would give up receiving Communion so that they could believe that they wouldn't have to receive except when everyone did. I told them we would all three die, for I thought doing so would be better than to start a custom like this in these houses where there were others who loved God as much as they and would want to do likewise.

12. The harm the custom had caused was so extreme—and the devil must have meddled—that since they did not receive Communion, they truly thought they would die. I showed great severity, because the more I saw that they were not submitting themselves to obedience (because in their opinion they could not do so) the more clearly I saw that the desire was a temptation. They passed through that day with a good

deal of difficulty; and another day, with a little less. And so the impulsion continued to diminish in such a way that even if I received Communion, because I was ordered to do so (for the confessor saw them so weak that he didn't give them the same order), they bore this very well.

13. Within a short time both they and everyone else recognized that this had been a temptation. And they realized how good it had been to remedy the situation in time, for a little later more things happened in that house that were disturbing to the superiors (not through the fault of these two nuns — perhaps later I may say something about it); and these superiors would not, in addition, have taken well to a custom like that, nor would they have tolerated it.

14. Oh, how many things of this sort I could mention. I'll mention only one other. It didn't happen in a monastery of ours but in a monastery of Bernardines. There was a nun there who was no less virtuous than those mentioned. Through disciplines and fasts she became so weak that each time she received Communion or had occasion to be enkindled in devotion she would immediately fall to the floor and there remain for eight or nine hours. It seemed to her and everyone else that she was experiencing a rapture. This happened so often that if a remedy had not been provided, much harm would have resulted. The report of the raptures spread through the whole locality. It saddened me to hear about her experience because, thanks be to the Lord, I understood its nature, and I feared about where it would end up. Her confessor was a close friend of mine, and he came to tell me about it. I told him what I understood and why the absorption was a waste of time and couldn't possibly be a rapture, but the result of weakness. I

told him to take away her fasts and disciplines and to distract her. She was obedient; she did as he said. As soon as she began to gain strength there was no more thought of rapture. And if indeed the experience had been one of rapture nothing would have sufficed to prevent it except the will of God, for the force of the spirit is so great that our efforts are not sufficient to resist. And, as I said,[10] a rapture leaves great effect in the soul; this other leaves no more effects than if it had not occurred, but tiredness in the body.

15. Let it, therefore, be understood from this example that anything that so controls us that we know our reason is not free should be held as suspect. Know that liberty of spirit will never be gained in this way. For one of the traits reason has is that it can find God in all things and be able to think about them. All the rest is subjection of spirit and, apart from the harm done to the body, so binds the soul as to hinder growth. The soul here resembles someone on a journey who enters a quagmire or swamp and thus cannot move onward. And, in order to advance, a soul must not only walk but fly. This immobility happens frequently when, as they say (and it seems to them), they are immersed in the divinity and cannot help themselves or find a remedy by diverting their attention because they are suspended.

16. Let them note that I again advise that in an instance of one day or four or eight there is nothing to fear, for it is not unusual for someone naturally weak to remain stunned for a number of days. If the matter goes beyond this, a remedy is necessary. The good in all this is that there is no sinful fault, nor will these souls fail to gain merit. But there are the difficulties I mentioned and many more. In the matter concerning

Communion, it will be a very great difficulty, because of the soul's love, if there is no submission in these things to the confessor and the prioress. Even though the soul feels drawn to solitude, it shouldn't go to the extreme of not consulting with them. It's necessary in this just as in other things that souls mortify themselves and be brought to understand that refraining from doing one's own will is more fitting than the experience of consolation.

17. Our self-love, too, can get mixed in with these experiences. It has happened to me sometimes that when I saw others receiving Communion just after I had received myself (to the point that the sacred species must have been still intact), I would desire not to have received so as to receive again. Since this happened to me so many times, I came afterward to notice (for at the time it didn't seem to me there was anything to give careful attention to) how the desire came more from wanting my own satisfaction than from love of God. Since in receiving Communion we, for the most part, experience tenderness and delight, that desire to receive again was taking hold of me. If its purpose was to have God within my soul, I already had Him; if it was to fulfill the obligation of going to Holy Communion, I had already done so; if to receive the favors that are bestowed with the Blessed Sacrament, I had already received them. Finally, I came to understand clearly that there was no other purpose in the desire than to experience again that sensible delight.

18. I remember that in a place where we had one of our monasteries I knew a woman who was a very great servant of God in the opinion of the whole town, and she must have been. She received Communion daily and did not have

a particular confessor; but on one day she would go to one church to receive Communion, and on another day to another. I noted this and wished more that she obey someone than receive Communion so often. She was in a house by herself and, in my opinion, doing whatever she wanted. But since she was good, all that she did was considered good. I told her of this at times, but she didn't pay any attention to me, and with reason, for she was much better than I. But in this matter I didn't think I was mistaken. The holy Fray Peter of Alcántara came to that place, and I arranged that he talk to her. I did not rest satisfied with the account she gave him. But perhaps she had nothing more to tell, for we are so miserable that we are never much satisfied except with those who follow our own way; for I believe that she had served the Lord more and done more penance in one year than I had in many.

19. But to come to the point, she fell sick with a fatal illness and diligently arranged that Mass be said in her house each day and that she receive the Blessed Sacrament. Since the sickness continued, a priest, a good servant of God, who often said the Mass for her, didn't think it was proper that she receive Communion daily in her house. The devil must have tempted her, because that day happened to be her last, the day on which she died. Since she saw the Mass ending and that she was deprived of the Lord, she became so greatly vexed and angry with the priest that he came to me, much scandalized, to tell me about it. I felt very sorry, for I still don't know if she was reconciled; it seems to me she died soon afterward.

20. Hence I came to understand the harm done by following our own will in no matter what; and especially in so important a matter. For it is right that those who approach

the Lord with such frequency should so understand their own unworthiness as to refuse to follow their own opinion, but supply, by obedience to a command, that which is lacking in order to approach so great a Lord—and what is lacking must be great. This good soul had the opportunity to humble herself very much, and perhaps she would have thereby merited more than by receiving Communion. It should be understood that the priest was not at fault, but that the Lord, seeing her misery and how unworthy she was, had thus ordained in order to enter so wretched a lodging. This is what a certain person did whom discreet confessors often refused to allow to receive Communion,[11] for she went frequently. This person, though she felt the loss very deeply, desired, on the other hand, the honor of God more than her own and did nothing but praise Him because He had awakened the confessor to look after her and not let His Majesty enter so wretched a lodging. And with these reflections she obeyed, with deep calm in her soul, although with a tender and loving pain. But not for the whole world together would she have gone against what was commanded her.

21. Believe me, it is clear that a love of God (I do not mean that it is really love but that in our opinion it is) that so stirs the passions that one ends up offending the Lord, or so alters the peace of the enamored soul that no attention is paid to reason, is in fact self-seeking. And the devil will be on the alert to afflict us when he thinks he can do us more harm, as he did to this woman. For certainly it frightened me very much, although not because I believed it would play a part in hindering her salvation, for the goodness of God is great, but because the temptation came at the worst time.

22. I have mentioned the matter here so that the prioresses might be warned and the Sisters might fear, reflect, and examine themselves on the manner in which they approach to receive so great a favor. If they approach in order to please God, they already know that He is pleased more by obedience than by sacrifice.[12] Well, if this is true and if I merit more, why am I disturbed? I do not say they are left without a humble distress, for not all souls have reached such perfection that they will be freed from suffering distress merely by the fact that they know they are doing what is more pleasing to God. Clearly, if the will is very detached from all self-interest, it will not feel anything. Rather it will rejoice that it is offered an occasion to please the Lord in something so costly, and it will humble itself and be just as satisfied by making a spiritual communion.

23. In the beginning of the spiritual life these great desires to approach the Lord are favors granted by God. This is true also at the end, but I say the beginning because at that time they should be more appreciated. Since in other things pertaining to perfection that I mentioned[13] these beginners are not so advanced, it may be readily granted them that they experience tenderness and feel pain when Communion is taken from them, provided the pain is borne with peace of soul and they draw forth acts of humility as a result. But when these souls experience some disturbance or passion and become angry with the prioress or confessors, they should believe that their desire to receive is an obvious temptation. This also holds true if someone decides to receive Communion even though the confessor says not to receive. I would not want the merit that is thereby derived, for in such matters we must not be

the judges of our own case. He who has the keys to bind and loose must be the one to judge.[14] That we might have understanding in things so important, may it please the Lord go give us light; and may His help not fail lest we cause Him displeasure through the favors He grants us.

ABSORPTION VERSES RAPTURE

Summary and Background: Chapter 6

Teresa begins this chapter by differentiating *absorption* from *rapture*. Absorption is a pleasant, dreamy state of consciousness that a soul tries to prolong. The soul abandons itself to the experience, spending hours absorbed in a peaceful, languid stupor. "The soul becomes so occupied in the pleasure that it does not want to stir or lose that experience for anything" (F. 6. 2.). Absorption occurs when a soul that has been weakened by penance and fasting experiences the prayer of quiet (the first degree of mystical prayer).

Teresa says that the state of absorption bears a superficial resemblance to the grace of rapture, in which *God* absorbs the soul. However, though absorption and rapture "are the same . . . in *appearance* [they are different] in *reality*" (F. 6. 4.) (italics added). What differentiates one from the other is their *effects*.

Absorption doesn't strengthen the soul's resolve to do the will of God. It weakens the mind and body and inclines the will to withdraw from the daily obligations of life. In contrast, rapture engenders virtues such as humility, detachment, and compassion (also see Teresa's *Life* ch. 20). "A rapture leaves great effects in the soul . . . [absorption leaves] tiredness in the body" (F. 6. 14.).

Teresa's advice to prioresses regarding nuns suffering from absorption is to "take away the fasts and disciplines

(I mean those that are not obligatory, and in time it could happen that all of them in good conscience may be taken away), and give these persons duties that will distract them" (F. 6. 5.). In addition, Teresa recommends that such nuns change the subject matter of their meditations to prevent them from becoming absorbed in *one thought*.

Next, Teresa writes of two nuns who began to experience deep desires for God. The problem wasn't the desires *per se*, for Teresa believed that their desires were the result of God's grace. The problem was their *interpretation* of their desires. Both actually believed that they would die if they did not receive communion every day. So they obtained permission from their confessor to do so. One of the nuns went so far as to insist that it was necessary for her to receive communion early in the morning to sustain her life.

Reflection. Teresa's treatment of rapture and absorption contains a basic truth about our lives. The *consequences* of our choices are different from their immediate *effects*. The immediate *effect* of absorption is an experience of peaceful languor. However, since the soul becomes attached to this experience, it wants to *rest* in its peaceful listlessness. It doesn't want to be disturbed. Therefore, the *consequence* of absorption is that the will is weakened; it develops a deep resistance to fulfilling the daily tasks of life.

We all share the desire of these souls. For who of us would not want to be exempt from the hassle, the mundane duties and chafing nitty-gritty of daily life? However, souls in the grip of absorption believe that their withdrawal is justifiable because they think that their experience is "spiritual." However, absorption counterfeits the spiritual by engendering a false sense of peace. In contrast, a truly spiritual experience *strengthens* us to do the will of God.

Teresa says that false peace in the spiritual life is a state of complacency, which is the result of two factors working together. The first is the untroubled conscience of a soul that has gradually grown lax in the obligations of life. The second is settling into a comfortable lifestyle. The false peace that is engendered by these two factors is not the peace that is the fruit of doing God's will but of the complacent soul that lives an unruffled, undisturbed life because it has cloistered itself from the demands of charity (See Teresa's *Meditations of Song of Songs*, ch. 2).

Questions. Have you become so attached to the consolations of your spiritual exercises that you have begun to neglect the duties and responsibilities of your state in life? Are there duties and responsibilities demanded by your state in life that you have neglected for so long that you no longer recognize your obligation to fulfill them? Have you become blind to the demands of charity?

Reflection. The real problem with the two nuns whom Teresa referred to in this chapter wasn't their *desire* to receive communion but the *extreme interpretation* that they attached to it; namely, if they did not receive communion every day, they would *die*. In consequence, they believed that they *needed* to receive communion daily. The underlying dynamic here is that a *want* can easily be interpreted as a *need*. This happens in two ways. First, we can make our emotions the criteria of reality. "If I *feel* that something is true, then it *must* be true." Second, we can indulge a desire for so long that we become dependent upon its fulfillment. Eventually, we believe that we cannot live without the object to which we have become attached. We become trapped by our desires. Or as Teresa writes, "The soul resembles someone on a journey who enters a quagmire or swamp and thus cannot move onward" (F. 6. 15.).

Question. Where in your life have you become stuck because you cannot give up something that you believe you *need*, when in fact you only *want* it?

Chapter 7

How one must deal with the nuns who have melancholy.[1] *This chapter is necessary for prioresses.*

1. These Sisters of mine at St. Joseph's in Salamanca, where I am staying while writing this, have repeatedly asked me to say something about how one must deal with the nuns who have that bodily humor called melancholy. For however much we strive not to accept those who have it, it is subtle and feigns death when it needs to, and thus we do not recognize it until the matter cannot be remedied. It seems to me that in a little book I said something about this;[2] I don't remember. Little is lost in saying something here, if the Lord be pleased that I succeed in doing so. It could be that I said something about this already, at another time. I would mention it another hundred times if I thought I could say something pertinent about the matter. So many are the contrivances that this humor seeks in order to do its own will that there is a need to search them out in order to know how to bear with those who have it and govern them so that no harm is done to the other nuns.

2. It must be pointed out that not all those who have this humor are so troublesome, for those who are humble and good-natured, even though they are disturbed within themselves, do not hurt others, especially if they possess sound intelligence. And also there are greater and lesser degrees of this humor. Certainly, I believe the devil takes melancholy as a means for trying to win over some persons. And if they do not walk with great care, he will do so. For since this humor can subdue reason, what won't our passions do once reason is

darkened? It seems that if reason is wanting, madness results, and so it does. But in those of whom we are now speaking, the melancholy doesn't reach the point of madness, which would be much less harmful. But to have to consider someone a rational person and deal with her as such even though she isn't is an unbearable burden. Those who are totally afflicted with this illness are to be pitied, but they do no harm, and if there is a means of bringing them under control, it is to put fear into them.

3. With those in whom this very harmful affliction has just begun, even though it is not so strong, the same remedy is necessary if other attempts prove insufficient. The affliction, in sum, springs from that humor or root and stems from that stock. And it is necessary that the prioress make use of the penances of the order and strive to bring these persons into submission in such a way as to make them understand they will obtain neither all nor part of what they want. For if they come to think that sometimes their cries, and the furies the devil speaks through them in order to bring them to ruin if he can, are sufficient for them to get what they want, they will be lost. And one such person is enough to disrupt the quiet of a monastery. Since the poor little thing has no one to help her defend herself from the things the devil puts before her, it is necessary for the prioress to proceed with the greatest care in governing her not only in exterior but also in interior matters. For since reason is obscured in the sick person, it must be clear in the prioress so that the devil doesn't begin to bring that soul under his control, taking that affliction as a means. Only at intervals does this humor afflict so much as to subdue reason. And then the person is not at fault, just as insane

people are not at fault for the foolish things they do. But those who are not insane have some fault. Thus it is a dangerous thing if during the times in which they are ill they begin to take liberties, which is a terrible artifice of the devil. It's necessary that they do not do so; otherwise, they will not be masters of themselves when they are well. If we consider the matter, that which interests these melancholic persons most is getting their own way, saying everything that comes to their lips, looking at the faults of others with which they hide their own, and finding rest in what gives them pleasure; in sum, they are like a person who cannot bear anyone who resists him. Well, if the passions go unmortified, and each passion seeks to get what it wants, what would happen if no one resisted them?

4. I repeat, as one who has seen and dealt with many persons having this affliction, that there is no other remedy for it than to make these persons submit in all the ways and means possible. If words do not suffice, use punishment; if light punishment is not enough, try heavy; if one month in the prison cell is not enough, try four months; no greater good can be done for their souls. For as I have said[3] and I repeat (and it is important for the afflicted themselves to understand this, even though at times they may be unable to help themselves), since the affliction is not confirmed madness of the kind that excuses one from any fault—although sometimes it may be, but it is not always so—the soul remains in much danger. But sometimes, as I say, reason is so overpowered that those afflicted will be forced to do or say what they did and said when they had no control. It is a great mercy from God toward those suffering this affliction that they may submit to someone who will govern them through this danger that I mentioned,[4]

for herein lies all their good. And, for the love of God, if anyone read this let her reflect that perhaps it is a matter of her
own salvation.

5. I know some persons who are on the borderline of
losing their minds completely. But they are humble and so
fearful of offending God that even though they may be dis-
solving in tears and grieving within themselves, they don't
do anything but what they are ordered to do. And they suffer
their illness as others do theirs; although this one is a greater
martyrdom. Thus they will have greater glory and have their
purgatory here in this life instead of the next. But I repeat that
those who do not submit willingly should be urged to do so
by the prioress. And let them not be deceived with indiscreet
pieties lest they end up disturbing all with their confusion.

6. There is another very great harm, leaving aside the danger that was mentioned:[5] Since the afflicted nun appears to be
good and the force the illness exercises interiorly is not understood, our nature is so miserable that each one will think that
she herself is melancholic and that thus others must bear with
her. And, in point of fact, the devil will cause the matter to
be thus understood, and he will bring about such havoc that
when one comes to recognize the fact there will be difficulty in
providing a remedy. This matter is so important that no negligence whatsoever should be allowed. But if the melancholic
nun should resist the prelate, who is the superior, she should
pay for it in the same way as the healthy nun and should not be
pardoned for anything. If she should utter an insulting word to
her Sister, the same holds true. So likewise in all similar things.

7. It seems to be unjust to punish a sick person, who
can't help it, just as one would a healthy person. Therefore,

it would also be unjust to bind and whip the insane, and the just thing would be to allow them to kill everyone. Believe me, I have tried and, in my opinion, attempted many remedies, and I find no other. It absolutely must not be tolerated that the prioress out of pity allow such nuns to begin taking liberties, for when she gets down to remedying the situation much harm will have already been done to others. If the insane are bound and chastised so that they will not kill others, and this is right and even seems to be a very compassionate thing to do since they cannot control themselves, how much more must one be careful not to allow these melancholic persons liberties by which they could harm souls. And I truly believe that this affliction is often, as I have said,[6] found in those whose dispositions are unrestrained, lacking in humility, and poorly disciplined; and the humor doesn't have as much strength as in the insane. I mean that "in some" the humor doesn't have as much strength, for I have seen that when there is someone to fear they do control themselves and they can. Well, why can't they do so for God? I fear that the devil, under the guise of this humor, as I have said,[7] wants to gain many souls.

8. Nowadays the term is used more than usual, and it happens that all self-will and freedom go by the name melancholy. Thus I have thought that in these houses and in all Religious houses, this term should not be uttered. For the term seems to bring along with it freedom from any control. Rather, the condition should be called a serious illness—and how truly it is one—and be cared for as such. For sometimes it is very necessary to reduce the humor by means of medicine in order that it be endured; and the nun must remain in the infirmary and understand that when she comes out and returns to the

community she must be humble like all and obey as do all. And she must understand that when she does not do so she may not use that humor as her defense. For the reasons that I have mentioned, and more could be said, this procedure is fitting. The prioress must, without letting these nuns realize it, lead them with much compassion, like a true mother, and seek whatever means she can to provide a remedy.

9. It seem that I am contradicting myself because up to now I said that these nuns must be dealt with strictly. So I repeat that they must not think they can come out and do what they want, nor should they be allowed out except under the condition that they must obey. For the harm lies in their thinking that they will be free to do whatever they want. But the prioress can refrain from ordering them to do what she sees they will be unable to do because of their not having the strength within themselves. She should lead them with all the skill and love necessary so that if possible they submit out of love, which would be much better, and usually happens. She should show that she greatly loves them and make this known through words and deeds. And she must note that the greatest remedy she has is to keep them much occupied with duties so that they do not have the opportunity to be imagining things, for herein lies all their trouble. And even though they may not perform these duties so well, she should suffer some defects so as not to have to suffer other greater ones that will arise if the melancholy overpowers them. I know that this is the most suitable remedy you can provide. And strive that they do not have long periods of prayer, not even those established in the constitutions, because, for the greater part, their imaginations

are weak and the long prayer will do them much harm. Otherwise, they will fancy things that neither they nor anyone who hears them will ever understand. Let her take care that they eat fish only rarely;[8] and also during the fasts, they ought not fast as much as do the others.

10. It seems excessive to give so much advice for this affliction and not for any other, there being so many serious ones in our miserable life, especially when considering the weakness of women. It is for two reasons that I do so: First, it seems these nuns are well, for they don't want to know that they have this affliction. Since it doesn't force them to stay in bed, because they do not have a fever, or to call the doctor, it's necessary for the prioress to be their doctor; for it is a sickness more prejudicial to all perfection than that of those who are in bed and in danger of death. Second, in the case of other illnesses it happens that either one is cured or one dies; with this illness, very seldom are the afflicted cured, nor do they die from it but they come to lose their minds completely—which is a death capable of killing all the nuns. They suffer more than death in themselves through afflictions, fantasies, and scruples, all of which they call temptations, and so they will have a great deal of merit. If they could come to understand that the illness is the cause of these, they would find much relief provided they paid no attention to them.

Indeed, I have great compassion for them, and it is also right that all those living with them have it. These latter should reflect that the Lord can give this compassion, and they should bear up with them, without letting this be known as I have said.[9] Please the Lord I may have succeeded in pointing out the proper thing to do in regard to so serious an illness.

MELANCHOLY

Summary and Background: Chapter 7

This chapter is a response to a request from the nuns of Salamanca. They need advice about how to deal with nuns suffering from melancholy. Melancholy refers to a whole range of mental and emotional disorders. Kavanaugh writes that "under the term 'melancholy,' Teresa includes a whole series of emotional and mental disorders."[10] To add to the confusion, Teresa also subsumes under the category of melancholy, nuns who want to live as they please and those who are afflicted with *acedia*, that weariness of spirit that afflicts solitaries. In consequence, since Teresa is dealing with different realities in this chapter or as she puts it, "there are greater and lesser degrees of this humor" (F. 7. 2.), she offers a variety of solutions to nuns who are "melancholic."

Melancholy can be so severe that it "can subdue reason . . . and madness results" (F. 7. 2.). When this is the case, Teresa advises that "If words do not suffice, use punishment; if light punishment is not enough, try heavy; if one month in the prison cell is not enough, try four months" (F. 7. 4.). These may seem like harsh measures. However, we are not privy to the medical condition to which Teresa is referring. Perhaps she is referring to persons who are suffering from bipolar conditions, who are both a danger to themselves and to others. If this is the case, locking a person up (there was no medication in those days) may have been the only option that was available.

However, Teresa's primary focus in this chapter is not on people who suffer such extremes of melancholy, but on nuns in whom "this harmful affliction has just begun" or nuns who "disrupt the quiet of the community" (F. 7. 3.) or those who have become "unbearable burdens" (F. 7. 2.). Teresa says that these nuns have to be made to conform to the rules of the community, so that they are made to "understand they will obtain neither all nor part of what they want . . . [through] their cries" (F. 7. 3.). On the other hand, Teresa says that "the prioress can refrain from ordering them to do what she sees they will be unable to do because of their not having the strength within themselves" (F. 5. 9.).

Having said this, Teresa anticipates a sense of confusion on the part of her readers, for she writes, "It seems that I am contradicting myself because up to this point I said that these nuns must be dealt with strictly" (F. 7. 9.). However, there is no contradiction in Teresa's advice. She knows that you cannot treat two people the same way, for every situation is unique. Teresa's advice to the prioresses is for them to avoid two extremes—being either too indulgent or too coercive.

Finally, Teresa offers some advice, which is both realistic and practical. She tells the prioresses not to expect the impossible because "very seldom are the afflicted cured" (F. 7. 10.). However, this does not mean that nothing can be done. Teresa knows that what deepens

melancholy is having too much time to ruminate. Therefore, the prioress should make sure that those afflicted
with melancholy are adequately employed with doing the
work of the community.

She [the prioress] should lead them with all the skill and
love necessary so that if possible they submit out of love,
which would be much better, and usually happens. She
should show that she greatly loves them and make this
known through words and deeds. And she must note
that the greatest remedy she has is to keep them much
occupied with duties so that they do not have the opportunities to be imagining things, for herein lies all the
trouble. And even though they may not perform these
duties so well, she should suffer some defects so as not
to have to suffer greater ones that will arise if the melancholy overpowers them. I know that this is the most suitable remedy you can provide. And strive that they do not
have long periods of prayer, not even those established
by the constitutions. (F. 7. 9.)

Reflection. As we read this chapter, we get the distinct
impression that Teresa is struggling with what advice to
give to prioresses. Perhaps, the struggle arises because
Teresa realizes that life is complex and that there are no
simple solutions when dealing with people. The underlying questions that Teresa deals with are relevant today
in community, family life, and the workplace. For example, when does a community have an obligation to dismiss
a member? When does one confront a situation, and when

would doing so make matters worse? Which behaviors should a group tolerate and which ones should be considered unacceptable? When should you be strict, and when should you be lenient? When do you lay down the law, and what constitutes a valid exception to the norm? As Teresa puts it, "[melancholic nuns] must not think they can come out and do what they want . . . but the prioress can refrain from ordering them to do what she sees they will be unable to do because of their not having the strength within themselves" (F. 5. 9.).

Questions. How often, like St. Teresa, have you had to struggle with how to deal with a difficult or disruptive person either in your family or in the workplace? What factors do you consider in determining whether you will be lenient or firm? Have you ever failed to confront someone for intolerable behavior? Have you ever demanded from someone more than he or she had the capacity to handle?

Reflection. The path of virtue is a *via media*, a mean between the extremes of excess and defect. Too much or too little of anything is not healthy. Throughout her writings, we see Teresa trying to steer a midcourse between the extremes of coddling oneself and neglecting one's health.

In *The Way of Perfection*, Teresa warns her nuns about the insidious danger of bodily comfort. "A fault this body has is that the more comfort we try to give it the more needs it discovers. It is amazing how much comfort it wants" (W. 11. 2.). She also writes, quite humorously, about paying undue attention to every little ache and pain. "Hardly does our head begin to ache than we stop going to choir, which won't kill us either. We stay away one day because our head ached, another because it was just now aching, and three more so that it won't ache again" (W. 10. 6.).

However, Teresa is not unmindful of the consequences of excessive mortification. She writes the following to her brother Lorenzo, who is seeking spiritual advice. "God desires your health more than your penance . . . Take great care not to give up sleep and to eat enough at your collation, for with your desire to do something for God you will not notice anything until the harm is done" (LE. 1. 506.).

We are presented with an image of the *via media* that avoids the two extremes of softness and hardness in the life of Siddharta Gautanma (Buddha). Siddharta was a prince raised in the lap of luxury. Having discovered that such an opulent life could not bring him wisdom, he left his father's house to live a life of extreme asceticism. However, this extreme did not yield him the wisdom that he sought. One day, as he was sitting on the bank of a river, a boat passed by. In the boat, a father was teaching his son how to play a lute. The father told his son that if the strings of the lute were too slack, poor music would be produced, but if they were stretched too tight, they would break. Thus, Siddharta discovered his "middle way."

Questions. Temperance is the virtue that moderates our behavior. It tightens behaviors that are self-indulgent and loosens those that are inflexible. Where in your life do you need to exercise the virtue of temperance? In what areas are you too lax or too rigid?

Reflection. St. Augustine formed a monastic community composed of people from the highest to the lowest stratum of Roman society. In consideration of the great diversity of their backgrounds, Augustine incorporated into his monastic rule the wisdom of the early Church. "Those who believed held all things in common . . . and all things *were distributed according to each one's need"* (Acts 2:44) (italics added).

> If special treatment in the way of diet is given to those who are not strong as a result of their former way of life, others who are stronger because they have had a different manner of life must not be aggrieved or think it unfair. Nor should they think the former luckier in getting something that they themselves do not get. Rather, they should be thankful that they are strong enough to do what others cannot. When those who have entered the monastery from a more luxurious way of life are given any food, clothing, bedding or covering that is not given to others who are stronger and more fortunate, these latter should consider how far the former have come down from their previous way of life in the world even though they cannot reach the simplicity in living which is possible for those who are stronger in body. All should not desire to receive the extra things which they see given to the few; such things are a concession, not an honor. Otherwise, a detestable disorder would arise in

the monastery, if the rich work there as hard as they can while the poor, who have greater strength, become soft.[11]

The principle contained in this passage is germane to the advice that Teresa gives to prioresses, namely, that a prioress should *not* treat the nuns *equally* but according to their *needs* and *capacities*. "The prioress can refrain from ordering them to do what she sees they will be *unable to do* because of their not having the strength within themselves" (F. 5. 9.) (italics added). What this means in practice is that the prioress will exempt certain nuns from the rigors of the rule in the same manner that Augustine recommends that "extra things [be] given to the few." In both Teresa's advice and Augustine's rule, the principle is the same—allowances and exceptions should be made for certain individuals.

Teresa is explicit in regard to nuns suffering from melancholy, just as Augustine is in regard to members of his community who belonged to the upper echelon of Roman society. Teresa writes, "And strive that they do not have long periods of prayer, not even those established by the constitutions. Let her [the prioress] take care that they eat fish only rarely; also during the fasts, they ought not to fast *as much as do the others* (F. 7. 9.) (italics added). In addition, Teresa tells the prioresses that certain nuns need not be required to be in chapel at the set times of prayer and that they can be given a dispensation from abstaining from meat.

Augustine anticipated resentment as a result of making allowances and exceptions. "If special treatment [is shown to some] . . . you must not be aggrieved or think it unfair."

It is not hard to imagine similar ill feelings engendered toward both the prioress and the melancholic nun who has been exempted from some of the strictures of the rule. Picture two nuns whispering to one another in the cloister. "Why does the prioress exempt Sr. Anna from making prayer in choir? It's not fair. All of us would like to sit in the cool shade of the cloister garden during prayer, instead of being cooped up in the hot choir. I think it's unfair. Quiet, here she comes. 'Good morning, Sr. Anna. I hope that you had a pleasant time at prayer in the *garden* today.'"

Questions. How do you feel when someone is given preferential treatment? Do you feel resentment? What behaviors are engendered by these feelings? Do you gripe to others? Do you spit out catty remarks? Do you shun or snub people? How are such feelings and behaviors affecting you spiritually?

Chapter 8

Some counsels concerning revelations and visions.

1. Some persons seem to become frightened just in hearing the words "visions" and "revelations." I don't understand why they consider this path along which God leads a soul such a dangerous one, or from where this dread comes. I do not want to treat now of which ones are good and which bad, or with the signs for discernment that I have heard from very learned persons; but of what ought to be done by someone who sees herself in this situation, for few are the confessors who will not intimidate her. Indeed, it doesn't cause as much fear or scandal to say that the devil is representing many kinds of temptation, the spirit of blasphemy, and absurd and indecent things as it does to say that an angel appeared or spoke or that our Lord Jesus Christ crucified was seen.

2. Nor do I want to treat at present of the revelations that are from God (for by now the fact that these bring great blessings to the soul goes without saying), but of the representations made by the devil in order to deceive and of how he makes use of the image of Christ our Lord, or of His saints. I hold that His Majesty will not give the devil the power to deceive a person by means of similar figures unless through that person's own fault, but that the devil himself will be the one deceived. (I mean, he will not deceive where there is humility).[1] Thus, there is no reason to be terrified but to trust in the Lord and pay little attention to these things except for the sake of praising the Lord more.

3. I know a person whose confessors caused her much distress over similar things; but afterward, from what she could understand through the great effects and good works that resulted, she judged that her experiences were from God. And she was very distressed that because of the command they gave her she had to bless herself and make the fig when she saw a vision.[2] Later, in talking with a highly learned Dominican,[3] she was told by him that this was wrong, that no one should do so, for wherever we see the image of our Lord, it is good to pay it reverence, even if the devil may have painted it. The devil is a great painter, and in wanting to do us an evil deed, he rather does us a good one if he paints a crucifix or other image so lifelike that he leaves it engraven in our heart. This reasoning pleased me much, for when we see a very good painting, even though we might know that a bad man did it, we wouldn't fail to esteem the image that was painted nor would we pay attention to the painter and lose our devotion. For the good or the evil does not lie in the vision but in the one who sees it and in whether or not she profits by it with humility; for if humility is present, no harm can be done not even by the devil. And if humility is not present, even if the visions be from God they will be of no benefit. For if that favor which should humble a nun when she sees she is unworthy of it makes her proud, she will be like the spider that converts everything it eats into poison; or like the bee that converts it all into honey.

4. I want to explain myself further: Our Lord, through His goodness, may wish to represent Himself to a soul so that it might know or love Him more, or that He might show it one of His secrets, or grant it some particular gifts or favors. And

if the soul, as I have said,[4] considers itself a saint because of a favor (for it should be confounded and know how little its lowliness deserves any favor) and thinks that this favor comes to it because of some service it has rendered, clearly the great good that could result is converted into evil, as in the example of the spider. Well now, let us suppose that the devil so as to incite pride causes these apparitions. The soul may think they are from God, humble itself, recognize its unworthiness to receive so great a favor, and strive to serve more. For in seeing itself rich, while not even deserving to eat the crumbs that fall from the table,[5] of the persons of whom it has heard that God grants these favors (I mean, not deserving to be a servant of any of them), it humbles itself, begins to force itself to do penance, prays more, and takes greater care not to offend this Lord. For it thinks it is He who grants this favor, and obeys with greater perfection. If it responds in these ways, I am sure the devil will not return, but will be put to shame, and that no harm will be left in the soul.

5. When she is told some things to do, or about the future, the nun should speak about the matter with a discreet and learned confessor, and not do or believe anything other than what he tells her. She can communicate about it with the prioress so that the latter might provide her with such a confessor. And let her be careful, for if she doesn't obey what the confessor tells her and fails to be guided by him, the experience comes from either the bad spirit or dreadful melancholy. Even if the confessor may not be right, she will be more right in not departing from what he tells her, even though it may be an angel of God who speaks to her in the favor. For His Majesty will enlighten the confessor or ordain how the task

may be carried out. In following the above advice, there is no danger; in doing otherwise, there can be many dangers and much harm.

6. Let us keep in mind that human nature is very weak, especially in women, and in this way of prayer weakness show itself more. Thus it is necessary that we don't immediately think that every little thing that comes to our fancy is a vision, and we should believe that when a vision does occur, this will be clearly known. Where some melancholy is present, there is need for much greater care. For in regard to these fancies, things have been told to me that have left me amazed at how it is possible for such persons truly to think that they see what they do not see.

7. Once a confessor, who was much admired, came to see me, for he was confessor to a person who told him that for many days our Lady appeared to her, sat on her bed, and spoke for over an hour telling her about future events and a great deal more. Among many absurdities there were some predictions that turned out to be right, and as a result the apparitions were thought to be true. I understood immediately the nature of the experience, although I did not dare say so. For we are in a world in which it is necessary to consider the opinions others have of us in order that our words take effect. So I told him to wait to see if the prophecies would prove true and to look for other effects and inquire into the life of that person. In the end he came to understand that the whole thing was nonsense.

8. I could tell of so many things like this that would more than justify my advice, that is: that a soul should not believe things at once, but that it wait for time to pass and understand itself well before telling the confessor so that it doesn't deceive

him without wanting to deceive him. For if he doesn't have experience of these things, his learning however great will not suffice for him to understand them. Not so long ago (in fact, very recently) there was a man who spoke much nonsense about things like these to some very learned and spiritual men. When he spoke with a person who had experienced such favors from the Lord, she saw clearly that he was suffering from madness together with illusion. Although the illusion wasn't then manifest but very dissimulated, the Lord after a while revealed it clearly; but this person who understood what the cause was had first to suffer much in not being believed.[6]

9. For these reasons and other similar ones it's very necessary for each Sister to speak clearly about her prayer to the prioress. The prioress should carefully consider the temperament and perfection in virtue of that Sister so that she might advise the confessor and provide for better understanding. She should choose a confessor for this particular purpose if the ordinary confessor is not sufficient for such matters. Let the Sisters be very careful that things like these, even though very truly from God, or favors recognized as miraculous, be not communicated to outsiders or to confessors who don't have the prudence to be silent. This is most important, more so than they may think, and it's important that the Sisters not discuss these things among themselves. And the prioress, with prudence, should always be seen as tending more to praise those who distinguish themselves in matters pertaining to humility, mortification, and obedience than those God leads by this very supernatural path of prayer, even though the latter may have all these other virtues. For if this path is from the spirit of the Lord, it brings with it the humility to like being despised. And

the praise of the above virtues will not harm the person who is led by this path and will benefit others. For since the others cannot attain to these things, for God gives to whomever He wants, let them flee sadness and seek to have the other virtues. Although God also gives these other virtues, they can in addition be the objects of our striving, and they are of great value for the Religious life. May His Majesty give them to us since no one who strives for them with effort, solitude, prayer, and confidence in His mercy will be denied by Him.

COUNSELS ON VISIONS AND REVELATIONS
Summary and Background: Chapter 8

This chapter concerns visions produced by the devil and by God. Teresa says that we should not fear visions that come from the devil; rather, we should fear how *we relate* to them. If we relate to these visions with pride, we become vulnerable to the deceptions of the devil. Conversely, if we relate them with humility, we can profit from them. Talking about herself in the third person, Teresa writes,

> I know a person whose confessors caused her much distress over similar things [said that her visions were from the devil]; but afterward, from what she could understand through the great effects and good works that resulted, she judged that her experiences were from God. And she was very distressed that because of the command they gave her she had to bless herself and make the fig when she saw a vision. Later, in talking with a highly learned Dominican, she was told by him that this was wrong, that no one should do so, for wherever we see the image of our Lord, it is good to pay it reverence, even if the devil may have painted it. The devil is a great painter, and in wanting to do us an evil deed, he rather does us a good one if he paints a crucifix or other image so lifelike that he leaves it engraven in our heart. This reasoning pleased me much, for when we see a very good painting, even though we might know that a bad man did it, we

wouldn't fail to esteem the image that was painted nor would we pay attention to the painter and lose our devotion. For the good or the evil does not lie in the vision but in the one who sees it and in whether or not she profits by it with humility; for if humility is present, no harm can be done not even by the devil. And if humility is not present, even if the visions be from God they will be of no benefit. For if that favor which should humble a nun when she sees she is unworthy of it makes her proud, she will be like the spider that converts everything it eats into poison; or like the bee that converts it all into honey. (F. 8. 3.)

What Teresa is saying in this passage is that just because something comes from the devil, it does not mean that it will have a bad effect, or if something comes from God, it does not mean that it will have a good effect. It all depends upon how we relate to what is presented to us.

Next, Teresa gives advice to souls that believe that God has told them "some things to do" (F. 8. 5.). Teresa, knowing that it is dangerous to act upon *our interpretations* of visions, counsels that we "should speak about the matter with a discreet and learned confessor" (F. 8. 5.).

In addition to the qualities of being discreet and learned, Teresa underlines the importance that the confessor also have *experience* in such matters. This is because "if [the confessor] doesn't have experience of these things, his learning however great will not suffice for him to understand them" (F. 8. 8.).

Finally, Teresa ends this chapter by giving an admonition regarding discretion and prudence. She counsels her nuns not to tell people outside the monastery about the favors that God has granted them, especially "confessors who don't have the prudence to be silent" (F. 8. 9.). Furthermore, she advises the prioresses not to draw attention to nuns who have received these graces but to praise those who practice virtue. To do the opposite would be to send the wrong message, namely, that spiritual experiences are more important than living a life of virtue.

Reflection. Abstracting from the subject matter of visions, we may summarize the underlying principle of Teresa's teaching in the first half of this chapter as follows—don't consider the *source*, consider the *effect*. What determines whether something will help or harm us depends upon us. For example, if someone insults you, the insult can harm you, only if you harbor a grudge or seek revenge. However, the insult can help you grow, if by God's grace, you are able to forgive the person who has insulted you. To use Teresa's image, in the first instance, we are like the spider that converts the insult into poison. In the second instance, we are like the bee that converts it into honey.

St. Francis de Sales uses a metaphor similar to Teresa's image of the spider and the bee.

Remember that while bees are making honey they live and feed on bitter food, and that we can never perform acts of greater sweetness and patience, or better, compose honey of excellent virtues, than while we eat the bread of bitterness and live amid afflictions. Just as the best honey is gathered from the blossoms of thyme, a small bitter herb, so also the virtue practiced in the bitterness of the most vile, low, and abject humiliations is the most excellent of all.[7]

The art of the saints is the ability to draw good out of every situation, no matter how bitter or painful. They knew that nothing could separate them from the love of Christ, if they accepted God's grace to respond in love in the face of suffering.

Questions. We can either be helped or harmed by any experience in life, depending upon how we respond to it. Like the saints, we too can draw good out of every situation, if we accept God's grace to respond in love. Where in your life is God offering you the grace to respond more like the bee than the spider?

Reflection. "Give every man thine ear, but few thy voice" (Hamlet, I 3, 68). Teresa's version of Polonius's advice to his son Laertes may be as follows. "Give every priest your ear but disclose your heart to few of them." In short, be very selective about persons to whom you open your heart. One of the reasons that Teresa counsels caution in this regard is that even though a confessor is educated, he may be ignorant in spiritual matters. "If [the confessor] doesn't have experience of these things, his learning however great will not suffice for him to understand them" (F. 8. 8.). In consequence, he may misinterpret a penitent's experiences and give bad advice.

Teresa is telling her sisters not to give credence to someone's interpretation of their spiritual experiences merely because he is a priest. This caution is based upon Teresa's own experience with priests. Some were good spiritual directors and others proved to be incompetent; some gave good advice and others gave bad advice. Teresa's teaching is very important in our own day.

I have often heard people espouse the belief that "the priest stands in the place of God," without ever asking what this *means*. To help us to differentiate what this statement *means* from what it does *not mean*, let us take the example of the Sacrament of Reconciliation. In the confessional, the priest stands in the place of God because he has been given the power to forgive sins. The absolution that he gives is valid because he is the ordained instrument *through which* God's forgiveness is granted. The absolution is valid regardless of the priest's state of soul, even if the priest is in the state of mortal sin. In this sense, we can say that the priest stands in the place of God.

However, we cannot apply this statement to the human attributes of a priest. A priest's authority to give absolution in the confessional does not validate the truth of the *advice* that he gives to a penitent. To believe that the priest stands in the place of God regarding the *counsel* that he gives is a very dangerous belief, for there are many holy priests who give bad spiritual advice. "If [the confessor] doesn't have experience of these things, his learning however great will not suffice for him to understand them" (F. 8. 8.). The essence of Teresa's advice is this. Be cautious with whom you share your inner life. Just because a person is either intelligent or in a position of authority, do not assume that he or she can understand your soul.

Questions. Have you ever been imprudent by sharing the secrets of your heart with someone who did not have the capacity to understand you? What was the effect?

Chapter 9

Deals with how she left Medina del Campo for the foundation of St. Joseph in Malagón.

1. How far I've wandered from my subject! And yet, it could be that some of these counsels that were mentioned were more opportune than my telling about the foundations. Well now, while at St. Joseph's in Medina del Campo I observed with great consolation how those Sisters were following in the footsteps of the Sisters of St. Joseph's in Avila through complete religious dedication, sisterly love, and spirituality. I observed, too, how our Lord provided for His house, for the needs of the chapel as well as for those of the Sisters. Some of the new ones entering the monastery it seemed the Lord had chosen as the kind of cement that is suited to an edifice like this. In these beginning stages, all the good, I think, will be for the sake of the future. For since these Sisters find the path, those who are to come will follow it.

2. There was a lady in Toledo, a sister of the Duke of Medinaceli, in whose home I had stayed by order of my superiors, as I mentioned more at length in writing about the foundation of St. Joseph's.[1] While I was in her home, she got to like me in a special way, which in turn must have been a means by which this lady was stirred to do what she did. For His Majesty often makes use of means like these that seem fruitless to us who don't know the future. Since this lady knew that I had permission to found monasteries, she began to urge me very much to make a foundation in her town of Malagón.[2] I in no way wanted to accept since the town was so small that we would be forced

126

to have an income in order to support ourselves—something to which I was very much opposed.

3. Both my confessor[3] and other learned men with whom I discussed the matter told me that I was doing wrong, that since the holy Council had given permission to have an income, I shouldn't, because of my own opinion, fail to found a monastery where God could be so much served. To this were added the many urgings of this lady which I could not resist. She provided a sufficient income, for I am always in favor of monasteries being either completely poor or maintained in such a way that the nuns will not need to beg from anyone for their needs.

4. I made every effort I could so that none of the nuns would possess anything, but that they would observe the constitutions in their entirety as in our other monasteries founded in poverty. Having completed all the paper work, I sent for some Sisters to make the foundation, and along with that lady we went to Malagón. When we got there, the house was not yet ready for us to move in. And so we were detained for more than eight days in an apartment of this lady's castle.

5. On Palm Sunday,[4] in the year 1568, with the people of the town, we went in procession to the church, in our white mantles and with veils covering our faces. A sermon was preached there, and from that church the Blessed Sacrament was brought to our monastery. This inspired great devotion in everybody. I stayed there for some days. On one of those days, while in prayer after having received Communion, I understood from our Lord that He would be served in that house. I don't think I was there quite two months, for my spirit was eager to go and found a house in Valladolid, and the reason was the one I will now mention.

MALAGÓN (1568)

Summary and Background: Chapter 9

"How far I've wandered from my subject! And yet, it could be that some of these counsels that were mentioned were more opportune than my telling about the foundations" (F. 9. 1.). After taking an extended but fruitful detour from her account of the founding of her convents, Teresa returns to her subject matter, the founding of her next monastery in Malagón.

However, before dealing with Malagón, Teresa makes the following statement about the quality of the nuns in the community of Medina del Campo. "Some of the new ones entering the monastery it seemed the Lord had chosen as the kind of cement that is suited to an edifice like this. In these beginning stages, all the good, I think, will be for the sake of the future. For since these Sisters find the path, those who are to come will follow it" (F. 9. 1.). In short, what will ensure the survival of the community is the holiness of its members that will attract vocations.

While Teresa was in Medina del Campo, she received two offers from rich benefactors to found two more monasteries. The first was from Don Bernardino de Mendoza, the brother of Don Alvaro de Mendoza, the bishop of Avila. Don Bernardino offered Teresa his country villa on the outskirts of Valladolid. We will say more about Don Bernardino, in chapter ten, where Teresa discusses the foundation at Valladolid.

The second benefactor was Doña Luisa de la Cerda, a very rich noblewoman, who wanted Teresa to found a convent in Malagón in memory of her deceased husband Arias Pardo de Savedra. Malagón was the city in which Arias had been lord. Teresa had become acquainted with Doña Luisa at the time of her husband's death in 1562. In her grief, Doña Luisa wanted a spiritual companion to give her solace. Having heard of a holy Carmelite nun in Avila named Teresa, Doña Luisa approached Angel de Salazar, Teresa's provincial. She requested that Teresa come to live with her in Toledo. Because Doña Luisa was a very generous benefactor, Salazar did not want to refuse her request. Therefore, he ordered Teresa to go to Toledo, where she stayed with Doña Luisa from January to July of 1562 (The account of Teresa's stay can be found in *The Book of Her Life*, chapter 34).

Now, six years later, Doña Luisa wants Teresa to found a monastery in Malagón. Teresa decided to go to Toledo to see Doña Luisa about her offer. However, first she had to make a side trip to Alcalá at the request of another influential woman, Doña Leonor de Mascareñas, who had been the governess of both King Phillip II and Charles V.

In 1562 (the same year that Teresa founded St. Joseph's in Avila), Doña Leonor had helped a *beata*, María of Jesus, to found a convent in Alcalá, based upon the primitive rule of Carmel. María of Jesus was an extremely fervent (some would contend unbalanced), pious women. She was a widow who decided to become a religious. She donned sackcloth and walked to Rome barefoot to obtain permission to found a monastery. There is a story, be it real or apocryphal, that as she was setting out on her pilgrimage, her little boy came running up behind her, crying for his mother. Undeterred by motherly affection, she put her son in the custody of an aunt and resolutely set her face like flint toward the Eternal City.

Apocryphal or not, this story speaks of María's commitment to actualize her vision, which unfortunately included a brutal penitential way of life. The inhumanity of the convent's asceticism plus the fact that the convent was deep in debt so concerned Doña Leonor that she asked Teresa to go to Alcalá to see what could be done.

Besides the fact that Teresa was known for her intelligence and common sense, there was a specific reason why Doña Leonor implored Teresa's assistance. While Teresa lived with Doña Luisa in 1562, Teresa had became acquainted with María of Jesus. It was Doña Leonor's hope that since they knew one another and shared a common value, namely, wanting to live a stricter form of the Carmelite life, that María would listen to Teresa's advice.

Teresa went to Alcalá and spoke to María. However, we do not know the outcome of their meeting. Many believe that it was fruitless because Teresa never refers to it, either in the *Foundations* or in any of her letters. However, this argument from silence is not conclusive, for Maria's convent that had been on the verge of collapse still exists today. Some believe that the weeks that Teresa spent at Alcalá permeated the convent with her common sense, which tempered the community's approach to excessive penances.

After Teresa left Alcalá, she traveled to Toledo, where Doña Luisa welcomed her warmly. Doña Luisa offered Teresa both a building to live in and an income to support the community. While Teresa was grateful for the offer, she hesitated for two reasons. First, she did not want to accept the offer of an income for the nuns, for she wanted the convent to be founded in poverty, that is, supported by alms and the work of the nuns. Second, Teresa was wary of establishing a convent in Malagón because it was a poor town. Could a convent founded in poverty survive in this locale? Could the populace afford to purchase the handiwork of the nuns? Would there be sufficient alms?

In the face of Teresa's resistance, "[Doña Luisa] began to urge (*importunar*) me very much to make a foundation in her town of Malagón" (F. 9. 2.). *Importunar* can be translated in various ways. It can mean to urge, to ask persistently, to disturb by reiterating the same request, and even to harass. Perhaps the best translation is "to pester."

In addition to Doña Luisa's pestering, Domingo Báñez, O.P., Teresa's confessor, told her that she was allowing her ideal to get in the way of founding another convent. "Both my confessor and other learned men with whom I discussed the matter told me that I was doing wrong, that since the holy Council [The Council of Trent 1554–1563] had given permission to have an income, I shouldn't, because of my own opinion, fail to found a monastery where God could be so much served" (F. 9. 3.).

In the end, Teresa acquiesced. Teresa, Doña Luisa, and her retinue set out for Malagón. They arrived on

April 1, 1568, and stayed at Doña Luisa's castle. The convent of Malagón was founded on Palm Sunday, April 11. However, in a short period of time, it became evident that a mistake had been made. The monastery was situated so close to the marketplace that the noise from the streets was a source of continual distraction. Teresa brought this to Doña Luisa's attention. After hearing Teresa's concern, Doña Luisa permitted Teresa to choose a more suitable site. Teresa designed the new monastery herself. It was exactly what she wanted. However, it was another eleven years before the monastery was completed.

Reflection. At the beginning of this chapter, Teresa states that since the nuns in Medina del Campo had found the right path "those who are to come will follow it" (F. 9. 1.). This testament to the power of virtue and good example is so fundamental to Teresa's teaching that we see it throughout her writings. For example, in *The Interior Castle*, we read, "Do you think such humility, your mortification, service of all and great charity toward them, and love of the Lord is of little benefit? This fire of love in *you* enkindles *their* souls, and with every other virtue, *you* will always be awakening *them* (IC. 7. 4. 14.) (italics added). Likewise, in *The Way of Perfection*, Teresa writes, "when virtue is placed before our eyes, the one who desires it grows fond of it and seeks to gain it" (W. 6. 1.). These passages speak of the power of good example. By observing the lives of others, not only do we find instruction on how to live a virtuous life, but, more importantly, we begin to *desire* to live virtuously. It is within this perspective that we should take care in how we live. As Cardinal Suenens once said, "Be careful in the way that you live, for your life may be the only gospel that your neighbor ever reads."

Questions. Have you ever considered that your quiet fidelity to your calling in life enkindles in others the desire to do good? Who are the people in your life who enkindle in your soul the desire to grow in virtue?

Reflection. Teresa spends only one chapter (one and a half pages) on the foundation of Malagón. Nevertheless, this chapter is important. It deals with a conflict that Teresa struggled with most of her life—the conflict between her ideal of founding monasteries in poverty and accepting endowments from rich benefactors who would ensure a fixed income for her nuns. If Teresa accepted endowments from rich benefactors, she would not be living her ideal. If she adhered to her ideal, she would found fewer monasteries.

This conflict raises several important questions. When Teresa acquiesced, was she caving in to Doña Luisa's pressure? By accepting Doña Luisa's offer, would she be abandoning the very reason why she had left the Incarnation? Was Teresa watering down her ideal or was she accepting reality? Was she *giving in* or *letting go*? When is being adamant in adhering to one's ideal doing the will of God, and when is it being obstinate?

Questions. Have you ever been in a situation similar to Teresa's, namely, struggling with the choice between adhering inflexibly to your ideals and allowing them to be tempered by reality? Teresa was able to temper her ideal when she accepted the fact "that she was allowing her ideal to get in the way" (F. 9. 3.) of serving God. Have you ever considered that adhering rigidly to your ideal is an obstacle to seeing and doing the will of God?

Reflection. Consider the following scenario. As a result of Domingo Báñez's persuasive argument, Teresa is now inclined to make a foundation in Malagón. However, as Doña Luisa continues to pressure Teresa, she is tempted to refuse the offer in order to spite Doña Luisa. Teresa doesn't want to give Doña Luisa the satisfaction that she has won.

We sometimes find ourselves in similar situations. Let us say that you are thinking of repainting the outside of your house and a snooty neighbor makes the suggestion that white with green shutters would be the perfect combination. You resent your neighbor's suggestion because he has always given the impression that his aesthetic taste is far superior to yours. Unfortunately, before he gave his suggestion, you had already decided to paint your house white with green shutters. You're furious and feel caught in a bind. You *want* to paint your house white with green shutters; however, you *don't want* to give the impression that you are doing so because of your neighbor's suggestion. You dread the endless comments that he will make to you and your neighbors about how his "exquisite taste" informed your decision.

The danger at this juncture is that you will *deprive yourself* of what you want because you want to *withhold from* your neighbor the satisfaction that he wants. However, whenever you grudgingly withhold something from another, you are held fast in the grip of a grudge, and you only do harm to yourself.

Conversely, there is a great opportunity at this juncture. If you choose to paint your house white with green shutters, without caring if your neighbor believes that you did so because of his suggestion, then you have taken the first step in becoming free of what your neighbor thinks. It takes a special form of courage to allow people to think what they want of you.

Questions. Have you ever deprived yourself of what you wanted in order to spite someone else? In contrast, have you ever experienced the peace of not giving in to the desire to spite another?

Chapter 10

Deals with the foundation of the house in Valladolid. Its title is The Conception of Our Lady of Mount Carmel.

1. Four or five months before this monastery of St. Joseph's in Malagón was founded, I was speaking with a distinguished young gentleman[1] who told me that if I wanted to establish a monastery in Valladolid he would most willingly give me a house he owned with a large and good garden containing a vineyard. He wanted to give away the property immediately; it was very valuable. I accepted his offer, although I wasn't too decided on making a foundation where the property was, since the place was about a quarter of a league outside the city. But it seemed to me that we could move to the city once the possession of a house had been taken in that district. And since he offended it so willingly, I did not want to refuse his good deed or hinder his devotion.[2]

2. Two months later, more or less, he was struck by a sudden illness that took away his speech, and he could not confess well, although he made many signs to ask the Lord's pardon. He died shortly afterward, very far from where I was.[3] The Lord told me that the young man's salvation had been in great jeopardy but that he had received mercy for the service he had rendered to the Blessed Mother in giving that house to be a monastery of her order; however, that he would not leave purgatory until the first Mass was said there, that then he would leave. I was so conscious of the grievous afflictions of this soul that even though I wanted to make a foundation in

Toledo, I set it aside for then and hastened as much as I could to found a house in Valladolid.

3. It couldn't be made as quickly as I desired, for I was forced to delay a number of days as St. Joseph's in Avila, which was under my charge, and afterward at St. Joseph's in Medina del Campo, for I passed by there. I was in prayer one day in Medina when the Lord told me to hurry because that soul was suffering very much. Although I didn't have the means available, I set to work and entered Valladolid on the feast of St. Lawrence.[4] And when I saw the house, I was dismayed; I knew that it would be a foolish mistake for nuns to stay there. The cost to them would be very great. For although the site was most gratifying on account of the garden which was so delightful, the nuns would certainly become sick, for it was near a river.

4. Though tired out, I had to go to Mass at a monastery of our order. I saw that the monastery was at the entrance to the city,[5] and this was so far away that my distress was doubled. Nonetheless, I said nothing to my companions[6] so as not to discourage them. Although weak, I had some faith that the Lord, by whom I had been told what was just mentioned, would provide a remedy. I arranged very secretly for workmen to come and begin building walls to provide for recollection, and other necessary things. With us, were the priest I mentioned, Julián de Avila,[7] and one of the friars mentioned,[8] who desired to be discalced and who was learning about our method of procedure in these houses. Julián de Avila was engaged in seeking to obtain the license from the bishop, who, before I arrived, had given us reason to hope that it would be

granted. The license could not be gotten so quickly as to prevent a Sunday from coming along first. But permission was granted to say Mass where the church would be, and thus it was said for us.

5. I had forgotten that what was told to me about that soul would then be accomplished.[9] For, although I was told "at the first Mass," I thought that it would be at the one in which the Blessed Sacrament would be reserved. When the priest[10] came with the Blessed Sacrament to the place where we were to receive Communion and I approached to receive it, the gentleman I mentioned appeared beside him, his face joyful and resplendent. With hands folded, he thanked me for what I had done so that he could leave purgatory and go to heaven. And indeed before the first locution, when I heard that he was on the way to salvation, I had not had such a thing in mind and was consequently much afflicted. It seemed to me that another way of dying would have been necessary in view of the way he had lived. For although he had performed many good deeds, he was much involved in the things of the world. True, though, he had told my companions that he kept death very much before him. It is important to know that our Lord is pleased with any service rendered to His Mother, and great is His mercy. May He be blessed and praised for everything. For He repays our lowly deeds with eternal life and glory, and He makes them great while they are in fact of little value.

6. Well, when the feastday of our Lady's Assumption arrived, which was August 15, 1568, we took possession of this monastery. We were there only a short while[11] because almost all of us fell very sick. This was seen by a lady from that city, Doña María de Mendoza, who is the wife of

Commander Cobos[12] and mother of the marquis of Camarasa. She is a very Christian woman and most charitable. The superabundance of alms she gave away made this clear. When she saw the situation, and before I spoke to her about the matter, she showed me much charity; for she is the sister of the bishop of Avila who was very favorable toward us in the foundation of the first monastery and is still so in all that pertains to our order.[13] Since she is very charitable and saw that we could not remain there without great hardship and also that the site was far from where we could receive alms, as well as unhealthy, she told us to give that house to her and that she would buy us another. And this she did. The one she gave us was worth much more, and in addition she has given all that is necessary up till now, and she will do so as long as she lives.

7. On the feast of St. Blaise[14] we moved there in a large procession, and with great devotion shown on the part of the people; and their devotedness continues even to this day, for the Lord grants many favors in that house. And He has brought souls whose sanctity in due time will be recounted so that He may be praised. For it is by such means that the Lord desires to magnify His works and favor His creatures. In fact, a very young girl entered there and showed what the world is by despising it. It has occurred to me to speak of her here so that those who have great love for the world will be put to shame and that young girls to whom the Lord may give good desires and inspirations will take her example and carry them out.

8. There is in this place a lady named Doña María de Acuña, a sister of the Count of Buendía. She was married to the governor of Castile. When he died, she was left, while still

quite young, with a son and two daughters. She began to live so holy a life and rear her children in such virtue that she merited from the Lord that He desire these children for Himself. (I was mistaken, for she was left with three daughters.) The one daughter became a nun immediately. The other one did not want to marry but lived a very edifying life with her mother.[15] The son at an early age began to understand what the world was and felt so intensely God's call to enter religious life that no one was able to prevent him from following it. His mother was so delighted with his vocation that she helped him very much by her prayers to our Lord, although for fear of his relatives she did not show this openly. In sum, when the Lord wants a soul for Himself, creatures have little strength to prevent this. So it happened in this case, for after having been delayed for three years and strongly urged to change his mind, he entered the Society of Jesus.[16] A confessor of this lady[17] told me that he had been informed by her that she had never in her life experienced such joy in her heart as on the day her son made his profession.

9. O Lord! What a great favor You grant to those children whose parents love them so much as to want them to possess their estates, inheritance, and riches in that blessed life that has no end! It is a great pity the world is now so unfortunate and blind that it seems to parents their honor lies in not letting the dung of this world's goods be forgotten and in not remembering that sooner or later these things will come to an end. And everything that has limits, even though it lasts a while, will eventually come to an end; and little importance should be given to it. Such parents want to sustain their own vanities at a cost to their children, and very boldly take from God souls

that He wants for Himself. And they take from these souls a good so great (God inviting them to be His guest) that, even were the good not to last forever, it would still be extraordinary to see oneself freed from the tiresomeness of the world and its laws; and the more goods people possess, the greater the tedium. Open the eyes of parents, my God. Make them understand the kind of love they are obliged to have for their children so that they do not do these children so much wrong and are not complained about before God in that final judgment where, even though they may not want to know it, the value of each thing will be understood.

10. Well, this gentleman, who was the son of this Doña María de Acuña (his name was Don Antonio de Padilla), at the age of seventeen, more or less, was mercifully drawn by God from the world. Hence, the estates went to the oldest daughter, whose name was Doña Luisa de Padilla. For the Count of Buendía had no sons, and Don Antonio was heir to both the earldom and the governorship of Castile. I will not mention the many things Don Antonio suffered from his relatives before going on with his plan, because this is not my purpose in writing. Whoever knows how much value those of the world place on their having an heir to their properties will fully understand.

11. O Son of the Eternal Father, Jesus Christ, our Lord, true King of all! What did You leave in the world? What could we, your descendants, inherit from You? What did You possess, my Lord, but trials, sufferings, and dishonor? You had nothing but a wooden beam on which to swallow the painfully difficult drink of death. In sum, my God, it does not fit those of us who want to be your true children, and hold on to their inheritance,

to flee suffering. Your heraldry consists of five wounds. Courage, then, my daughters; this must be our badge if we are to inherit His kingdom. Not with rest, not with favors, not with honors, not with riches will that which He bought with so much blood by gained. O illustrious people! Open your eyes for the love of God; behold that the true knights of Jesus Christ and the princes of His Church, a St. Peter and a St. Paul, did not follow the road you follow. Do you think perhaps there will be a new road for you? Do not believe it. Behold the Lord is beginning to show it to you through such young persons as those of whom we are now speaking.

12. At times I have seen and spoken to this Don Antonio. He would have wanted even many more possessions so as to leave them all. Blessed the young man and blessed the young girl who have merited so much from God that at the age in which people are usually overpowered by the world, they trampled on it. Blessed be He who bestowed on them so much good.

13. Well since the estates were left to the older sister, it happened that she didn't attribute any more importance to them than did her brother. For from the time she was a child she gave herself so much to prayer (which is the place where the Lord gives the light to understand truths) that she esteemed these things as little as did her brother. Oh, God help me, how many trials, torments, litigations, and even risking of lives and honor many would undergo to be heir to this inheritance. She suffered greatly in order to be allowed to renounce it. So goes this world; it would clearly show us its frenzy if we were not blind. Very willingly, so that they might leave her free from this inheritance, she renounced it in favor of her sister—for there

was no one else—who was ten or eleven years old. Immediately, in order to perpetuate their miserable family name, her relatives arranged to have this young girl marry an uncle of hers, the brother of her father, and obtained a dispensation from the Supreme Pontiff; and the two were engaged.

14. The Lord did not desire that the daughter of such a mother and the sister of both such a brother and such sisters be left more deceived than they, and thus what I will now relate happened. When the girl began to enjoy the worldly clothes and finery that, in accord with her status, would attract the fancy of a girl at that tender age (two months had not yet gone by from the time of her engagement), the Lord began to give her light, although she was not then aware of what He was doing. Once at the close of a day she had spent most happily with her fiancé, whom she loved more intensely than her age warranted, she became extremely sad at seeing how the day came to an end and that likewise all days would come to an end. Oh, greatness of God! That very happiness that the joys of perishable things gave her, she came to abhor! She began to experience such great sadness that she couldn't hide it from her fiancé, nor did she know how to tell him, nor could she, even though he was questioning her.

15. At that time she had to go on an unavoidable journey to a place far from where she lived. She felt very sorry since she loved him so much. But soon the Lord revealed to her the cause of her affliction; it was, in fact, that her soul was inclined toward that which would have no end. She began to consider how her brother and sister had chosen the safer path and left her amid the world's dangers. This, on the one hand; on the other hand, the fact that it seemed there was no remedy was

exhausting her (for she wasn't aware, until she asked, that even though she was engaged it was still possible for her to become a nun). And above all, the love she had for her fiancé did not allow her to come to a decision. So she was suffering much distress.

16. Since the Lord wanted her for Himself, He gradually took away this love she had for her fiancé and increased her desire to give up everything. At this time she was moved only by the desire to be saved and to seek the best means. For it seemed to her that in the midst of the things of the world she would forget to seek that which is eternal. This is the wisdom God infused in her at so early an age; to seek how to gain that which is without end. Fortunate soul that so early in life freed itself from the blindness in which many old people die! Once she saw that her will was free, she resolved to occupy it completely in God. Until that time she had remained silent; now she began to speak of the matter to her sister. Her sister, thinking it was a childish trifle, tried to dissuade her and told her some things about how she could be saved even though married. The young girl responded by asking her sister why she herself had given up marriage. Some days passed, and her desire went on increasing. She didn't say anything to her mother, but perhaps it was the mother who through her prayers was causing this battle in her daughter.

Chapter 11

Continues the subject that was begun about how Doña Casilda de Padilla attained her holy desires of entering religious life.

1. At this time the habit was received by a lay Sister in this monastery of the Immaculate Conception about whose vocation I should perhaps say something.[1] Although she is from a different background (a little peasant girl), she is so virtuous, because of the great favors God has granted her, that she deserves to be remembered here in praise of Him. And when Doña Casilda (the name of this girl beloved of the Lord) went with her grandmother,[2] who was her fiancé's mother, to this lay Sister's reception of the habit, she felt intensely drawn to this monastery, thinking that since it was small and the nuns were few they could serve the Lord better. But she still had not reached the decision to leave her fiancé, which, as I said,[3] was what most held her back.

2. She recalled how before she was engaged she used to spend periods of time in prayer. Her mother in her goodness and holiness had brought her children up this way, for once they reached the age of seven she would make them enter an oratory from time to time, and she taught them how to reflect on the Passion of the Lord and made them to go to confession frequently. And thus she witnessed this happy outcome of her desires, that her children belong only to God. She told me herself that she had always offered them to God and begged Him to take them out of the world, for she was already disillusioned and knew how little it should be esteemed. I sometimes reflect on the accidental joy that will be hers when she

sees them rejoicing in eternal joys and that she was the means, and on the gratitude they will have toward her, and how on the contrary those parents who did not bring their children up as children of God (for they are children more of God than of their parents) will find themselves, together with their children, in hell, and the maledictions they will spew forth and the despair they will experience.

3. Well, to return to what I was saying, since Doña Casilda realized that she was now reluctant even to recite the rosary, she had great fear that things would always get worse. It seemed to her she saw clearly that by coming to this house her salvation would be assured. And thus she reached an unwavering decision. One morning when she came here with her sister and mother, the occasion arose for their entering inside the monastery; indeed without any worry that the young girl would do what she did. Once she saw herself inside, no one was able to get her to leave the house. So many were the tears and words with which she begged them to allow her to stay that all were frightened. Her mother, although interiorly rejoicing, feared the relatives and did not want her to remain in this way lest they say that the daughter had been persuaded by her mother. And the prioress,[4] too, felt like this, for it seemed to her that the girl was but a child and that more testing was needed. This took place in the morning. They had to stay until evening, and they sent for the girl's confessor and for Father Maestro Fray Domingo (the Dominican whom I mentioned in the beginning),[5] who was my confessor, although I was not here then.[6] This Father understood at once that it was the Spirit of the Lord. He helped her very much, suffering a good deal from her relatives, promising to help

her so that she could return another day. (That is the way all
those who seek to serve God must act. They must strive not
to consider human prudence so much when they see a soul
called by God).

4. After a great deal of persuasion, and so that blame
would not be placed on her mother, she came out this time.
Her desires continued to increase. Her mother began to inform
her relatives secretly so that the fiancé would not learn of it.
They said her desire was a childish whim and that she should
wait until she was of age, for she wasn't yet twelve years old.
She asked why, since they found her old enough to be married and left to the world, they didn't find her old enough to
give herself to God. The things she said made it appear that it
wasn't she who was speaking.

5. The matter couldn't be kept so secret that her fiancé
was not informed. Since she knew about this, it seemed to her
that she couldn't bear waiting for him to give his consent to
her entering religious life. On the feast of the Immaculate
Conception, when she was in the house of her grandmother
(who was also her mother-in-law to be), who didn't know
anything about her desires, she begged to be allowed to go
to the country with her governess to relax a while. Her grandmother, to please her, allowed her to go, in a carriage along
with her servants. Giving one of the servants some money, the
girl asked him to wait for her at the entrance of this monastery
with some bundles of twigs or vine branches. She arranged to
go in a roundabout way so that they would pass by this house.
When she arrived at the entrance, she told the servants to ask
at the turn for a jug of water and not to tell who it was for, and
she quickly got down from the carriage. The servants told her

not to get down, that they would bring the water to her, but she refused. The bundles were already there. She told them to tell the nuns to come to the door to get those bundles, and she stood waiting there. When the nuns opened, she entered inside and went and embraced the statue of our Lady, weeping and begging the prioress not to throw her out. The shouts of the servants were loud as was also their pounding on the door. She went to speak to them at the grille and told them that she would by no means come out and that they should go and tell her mother. The women that had gone with her broke into loud laments. She made little of it all. Her grandmother, when told the news, decided to go at once.

6. In sum, neither the girl's grandmother, nor her uncle, nor her fiancé (who came to the grille and tried to get her to change her mind) could do any more than torment her when with her, and afterward she would be stronger in her resolve. Her fiancé, after much moaning, told her that she could serve God more by giving alms. She answered that he could give them. And, in response to his other arguments, she told him that she was more obliged to seek her salvation and that she saw she was weak and that she could not be saved amid worldly occasions of sin, and that he should not complain about her because she hadn't left him except for God, and that because of this she was not offending him. Once she saw that nothing satisfied him, she got up and left him.

7. He made no impression on her; rather, she felt totally displeased with him. When God enlightens the soul with truth, temptations and stumbling blocks set by the devil help it more. For it is His Majesty who fights for the soul, and thus she saw clearly here that it was not she who was speaking.

8. Since her fiancé and relatives saw how little they accomplished in trying to get her to leave willingly, they turned to force. Thus, they obtained a court order to take her out of the monastery and that the nuns allow her to leave. During the whole time, from the feast of the Immaculate Conception to that of the Holy Innocents[7] (when they took her away), she remained in the monastery, without receiving the habit, but following all the religious observances as though she had received it, and with the greatest happiness. On the day the law officers took her away she was brought to the house of a gentleman. She was in tears, asking why they were tormenting her since it would be no avail. In the gentleman's house men religious as well as other persons tried hard to persuade her. Some thought it was all childish, others wanted her to enjoy the married state. I'd have to go on at great length if I were to tell about the arguments she was confronted with and the way she got out of them all. She left them astonished by the things she said.

9. Since they saw they were getting no where, they brought her to her mother's house so as to detain her there for a while. Her mother was now tired of seeing so much disturbance, but did not by any means help her; rather, from what appeared, she was against her. It could be that she was against her so as to test her further. At least that's what she told me afterward, and she is so holy one cannot but believe what she says. But the girl did not know this. Moreover, the girl's confessor was extremely opposed. As a result, she had only God, and one of her mother's maids, who was one in whom she confided. Thus she underwent much trial and hardship until her twelfth year, when she learned that, since they couldn't get her to give up the idea, they were planning to bring her to be a nun at

the monastery where her sister was,[8] for not so much austerity was practiced there.

10. Knowing about this, she was determined to strive through every means she could to obtain her happiness by going ahead with her own plan. And thus, one day when she went to Mass with her mother, her mother went to confess in one of the confessionals. Doña Casilda then asked her governess to go to one of the Fathers and ask him to say a Mass. When she saw that the governess was gone, she placed her chopines in her sleeves, lifted her skirt and hastened as quickly as she could to this monastery, which was quite far away. Her governess, when she didn't find her, went after her; once she got near, she asked a man to catch hold of her. He said afterward that he wasn't able to move, and so he let her get away. The girl entered the first gate of the monastery, closed it, and began to shout; when the governess arrived, this young girl was already inside the monastery. They gave her the habit immediately. And thus she fulfilled the good inspirations the Lord had placed within her. His Majesty began very shortly to repay her with spiritual favors, and she to serve Him with the greatest happiness, humility, and detachment from everything.

11. May He be blessed forever! For thus, through the rough, woolen dress of the poor He gives pleasure to one who was so attached to very costly and elegant clothes; although the dress of the poor played no part in hiding her beauty. For the Lord distributed natural graces to her as well as spiritual: a temperament and intelligence so agreeable as to awaken all to praise His Majesty. May it please Him that there be many who will thus answer His call.[9]

DON BERNARDINO AND
DOÑA CASILDA DE PADILLA

Summary and Background: Chapters 10 and 11

Teresa begins chapter ten as follows: "Four or five months before this monastery of St. Joseph's in Malagón was founded, I was speaking with a distinguished young gentleman [Don Bernardino] who told me that if I wanted to establish a monastery in Valladolid he would most willingly give me a house he owned with a large and good garden containing a vineyard" (F. 10. 1.). Two months later Don Bernardino died.

Because Don Bernardino had lived a dissolute life, his salvation was in question. However, God revealed to Teresa that he had received mercy on his deathbed and was saved but that "he would not leave purgatory until the first Mass was said there" [the foundation at Valladolid] (F. 10. 2.).

As a result of this revelation, Teresa was anxious that the foundation be established as soon as possible. However, because she was still the prioress of St. Joseph's, she had to return to Avila on business. She left Malagón a month after its foundation (May 19, 1568) and worked her way back to Avila. She arrived in Avila on June 2, stayed until the end of the month, and then began the long trek to Valladolid.

Teresa chose three nuns to be members of the new foundation. On route to Valladolid, the party stopped at

Medina del Campo, where they were joined by three addition nuns and St. John of the Cross. Six months later, John would be instrumental in founding the first monastery of Discalced Carmelite friars at Duruelo (chapters 13 and 14). Shortly after Teresa arrived at Valladolid (August 10), Mass was celebrated. As Teresa received communion, she saw Don Bernardino standing beside the priest "his face joyful and resplendent. With hands folded, he thanked me for what I had done so that he could leave purgatory and go to heaven" (F. 10. 5.).

By August 15, the community was established. Unfortunately, they had to vacate the premises by October. Because the monastery was located near the Pisuerga river, it proved to be a very unhealthy place to live. Most of the nuns became "very sick" (F. 10. 6.). In addition, the monastery was located south of Valladolid, which posed a formidable obstacle for a convent dependent upon alms.

Doña María de Mendoza, Don Bernardino's sister, saw the plight of the nuns, so she took over her brother's estate and purchased a house for them inside Valladolid. The community moved into their permanent residence the following year, on the feast of St. Blaise, February 3, 1569. For the rest of chapter ten and the whole of chapter eleven, Teresa chronicles the story of a young noblewoman named Doña Casilda.

Doña María de Acuña, Doña Casilda's mother, married the Governor of Castile. When her husband died, she began living a very pious life and reared her four children in the practice of virtue. Antonio, her eldest child, renouncing his claim to his inheritance, became a Jesuit. Luisa, the next oldest, also renounced the family's inheritance when she took a perpetual vow of virginity. María, the third child, became a Dominican nun in Valladolid. In consequence, the whole of the family's wealth was earmarked for Doña Casilda, the youngest child. Doña María had arranged a marriage between Doña Casilda and her uncle Martin (her father's brother). By doing so, both the family fortune and the title of Governor would be retained.

Doña Casilda loved her uncle and they became engaged. Everything looked as if the marriage would go forward, until one day Doña Casilda had a life-altering experience.

> Once at the close of a day she had spent most happily with her fiancé, whom she loved more intensely than her age warranted, she became extremely sad at seeing how the day came to an end and that likewise all days would come to an end. Oh, greatness of God! That very happiness that the joys of perishable things gave her, she came to abhor! She began to experience such a great sadness that she couldn't hide it from her fiancé, nor did she know how to tell him, nor could she, even though he was questioning her. (F. 10. 14.)

After this experience, Doña Casilda's soul became more inclined toward the things of eternity than those of time. Gradually, as her desire to become detached from this world increased, her desire to marry decreased. One day, while she was attending a clothing ceremony at the

Carmelite monastery in Valladolid, a desire to enter the community was awakened. However, the last threads of her love for her fiancé prevented her from asking for admittance. But these threads were severed when Doña Casilda began to reflect upon the contrast between how she was *before* she had become engaged and how she was *afterward*. "She recalled how *before* she was engaged she used to spend periods of time in prayer . . . She was *now* reluctant even to recite the rosary" (F. 11. 10–11.) (italics added).

Soon afterward, Doña Casilda's desire to enter Carmel became known to her family and relatives, who tried to dissuade her." [Doña Casilda's] sister, thinking it was a childish trifle, tried to dissuade her and told her some things about how she could be saved even though married" (F. 11. 16.). "[Her relatives] said that her desire was a childish whim and that she should wait until she was of age." But Doña Casilda retorted, "Why, since [you find me] old enough to be married" (F. 11. 4.)? Doña Casilda's fiancé also tried to dissuade her with the argument that "she could serve God more by giving alms." She responded, in that case "[you] could give them" (F. 11. 6.). Doña Casilda was not to be deterred. She entered Carmel on January 13, 1577, a week after her fifteenth birthday. However, there is an epilogue to this story.

Five years later, Doña Casilda left Carmel and joined the Franciscan nuns of Santa Gadea del Cid, where she eventually became the abbess. The exact reason why she left Carmel is not entirely clear, but there are indications that she was pressured to do so by her mother and relatives on account of issues regarding inheritance.

When Doña Casilda entered Carmel, she did not renounce her claim to her inheritance. This meant that if she died in Carmel, the monastery would receive the inheritance as a dowry, but if she left the convent, it would receive nothing. St. Teresa left the decision whether or not to renounce her inheritance in the hands of Doña Casilda. Teresa even gave María Bautista, the prioress of Valladolid, the advice, "I would not interfere in the matter" (LE. 1. 164. 1.).

It seems that originally Doña Casilda's mother was in favor of the inheritance being used as a dowry for the convent, as indicated by Teresa in a letter that she sent to María Bautista shortly before Doña Casilda's profession. "Doña María now wants her to renounce her possessions in favor of the house [the convent of Valladolid]" (LE. 1. 164. 4.). However, five years later, Doña María had a change of heart. She persuaded her daughter to leave Carmel and obtained permission from Rome for Doña Casilda to be transferred to a Franciscan monastery in Burgos. Eventually, Doña Casilda became the abbess there.

Also, Doña María persuaded her daughter María to leave the Dominicans and obtained a dispensation for her daughter Luisa from her perpetual vow of virginity. Doña María then proceeded to arrange Luisa's marriage to her uncle Martin, who had first been betrothed to Doña Casilda.

Lurking in the background of "this intrigue," and these "strange reversals," to use St. Teresa's expressions

(LE. 2. 408. 3.), were some Jesuits who had a vested interest in acquiring Doña Casilda's inheritance. They persuaded Doña María that the money would be better spent by financing a new Jesuit university rather than by supporting the Carmelite nuns of Valladolid. There was much litigation between the Jesuits and the Carmel of Vallidolid over the inheritance. The Carmelites lost. Doña María's Jesuit son, Antonio, received a large share of the inheritance, which was used to finance the Jesuit college at Valladolid.

Teresa's reaction to this whole sordid episode was one of abhorrence, bordering on disgust. She writes, "I don't know what to say about this world, for where there is a question of self-interest there is no holiness, and this makes me want to abhor everything in it" (LE. 1. 164. 4.).

One final note. After Luisa's husband (uncle Martin) died, Luisa provided for her children and entered the Carmelite monastery at Talavera.

Reflection. Flannery O'Connor's short story, "Parker's Back," is a symbol of how the mysterious designs of God's providence are woven into the daily events of our lives. The story begins when a fourteen-year-old boy, named Obadiah Elihue Parker (known simply as Parker), goes to the circus. There he sees a man tattooed from head to foot. The intricate designs and brilliant colors of the various tattoos formed a unity that awakened such a deep sense of wonder in Parker that it changed the whole direction of his life. However, he was unaware of this change at the time it happened. "Parker had never before felt the least motion of wonder in himself. Until he saw the man at the fair . . . when a peculiar unease settled in him. It was as if a blind boy had been turned so gently in a direction that he did not know his destination had been changed."[10]

The experience awakened in Parker a restlessness and a longing, a "peculiar unease" for something that he could not name. He tried to recapture the experience of wonder that he had felt that day at the circus by having his own body tattooed. However, all of his tattoos ultimately left him dissatisfied. "Parker would be satisfied with each tattoo about a month, when something about it that had attracted him would wear off. Whenever a decent-sized mirror was available, he would get in front of it and study his overall look. The effect was not one intricate arabesque of colors but of something haphazard and botched. A huge dissatisfaction would come over him and he would go off and find another tattooist and have another space filled up."[11]

The experiences of Parker and Doña Casilda have three things in common. First, both were triggered unexpectedly by daily events, one by viewing a tattooed man, the other by the evening twilight. Second, both experiences evoked a longing for something they could not name. Parker's longing was experienced in a stirring of wonder; whereas Doña Casilda's longing was cloaked in a sadness that came from the realization "that all days would come to an end" (F. 10. 14.). Third, neither realized that God was the source of their experiences *at the time* they occurred. Parker's experience "was as if a blind boy had been turned so gently in a direction that he did not know his destination had been changed." Similarly, for Doña Casilda "[t]he Lord began to give her light, although she was not then aware of what He was doing" (F. 10. 14.).

We would not think of Doña Casilda's experience as strange, for it is not uncommon to feel the sadness of the shortness of life in the waning dusk. Conversely, Parker's experience strikes us as somewhat bizarre, for we do not associate an experience of God's grace with circuses and tattooed men.

In a letter to her friend Elizabeth Hester, O'Connor writes, "Part of the difficulty of [writing about the action of grace upon a character] is that you write for an audience who doesn't know what grace is and don't recognize it when they see it."[12] It is not difficult to recognize the workings of grace in places and at times that we expect. We would expect God's grace to touch us in church, at significant crossroads of our lives, but not while looking at a tattooed man in a circus tent. However, the Gospel bids us to look for God in the most unexpected places, for it proclaims that the central event of human history unfolded in a mud-filled stable in Bethlehem. God invites us to see what is hidden in full view.

Questions. God can use anything, even the most unlikely object or circumstance to communicate his grace to us. Have you ever experienced the gift of God's grace through an unlikely source? Is there something in your life that is preventing you from recognizing God's grace that is hidden in full view?

Reflection. Everyone was trying to dissuade Doña Casilda from following God's call in her life. "Her mother began to inform her relatives and they said her desire was a childish whim and that she should wait until she was of age" (F. 11. 4.). "Her sister thinking it was a childish trifle, tried to dissuade her and told her some things about how she could be saved even though married" (F. 10. 16.). "Her fiancé told her that she could serve God more by giving alms" (F. 11. 6.).

Their motives for trying to make Doña Casilda change her mind are complex. Their concern that she was too young to enter the convent and might be making a decision that she would later regret was legitimate. However, there were other reasons why they wanted to dissuade her from becoming a nun, namely, to secure the family fortune and retain the title of Governor by means of marriage.

Sometimes we find ourselves in Doña Casilda's situation. People can both discourage us from following our heart's desire and try to pressure us into doing something that is at odds with what we believe that we are called to do. This pressure can be manifested in many ways. Take parents who try to persuade their son to carry on the family business or to pursue a career that promises either money or prestige. Or take the example of a parent who tries to steer their daughter into marrying a man because he is a member of an influential family. These dynamics apply to any person—a mentor, a colleague, a teacher, or close friend who exerts undue pressure on another person for the sake of fulfilling his or her desires or needs. How often have we felt that there was a hidden agenda lurking beneath the statement, "My only concern is what is best for you."

Questions. "To be nobody-but-yourself in a world which is doing its best, night and day, to make you everybody else—means to fight the hardest battle which any human being can fight."[13] While E. E. Cummings' assertion may be an overstatement of the human condition; nevertheless, it speaks of a basic struggle in life. To be true to the person God wants you to be is a hard battle. Have you ever felt that you were being pressured into doing something that was against your will? Have you ever given in to pressure from others and then deeply regretted your action?

Chapter 12

Tells about the life and death of a religious, Beatriz de la Encarnación, whom our Lord brought to this same house. Her life was one of high perfection, and her death was of a kind that makes it fitting for us to remember her.[1]

1. Some years before, a young girl, Doña Beatriz, a distant relative of Doña Casilda, entered this monastery to become a nun.[2] She amazed all when they saw the great virtues the Lord was forming in her. And both the nuns and the prioress affirmed that they had never noticed in any aspect of her life anything they would consider an imperfection. Nor did they ever see any other expression on her face than a modest happiness that well revealed the inner joy of her soul. With an untroubled quiet she kept strict silence in such a way that nothing singular was noticed about it. Never was she known to have spoken a reprehensible word, nor was any obstinacy seen in her, nor did she ever make an excuse, even though, as is the custom in these houses in order to practice mortification, the prioress to test her tried to blame her for something she had not done. Never did she complain about anything, or of any Sister. Nor by her expression or word did she in the office she held give displeasure to anyone or occasion to attribute some imperfection to her. Neither was any reason found for accusing her of some fault in chapter, even though the defects the monitors would point out during chapter were very minute.[3] In all events her interior and exterior composure was unusual. This arose from her keeping eternity very much in mind and the end for which God created us. She always bore

the praises of God on her lips and the greatest spirit of gratitude; in sum, hers was a perpetual prayer.

2. In matters of obedience she was never at fault, but showed a readiness, perfection, and joyfulness in all that she was ordered to do. She practiced the greatest charity toward her neighbor—this was shown in such a way that she said that she would allow herself to be broken into a thousand pieces to keep any soul from being lost and so that thus all souls might find joy in their Brother, Jesus Christ (which is how she referred to our Lord). As for her trials, which were very severe, there were terrible illnesses, as I shall say afterward,[4] with intense pain, and she suffered them with the greatest willingness and happiness, as if they were choice favors and delights. Our Lord must have given her spiritual favors and delights, for otherwise it would have been impossible for her to bear her illnesses as cheerfully as she did.

3. It happened that in this city of Valladolid some men were going to be burned because of their great crimes. She must have known that these men were not approaching their death with as good a disposition as was fitting, and this caused her the greatest affliction; with much anguish she went to our Lord and begged Him very earnestly for the salvation of those souls. And in exchange for what they deserved (or that she might obtain that grace—I don't remember the precise words), she promised to give her whole life, all the trials and sufferings she could bear. That same night the first fever struck her, and until she died she was always suffering. The condemned men, in turn, died well; hence it seems that God heard her prayer.

4. She was next afflicted with an intestinal abscess causing the severest suffering. The patience the Lord had placed in her soul was indeed necessary in order for her endure it. This abscess was so internally located that the medicines they gave were of no help until the Lord willed that it come to a head and drain, and thus she improved somewhat from this illness. With that desire for suffering given to her, she was unable to be satisfied with little, and thus once, while she was listening to a sermon on the feast of the Cross, her desire so increased that when the sermon was over she went in a tearful impulse and threw herself on her bed. When they asked her what was the matter, she answered that they should beseech God to give her many trials and that with this she would be content.

5. She spoke with the prioress about all these interior matters and in this practice found comfort. Throughout her illness, she never gave the least trouble to anyone, nor did she do anything but what the infirmarian wanted, even if it was something as slight as drinking a little water. It is very common for souls who practice prayer to desire trials when they do not have any. But when they do and are in the midst of these very trials, it is not common for them to rejoice. And thus, once when she was afflicted, though the affliction did not last long, and suffering extreme pain from an abscess in her throat so that she could not swallow, she told the prioress in the presence of the Sisters (since the prioress's duty was to console and encourage her to bear so much sickness) that she had no pain and that she would not change places with any of the Sisters who were very well. She kept the Lord, for whom she was suffering, so present before her that she tried to cover up her suffering as much as possible that others would not

know how great it was. And this, except when the pain grew intense, she complained very little.

6. It seemed to her there was no one on earth as wretched as she; thus, insofar as one could understand, her humility was great. In speaking of the virtues of other persons, she was very joyful. In matters concerning mortification she was persistent. Without letting it be noticed, she avoided what afforded her recreation, for unless one were watching closely, this would not be known. It didn't seem she lived or conversed with creatures, so little did she care about anything. However things went, she bore them with peace. She was always composed; so much so that once a Sister said to her that she seemed to be like one of those persons of nobility so proud that they would rather die from their hunger than let anyone outside know about it. For they couldn't believe that she failed to feel some things, although it hardly seemed so.

7. She performed all her work and duties with the goal of not losing any merit, and so she used to say to the Sisters: "The smallest thing when done for the love of God is priceless; we should set our eyes, Sisters, only on this goal of love and on pleasing Him." She never meddled in things that were not her responsibility; thus she found fault with no one but herself. So strongly did she feel that no good should be said of her that she was careful not to speak well of others in their presence so as not to cause them pain. She never sought consolation (neither by going to the garden nor in any created thing), for she said it would be rude to seek relief from the sufferings that our Lord gave her. Thus she never asked for anything, but got along with what was given her. She also said that it would be a cross for her to find consolation in anything that was not

God. The fact is that when I inquired from those in the house, no one had seen in her anything other than what would be seen in someone of great perfection.

8. Well, when the time arrived in which our Lord desired to take her from this life, the sufferings increased; so many illnesses came upon her together that others, in order to praise our Lord at observing the happiness with which she bore them, went at times to see her. The chaplain especially, who is the confessor in that monastery and a true servant of God, had a great desire to be present at her death. Being her confessor, he considered her a saint. God was pleased to grant him this desire. For since she was in so much pain, and although she had already been anointed they called him in case there would be need that night for her to be reconciled or helped to die. A little before nine while all were with her (and he too), about a quarter of an hour before she died, she raised her eyes, and a happiness like a shining light came over her countenance. She remained as would someone gazing on an object that gives profound joy, for she smiled twice. All those who were there, and the priest himself, received so much spiritual delight and happiness that they didn't know what else to say than that it seemed to them they were in heaven. And with this happiness that I mention, her eyes fixed on heaven, she died, looking like an angel. Thus we are able to believe, according to our faith and according to her life, that the Lord brought her to rest in payment for the many things she had desired to suffer for Him.

9. The chaplain affirms, and has told many persons, that at the time of her burial he perceived an extremely sweet fragrance coming from her body. The Sister sacristan also affirms

that despite all the candles that burned at the funeral and burial, not one of them grew smaller in size. All this can be believed as coming from the mercy of God. In speaking of these things with a confessor of hers from the Society of Jesus with whom for many years she discussed her soul, I was told that they didn't amount to much; and he said he was not surprised because he knew that our Lord communicated a great deal with her.

10. May it please His Majesty, my daughters, that we know how to profit from companionship as good as this and from many other persons whom our Lord gives us in these houses. It may be that I will say something about them so that those who are a bit lukewarm will be strengthened and that we may all praise the Lord who in this way lets His magnificent riches show forth in us weak, little women.

BEATRIZ DE LA ENCARNACIÓN

Summary and Background: Chapter 12

The underlying purpose for Teresa's writing this chapter is to correct Sr. Juliana's account of Sr. Beatriz's life. Teresa writes the following to the prioress of Valladolid regarding an obituary that was to be written for a nun who recently had died. "And don't entrust it to Juliana, for because of exaggeration, the silly and nonsensical things she said in the report about Beatriz de la Encarnación were unbearable" (LE. 1. 143. 6.).

Teresa's account is more reflective of the truth of Beatriz's life. Teresa focuses upon her virtues, most notably, her restraint regarding speech. Beatriz never uttered "a reprehensible word," and "never did she complain about anything" (F. 12. 1.). In addition, she had great zeal for the eternal welfare of souls (F. 12. 1.). Teresa expounds upon these virtues within the context of the great physical sufferings that Beatriz endured during her brief time in Carmel.

All of Beatriz's ailments began the night after some heretics were burned at the stake in Valladolid. Beatriz begged God for the salvation of their souls, and in exchange she promised God that she would bear with patient resignation all the trials and sufferings of her life. On the night of the execution (the condemned men gave signs of repentance before they died), Beatriz was afflicted with an intestinal abscess that caused her much suffering. As time went on, she suffered many other ailments.

There are two things that Teresa emphasizes in this chapter. First, she states that what God sent Beatriz was not her *sufferings* but rather the *patience* to endure them. "The patience the Lord had placed in her soul was indeed necessary in order for her to endure [her sufferings]" (F. 12. 4.). Second, Teresa does not dwell upon *what* she suffered but *how* she bore her sufferings—with great patience. "However things went, she bore them with peace. She was always composed" (F. 12. 6.).

Reflection. In the prologue of *The Way of Perfection*, Teresa says that she is thinking of listing some remedies for certain "common, small temptations" because "since they are so common perhaps little attention is paid to them" (W. Pro. 2.). There is a basic truth of human nature contained in these words, namely, that ingrained habits resist reflection. When a bad habit has taken root in us, we indulge in it without thinking. And when a community participates in the same bad habit, even less attention is paid to it. One such habit that Teresa writes of in this regard is that of chronic complaining.

> It seems to me an imperfection to be always complaining (*quejarnos*) about light illnesses. If you can tolerate them, don't complain about them. When the sickness is serious, it does the complaining itself; this is different and the sickness is immediately obvious. Consider that you are few, and if one has this habit of complaining, it wears (*fatigadas*) everyone out . . . If you do

not lose the habit of speaking and complaining about everything you will never finish your lamenting. (W. 11. 1–2.)

Quejarse, the infinitive of *quejarnos*, can mean "to complain," "to lament" "to murmur," "to gripe," or "to grumble." We are all prone to complain and grouse about many things. And complaining can become addictive because it temporarily relieves tension. In consequence, it can become habit forming.

We all know how hard it is to break the habit of complaining. At times, nothing seems to work. Teresa doesn't provide us with a solution; nevertheless, she offers us something to reflect upon that may provide us with an incentive to change. She points out one of the effects that complaining has upon others. "It wears (*fatigadas*) everyone out." *Fatigar*, the infinitive of *fatigadas*, means "to tire," "to weary," "to fatigue," "to gall."

How would you feel if you accidentally overheard the following conversation about yourself? "He is so tiresome. He goes on and on and on, complaining about everything and everyone. I cringe when I see him coming. He is so draining and such a tedious bore." Wouldn't you be devastated, knowing that this is what people really think about you? What effect do you think this knowledge would have upon your habit of complaining? Conversely, how would you feel if you heard that someone had said of you what Teresa said of Sr. Beatriz? "Never did she complain about anything" (F. 12. 1.).

Questions. Is there something that you are always complaining about? Have you ever considered the impact that your complaining has upon others? What impact does chronic complaining have upon you?

Chapter 13

Treats of how and by whom in the year 1568 the first house for the observance of the primitive rule by discalced Carmelite friars was founded.

1. Before making the foundation of Valladolid, I had already agreed with both Father Fray Antonio de Jesús, who was then prior of the Carmelite monastery of St. Anne in Medina, and Fray John of the Cross, as I have already mentioned,[1] that they would be the first to enter if a monastery for discalced friars were founded for the observance of the primitive rule. Since I had no resources for acquiring a house, I did nothing but commend the matter to our Lord. For, as I have said, I was now satisfied with these Fathers.[2] The Lord had indeed exercised Father Fray Antonio de Jesús in trials during the year since I had spoken with him; and he suffered them with much perfection. As for Father Fray John of the Cross, no trial was necessary. Even though he had lived among the calced friars, those of the cloth,[3] he always lived a life of great perfection and religious observance. Since the Lord had given me the chief requirement for a beginning, which was friars, He was pleased to arrange the rest.

2. A gentleman from Avila, named Don Rafael,[4] with whom I had never spoken, found out, I don't know how (for I don't remember), about my desire to make a foundation for discalced friars. He came and offered me a house he owned in a little town[5] of very few inhabitants (I don't think even twenty, but I don't remember now). He kept the house there for an administrator who collected the revenue from his grain fields.

Although I imagined how it might look, I praised our Lord and thanked this gentleman very much. He told me it was on the direct route to Medina del Campo and that since I had to pass by there to make the foundation in Valladolid I could see it. I told him I would, and indeed that is what I did. I left Avila with a nun companion and with Father Julián de Avila, the chaplain at St. Joseph's in Avila, the priest I mentioned who helped me in these travels.

3. Although we left in the morning, we got lost because we didn't know the road; and since the place is little known, we couldn't get much information about where it was. Thus, our traveling that day was very trying and the sun was very hot. When we thought we were near, we discovered we had just as far to go. I always remember the tiredness we felt and the wrong roads we took on that journey. The result was that we arrived shortly before nightfall.

When we entered the house it was in such a state that we dared not remain there that night; it wasn't at all clean and was filled with vermin. It had a fairly good entrance way, a room double in size, a loft, and a small kitchen. This was all we had for our monastery. I figured that the entrance way could serve as the chapel, the loft as the choir, which would adapt well, and the room for sleeping.

My companion, although much better than I and very fond of penance, couldn't bear the thought of my planning to found a monastery there and said to me: "Surely, Mother, there isn't a soul, however good, that could put up with this. Don't even consider it." The Father who came with me, although he agreed with my companion, did not oppose me since I had told him my intentions.[6] We went to spend the night in the church, although not in vigil because we were exhausted.

4. When we arrived in Medina, I spoke immediately with Father Fray Antonio, and I told him what took place and that if he would have the courage to stay there for a while, I was certain God would soon provide a remedy, and that the important thing was to begin. It seems to me I was most aware of what the Lord had done and was feeling sure, so to speak; just as I do now from what I see and even much more so because of what up till now I have seen, for at the time of my writing this there are, through the goodness of God, ten monasteries of discalced friars.[7] And I told him he should realize that neither the provincial at that time nor the previous one would give permission—for the foundation needed their consent, as I said at the beginning—if we were seen living in a well established house.[8] This was apart from the fact that we did not have the means for such a house. And I pointed out that in that little place and house the foundation would not attract attention. And so Fray Antonio told me that he would be willing to live not only there but in a pigsty. Fray John of the Cross was of the same mind.

5. Now what remained was to obtain the consent of the two Fathers I mentioned because this was the condition under which our Father General granted the permission.[9] I hoped in our Lord to obtain it, and so I told Father Fray Antonio to take care to do all he could to gather something together for this house. I went with Fray John of the Cross to the foundation of Valladolid about which I have written.[10] And since we spent some days before establishing the enclosure on account of the workmen who were getting the house ready, there was

an opportunity to teach Father Fray John of the Cross about our way of life so that he would have a clear understanding of everything, whether it concerned mortification or the style of both our community life and the recreation we have together. The recreation is taken with such moderation that it only serves to reveal the Sisters' faults and to provide a little relief so that the rule may be kept in its strictness. He was so good that I, at least, could have learned much more from him than he from me. Yet this is not what I did, but I taught him about the lifestyle of the Sisters.[11]

6. It pleased God that the provincial, Fray Alonso González, from whom I had to obtain approbation, was there. He was elderly, good natured, and without malice. I told him many things, and reminded him of the account he would have to give if he hindered a work as good as this when asked by God to carry it out. His Majesty, wanting the foundation, put him in the right disposition, for he mellowed very much. When Doña María de Mendoza and the bishop of Avila, her brother (who is the one who always favored and protected us) came, they convinced both him and Father Fray Angel de Salazar, the previous provincial, the one from whom I feared all the difficulty. Moreover, a certain need arose at the time for which the latter provincial had need of assistance from Doña María de Mendoza. This fact, I believe, helped a great deal, although even if this opportunity had not been present, our Lord would have moved the provincial's heart just as He did the heart of Father General which was anything but inclined to the idea.

7. Oh, God help me, how many obstacles I have seen in these business matters that seemed impossible to overcome, and how easy it was for His Majesty to remove them. And

how ashamed I am not to be better after seeing what I have seen. For now as I am writing, I am growing fearful and want our Lord to make known to everyone how in these foundations we creatures have done next to nothing. The Lord has directed all by means of such lowly beginnings that only His Majesty could have raised the work to what it now is. May He be always blessed, amen.

Chapter 14

Continues to speak of the foundation of the first monastery of discalced Carmelite friars. For the honor and glory of God, tells something about both the kind of life lived there and the good our Lord began to do in those surroundings.

1. Having the permission of these two provincials, I now figured that nothing was lacking. We arranged that Father Fray John of the Cross would go to the house and get it ready so that, in spite of all, it could be lived in. For me, what was most urgent was that the friars begin, for I was very fearful lest some obstacle would come along our path. And this they did. Father Fray Antonio had already gathered some of the things necessary. Insofar as we could, we helped him; although our help amounted to little. He came to Valladolid with great happiness to speak to me and told me what he had collected, which was very little. It was only with clocks that he was well provided, for he had five of them; this greatly amused me. He told me they were meant as a help to follow the daily schedule, which he wanted well fixed; I don't think he even had any bed yet to sleep in.

2. Although they had wanted to do a great deal with the house, not much time was required to prepare it because there was no money. When it was ready, Father Fray Antonio happily renounced his priorship and promised to observe the primitive rule. Although he was told to try the new way of life first, he did not want to. He went to his little house with the greatest happiness in the world. Fray John was already there.

3. Father Fray Antonio has told me that when he first came near the little place he felt a great inner joy, and it seemed to him that he was now through with the world by leaving it all and placing himself in that solitude. Neither of the two found the house unfit; rather, it seemed to them they were living in the midst of great pleasures.

4. Oh, God help me! What little these buildings and exterior comforts do interiorly. Out of love for Him, I ask you my Sisters and Fathers, that you never fail to be very moderate in this matter of large and magnificent houses. Let us keep before us our true founders, those holy fathers from whom we descend, for we know that by means of that path of poverty and humility they now enjoy God.

5. Truly I have seen that there is more spirituality and even inner happiness when suitable accommodations for the body are seemingly lacking than afterward when the house is large and the accommodations good. What benefit is it to us that the house be large since it is only one small room that each one habitually uses? That it be well designed—what help is that to us? Indeed, if it isn't well designed, we won't then have to go around looking at the walls. By considering that the house will not be ours forever, but ours only for as short a time as this life lasts, even though that may be long, everything will be easy for us. We will see that the less we have here below, the more we will enjoy in eternity, where the dwelling places will be in conformity with the love with which we have imitated the life of our good Jesus. If we say that these are the beginning steps in order to renew the rule of the Virgin, His Mother, our Lady and Patroness, let us not be offensive to her or to our holy fathers of the past as to fail to live as they did. Since, because

of our weakness, we cannot do so in every way, in matters that are not essential for sustaining life, we must proceed very carefully. For it is all a matter of but a little effort, and that becomes delightful, as was the case with these two Fathers. And once we are determined to undergo this effort, the difficulty passes, for all the pain is but a little in the beginning.

6. On the First or Second Sunday of Advent (I don't remember which of these Sundays it was), in the year 1568, the first Mass was said in that little stable of Bethlehem, for it doesn't seem to me the house was any better.[1] The following Lent, while on my way to the foundation in Toledo, I passed by there.[2] When I arrived in the morning, Father Fray Antonio was sweeping the doorway to the church with that joyful expression on his face that he always has. I said to him: "What's this, my Father; what has become of your honor?" Telling me of his great happiness, he answered with these words: "I curse the day I had any."

When I entered the little church, I was astonished to see the spirit the Lord had put there. And it wasn't only I, for the two merchants, my friends from Medina who had accompanied me there, did nothing else but weep. There were so many crosses, so many skulls! I never forget a little cross made for the holy water fount from sticks with a paper image of Christ attached to it; it inspired more devotion than if it had been something very expertly carved.

7. The choir was in the loft. In the middle of the loft the ceiling was high enough to allow for the recitation of the Hours, but one had to stoop low in order to enter and to hear Mass. There were in the two corners facing the church two little hermitages, where one could do no more than either lie

down or sit. Both were filled with hay because the place was very cold, and the roof almost touched one's head. Each had a little window facing the altar and a stone for a pillow; and there, too, the crosses and skulls. I learned that after the friars finished Matins they did not leave the choir before Prime but remained there in prayer, for their prayer was so deep that when it came time to say Prime their habits were covered with snow without their having become aware of the fact. The two Fathers recited the Hours with another Father from among those of the cloth who went to stay with them (although he didn't change his habit because he was very sickly) and another young, unordained brother who was also there.[3]

8. They used to go preach in many of the neighboring towns where the people were left without any instructions in Christian doctrine. On this account also I rejoiced that the house had been founded there. For I had been told that there was no monastery nearby nor any place from which the people could get instructions, which was a great pity. In a short time the reputation the Fathers had was so great that I experienced the deepest consolation when I learned of it. For their preaching, as I say, they journeyed barefoot a league and a half, or two, for at the time they did not yet wear sandals (afterward they were ordered to wear them), and in much snow and cold. When finished with their preaching and confessing, they returned very late to their house for supper. In their happiness, all they did seemed small to them.

9. As for food, they had a surplus, for the people in the neighboring towns provided them with more than they needed. And some gentlemen from those towns came there to confession and offered them better houses and sites. Among

those gentlemen was a Don Luis, lord of five towns.[4] This particular gentleman had built a church to honor an image of our Lady, which was indeed worthy of being venerated. His father had sent it through a merchant from Flanders to his grandmother or mother (I don't remember which). The merchant liked it so much that he kept it for many years, and afterward at the hour of his death ordered that it be sent to Don Luis. It is a large altarpiece; I haven't seen anything better in my life—and others say the same. Father Fray Antonio went to that place at the request of this gentleman and saw the image; he liked it so much, and rightly so, that he agreed to transfer the monastery there. This town is called Mancera.[5] Although there was no well in that place, nor did it seem that any could be found there, this gentleman built the friars a monastery, small and in keeping with their profession, and gave them furnishings. He did everything very well.

10. I don't want to fail to mention the way, considered to be miraculous, in which the Lord gave them water. One day after supper, while the prior, Father Fray Antonio, was talking in the cloister with his friars about the need for water, he rose and took a staff he was holding in his hands and made a sign of the cross on one part of it (I think he made the sign of the cross, although I don't remember well whether he did or not); but anyway he pointed with the stick and said: "Now, dig here." After they had dug only a little, so much water came out that it is now even difficult to drain the well so as to clean it. The water is very good for drinking, and all that was needed for the remaining construction work was taken from there, and never, as I say, does the well empty out. After they had enclosed a garden with a wall, they sought to get water

for the garden and made a water wheel and went to much expense; up till now, they have not been able to find any more, not even a little.

11. I couldn't thank our Lord enough when I saw that little house,[6] which shortly before was uninhabitable, with such a spirit that everywhere I looked I found something edifying. And by the way they were living, I learned of the mortification, prayer, and good example they were giving. A gentleman and his wife, whom I knew and who lived in a nearby town, came to see me there, and they never stopped telling me about the sanctify of these Fathers and the great good they were doing in those towns. I experienced the greatest interior joy, for it seemed to me that I saw a beginning that would be of much benefit to our order and service to our Lord. May it please His Majesty that things will continue as they are now, and that my plan will indeed by realized.

The merchants who had accompanied me told me that not for all the world would they have missed having gone there. What a thing virtue is, for that poverty pleased those merchants more than all their riches, and their souls were left satisfied and comforted.

12. After conversing with those Fathers, I spoke of some things and begged them especially—since I am weak and wretched—not to be so rigorous in penitential practices, for what they were doing was severe. Since it had cost me so much in desire and prayer for the Lord to give me some friars to begin with and I saw such a good start, I feared lest the devil would attempt to put an end to this beginning before what I hoped for could be accomplished. As one who is imperfect and of little faith, I did not observe that this was God's work and

that His Majesty would carry it forward. Since they engaged in practices in which I did not, they paid little attention to my words about giving them up. And thus I went away greatly consoled, although I did not give God the praise so great a favor deserved.

May it please His Majesty, in His goodness, that I be able to serve somehow for the very many things I owe Him, amen. For, indeed, I understood that this foundation was a much greater grace than the favor He granted me to found houses of nuns.

DURUELO, THE FIRST FOUNDATION OF FRIARS

Summary and Background: Chapters 13 and 14

We begin our consideration of these chapters by recalling that in 1567, Teresa obtained permission to found more convents of nuns and two monasteries of reformed Carmelite friars from Rossi, the Carmelite General. Chapters thirteen and fourteen recount the establishment of the first foundation of Carmelite friars in the village of Duruelo (1568).

While Teresa was founding Medina del Campo in 1567, she told Fr. Antonio de Heredia, a Carmelite priest, that she had been given permission from Rossi to found a monastery of Discalced friars and that she was praying to find at least one candidate for this new venture. Antonio volunteered. Teresa was not heartened. "I took it that he was joking with me and told him so . . . it didn't seem to me he was the one for a beginning like this" (F. 3. 16.). In spite of her incredulousness, Teresa was willing to give Antonio an opportunity to prove himself.

As time passed, she saw evidence that Antonio might prove to be a suitable candidate.

"For a year passed and during that year so many trials and persecutions from many false accusations came upon him that it seems the Lord wanted to test him. He bore it all so well and was making such progress that I praised our Lord, and it seemed to me His Majesty was preparing him for the new foundation" (F. 3. 16.).

Providentially, while Teresa was still in Medina, a young Carmelite friar, John of St. Matthias (St. John of the Cross) arrived in Medina. He had come home to celebrate his first Mass. Teresa was introduced to John by Antonio, and she persuaded John to become a member of her new venture. Now Teresa had two candidates, one promising, the other not so promising, for in spite of the change that Teresa had witnessed in Antonio, she still had her reservations about him. "I still wasn't so satisfied with the prior [Antonio]" (F. 3. 17.).

Nevertheless, Teresa accepted whom God had sent her and exclaimed to her nuns, "Daughters, I have a friar and a half!" It has been commonly assumed that the half-friar refers to John of the Cross, because of his short stature. However, Teresa may have been referring to Antonio as the "half friar." Even though Antonio was tall in stature, in Teresa's eyes, he was only half the friar that John was.

After saying his first Mass in Medina, John returned to Salamanca to finish his final year of study. During this time (1567–1568), Teresa established the foundation of Malagón, then traveled back to Avila to attend to her duties as prioress of St. Joseph's and to prepare to travel to Valladolid, where she would found her next convent.

While in Avila, Teresa was offered a house in the village of Duruelo by Don Rafael, for the expressed purpose of founding a monastery of Discalced Carmelite friars. Because Duruelo was on route to Valladolid, Teresa stopped to see Don Rafael's gift. It was a filthy, tumbled down shack filled with vermin. The conditions were so wretched that one of Teresa's traveling companions exclaimed, "Surely, Mother, there isn't a soul, however good, that could put up with this. Don't even consider it" (F. 13. 3.). In spite of these conditions, Teresa decided to make the foundation in Duruelo.

Teresa instructed Antonio to gather objects that would be useful in making the foundation in Duruelo and then continued on to Valladolid with John of the Cross. Because the monastery's cloister in Valladolid had not yet been established, John lived with the nuns from August 10 to September 30, 1568. During this time, Teresa "taught him about the lifestyle of the nuns" (F. 13. 5.). This "on site" education has frequently been referred to as John's "second novitiate." It was also during John's time at Valladolid that Teresa intuited that John had a bent toward severe penitential practices.

After John's "second novitiate," Teresa sent him to Duruelo to assist Antonio with the new foundation. Since Avila was on route to Duruelo, Teresa saw an opportunity to help correct John's bent toward severe asceticism. She had John personally deliver a letter to Don Francisco de Salcedo, her former spiritual director. In the letter, Teresa implored: "I beg again as an alms of you that you speak to this padre and counsel him on what you think about his mode of life" (LE. 1. 13. 5.). Since Teresa knew from personal experience that Don Francisco was a wise and prudent spiritual director, she believed that he would be able to temper John's bent toward rigorous penitential practices.

Teresa first met Don Francisco in 1554, before she left the Incarnation to found St. Joseph's. During this time, Teresa had begun to receive visions and mystical graces. Because she was afraid of being deceived by the devil, she consulted Fr. Gaspar Daza, a diocesan priest, noted for his learning.

Daza was *too enthusiastic* about Teresa's spiritual progress. He told her that she must die to self *all at once*. This overwhelmed Teresa. "If I were to have no one else but him to speak to, I believe that my soul would have never improved. For the affliction I felt in seeing what I did not do—nor did it seem I could do—that which he told me would have been enough to make me lose hope and give up everything" (L. 23. 9.).

In her discouragement, Teresa turned to Don Francisco de Salcedo for guidance. His guidance was both wise and prudent. "He began to visit me, encourage me, and tell me that I shouldn't think I could give up everything in a day, that little by little God would do the work . . . He proceeded with discretion little by little showing me ways to conquer evil" (L. 23. 10.). Thus, knowing by experience that Don Francisco was a wise and prudent man, Teresa believed that he could have a softening influence upon John's harshness. However, this does not seem to have been the case.

Five months later, in February 1569, Teresa visited Duruelo. Although she was edified by John and Antonio's zeal for mortification, she was still apprehensive about its excessiveness. Teresa voiced her concern. John and

Antonio listened respectfully. However, they had minds of their own. "After conversing with those Fathers, I spoke of some things and begged them especially not to be so rigorous in penitential practices, for what they were doing was severe . . . Since they engaged in practices in which I did not, *they paid little attention to my words about giving them up*" (F. 14. 12.) (italics added).

In addition to her apprehensions about John's asceticism, Teresa also had concerns about Antonio's impracticality. From the beginning, he had exhibited a lack of judgment. This was manifested in the house that he had procured for the foundation of Medina del Campo. "[It was] completely collapsed except for one room"(F. 3. 3.). Another example of Antonio's impractical nature manifested itself in his procurement of what he thought was *necessary* for the establishment of Duruelo. "[Antonio] came here to Valladolid to speak to me with great satisfaction, and told me what he had got together [for the new foundation of Duruelo], and it was little enough; he had provided himself with nothing but clocks—he took five of them, which struck me as funny. He told me this was so he could keep regular hours, for he did not wish to live carelessly; yet I believe he didn't have anything to sleep on."[7]

Sometimes, Antonio's decisions, though well meaning, did not take into consideration the practicalities of life. We have an example of this in his decision to move the community from Duruelo to Mancera. It wasn't the move *per se* that exhibited his poor judgment, for it became evident that Duruelo was unhealthy and uninhabitable. Rather, it was the *basis* upon which Antonio (the local superior) chose the site for the new monastery.

Don Luis de Toledo offered Antonio a church in the town of Mancera and an adjacent building that would function as a monastery. The church contained a beautiful altarpiece. Antonio was so taken with the beauty of the altarpiece that he decided to transfer the community to Mancera without considering that the place had neither a well nor a likelihood that water could be obtained. This incident echoes Antonio's choice of the house that he had purchased at Medina del Campo, a dilapidated structure that he described to Teresa as needing "only minor repairs."

In charity, Teresa redeems Antonio by ending chapter fourteen by recording the "miraculous" way in which the new community at Mancera obtained water, reminiscent of Moses striking the rock in the desert with his staff.

I don't want to fail to mention the way, considered miraculous, in which the Lord gave them water. One day after supper, while the prior, Father Fray Antonio, was talking in the cloister with his friars about the need for water, he rose and took a staff he was holding in his hands and made a sign of the cross on one part of it (I think he made the sign of the cross, although I don't remember well whether he did or not); but anyway he pointed with the stick and said: "Now, dig here." After they had dug only a little, so much water came out that it is now even difficult to drain the well so as to clean it. (F. 14. 10.)

Was this divine providence or just sheer dumb luck? Perhaps it was both. The jury is still out.

Reflection. The one image of Antonio that most people remember is when Teresa arrives in Duruelo, sees him sweeping the steps of the monastery, and asks him what has become of his honor. Antonio replies, "I curse the day I had any" (F. 14. 6.). However, this image of Antonio as a poor, humble, simple friar does not tell the whole story. Fr. Kieran Kavanaugh, O.C.D., writes the following about Antonio.

Although he was learned and a good preacher, he tended to be touchy, quarrelsome and a bit of a gossip. Not always showing good judgment in the delicate situations preceding the separation of the discalced friars and nuns into separate provinces, he showed poor judgment as well in his ascetical practices. Thus, after the chapter of 1581, they had to forbid him to go about barefoot and made him wear hemp sandals like the others. In his relations with Teresa he manifested a jealous immaturity. Although he esteemed her highly, he thought she should prefer him to others who joined her reform after himself. Since she was obliged to write much more to Gracian than to him, she cautioned Gracian to avoid letting him know how often she wrote. Sometimes in his childishness he would refuse to write to her for months, nor would he answer the letters written by her to him, which presumably overflowed with warmth and love and good humor. He never saved any of her letters to him. It was he who as vicar provincial ordered Teresa at the end of her life to go to Alba de Tormes. By doing this he frustrated her avid plans to go to Avila for the profession of her niece Teresita. (LE. 1. 609.)

To say the least, Antonio was a complex individual. He was gifted but had emotional problems and often exhibited bad judgment. Yet, in spite of his limitations, he played an important role in Teresa's reform. And Teresa had the wisdom and humility to accept the imperfect instruments that God had sent her.

What we see in Antonio is an aspect of divine providence. The people that God chooses to do his work are often very wounded and sinful individuals. One obvious example is Jesus' selection of the twelve apostles. They were poor fisherman who did not grasp what Jesus was trying to teach them. They were ambitious men, often quarreling among themselves regarding who of them was the greatest.

The Church has always been a community of wounded sinners. St. Augustine warns catechumens, who are about to enter the Church, not to expect to see a church of saints within its walls. To do so is to risk being scandalized. He writes,

> Accordingly you will have to witness many drunkards, covetous men, deceivers, gamesters, adulterers, fornicators, men who bind upon their persons sacrilegious charms, and others given up to sorcerers and astrologers and diviners practiced in all kinds of impious arts. You will also have to observe how those very crowds which

fill the theatres on the festal days of the pagans also fill
the churches on the festal days of the Christians.[8]

There are many images of the Church—The Bride
of Christ, The Mystical Body of Christ, the Sealed Foun-
tain, to name a few. All of them symbolize a deep spiritual
dimension of the Church in which Christ dwells among his
people. However, we are also a community of wounded
sinners. In one of St. Augustine's sermons on the Parable
of the Good Samaritan, he compares the Church to a con-
valescent ward (the inn where the Samaritan recovered
from his wounds).

At first glance, this image seems pessimistic, but upon
reflection, it reveals itself as being both realistic and compassionate. Spiritually, we are all sick and infirm. Our task
upon this earth is to love our infirm neighbor with our
infirm heart. As W. H. Auden puts it, "You must learn to
love your crooked neighbor with all your crooked heart." In
short, we can only love our neighbor *as he is* and *as we are*.

Questions. In the above passage, St. Augustine is speaking
to the catechumens. He is basically warning them not to
have unrealistic expectations of the kind of people whom
they will find when they enter the Church. His advice may
be put in the form of a question: "What did you expect?"
To what degree are your harsh judgments of people the
result of your unrealistic expectations? In what specific
way is God asking you to love your crooked neighbor
with your crooked heart? Also, like Teresa, do you have
the capacity to work with deeply wounded people?

Chapter 15

Treats of the foundation of the monastery of the glorious St. Joseph made in the city of Toledo in 1569.

1. In the city of Toledo there was a merchant, a respected man and servant of God, who never wanted to marry but lived a very good Catholic life of great trustworthiness and virtue. Through honest trade he went about increasing his wealth with the intention of using it for some work very pleasing to the Lord. He was struck with a fatal illness. His name was Martín Ramírez.[1] A Father from the Society of Jesus named Pablo Hernández,[2] a confessor of mine when I was in Toledo arranging for the foundation of Malagón, was very eager that one of our monasteries be founded in Toledo. So he went to speak with the man and told him of the great service such a foundation would give our Lord and how the fund for chaplains and chaplaincies[3] that he wanted to establish could be left for this monastery and that the certain feast days and everything else he had resolved to leave to the care of a parish in that city would be taken care of by such a monastery.

2. The merchant was so sick that he saw there was no time to make such arrangements, and he left the whole matter in the hands of his brother, whose name was Alonso Alvarez Ramírez; once this was done, God took him. The right decision had been made, for this Alonso Alvarez is a very discreet God-fearing man, trustful and charitable in almsgiving, and open-minded. As one who has had many dealings with him, I can as an eyewitness say this in all truthfulness.

3. When Martín Ramírez died, I was still involved with the foundation at Valladolid. There I received a letter from Father Pablo Hernández of the Society and from Alonso Alvarez himself, giving me an account of what had happened and advising me that if I wanted to accept this foundation I should come quickly. So, shortly after the house in Valladolid was put in order, I left for Toledo. I arrived on the eve of Our Lady of the Incarnation⁴ and went to the house of Doña Luisa, which is where I stayed at other times. She was the foundress of Malagón. I was received with great joy, for she loves me very much. I brought with me two nuns from St. Joseph's in Avila, who were great servants of God.⁵ We were immediately given a suite of rooms, as was that lady's custom, where we remained with as much recollection as in a monastery.

4. I immediately began to take up the business matters with Alonso Alvarez and a son-in-law of his, named Diego Ortiz. The latter, although very good, and a theologian, was more unyielding in his opinion than Alonso Alvarez. He did not readily soften his demands. They began to ask for many conditions that I didn't think I could easily agree to. While engaged in these negotiations, I was looking for a house to rent so as to establish possession of the new foundation. But I was never able to find one that was suitable, although a great deal of searching had been done. Nor was I able to get the ecclesiastical administrator to give me the license (for at that time the archbishop was not there),⁶ although this lady in whose house I was staying tried hard, as did also a nobleman, a canon in this church, whose name was Don Pedro Manrique, son of the governor of Castile. Don Pedro was a very good servant of God, and still is (for he is alive, though he had poor health).

Some years after this house was founded, he entered the Society of Jesus where he is now.[7] He was an important person in this city because he is very intelligent and trustworthy. Nonetheless, he was unable to get me the license. For when the governor softened in his resistance, those on the council did not. To add to this, Alonso Alvarez and I couldn't come to an agreement because of his son-in-law to whom he gave much power. We ended up by disagreeing on everything.

5. I didn't know what to do, for I hadn't come for any other reason, and I saw that if I went away without making a foundation, the fact would be much publicized. Nonetheless, I was saddened more over their not giving me the license than by all the rest. I knew that once possession of the foundation was established, the Lord would provide as He had in other places. So I resolved to talk to the governor, and I went to a church that was next to his house and sent someone to beg him to be kind enough to speak with me. More than two months had passed in trying to obtain the license, and each day the matter got worse. When I saw him, I told him that it was hard to accept the fact that there were women who wanted to live with so much austerity, perfection, and withdrawal from the world while those who would bear nothing of this but lived in comfort wanted to hinder these works that were of such service to our Lord. These and many other things I told him with a great determination which was given me by the Lord. The governor's heart was so moved that before I left he gave me the license.

6. I went away very happy. It seemed to me I now had everything without having anything, for I must have had only about three or four ducats. With these I bought two paintings

done on canvas[8] (for I didn't have anything with an image to put on the altar), two straw mattresses and a woolen blanket. As for the house, we forgot about it since I was not in agreement with Alonso Alvarez. A merchant in the same city, a friend of mine named Alonso de Avila,[9] who had never wanted to marry and who thinks only of doing good for those in prison—and he does many other good works as well—told me not to be afflicted, that he would find a house for me; but he took sick. Some days before, a very holy Franciscan friar named Martín de la Cruz had come to that place. He was there for some days, and when he left he sent me a young man named Andrada[10] (by no means rich but very poor), asking him to do everything I told him. One day when Andrada was attending Mass in a church, he came to speak to me and tell me what he had been told by that blessed man and that he was certainly ready to do everything he could for me; although only with his personal service could he help us. I thanked him and was amused, and my companions even more so, to see the kind of help that saintly man had sent us. The clothes this young man had on were not the kind one would wear when going to speak with discalced nuns.

7. Having the license but no one who would help me, I didn't know what to do or whom to entrust with the task of seeking a house for me to rent. I remembered the young man that Fray Martín de la Cruz had sent me and mentioned him to my companions. They laughed very much at me and told me not to do such a thing, that it would serve for no more than to make the secret plan public. I didn't want to listen to them. Since he was sent by the servant of God, I trusted that there was something for him to do and that this offer to help had a

mystery about it. Thus I sent for him and told him, placing him under all the secrecy I could, what was happening and asked that with this in mind he look for a house for me and that I would provide a guarantor for the rent. The guarantor of the rent was the good Alonso de Avila who, as I mentioned,[11] took sick. The task seemed a very easy one to Andrada and he told me that he would look for one. Right away, the day after the next, while I was attending Mass at the house of the Society of Jesus, he came to speak to me and said that he already had the house, that he had the keys, that it was nearby and that we should go to see it. And this we did. It was so nice that we stayed in it for almost a year.[12]

8. Frequently, when I reflect on this foundation, I am amazed by the designs of God. For almost three months—at least more than two, but I don't remember exactly—very wealthy persons had made the rounds of Toledo looking for a house for us and were never able to find one, as though there were no houses in the city. And then this youth comes along, not rich but very poor, and the Lord desired that he find one immediately. And though it could have been found without trouble if an agreement had been reached with Alonso Alvarez, not only did we fail to reach one but were far from doing so. Thus in God's design the foundation had to be made in poverty and with trial.

9. Well then, since the house pleased us, I gave the order at once to take possession before anything was done in it, lest some obstacle arise. Indeed, in a short while Andrada, who was mentioned, came to tell me that the house was being vacated that day, that we should bring our furniture. I told him there was little to do, for we had nothing but two straw

mattresses and a blanket. He must have been surprised. My companions regretted that I told him and said that since I had mentioned this to him and he thereby saw how poor we were, he would not want to help us. I had not thought of this, but he paid little attention to it. For the One who gave him that desire had to advance the work until it was completed. And indeed I don't think we ourselves could have done better than Andrada in preparing the house and getting workmen. We borrowed the things necessary for saying Mass, and, in order to take possession of the house, went with a workman at nightfall; and we brought a bell that is used at the elevation of the Blessed Sacrament, for we had no other. With much fear on my part, we spent the whole night getting everything in order. There was no place for a church except in one of the rooms of another little house next to this one and occupied at the time by some women; the owner had also rented this little house to us.

10. Since we had everything ready by dawn and we had not dared say anything to the women lest they reveal what we were doing, we began to make a door through a thin partition wall which led on to a very tiny patio. When the women, still in bed, heard the pounding, they got up terrified. We had all we could do to calm them down; but it was already time for Mass, and although they were hard to deal with, they did not do us any harm. And when they saw what our intention was the Lord pacified them.

11. Afterward, I realized how poorly we had proceeded; for at the time, with the absorption God gives in the work so that it will get done, one does not think of the difficulties. Well, when the owner of the house found out that it was made into a

church, the trouble began, for she was the wife of an heir to an entailed estate and was very much opposed to this. The Lord was pleased that when she learned we would buy the house if we were satisfied with it, she was appeased. But, when those on the council learned that the monastery, for which they had never wanted to give a license, was founded, they became very angry and went and complained to the canon (whom I had secretly informed), boasting to him that they would do everything in their power to destroy it. Since the ecclesiastical administrator had gone on a trip after having given me the permission and was not in the city, they went to complain to the canon I mentioned, astonished at such boldness that a useless little woman should found a monastery against their will. He pretended that he knew nothing and pacified them as best he could, telling them that she had done so in other cities and with due authorization.

12. After I don't know how many days, they sent us a notice of excommunication so that no Mass could be said until I presented the documents giving me authorization for what was done. I answered very meekly that I would do what they ordered, although I was not obliged to obey in that matter. And I asked Don Pedro Manrique, the gentleman I mentioned,[13] to go and speak to them and show them the documents. He appeased them since the deed was already done; otherwise, we would have been in deep trouble.

13. For some days we had no more than the straw mattresses and the blanket, and even that day we didn't have so much as a stick of wood to make a fire to cook a sardine. And I don't know who it was the Lord moved to leave a little bundle of wood in the church to help us. The nights were quite cold;

but with the blanket and the woolen mantles we wore, we kept ourselves warm, for these mantles often help us. It will seem impossible that though we had stayed in the house of that lady who loved me so much,[14] we had to enter the new foundation in so much poverty. I don't know the reason, except that God wanted us to experience the good that lies in this virtue. I did not ask for help, because I don't like to be a bother; and she perhaps wasn't aware. Moreover, I am indebted for what she was able to give us.

14. The experience was very good for us; the interior consolation and happiness we felt were so great that I often think about what the Lord keeps stored up within the virtues. It seems to me this lack we experienced was the cause of a sweet contemplation. But this poverty did not last long, for soon Alonso Alvarez himself as well as others were providing us with more than we needed. And, true to say, my sadness was such that it resembled that of discovering that many gold jewels in my possession were taken away and I left poor. Thus I felt sorry that they were bringing our poverty to an end, and my companions felt the same. Since I saw they were sad, I asked them what troubled them, and they answered: "What else could it be, Mother, for it no longer seems we are poor."

15. From then on my desire to be very poor increased. And I felt freedom in having so little esteem for temporal goods, for the lack of these goods brings an increase of interior good. Certainly, such a lack carries in its wake another kind of fullness and tranquility.

During those days in which I was discussing the foundation with Alonso Alvarez, there were many persons to whom the plan seemed wrong—and they told me so—since that

family was not from the nobility, although the family was
very good, regardless of its social status, as I have said.[15] They
thought that in a city as important as Toledo I would not lack
comfort. I did not pay much attention to this, because, glory to
God, I have always esteemed virtue more than lineage. But so
much was said to the ecclesiastical administrator that he gave
me the license under the condition that I make the foundation
as in other places.

16. I didn't know what to do, for after the foundation
was made they again took up the negotiations. But since the
house was already founded, I arranged to let them become the
patrons of the large chapel and settled things in such a way
that they would have no connection with what pertained to
the monastery, as is now the case. There was already someone
who wanted the large chapel, an important person; and there
were many opinions about this so that I didn't know what to
decide. Our Lord desired to give me light in this matter, and
so at one time He told me that lineage and social status mattered not at all in the judgment of God. He gave me a severe
reprimand for listening to those who spoke to me about this;
concerns of this sort were not for those of us who had already
despised the world.

17. With these and other reasons I was very humbled,
and I resolved to settle what had been begun and give them
the chapel. I never regretted it, for we have seen clearly what
poor assistance we would have received as far as buying a
house goes. But with the help of Alonso Alvarez we bought a
house in the place where we are now. It is one of the nicest in
Toledo, and cost twelve thousand ducats. Since, according to
the contract, so many Masses and feasts are to be celebrated,

the nuns as well as the people are much consoled. Had I paid attention to the vain opinions of the world, it would have been impossible, from what we can understand, for us to be so well provided for, and I would have offended the one who with so much good will did this charitable deed for us.

Chapter 16

Treats of some of the things that have taken place to the honor and glory of God, in this monastery of St. Joseph's in Toledo.

1. It has occurred to me to say something about what some of the nuns put into practice in the service of the Lord so that those who follow may strive to imitate the good things that were done in the beginning.

Before the house was bought, a nun named Ana de la Madre de Dios entered here at the age of forty. Her whole life had been spent in serving His Majesty. Although her house and way of life lacked no comfort because she lived alone and was well-to-do, she wanted instead to choose the poverty and submission of our order, and so she came to speak with me. Her health was poor. But since I saw she was so good and determined a soul, I thought she would be helpful for the beginning of the foundation; so I admitted her. God was pleased to give her much more health in the practice of austerity and submission than she had in her freedom and comfort.[1]

2. What edified me, and the reason I am recording this here, is that before she made her profession she offered everything she owned—and she was very rich—as an alms to the house. I was not happy about this and did not want to consent, telling her that perhaps afterward either she would be sorry she entered or we might not want to admit her to profession. And I added that what she did was imprudent, although we would not have let her go without giving the money back. But I wanted to overstate the point: first, so that there would be no occasion for temptation; second, in order to test her spirit. She answered

that if this were to happen she would beg for the money out of love of God. And I was unable to make her change her mind. She lived very happily and with much better health.

3. The mortification and the obedience that were practiced in this monastery were great. As a result, the several times that I was there the prioress had to be careful[2] about what she said. For even when she said something only casually, they would immediately carry it out. Once they were looking at a pond that was in the garden, and she said to a nun standing nearby: "But what would happen if I were to say, 'jump in'?" Hardly was this said, and the nun was in the pond and got so soaked that she had to change her clothes. At another time, when I was present, the nuns were going to confession, and one who was waiting for the other to finish came to speak to the prioress.[3] She asked her why she was doing that and if it was good way to recollect herself and told her to go stick her head in a well that was nearby and there think of her sins. The nun thought she was to jump into the well and went so quickly to do so that if they hadn't hurried to hold her back she would have done so thinking she was doing God the greatest service in the world. Other similar things, requiring much mortification, were done. This made it necessary for learned men to restrain the nuns and explain to them the matters in which they were obliged to obey. For these nuns did some things that were imprudent, so that if their good intention had not redeemed them, they would have lost rather than gained merit. The above is true not only of this monastery, but it occurred to me to speak of the matter here. Rather, in all the others there are so many things happening that I wish I had not a part in them so that I could freely tell about some of them for the praise of our Lord in His servants.

4. It happened that while I was here a fatal illness struck one of the Sisters. After receiving the sacraments and being anointed, her happiness and joy were so great that, as though she were going to another country, we were able to talk to her about how she should recommend us to God when in heaven and to the saints to whom we were devoted. A little before she died, I went to her room to be with her, for I had just gone before the Blessed Sacrament to beg the Lord to give her a good death. And when I entered I saw His Majesty at the head of the bed. His arms were partly opened as though He was protecting her, and He told me that I could be certain He would protect all the nuns that die in these monasteries and that they should not fear temptation at the hour of death. I was left very consoled and recollected. After a little while I began to speak to her, and she said to me: "O Mother, what great things I am going to see." Thus she died, like an angel.[4]

5. And I have noticed that some who have died since this occurred have done so with quiet and calm as though they were in rapture or in the prayer of quiet, without showing the least sign of any temptation. Thus I hope in the goodness of God that He will be merciful to us at the moment of death through the merits of His Son and those of His glorious Mother whose habit we wear. Therefore, my daughters, let us strive to be true Carmelites, for soon the day's journey will end. And if we were to know the affliction that many experience at the hour of death and the cunning deceit with which the devil tempts them, we would highly esteem this favor.

6. One thing occurs to me now that I want to tell you, for I knew the person, and indeed he was almost a relative of my relatives. He was a great gambler, who had taken some

theology by which the devil tried to deceive him, making him believe that the purpose of amendment at the hour of death was worth nothing. He had this so fixed in his mind that others could in no way get him to confess. Nor did anything suffice, though the poor man was extremely afflicted and repentant of the evil life he had lived. But he asked why he should confess since he saw that he was condemned. A learned Dominican friar who was his confessor did nothing but argue with him, but the devil taught him so many subtleties that the friar's arguments were insufficient. Thus for some days the confessor didn't know what to do; and, along with others, he must have recommended the matter urgently to the Lord since he had compassion on the man.

7. When the illness, which involved pain in the side, was beginning to afflict the man greatly, the confessor returned. He must have thought up other arguments, but they would have been of little benefit if the Lord had not taken pity on that man and softened his heart. And when the confessor began to speak to him and give him reasons, the man sat up in bed as though he were not sick at all and said to him: "What, in short, do you have to say that could help me benefit from my confession? For I want to make it." And he sent for a secretary or notary (I don't remember which) to record his testimony, and made a very solemn oath not to gamble any more and to amend his life. He confessed very well and received the sacraments with such devotion that from what we can understand according to our faith he was saved. May Our Lord be pleased, Sisters, that we live our lives as true daughters of the Blessed Virgin and keep our vows so that He may grant us the favor He has promised us. Amen.

TOLEDO (1569)

Summary and Background: Chapters 15 and 16

The founding of the monastery of Toledo (chapters 15 and 16) is an example of how personalities and cultural prejudices can make an ordinarily simple task very complex and vexing. The foundation of Toledo began simply enough. While Teresa was in the process of establishing a community in Valladolid, Pablo Hernandez, one of Teresa's confessors, asked Martin Ramírez, a rich merchant of Toledo, to endow a Carmelite monastery in Toledo. Ramírez agreed and Teresa accepted the offer. However, Martin Ramírez died. As a result, Teresa had to leave Valladolid before that foundation was established because she was advised by one of Ramírez's executors to come to Toledo as soon as possible, if she wanted to receive financial support for the new foundation.

Before leaving Valladolid, Teresa wrote to Doña Luisa de la Cerda in Toledo. Doña Luisa was the woman who had financed the monastery in Malagón. Teresa requested that she obtain a license to found the monastery in Toledo. Doña Luisa did nothing. The reason why Doña Luisa did not respond may have been due to the difficulties involved in obtaining the necessary permissions. Toledo already had twenty-four convents with over 1,200 nuns, and a new foundation could not be established without special permission from the city council, the Archbishop of Toledo, and King Philip.

However, bureaucratic and ecclesiastical red tape does not seem to have been the only reason for Doña Luisa's failure to act. This is indicated by the fact that even though she allowed Teresa to live in her residence in Toledo temporarily, while Teresa was in the process of procuring a building for her new monastery, Doña Luisa did not give Teresa any financial assistance. Doña Luisa's coldness toward this new foundation is evident in Teresa's remark. "It will seem impossible that though we had stayed in the house of that lady who loved me so much, we had to enter the new foundation in so much poverty" (F. 15. 13.).

There were two reasons that account for Doña Luisa's cold behavior. First, the aristocracy resented that a religious house be founded by someone below their social station. The aristocracy believed that it was their exclusive right to be the benefactors of religious institutions. Martin Ramírez was only a merchant. Doña Luisa's viewpoint was shared by many. "[T]here were many persons to whom the plan seemed wrong—and they told me—since the [Ramírez] family was not from the nobility" (F. 15. 15.).

The second reason was racial prejudice. Anti-Semitism was deeply rooted in the nobility of Toledo, and Ramírez was a *converso*, that is, a Jew who had "converted" to Catholicism. Parenthetically, Teresa's paternal grandfather was also a *converso* from Toledo, who had been persecuted by the Inquisition.

In spite of these problems, Teresa began to deal with Alonso Ramírez and his son-in-law Diego Ortiz, the executors of Martin Ramírez's estate. Ortiz insisted that the endowment be contingent upon certain conditions. Ortiz scrutinized Teresa's constitutions and quibbled over every aspect of them. He insisted that parts of the constitutions be changed. Teresa found this condition completely unacceptable. She refers to Ortiz as being "very good and a theologian" (F. 15. 4.). This statement may not have been meant as a compliment to Ortiz's theological astuteness but a comment upon his nit-picking. In the end, Teresa rejected the bequest.

Teresa was now faced with a threefold problem: first, obtaining permission for a foundation; second, raising adequate capital for her new project; and third, finding a suitable house. Teresa felt that obtaining permission was the first priority, and once she received it, God would provide. "I was saddened more over their not giving me the license than by all the rest. I knew that once possession of the foundation was established the Lord would provide as he had in other places" (F. 15. 5.).

Obtaining permission might have been easy for Teresa, for Bartolomé Carranza, the local bishop, was very liberal minded. However, there was a small hitch. Carranza was the son of poor parents. Members of the clergy who belonged to the aristocracy resented the fact that such a prestigious bishopric had been given to one not of their social class. As a result of their animosity, they accused Carranza of heresy. He was tried, found guilty of trumped-up charges, and imprisoned for seventeen years. He died a broken old man of seventy-three, a few days after he had been released from prison in 1576.[5]

Standing in for Carranza as the ecclesiastical governor of Toledo was Don Gomez Tello Giron. One day, Teresa cornered him in the church located next to his house. Don Gomez was truly moved by Teresa's plight. However, because he would have to give an account of his action to the city council, he granted Teresa permission to found a monastery but only on the condition that the monastery have no patrons. Thus, he could say to the city council, "Yes, I gave permission that the monastery be founded, but I made sure that neither Martin Ramírez nor any other *converso* merchant would be its patron." Little did Don Gomez realize that Martin Ramírez's offer to Teresa was a dead issue. In charity, Teresa did not feel that it was necessary to burden Don Gomez with this information.

So here is Teresa, in a situation similar to the one in Avila, when Rubeo, the Carmelite General, gave her permission to found more monasteries. Just as she wrote then, "Here I was, a poor discalced nun, without help from anywhere—only from the Lord—weighed down with patent letters and good desires, and without there being any possibility of my getting the work started" (F. 2. 6), now she writes, "It seemed to me I now had everything without having anything" (F. 15. 6.).

Having permission but being penniless, Teresa went in search of a house. As providence would have it, another *converso* merchant Alonso de Avila offered to both finance and find a house for Teresa. Unfortunately, he fell sick and was unable to look for a house. Subsequently, Martín de la Cruz, a Franciscan friar, offered Teresa assistance in the person of Andrada, a poor, young student. Martin told Teresa that Andrada would be able to find a house for her.

However, when Teresa met Andrada, she had severe reservations. "I thanked [Andrada] and was amused, and my companions even more so, to see the kind of help that saintly man [Martin] had sent us. The clothes this young man had on were not the kind one would wear when going to speak with discalced nuns . . . I mentioned [Andrada] to my companions. They laughed very much at me and told me not to do such a thing, that it would serve for no more than to make the secret plan public" (F. 15. 6–7.).

Her first impression told Teresa that her companions were right. However, Teresa's deep spiritual intuition told her something else. "The offer to help had a mystery about it. Thus I sent for [Andrada] and told him, placing him under all the secrecy I could, what was happening and asked that with this in mind he look for a house for me" (F. 15. 7.).

Within two days, Andrada found a suitable house to rent. It was located in the former Jewish ghetto of the city, perhaps, close to the ancestral home of Teresa's grandfather. The community moved in with a promise that the rent would be paid. The rent was paid with the money that Alonso de Avila, the *converso* merchant, had promised Teresa and, ironically, with money from the wife of Doña Luisa's butler.

Next, just as at Medina del Campo, Teresa and her companions, under the cloak of darkness, stealthily took possession of the house in Toledo. They brought in their scanty belongings (two straw mattresses and a blanket) and had workmen labor through the night to get the house ready by dawn, when the first Mass would be offered.

Doña Luisa and her maids attended the Mass. However, even though she saw the dire poverty of the community, she, who had financed the monastery at Malagón in honor of her late husband, would not offer the least amount of financial assistance to this new venture. Perhaps, Doña Luisa felt that Doña Teresa de Cepeda y Ahumada (St. Teresa) had violated an unwritten code of Spanish society by accepting the offer of a *converso* merchant to endow one of her monasteries. If this was true, how would Doña Luisa have treated Teresa if she had known that Teresa's grandfather was also a *converso*?

As Teresa and her companions were settling into their new home, another problem arose. The tenants next door informed the owner that his house had been turned into a church. The owner informed the city council. The council became irate with Don Gomez for giving Teresa a license without consulting them. Consequently, they leveled their complaint with the canon of the Cathedral because Don Gomez was out of town. The council complained to the canon that Teresa did not have authorization to make a foundation.

However, the council was unaware that by the time they lodged their complaint to the canon, Teresa already talked to him. Teresa had "secretly informed" (F. 15. 11.) the canon that the council would do anything to thwart her foundation. So being forewarned, the canon "pretended that he knew nothing" (F. 15. 11.) and pacified the council by saying that Teresa had obtained permission in other cities and most probably had obtained permission in Toledo.

There is a subscript to this incident between the city council and Teresa. What had fueled the council's opposition toward Teresa was a long-standing animosity between Don Gomez and both the city council and the chapter of the cathedral. Ever since Bishop Carranza had been imprisoned, Toledo had not had a bishop, only an administrator. Don Gomez, the present administrator, had continually tried to seize control of the diocese. In short, there was a power struggle. The city council felt that Don Gomez's decision to give Teresa permission to found a religious house, without consulting them, was just another way of exerting his power. Teresa was caught in the crossfire. As the old African proverb has it, "When two elephants fight, it is the grass that gets trampled."

After Teresa's foundation became a *fait accompli*, the executors of Martin Ramírez's estate became more amenable to Teresa's wishes. Teresa worked out an agreement with them by which they became patrons of the monastery's chapel and helped finance the convent's chaplaincies. In return, Diego Ortiz promised not to interfere in the life of the community.

This negotiated settlement proved beneficial to both parties. It defrayed an expense for the community, while providing the Ramírez family with a feather in its cap.

The Ramírez family could boast of being a benefactor of a religious house, a privilege reserved for the nobility. Eventually, the community was able to move into a permanent residence with the help of a legacy from the late Martin Ramírez.

Teresa's decision to accept the legacy of Martin Ramírez can be regarded as a deliberate choice, in light of the fact that a member of the nobility also had offered to be a benefactor of the convent's large chapel. Her choice was the result of God's enlightenment. "Our Lord desired to give me light in this matter, and so at one time He told me that lineage and social status mattered not at all in the judgment of God. He gave me a severe reprimand for listening to those who spoke to me about this; concerns of this sort were not for those of us who had already despised the world" (F. 15. 16.).

As a postscript, it should be mentioned that thirteen years after the foundation of Toledo, when Teresa's niece Beatrice of Jesus was prioress of the community, the community was able to move into a larger building, one that afforded the silence and solitude that their life required. The building was the former palace of Doña Luisa.

Chapter sixteen is a counterweight to chapter fifteen. To offset the frustration that Teresa had experienced in founding the Toledo Carmel, she now recounts the good that was being practiced by her sisters there. Thus, Teresa begins chapter sixteen with the following. "It has occurred to me to say something about what some of the nuns put into practice in the service of the Lord so that those who follow may strive to imitate the good things they were doing in the beginning" (F. 16. 1.).

The specific nun that Teresa focuses on in this chapter is Ana de la Madre de Dios. She was a rich noblewoman, whose husband had died when she was twenty-one. Teresa met her at Doña Luisa de la Cerda's palace. Ana entered Carmel and gave her wealth to the convent. Though Teresa was edified by her generosity, she was very reluctant to accept Ana's money before she made her profession, for Teresa knew that often two things happen. First, the person may feel very enthusiastic upon entering the monastery, only to discover that she does not want to stay. Second, the community may ask the fledging member to leave.

> What edified me, and the reason I am recording this here, is that before [Ana] made her profession she offered everything she owned—and she was very rich—as an alms to the house. I was not happy about this and did not want to consent, telling her that perhaps afterward either she would be sorry she entered or we might not want to admit her to profession. And I added that what she did was imprudent, although we would not have let her go without giving the money back. (F. 16. 2.)

Next, Teresa deals with blind obedience, which is not a virtue but an act of imprudence. For example, once when the prioress of Toledo was walking with another nun next to a pond in the cloister garden, the prioress said, "What would happen if I said 'jump in'? Hardly was this said, and the nun was in the pond and got so soaked that she had to change her clothes" (F. 16. 3.). Such an incident shows such a lack of common sense that "this made it necessary for learned men to restrain the nuns and explain to them the matters in which they were obliged to obey. For these nuns did some things that were imprudent, so that if their good intention had not redeemed them, they would have lost rather than gained merit" (F. 16. 3.).

Teresa ends chapter sixteen by contrasting the deaths of two individuals, one a nun of the Toledo community, the other a layman who was a gambler. Both are examples of God's mercy. Regarding the death of the nun, Teresa said that she saw a vision of Jesus at the head of the bed of the dying nun. Jesus had his arms outstretched. Jesus told Teresa that "He would protect all the nuns that die in these monasteries and that they should not fear temptation at the hour of death" (F. 16. 4.). The nun died in peace.

The gambler also died in the embrace of God's mercy but only after having been rescued from the brink of despair. He would not confess his sins on his deathbed because he believed that since he had lived such an evil life, it would be an exercise in futility. However, after his confessor talked to him several times, he was able to accept that he was not beyond the pale of God's mercy. He confessed his sins and died in peace.

Both stories must have touched Teresa deeply, for she knew that she, too, was a sinner saved by the mercy of God— "Forever I will sing the mercies of the Lord."

As a postscript to this chapter, a year after the chapel of the Toldeo convent had been endowed, Diego Ortiz demanded that the nuns sing extra Masses for members of the Ramírez family. Teresa resisted his demand claiming that it "would seriously inconvenience the nuns and be burdensome to them" (LE. 1. 33. 3.). Teresa knew that Diego was trying to bully her and that he did not have a canonical leg to stand on. So Teresa told him that the Father Visitator (Pedro Fernández, O.P.) would be passing through Toledo shortly and that she would talk to him about the matter and invited Diego to do likewise. "The visitator is very learned and well informed, and your honor will enjoy dealing with him" (LE. 1. 33. 4.). Diego declined the invitation.

Reflection. H. G. Wells's short story "The Country of the Blind" is a symbol of the human condition. It is about a mountaineer named Nunez, who is injured when he falls off a mountain cliff, in the jungles of Ecuador. He is rescued by men from a tribe that has lived in a hidden valley for generations. For some unknown reason, everyone in the tribe was born blind. The blindness that had struck the members of the tribe had happened so far in the past that even the concept of "seeing" was foreign to them.

> They would not even understand many of [Nunez's] words. For fourteen generations these people had been blind and cut off from all the seeing world; the names for all the things of sight had faded and changed; the story of the outer world was faded and changed to a child's story; and they had ceased to concern themselves with anything beyond the rocky slopes above their circling wall.

Blind men of genius had arisen among them and questioned the shreds of belief and tradition they had brought
with them from their seeing days, and had dismissed all
these things as idle fancies and replaced them with new
and saner explanations. Much of their imagination had
shriveled with their eyes, and they had made for themselves new imaginations with their ever more sensitive
ears and finger-tips.[6]

When we consider the behavior of Doña Luisa and
the nobility of Toledo toward Teresa and the Ramírez family, we may shake our heads in disbelief. "How can these
people be so blind? How can they justify their behavior
toward the *converses*? How can they call themselves good
Catholics and place their social status above the Gospel?"

Wells's story gives us one possible answer to these
questions, for there is a similarity between the blind people of the Ecuadorian tribe and the nobility of Spain. Both
belonged to "tribes." The beliefs of the individual members were formed by the group to which they belonged.
Over generations, their beliefs had become unquestionable and their imaginations shriveled.

Perhaps the greatest blindness is the arrogant assumption that *we* are less blind than those whom we are quick
to condemn for their obtuseness. We are all members of a
tribe; all of us hold as dogma mere human precepts.

Questions. Are there values that you have ingested from
your culture that you have never examined? What are the
unquestionable values and beliefs of your tribe (e.g., your

family of origin)? Have these values and beliefs engendered prejudices in you to which you are blind?

Reflection. In 1989, photographer Andres Serrano exhibited a controversial photograph entitled "Piss Christ." It depicts a plastic crucifix submerged in a glass of urine. Many Christians felt offended by the photo because they considered it blasphemous. However, there were other reactions.

In an interview with Bill Moyers, Sr. Wendy Beckett was asked about her reaction to Serrano's work. She said that while the photo left much to be desired from an artistic standpoint, she did not consider it blasphemous. Beckett said that the photo actually increased her devotion to Jesus because she saw it a symbol of what our culture has done to Christ. Beckett felt that the real problem with the photo was that people *reacted* to it instead of allowing it to *speak* to them.

It is so difficult to get beyond our first reactions. This is true for all of us, even saints like Teresa. We have an example of this when the young student Andrada offered his assistance to Teresa. At first, she did not take him seriously. In fact, she was amused. Teresa basically said to him, "Thanks but no thanks. Don't call us, we'll call you." "I thanked him and was amused, and my companions even more so, to see the kind of help that saintly man had sent us. The clothes this young man had on were not the kind one would wear when going to speak with discalced nuns" (F. 15. 6.). Teresa and her companions judged a book by its cover.

However, it's to Teresa's credit that she was able to get beyond her first reaction and listen to her heart. "The offer to help had a mystery about it. Thus I sent for [Andrada] and told him, placing him under all the secrecy I could, what was happening and asked that with this in mind he look for a house for me" (F. 15. 7.).

Teresa's extraordinary gift of common sense could have become a curse if practicality was the *only* criterion upon which she made decisions. Reason and faith are two voices of God. Teresa was "bilingual." She understood the language of the mind and the heart.

Questions. St. Thérèse wrote that "[God] teaches without noise of words. Never Have I heard Him speak, but I feel that he is within me at each moment . . . guiding and inspiring me with what I must say and do."[7] These words of St. Thérèse refer to her ability to perceive the language of the heart—God's voice within us. Considering all the voices of this world that compete for our attention, what practices help you to perceive God's guidance within the silence of your heart?

Chapter 17

Treats of the foundation of the two monasteries in Pastrana, one for the nuns and one for the friars. They were made in 1570, I mean 1569.

1. After the foundation of the house in Toledo, during the fifteen days preceding Pentecost, the little church, the grates, and other things had to be prepared. There was a great deal to do, for as I have said we remained in this house for almost a year. I was tired after those days from going about with the workmen. When the vigil of Pentecost came, all the work was done. That morning as we sat in the refectory to eat, great consolation came over me in seeing that I no longer had anything to do and that I could enjoy some time with the Lord on Pentecost; I was almost unable to eat so consoled did my soul feel.[1]

2. I did not deserve to have this consolation very long, for while I was in the midst of it, they came to tell me that a servant sent by the Princess of Eboli, the wife of Ruy Gómez de Silva, was there. I went to meet him and learned that the princess was sending him for me since I had been in communication with her for some time about the foundation of a monastery in Pastrana. I didn't think it was to come about so quickly. The idea made me uneasy because it would have been dangerous to leave a monastery founded so recently and in the midst of opposition. So I resolved not to go, and said so. The servant told me that this would not be acceptable, because the princess was already in Pastrana and had not gone for any other reason, that she would take a refusal as an insult. Despite all this, I had no thought of going, and so I told him to

go get something to eat and that I would write to the princess; and then he left. He was a very honorable man, and though he did not like it that I refused, once I explained the reasons to him, he went along with them.

3. Moreover, the nuns who were to make up the new community had just arrived, another reason why I did not see how I could leave so soon.[2] I went before the Blessed Sacrament to beg the Lord to help me write in such a way that the princess would not grow angry. That would have been very bad for us since the friars were then just beginning and, above all, it was good to keep in the favor of Ruy Gómez who had such strong influence with the king and with everyone. But I don't remember if I recalled the latter, although I know well that I did not want to displease Ruy Gómez.[3] While I was praying to the Lord, He told me not to fail to go, that I was going for more than that foundation and that I should bring the rule and constitutions.

4. Since I heard this—although for myself I saw serious reasons for not going—I didn't dare but do what I usually do in similar instances, which was to follow the counsel of my confessor. And so I sent for him. I did not tell him what I had heard in prayer.[4] In this way I am always left more satisfied, for I beg the Lord to give my confessors light in conformity with what they can know naturally. And when His Majesty wants something to be done, He puts it in their heart. This has happened to me many times. So it happened this time, for after considering everything, he thought I should go, and with that I decided to leave.

5. I sent out from Toledo the second day after Pentecost traveling by way of Madrid. There my companions and I went

for lodging to a monastery of Franciscan nuns, with a lady, who had founded it and lived in it, named Doña Leonar Mascareñas.[5] She had been the king's governess and is a very good servant of our Lord. I had lodged there at other times when on certain occasions I had to pass by, and she always showed me much kindness.

6. This lady told me she was happy I had come at that time because a hermit was there who eagerly desired to meet me[6] and that it seemed to her the life he and his companions were living was very similar to that of our rule. The thought came to me that if this were so it would be a good thing since I had only two friars, and so I begged her to arrange for us to speak. He was staying in a room given him by this lady. He was there with another young brother named Fray Juan de la Miseria, a great servant of God and very simple with regard to the things of the world.[7] While we were speaking together, this hermit told me that he wanted to go to Rome.

7. Before going on, I want to mention what I know about this Father, named Mariano de San Benito. He was Italian, a doctor, and very intelligent and talented. While he was living as the supervisor of the entire household of the queen of Poland, our Lord called him to leave all so as to better obtain his salvation. He had not been inclined to marry, but was a knight of the Order of St. John of Jerusalem. He had undergone some trials in which he had been falsely accused of being involved in a man's death and thus put in prison for two years. While there, he didn't want to be defended by any learned man or anyone else, but only by God and His justice, for there were witnesses who said that he had ordered them to kill the man. Resembling the old men in the story about Saint Susanna,[8]

when each was asked where the accused was at the time, one said that he was seated on a bed; and the other, at a window. In the end they confessed to having calumniated him. And he assured me that he had spent much money to free them so that they would not be punished, and that certain information had come into his possession against the one who had caused him the trouble and that he likewise did as much as he could not to do that one any harm.

8. Through these and other virtues—for he is a clean-living and chaste man, unwilling to have any dealings with women—he must have merited from our Lord knowledge of what the world is so that he would strive to withdraw from it. And thus he began to think about which religious order to join. And, from what he told me, in thinking about the different orders, he found in each one some difficulty for his temperament. He learned that near Seville some hermits had come together to live in a desert called El Tardon, under a very holy man, named Padre Mateo,[9] whom they took as their superior. Each one lived apart in a cell. They did not recite the divine office together but did gather in an oratory for Mass. They had no fixed income; neither did they want to receive alms, nor did they. But they supported themselves by the work of their hands, and each one ate alone and very poorly. When I heard about this, it seemed to me to be a living picture of the life of our own holy fathers. Father Mariano had spent eight years in this manner of life. When the holy Council of Trent came and took away authorization for the eremitical life, he wanted to go to Rome to seek permission that they might continue as they were, and this was his intention when I spoke to him.[10]

9. Well now, when he told me the manner of his life, I showed him our primitive rule and told him that without so much trouble he could observe all of that since his life was the same as that prescribed in the rule, especially living by the work of one's hands. He was very much inclined to the latter and told me that the world was lost because of greed and that this was why religious life was not valued. Since I felt the same, we quickly agreed in this and even in everything else. When I gave him reasons about how much he could serve God in this habit, he told me that he would think over the matter that night. I already saw that he was nearly decided, and I understood that what I had learned in prayer (that I was going to Pastrana for more than the foundation of a monastery of nuns)[11] referred to this. The thought gave me the greatest happiness since it seemed to me that the Lord would be much served if this hermit were to enter the order. He was so moved that night by His Majesty, who desired this, that the next day he called for me, now very determined and even very surprised to see how quickly he himself had changed, especially through the instrumentality of a woman, for even now he sometimes mentions this to me, as though what I said were the cause and not the Lord who can change hearts.

10. Great are God's judgments. Mariano had gone many years without knowing what to decide concerning his state, for the life he had been living was not that of a religious, since the hermits did not make vows and take on any obligation other than to remain there in solitude. And God quickly moved him and revealed how much His Majesty would be served by him in this state and the need for him in order to carry on what had been begun. For he has helped a great deal,

and up to now it has cost him many trials. And by what can be seen from the opposition the followers of this primitive rule now experience,[12] the work will cost him more until it is firmly established. For through his talent, intelligence, and good life he is influential with many persons who favor and defend us.

11. Well then, he told me how Ruy Gómez had given him a good hermitage and site in Pastrana, the place where I was going, for a settlement of hermits and that he wanted to accept it for this order and receive the habit. I thanked him and praised our Lord greatly. For of the two monasteries for which our Most Reverend Father General had sent permission, only one had been founded.[13] From there I sent a message to the two Fathers that were mentioned, the present provincial and the previous one,[14] begging them to give me permission since the monastery could not be founded without their consent. And I wrote to the bishop of Avila, Don Alvaro de Mendoza, who was very favorable toward us, to try to get them to grant it.

12. God was pleased that they look favorably on my request. It seemed to them that in a place so isolated the foundation could do them little harm. Mariano gave me his word that he would go there when the permission came. Thus, I was extremely happy. Once there, I met the princess and the prince, Ruy Gómez, who received me very cordially. They gave us a separate apartment, where we stayed longer than I had expected. For the house where we were to live was so small that the princess had ordered much of it to be torn down and many things built anew, but not the walls.

13. I spent three months[15] there during which many trials were suffered, since the princess asked me to do things that were not fitting for our form of religious life, and so I decided,

rather than make the foundation, to leave. The prince, Ruy Gómez, with both his common sense, which was very great, and his reasonableness, got his wife to agree with us. And I bore with some things because I was more desirous that the monastery of friars be founded than that of the nuns. I knew how important this was, and the importance afterward became clear.

14. At this time Mariano with his companion (the two hermits that were mentioned)[16] came, and when the permission arrived, the prince and princess were glad to agree that the hermitage they had given him for hermits be used by discalced friars. I sent for Father Fray Antonio de Jesús, who was the first discalced and was in Mancera so that he might get the foundation started. I made habits and white mantles and did all I could so that they might take the habit at once.

15. At this time I had sent to Medina del Campo for more nuns, for I had brought only two with me. There was a Father in Medina, about middle-aged, not too old, not too young, and a very good preacher, whose name was Baltasar de Jesús.[17] Since he knew that the monastery was being founded, he came with the nuns and desired to become a discalced. This he did after he arrived, and when he told me, I praised God. He gave the habit to Father Mariano and his companion. Both of them became lay brothers, for Father Mariano did not want to become a priest, but wanted to be the least of all; nor could I convince him otherwise. Afterward, by order of our Most Reverend Father General, he was ordained a priest.[18] Once the two monasteries were established and Father Fray Antonio de Jesús had come, novices began to enter, of whom I shall give some examples later on. And they began to serve our Lord so

authentically that, if He be pleased, someone more capable than I of telling about it, will put it in writing. For such a task, I would fall short.

16. As for the nuns, the monastery there received much kindness from the prince and princess. And the princess favored them and treated them well until the prince, Ruy Gómez, died.[19] Tempted by the devil, or perhaps because the Lord permitted it—His Majesty knows why—the princess in the intense emotion felt from her husband's death entered to be a nun. With the affliction she was experiencing, the practices of enclosure to which she was not accustomed could only displease her, and because of the holy Council the prioress could not give the liberties the princess wanted.

17. The princess came to dislike both the prioress and all the rest of the nuns along with her. Such was her dislike that even after she discarded the habit and lived in her own house she caused them trouble. And the poor nuns were so disturbed that I strove in every way I could, begging the superiors to move the monastery from there and found one in Segovia. As will be said later,[20] they did move to Segovia, and left behind all that the princess had given them, but brought along some nuns she had ordered them to accept without any dowry. The beds and other little things that the nuns had brought there with them they also took along. Their departures left the townspeople very sorry. As for me, seeing the nuns in peace left me with the greatest happiness in the world. For I was very well informed that they were in no way at fault for the displeasure of the princess. On the contrary, they served her as much when she had the habit as they did before she received it. The only occasion for her displeasure was the one

I mentioned[21] plus the hardship both she and the servant she had brought with her experienced. For, from what is known, she was entirely at fault. In sum, the Lord permitted it. He must have seen that it was not proper for that monastery to be there, for His judgments are great and beyond all our understanding. I, on my own account, would not dare do anything without consulting learned and holy persons.

PASTRANA (1570)

Summary and Background: Chapter 17

In September 1568, when John of the Cross's "second novitiate" was over, Teresa sent him from Valladolid to Duruelo to help Antonio set up the new monastery. On route, John stopped at Avila to deliver a letter from Teresa to Don Francisco de Salcedo, a holy man, who had once given Teresa spiritual direction. At the end of the letter, Teresa bemoans the fact that because of pressing matters, it might not be possible for her to return to Avila for at least a year. "For, in passing, it might be said that this year could be without my seeing you again, the Princess of Eboli being in such a hurry" (LE. 1. 13. 61.).

This passage refers the Princess's offer to found a convent at Pastrana, where she and her husband had been in the process of creating a model city in Spain. They had already established hospitals, churches, funded various charities, and helped to support the agriculture of the region. And as a crowning touch, the Princess wanted Pastrana to be enhanced by a convent, founded by no less than the much sought after saint of Avila.

However, as Teresa would soon discover, the Princess's "offer" was not a request but a demand.

The Princess of Eboli, a cousin of Doña Luisa de la Cerda, was married to Ruy Gómez de Silva, a personal friend of King Philip II. The Princess was known for her beauty. She is portrayed as wearing an eye-patch.

Historians are divided over the reason for the patch. Some say that she wore it as the result of a childhood injury; others believe that its purpose was to hide a squint whereas still others thought that it was an accessory that added a mysterious allure to her beauty. She was also haughty, capricious, irascible, ambitious, had a deep sense of entitlement, and wielded her influence with very little regard for the lives of others.

This last characteristic is seen in the opening paragraphs of this chapter. One day as Teresa is in the process of establishing the convent of Toledo, the Princess's servant shows up at the front door unannounced. He tells Teresa to come with him to Pastrana *immediately* because the Princess had decided to found a monastery. A failure to comply would be taken "as an insult" (F. 17. 2.).

Teresa tells us that she didn't know what to do. She was afraid to leave her fledging community in Toledo, but she did not want to refuse, principally because the Princess's husband had such a great influence on King Philip. Teresa knew that the king's support was necessary for the continued expansion of her reform. Bewildered, Teresa prayed for guidance. The Lord instructed her to go to Pastrana. Teresa writes, "I was going for more than that foundation and that I should bring the rule and constitutions" (F. 17. 3.).

Teresa knew that voices she heard in prayer should not be too readily believed; they needed to be tested. She believed that if what she had heard was truly from God, then God would confirm this through one of his human instruments. Thus, as was her custom, Teresa consulted her confessor.

> Since I heard [what the Lord had said to me in prayer]—although for myself I saw serious reasons for not going—I didn't dare but do what I usually do in similar instances, which was to follow the counsel of my confessor. And so I sent for him. I did not tell him what I had heard in prayer. In this way I am always left more satisfied, for I beg the Lord to give my confessors light in conformity with what they can know naturally. And when His Majesty wants something to be done, He puts it in their heart. This had happened to me many times. So it happened this time, for after considering everything, he thought I should go, and with that I decided to leave. (F. 17. 4.)

So at the end of May 1569, Teresa with her companion Sr. Isabel de Santo Domingo and Pedro Muriel, a Calced Carmelite priest, set out for Pastrana. On route, they stopped at Madrid at the request of another noblewoman, Doña Leonor de Mascareñas. During their three-day stay, Teresa was introduced to two Italian hermits, Mariano Azzaro and Giovanni Narduch. Azzaro told Teresa that Ruy Gomez had given him a hermitage and a piece of land in Pastrana. When Teresa heard this, she persuaded the two hermits to become Carmelites. It was only then that Teresa realized the meaning of the words that the Lord had spoken to her. "That I was going to Pastrana for more than the foundation of a monastery of nuns" (F. 17. 9.). Three months later, the hermits would follow Teresa to Pastrana and found the second house of Discalced Friars.

Parenthetically, Narduch (Juan de la Miseria) was a painter of some repute. He was the one who painted the most famous portrait of Teresa. Teresa, at the command of her confessor, sat for days while her portrait was being painted. After looking at the completed work, she exclaimed, "God forgive you, Fr. Juan! To think that after all I have suffered at your hands you should paint me so bleary eyed and ugly!"

When Teresa arrived in Pastrana, she realized that the populace would be too small to support a convent founded in poverty and that the endowment that the Princess was willing to give would not be adequate to support the community. Going against her ideals, Teresa insisted that a fixed income was required. Teresa was well aware of the Princess's capriciousness and did not want her convent to be dependent upon her mercurial moods. At first, the Princess was appalled by Teresa's demand but eventually acquiesced. However, this was not the end of the friction between the Princess and Teresa.

The Princess insisted that a personal friend, Catalina Machuca, a rather unstable Augustinian nun, be admitted to the new foundation at Pastrana. Teresa flatly refused and held her ground. The Princess was furious at Teresa's refusal but was powerless to change her mind. However, the Princess had one avenue of revenge open to her.

She had heard from her cousin Doña Luisa that Teresa had written an account of her life and mystical graces

(*The Book of Her Life*). The Princess pleaded that Teresa allow her to read it. Teresa was very reluctant, but after the Princess promised that only she and her husband would see it, Teresa acquiesced to her wishes. This proved to be a mistake. The Princess gave the book to everyone in her house to read, even the servants. They laughed at passages and made Teresa out to be a pious fool. Teresa was mortified and was tempted to leave Pastrana but endured her humiliations because she did not want to risk the foundations, especially the friars. "I bore with some things because I was more desirous that the monastery of friars be founded than that of the nuns" (F. 17. 13.).

By mid-July, both foundations had been established and Teresa left Pastrana for Toledo. Four years later, on July 29, 1573, Ruy Gómez died in Madrid. At the funeral, the Princess ordered Mariano Azzaro to take off his Carmelite habit and drape it over her shoulders. She then denounced the riches of this world and declared that she would become a Discalced Carmelite nun. When the prioress of Pastrana learned of this, she exclaimed, "The princess a nun! That will be the end of this house."

This statement proved to be prophetic. The Princess arrived at the doors of the convent five months pregnant, accompanied by her maids and so much luggage that the convent had no room for it. She ordered everyone around and demanded that she be addressed by the nuns on their knees. The Princess made it clear that she would not be subservient to anyone—even the prioress. She insisted that her two maids be accepted as nuns and demanded that her visitors, who were many, be permitted to enter the cloister.

However, even with these accommodations, the Princess still felt that she was being denied what was due to her. In consequence, she moved to one of the hermitages in the convent garden outside the cloister. There she held court; she daily received members of the aristocracy. This was a relief to the nuns. However, when the Princess moved to the hermitage, she cut off the nuns' daily allowance for food. When King Phillip II heard of the situation, he ordered the Princess to leave the convent. In spite of this, the Princess still made the lives of the nuns miserable. As Teresa puts it, "Even though the princess has returned home, [the nuns] are like captives . . . Now she is also mad at the friars" (LE. 1. 58. 6.).

Teresa was aware of the situation but had to wait several months until she had a place to move the community. In March 1574, the foundation of Segovia was established. Segovia was relatively close to Pastrana, and since Teresa needed nuns to form the new community, the transfer of the nuns from Pastrana to Segovia proved to be the perfect solution to both of her problems.

By April 1574, Teresa had arranged for the transfer of the nuns. One night, under the cover of darkness, five ox carts arrived at the outskirts of Pastrana. Reminiscent of the foundation of Medina del Campo, the nuns tiptoed through the darkened streets of Pastrana to the carts and made their escape to Segovia.

However, hell hath no fury like a princess scorned. When the Princess discovered that the nuns had abandoned the convent, she denounced Teresa's *Book of Her Life* to the Inquisition as being a heretical text. Teresa was never brought to trial, and though no charges were officially formulated by the Inquisition, Teresa's autobiography was never returned to her.

Years later, while at the royal court of Madrid, the Princess formed a political alliance with Antonio Pérez, the King's undersecretary of state. Pérez and the Princess fell under suspicion of betraying state secrets to a foreign government. Pérez was put under house arrest and the Princess was sent to prison. However, when she fell ill, King Phillip allowed her to return to her palace in Pastrana. Because of her extravagant lifestyle and unbecoming behavior, King Philip deprived her of the custody of her children and appointed an administrator for her property.

Meanwhile, Pérez, who was now in prison on suspicion of murder, escaped and fled to Aragon. King Philip, fearing that the Princess would also escape, had all the doors, windows, and skylights of her palace barred. In addition, he severed her communication with the outside world. The year was 1590. She lived in this condition until she died in 1592. As one historian writes, "[Philip] transformed her apartments into a sombre prison, with little air and almost no light—a 'dungeon of death,'" as his prisoner said. The Princess died there on February 2, 1592, at the age of fifty-two, after one-and-twenty months of this cruel seclusion."[22]

Reflection. In *The Way of Perfection* Teresa writes: "What I ask of you, Sisters, is that if anyone sees within herself that she is unable to follow what is customarily practiced here she should say so; there are other monasteries where the Lord is also served. Do not disturb these few nuns brought here together by His Majesty. In other places there is the freedom to find relief by being with relatives" (W. 8. 3.).

This passage can be best understood within its historical context. Four years before Teresa wrote the *Way*, she left the convent of the Incarnation and founded St. Joseph's in Avila. In the Incarnation, it was the custom of the nuns to carry on lengthy visits with their friends and relatives both inside and outside of the monastery. One of the reasons why Teresa founded St. Joseph's was to establish a lifestyle that would ensure the silence and solitude necessary to lead a contemplative life. In consequence, the cloister was more strictly enforced, and visits to the front parlor were reduced substantially. These changes put strictures on the freedom of the nuns. There were many woman, both nuns from the Incarnation and those attempting to enter religious life for the first time, who had a great *desire* to live Teresa's new way of life. However, once they entered St. Joseph's, they realized that they did not have the *capacity* to live the life to which they aspired. However, some of these nuns couldn't admit this fact and complained about what they were not permitted to do. Teresa is saying to these nuns that it would be best that they leave because they are making everyone miserable.

"Do not disturb these few nuns brought here together by His Majesty. In other places there is the freedom to find relief by being with relatives" (W. 8. 3.).

In the person of the Princess of Eboli, we have an extreme example of someone who could not accept the fact that she did not have the capacity to live the life to which she aspired. Her pampered self could not endure the rigors of the convent. In consequence, she made everyone around her miserable. Her desire to live the life of a nun was an impulse of her imagination. Teresa writes that, "big plans sometimes come to us during prayer" (IC. 5. 3. 8.). However, we soon discover that "the determination was not in the *will* . . . but a work of the *imagination*" (IC. 5. 3. 10.) (italics added).

Questions. We all have dreams that spin around in our minds. But what happens when they hit the hard wall of reality? Can we accept who we are? Can we accept the fact that we are not gifted in a certain area of life? How do we relate to people who are living our dreams? Can we rejoice with them or do we try to undermine their confidence and spoil their happiness?

Reflection. In Act IV of Verdi's opera, *Don Carlos*, the treachery of the Princess of Eboli is exposed. While imprisoned, she bemoans her fate in the aria "O don fatal" (O fatal beauty). "O fatal gift, O cruel gift . . . You make us so vain and proud. I curse you, I curse you, O beauty!"

Here is a pitiful example of someone who cannot take responsibility for the consequences of her choices. It is almost as if the Princess is saying that it was beauty that *made* her vain. Her vanity was not a choice; it was foisted upon her. However, the truth is that she was cursed, not because she was *gifted* with beauty, intelligence, and power, but because she *misused* her gifts for her own selfish ends.

Questions. Do you have a gift, be it beauty, strength, intelligence, prestige that you are tempted to misuse? If you misuse your gift, can you accept responsibility for your actions?

Chapter 18

Treats of the foundation of the monastery of St. Joseph in Salamanca in the year 1570. Deals with some important counsels for prioresses.

1. After these two foundations were made, I returned to the city of Toledo, where I remained some months until the house, which I mentioned, was bought and everything was left in order.[1] While I was engaged in these things, a rector of the Society of Jesus wrote me from Salamanca, telling me that it would be very good to have one of these monasteries there, giving me reasons for this.[2] But since the town was very poor, I resisted founding a monastery there in poverty.[3] In considering that Avila is just as poor, and the monastery there is never in want, nor do I believe that God will fail those who serve Him, if they live as moderately as we do, and that the nuns are so few and help themselves through the labor of their hands, I decided to make the foundation. And going from Toledo to Avila, I sought there to obtain permission from the bishop who was then . . .[4] Since the Father Rector had informed him about our order and that the foundation would render service to God, he responded very favorably and gave the permission without delay.

2. It seemed to me that once I had permission from the ordinary, the monastery was a much as founded, so easy did the rest seem to me. Thus, I immediately sought to rent a house that a lady, whom I knew,[5] would let me have. But this was a difficult thing to do because the time was not the proper one for renting and the student occupants agreed to leave only when the new occupants arrived. They did not know who the

new ones would be, for I took the greatest care so that nothing would be known until I took possession of the foundation. I already have experience of what the devil stirs up to hinder one of these monasteries. And although with this one God, desiring it to be founded, did not allow him to cause trouble in the beginning, the trials and contradictions were so great afterward that they are still not completely overcome—and some years have passed between the time it was founded and my writing this account.[6] Thus, I believe that God is served very much in it since the devil cannot bear it.

3. Well now, having obtained the permission and being certain of a house to rent, I left for Salamanca. I trusted in the mercy of God because there wasn't a person there who could in any way help me with the great deal that had to be done in order to make the proper adaptions in the house. For the sake of secrecy, I took with me only one other nun as companion,[7] for I found this to be better than bringing the nuns before taking possession. I had learned from experience through what had happened to me in Medina del Campo; there I got myself into much trouble.[8] Thus, if there were some obstacle, I could undergo the trial alone, with no one other than the one required companion. We arrived on the vigil of All Saints.[9] The previous night we had traveled a good deal before coming to a place to sleep. The weather was cold; and I, very sick.

4. I am not recording in these foundations the great hardships endured in the traveling: the cold, the heat, the snow (once it didn't stop snowing the whole day); sometimes getting lost, and at other times, being very sick and having a fever (for, glory to God, I usually have poor health). But I saw clearly that our Lord was giving me strength. It happened

to me at times when a foundation was being planned that I would be so sick and have so many pains that I would get very anxious. It seemed to me that I wasn't even able to remain in my cell without lying down. I would turn to our Lord, complain to His Majesty, and ask how He desired me to do what I couldn't. Afterward, although I still felt the hardship, His Majesty gave me strength, and with the fervor and solicitude He gave, it seems I forgot about myself.

5. From what I now remember, fear of the hardship involved never prevented me from making a foundation even though I felt strong aversion to the traveling, especially the long journeys. But once we got started, the journey seemed easy to me, and I considered for whose service it was made and reflected that in that house the Lord would be praised and the Blessed Sacrament reserved. This is a special consolation for me: to see one more church, particularly when I recall the many that the Lutherans are suppressing. I don't know what trials, however great, should be feared if in exchange something so good comes about for Christianity. For although we often do not take note, it ought to be a great consolation for us that Jesus Christ, true God and true man, is present in the most Blessed Sacrament in many places. Certainly I am very often consoled in the choir when I see these very pure souls praising God, for one cannot help but recognize their holiness in many things, seeing their obedience, the joy so much enclosure and solitude give them, and their happiness when some opportunities for mortification come along. In places where the Lord gives the prioress more grace in exercising them in mortification, I see greater happiness. And the result is that the prioresses tire more easily in thus exercising them than these

souls do in obeying, for never in this matter of mortification do the desires of these nuns cease.

6. Although this subject is foreign to the one concerning the foundation that I began discussing, some things are coming to my mind now about this matter of mortification. Perhaps, daughters, they will be important for the prioresses, and so lest I forget I'll mention them now. For since the prioresses have different talents and virtues, they seek to lead their nuns along their own way. The one who is very mortified thinks that anything she commands is easy to submit to, as it would be for her, but perhaps it would be very harmful for the nun to whom she gives the orders. We must be careful about this. If for ourselves something would be harsh, we must not order others to do it. Discretion is an important aspect of government, and very necessary in these houses. I would say much more necessary than in other houses, for the account one must render concerning one's subjects is greater. This applies in interior as well as exterior matters.

Other prioresses, who are very spiritual, would like to reduce everything to prayer; in sum, the Lord leads souls by different paths. But the prioresses must remember that they are not there for the purpose of choosing a path for others according to their own liking but so as to lead subjects by the path of the rule and constitutions even though they themselves might desire and feel urged to do something else.

7. Once I was living in one of these houses with a prioress who was fond of penance; she led all the others along this path. She once had the entire community take the discipline while reciting the seven penitential psalms with their accompanying prayers, and things of this sort. Thus it happens that

if a prioress is absorbed in prayer, even though the hour is not one set apart for prayer, but after Matins, she keeps the whole community there even though it would be much better if the Sisters went to bed. If, as I say, she is fond of mortification, everyone has to follow suit, and these little sheep of the Virgin keep silent like little lambs; as for me, certainly, it causes much devotion, and embarrassment, and, at times, much temptation. The Sisters don't understand, for they are all absorbed in God. But I fear for their health and would want them to observe the rule, for with that there is plenty to do; and the rest should be done with gentleness. This is especially important in what pertains to mortification. For love of our Lord, the prioresses should be attentive in this, for discretion and knowledge of each one's talents are very important in these matters. If the prioresses are not carefully attentive, they will do the nuns much harm and leave them disturbed instead of helping them.

8. They must reflect that this mortification is not a matter of obligation; this is the first thing they must consider. Although mortification is very necessary in order that the soul gain freedom and high perfection, it is not accomplished in a short time. Rather, little by little, the prioress should help each one according to the spirituality and amount of intelligence God gives. It might seem to prioresses that intelligence is not necessary for this mortification, but they are mistaken. For with some nuns, much time will pass before they come to understand perfection and even the spirit of our rule (and perhaps they will afterward be the holiest), for they will not know when it is good to excuse oneself, and when not, or other trifling matters that if they understood they would perhaps carry

out with ease. And such nuns do not completely understand, nor does it seem to them that these are matters pertaining to perfection, which is worse.

9. There is a nun in one of these houses who is among the best servants of God in them, insofar as I can tell. She has a deep spirituality, receives favors from His Majesty, and has a spirit of penance and humility; yet, she does not completely understand some points in the constitutions. The accusation of faults in chapter[10] seems to her uncharitable, and she wonders how anyone can say anything against the Sisters and similar things and says that she could say some things against some Sisters who are very good servants of God; and in other matters I see that she is ahead of those who understand this well. The prioress must not then think that she understands a soul at once. Let her leave this to God, for it is He alone who can understand it. Rather, the prioress should strive to guide each nun along the way His Majesty is leading that one, provided that the nun is not failing in obedience or in the more essential matters of the rule and constitutions. That virgin martyr, from the eleven thousand, who hid herself did not fail to be a saint; on the contrary, by coming alone afterward to offer herself to be martyred, she perhaps suffered more than the rest of the virgins.[11]

10. Now, then, let us return to the subject of mortification. The prioress may ask something of a nun in order to mortify her, and although it is a little thing it may be a heavy burden to the nun. And even though the Sister does it, she is left so disturbed and tempted that it would have been better had she not been told to do it; I mean, to do it right away. The prioress should take heed not to try to make such a one perfect

by force but should allow her to proceed gradually until the Lord does the work in her. For that which is done to help her advance shouldn't be for her a cause of disturbance and spiritual distress, which is a very terrible thing, for she will be a very good nun without that perfection. Observing the others, she will gradually do as they do, as we have seen. And if she doesn't, she will be saved without this virtue of mortification. For I know one of these nuns who all her life practiced great virtue, and for some years now has served our Lord in many ways, and she often experiences some feelings and imperfections that she cannot do anything about, and she complained about them to me and is aware of them. I think that God allows her to fall into these sinless faults (for there is no sin in them) so that she might humble herself and realize that she is not totally perfect.

Therefore, some nuns will suffer great mortifications, and the greater the mortifications they are ordered to perform the more they will enjoy them because the Lord has given them the strength of soul to surrender their wills. Others will not suffer even little ones; and to impose mortifications on them would be comparable to loading a child down with two sacks of wheat. Not only will the child be unable to carry them, but he will bow under the weight and fall to the ground. Therefore, my daughters—I am speaking with prioresses—pardon me, for the things I have seen that happen to some make me to go on at greater length in this matter.

11. Another counsel I give you, and it is a very important one. Do not give any order that could be a sin (even venial) if carried out, and not even if you do so just to test obedience. (I've heard that some things would have involved mortal sin

if done). At least the nuns, because of their innocence perhaps are without blame; but not the prioress, because there is no order she gives that they will not carry out immediately. And since they hear and read about what the saints of the desert did, everything seems to them well done if ordered by obedience, at least in their own case. And also let subjects be advised that anything that would be a mortal sin when not ordered by the superior would still be one if the superior orders it, unless the matter involves omitting Mass or the Church fast, or things like that, in which the prioress may have reasons for dispensing. But something like jumping into the well and things of that sort are wrong to do. No one should think that God must work miracles, as He did with the saints; there are many other things in which perfect obedience may be practiced.

12. All the mortification in which these dangers are not present, I praise. Once a Sister in Malagón asked permission to take a discipline, and the prioress (she must have been asked more than once) answered: "Don't bother me." Since the nun persisted, the prioress said: "Go on, keep walking; don't bother me." With great simplicity, the nun went walking for several hours until another Sister asked her why she was walking so much, or something like that. And she replied that she had been ordered to do so. When the bell was rung for Matins and the prioress asked where she was, the other nun told her what had taken place.

13. Thus it's necessary, as I have mentioned at another time, that the prioresses be careful about what they do with souls that they see are so obedient. For another Sister showed a nun one of those very large worms, telling her to observe how pretty it was. The prioress said to the nun jokingly, well,

let Sister eat it. The Sister went and fried it very well. The cook asked her why she was frying it. She told her she was frying it so that she could eat it, and this she wanted to do. And the prioress, being very careless, could have done her much harm. I find I'm happier that they go to excess in matters of obedience because I am particularly devoted to this virtue, and so I have put down all I could so that the nuns might possess it. But it would profit me little to do so if the Lord through His supreme mercy had not given the grace for all in general to be inclined toward this virtue. May it please His Majesty to continue to give this grace long into the future. Amen.

Chapter 19

Continues the account of the foundation of the monastery of St. Joseph in the city of Salamanca.

1. I have digressed much. When something presents itself that by the Lord's will I come to understand through experience, it bothers me not give advice about it. It could be that what I think about the matter is worthwhile. Always inquire, daughters, from those who are learned, for through them you will learn how to advance along the way of perfection with discretion and in truth. If prioresses want to fulfill their duties well, they have great need to go to confession to a learned man (and if they don't, they will make many mistakes in the interests of sanctity); and they should strive also that their nuns confess to a learned man.

2. Well, on the vigil of All Saints, in the year that was mentioned,[1] we arrived at noon in the city of Salamanca. From an inn I sought to find out through a good man there if the house was free. He was a great servant of God, named Nicolás Gutiérrez,[2] to whom I had entrusted the task of making sure that it would be occupied. This man had won from His Majesty through his good life a great peace and happiness in the midst of trials, for he had undergone many trials. Having once enjoyed great prosperity, he was left very poor, but he bore the poverty with as much joy as he did the riches. The good man worked very hard for this foundation, with much dedication and willingness. When he came, he told me that the house was occupied, that he hadn't been able to get the students to leave. I told him how important it was that they vacate immediately,

248

before my presence in that city became known, for I am always afraid lest some obstacles arise, as I have said.[3] He went to the one who owned the house and insisted so much that it was vacated that afternoon. When it was almost night, we entered.

3. It was the first monastery I founded without reserving the Blessed Sacrament, for I had previously thought that a foundation was not official until the Blessed Sacrament was reserved. And I had now leaned that this wasn't necessary. That was a great consolation to me, for the house was in bad condition because of those students who had previously occupied it. Since they must not have had a gift for cleanliness, the whole house was in such a state that we did no small amount of work that night. The next morning the first Mass was said, and I arranged for more nuns to come from Medina del Campo.[4] My companion and I spent the night of All Saints alone. I tell you, daughters, I have to laugh when I recall the fear of my companion, who was María del Sacramento, a nun older than I and a great servant of God.[5]

4. The house was very large, was in a mess, and had many garrets. My companion couldn't get the students out of her mind, thinking that since they were so angry for having had to leave the house, one of them may have hidden there. They could have done this very easily, for there were many possibilities. We locked ourselves in a room where there was some straw, which was the first thing I provided for the founding of the house, because in having straw we would have a bed. We slept there that night with two borrowed blankets. The next day some nuns that were nearby, who we thought would be very displeased, lent us furnishings for our companions, who were to come, and sent us alms.[6] Their monastery was called

St. Isabel's and all the time we were there they gave us alms and did many favors for us.

5. Once my companion was locked in that room, it seems she calmed down a little with regard to the students, although she didn't do anything but look about from side to side, still fearful. And the devil must have helped by bringing to her mind thoughts about the danger. Her thoughts then began to disturb me, for with my weak heart, not much was needed. I asked her why she was looking around since no one could get in there. She answered: "Mother, I was wondering what would happen if I were to die now; what would you do here all alone?" If that had happened it would have been a hard thing for me to take. And I began to think a little about it and even become afraid. Because as for dead bodies, although I am not afraid of them, my heart gets weak even when I'm not alone. And since the tolling of the bells helped matters along, for, as I said, it was the vigil of All Souls,[7] the devil had a good means of making us squander our thoughts on trifles. When he sees that one has no fear of him, he looks for other devices. I said to her: "Sister, when this happens, I'll think about what to do; now, let me sleep." Since we had just spent two bad nights, sleep came soon and took away our fears. The next day more nuns arrived, and with them present, the fears left.

6. The monastery was in this house for about three years—I don't recall whether or not it was four, for I don't remember well since they sent me to the Incarnation in Avila.[8] I never would, or did, leave any monastery until it was in fit condition, had a spirit of recollection, and was adapted according to my wishes. In this matter God greatly favored me, for when

there was question of work to be done I enjoyed being the first. And as though I were to live in that house for the rest of my life, I sought to obtain everything, even the smallest thing that would contribute to the tranquility suitable for the life, and so it gave me great happiness to see that everything was in good shape. I very much regretted to see what these Sisters suffered, although not from a lack of sustenance (I took care of this from where I was, for the house was not located in a place suitable for receiving alms), but from a location that was unhealthy because of the humidity and cold. Since it was so large a house it could not be repaired. And, what was worse, the Blessed Sacrament was not reserved, which is a great affliction when so much enclosure is practiced. The Sisters were not unhappy but bore everything with a joy that moved one to praise God. Some told me that they thought it would be an imperfection to desire a house, that they were as happy there as they would be if they had the Blessed Sacrament.

7. Well, when the superior[9] saw their perfection and the trial they were undergoing, he was moved with pity and ordered me to come from the Incarnation. They had already reached an agreement with a gentleman there who was going to sell them a house.[10] But it was in such condition that they would have had to spend a thousand ducats before entering it. It belonged to an entailed estate, but the gentleman decided to allow us both to occupy it without first obtaining permission from the king and to put up partition walls. I got Father Julián de Avila,[11] who is the one I said came with me on these foundations, and we looked at the house so as to decide what had to be done, for experience has taught me much about these things.

8. We went in August and hurried as much as we could. The nuns were able to stay where they were until the feast of St. Michael, the time when houses were rented there. But the house was still far from being finished. Since we had not rented for another year, the one in which we were staying had another renter already. We were in a great hurry. The white-washing of the church was about finished. The gentleman who had sold us the house was not there. Some persons who wished us well told us that we had done wrong in coming so soon, but where there is need one takes poorly any advice that doesn't provide some help.

9. We moved on the eve of St. Michael, a little before dawn. The news had already been spread that the Blessed Sacrament would be reserved on the feast of St. Michael and that a sermon would be preached.[12] Our Lord was pleased that on the afternoon of the day we moved it rained so hard that it was most difficult to bring the things we needed. The chapel had been newly fixed up, but the roof was so poorly tiled the rain came through most of it. I tell you, daughters, I felt very imperfect that day. Since the news had already been spread about, I didn't know what to do. I became so distressed that I said to the Lord, almost complaining, that either He not order me to get involved in repair works or He help me in this need. The good man Nicolás Gutiérrez, with his equanimity, as though nothing had happened, told me very meekly not to be disturbed, that God would provide a remedy. And so it happened. On the feast of St. Michael, when it was time for the people to come, the sun began to shine, which filled me with devotion, and I saw how much better that blessed man had done by trusting in our Lord than I with my disturbance.

10. There were many people, and there was music, and the Blessed Sacrament was reserved with great solemnity. Since this house is in a good location, the people began to know about it and be devoted to it. In particular, the Countess of Monterrey, Doña María Pimentel,[13] favored us, as well as a lady, whose husband was the magistrate there, whose name was Doña Mariana. The very next day, as though to temper our happiness in having the Blessed Sacrament, the gentleman to whom the house belonged came. He was so furious that I didn't know what to do with him. And the devil made sure that he couldn't be reasoned with, for we had fulfilled all that we had agreed upon with him. There was little use in trying to explain to him. When some other persons spoke to him, he was a little appeased; but afterward he changed his mind again. I had already decided to leave the house. He didn't want this either, because he wanted to be given the money at once. His wife to whom the house belonged had desired to sell it in order to provide for two daughters, and this was the reason given in asking for the license to sell it. The money had already been deposited with a person chosen by the husband.

11. The fact is that even though this happened more than three years ago, the purchase of the house is not finalized, nor do I know whether the monastery will remain there; and this is why I have mentioned these things.[14]

12. What I do know is that in none of the monasteries of the primitive rule that up to now the Lord has founded did the nuns come near to suffering trials as great as these. Through the mercy of God, those who are there are so good, for they bear everything happily. May it please His Majesty to lead them on, for whether or not they have a good house matters

little. Rather, it gives us great pleasure to find we are in a house that we can be thrown out of, for we remember how the Lord of the world didn't have any. It has happened to us at times in these foundations that we were in a house that we didn't own, and the truth is that I never saw a nun distressed about that. May it please His Majesty that through His infinite goodness and mercy we will not be in want of the eternal dwelling places, amen, amen.

SALAMANCA, (ADVICE TO PRIORESSES) (1570)

Summary and Background: Chapters 18 and 19

Shortly after Teresa returned to Toledo from Pastrana (July 21, 1569), she received a letter from Martin Guitierrez S.J., the rector of the new Jesuit college in Salamanca. He requested that Teresa found a house in Salamanca. Teresa hesitated. "Since the town was poor, I resisted founding a monastery there in poverty" (F. 18. 1.). This statement may strike us as strange since Salamanca was a leading center of learning in Europe. However, Teresa knew that students and professors were generally poor and that Salamanca was devoid of merchants (those who had the capital to afford to give alms).

However, on second thought, Teresa decided to take up Guitierrez's offer. Teresa believed that God would provide the necessary funds in Salamanca, just as he had in the establishment of St. Joseph's in Avila, which was also a very poor town. Having obtained permission from the bishop of Salamanca, Teresa rented a house that was occupied by students. They *said* that they would vacate the premises when Teresa arrived.

In mid-August, Teresa set out from Toledo for Salamanca. She purposely took with her only *one* nun. "I found this to be better than bringing the nuns before taking possession [of the house]. I had learned from experience through what happened to me in Medina del Campo; there I got myself into much trouble. Thus, if there were some obstacle, I could undergo the trial alone, with no one other than the one required companion" (F. 18. 3.).

Here we see an example of Teresa's practical wisdom. Every one of her foundations presented difficulties. Therefore, she anticipated problems. For example, Teresa took it for granted that the house she rented would need some repairs before it would be habitable. This would require time, energy, and the hassle of finding laborers to do the work. "[There] wasn't a person there who could in any way help me with the great deal that had to be done in order to make the proper adaptations in the house" (F. 18. 3.). Taking only one companion would make it easier for Teresa, for while she was engaged in the nitty-gritty of setting up the house, she wouldn't have to worry about attending to the needs of several nuns. But there was another reason why Teresa took only one nun with her—"For the sake of secrecy" (F. 18. 3.). Since the monastery was to be founded in poverty, Teresa wanted to avoid drawing attention to herself and thus prevent arousing opposition from the populace.

In typical fashion, Teresa begins her account of the foundation of Salamanca only to get sidetracked by a train of thought—the conduct of prioresses. The core of Teresa's concern is with prioresses who "seek to lead their nuns along their own way" without considering that "the Lord leads souls by different paths" (F. 18. 6.). Teresa reminds those in authority that "they are not there for the purpose of choosing a path for others according to their own liking" (F. 18. 6.). The prioress should take it for granted that *her* way to God is not for everyone rather than to presuppose that she knows what is best for others. "The prioress must not think that she understands a soul at once. Let her leave this to God, for it is He alone who can understand it. Rather, the prioress should strive to guide each nun along the way His Majesty is leading that one" (F. 18. 9.).

In addition, the prioress should be cognizant of the fact that when she asks a nun to do something for the sake of mortification "although it is a little thing it may be a heavy burden to the nun" (F. 18. 10.). In consequence, "The prioress should take heed not to try to make such a one perfect by force but should allow her to proceed gradually until the Lord does the work in her. For that which is done to help her advance shouldn't be for her a cause of disturbance and spiritual distress, which is a terrible thing, for she will be a very good nun without that perfection" (F. 18. 10.).

Next, Teresa writes of nuns who are upset because they are not perfect. "I know one of these nuns who all her life practiced great virtue, and for some years now has served our Lord in many ways, and she often experiences some feelings and imperfections that she cannot do anything about, and she complained about them to me and is aware of them. I think that God allows her to fall into these sinless faults (for there is not sin in them) so that she might humble herself and realize that she is not totally perfect" (F. 18. 10.). In short, Teresa is telling us that sometimes our imperfections can save us from spiritual pride.

Finally, Teresa touches upon a matter that is very similar, if not identical, to the one that she dealt with in chapter sixteen, namely, simpleminded nuns, who carry out *literally* what the prioress tells them to do. Teresa gives the example of a nun who asks the prioress permission to perform some mortification. When the prioress told her, "Don't bother me," the nun persisted. In exasperation, the prioress said, "Go on, keep on walking; don't bother me." In short, the prioress told the nun, as we would say in our modern vernacular, "Take a walk." In consequence, "the nun went walking for several hours" (F. 18. 12.). Teresa's advice to prioresses is that they have to be cognizant *to whom* they are speaking because certain nuns will misinterpret their words.

After spending the whole of chapter eighteen giving advice to prioresses, Teresa begins chapter nineteen with the statement, "I have digressed much" (F. 19. 1.). Thank God for these digressions, for the Church has been enriched by them.

At high noon, on October 31, 1570, after "the great hardships endured in traveling: cold, the heat, the snow, sometimes getting lost [and] in poor health" (F. 18. 4.), Teresa and Sr. María del Sacramento, her companion, arrived in Salamanca, only to discover that the house that Teresa had rented was still occupied by the students. Teresa explained to the landlord that it was imperative that she take possession of the house immediately before her presence in the city became known. "I am always afraid lest some obstacle arise" (F. 18. 2.).

The students were evicted, but it wasn't until almost nightfall that Teresa and her companion could take possession of their house which "was in a mess" (F. 18. 4.). Because the house was a big ramshackle structure with many nooks and crannies and Sr. María was timid, she was afraid that one of the students was hiding in the house and meant to do them harm. To allay her fears, Teresa put down straw for bedding and locked the door of the room in which they would sleep. This helped to calm Sr. María's nerves.

The next day, they were visited by some Poor Clare nuns who lived in the neighborhood. Teresa thought that they "would be very displeased" (F. 19. 4.). She was probably having a flashback of her run-in with the Augustinian friars at Medina del Campo. However, to Teresa's pleasant surprise, the Poor Clares not only lent them furnishings but gave them alms.

After the community at Salamanca was established, it became evident in a short period of time that they would have to find another location. The structure of the building was unsound, and its proximity to the river proved to be a health hazard. The nuns began to get sick. Unfortunately, for various factors beyond Teresa's control, the community was not able to transfer to another location for three years, at which time Teresa entered into negotiations with Pedro de la Banda for the purchase of a house. The negotiations were interminable; they dragged on for years.

The house to be purchased was part of an entailed estate, which meant it could only be sold by obtaining a royal decree. However, Banda had led Teresa to believe that this was not the case. Teresa, believing Banda, began to have necessary renovations made in Banda's house. However, when Banda realized that he could not obtain permission to sell the house, he became furious at Teresa for ruining his property. Teresa wanted to cut her losses and look for another place, but Banda would not release her from the contract she had signed.

For years, Banda had the nuns pay rent on his house while he was in the process of obtaining the necessary permission for the house to be sold. In a letter to Fr. Jerome Gracián, dated September 1, 1582, approximately a month before she died, Teresa mentions that she was able to "rent [Banda's] house for another year" (LE. 2. 465. 8.). Teresa never saw the last chapter in the Banda saga. It took forty-four years before the situation was finally settled, during which time, the nuns were evicted twice.

Reflection. "[A]lthough it is a little thing it may be a heavy burden to the nun . . . [S]ome nuns will suffer great mortifications, and the greater they are ordered to perform the more they will enjoy them because the Lord has given them the strength of soul to surrender their wills. Others will not suffer even little ones; and to impose mortifications on them would be comparable to loading a child down with two sacks of wheat. Not only will the child be unable to carry them, but he will bow under the weight and fall to the ground" (F. 18. 10.). Teresa says something similar in *The Way of Perfection*. "For at times it happens that some trifle will cause as much suffering to one as a great trial will to another . . . And those sufferings that for us are heavy may be light for another. So in these matters let us not judge from ourselves . . . Consider that this advice is important for knowing how to sympathize with your neighbor who is having trials, however small they may be" (W. 7. 5–6.).

The truth that underlies both passages is that God has not endowed each of us with the same strengths. Teresa is telling us that if we do not take this fact into consideration, then we will either impose burdens upon people that they cannot bear or we will judge others according to our own yardstick, or both.

How often do we judge others from ourselves? "If I can do it, he can do it." Or how often do we become angry in disbelief, thinking that someone could do something *only if she tried harder*? Even though in some cases this may be true, the fact of the matter remains, we all have different strengths.

Also, we can be harsh in our judgments toward someone's moral failings in an area that we have never had to struggle. For example, if you have never had to struggle with overeating, lust, an addiction to alcohol, etc., you may be unsympathetic to these or other human weaknesses.

Questions. Does your inability to understand the limitations and weaknesses of others cause you to judge them harshly? Have you ever been judged harshly because a person was unable to understand your limitations or weaknesses?

Reflection.

> I know one of these nuns who all her life practiced great virtue, and for some years now has served our Lord in many ways, and she often experiences some feelings and imperfections that she cannot do anything about, and she complained about them to me and is aware of them. I think that God allows her to fall into these sinless faults (for there is not sin in them) so that she might humble herself and realize that she is not totally perfect. (F. 18. 10.)

This passage discloses the insidiousness of pride. At first glance, it might seem that the nun's concern about not being able to overcome her imperfections is an expression of her holiness. While this may be true to a certain extent, Teresa's remark about God allowing this nun to fall into certain faults as a means of keeping her humble indicates Teresa's concern about her spiritual pride, which takes the form of being overly distressed about her "sinless faults." It is as if the nun cannot accept that she is a human being—"not totally perfect" (F. 18. 10.).

Being upset over not being perfect is itself an imperfection. St. Francis de Sales writes in this regard, "It is a great failing to be angry with oneself for giving way to anger, impatience with one's impatience and so on . . . This sort of annoyance and bitterness with ourselves springs from self-love and leads to pride, for we are merely upset and disturbed at finding ourselves imperfect."[15]

However, pride will attempt to use these feelings of being upset with oneself as a means to gain recognition for being holy. Perhaps this is why the nun "complained about [her imperfections to Teresa]" (F. 18. 10.). The message that is being communicated is "Look how holy I am because I'm so concerned about the slightest imperfection."

Questions. In what area of your life are you unable to accept that you are "not totally perfect" (F. 18. 10.)? Have you ever considered that your inability to accept that you are not totally perfect is rooted in pride?

Chapter 20

Treats of the foundation of the monastery, Our Lady of the Annunciation, in Alba de Tormes. It was made in the year 1571.

1. Two months had not yet passed since the feast of All Saints (the day on which possession was taken of the house in Salamanca) when I received an urgent request from the administrator for the Duke of Alba and his wife that a monastery be founded in the town of Alba. I was not too keen about the idea because the town was a small one, which would make it necessary for us to have an income, and my inclination was not to have one. Father Master Fray Domingo Báñez (who had been my confessor, whom I consulted when beginning these foundations) happened to be in Salamanca, and he reprimanded me and told me that since the Council had given permission it would not be right to forego the foundation of a monastery because of a need for an income.[1] He said further that I failed to understand that whether the monastery had an income or not made little difference in regard to nuns being poor and very perfect.

Before I say more, I shall mention who the foundress was and how the Lord moved her to make the foundation.

2. The foundress of the monastery, Our Lady of the Annunciation, was Teresa de Layz, a daughter of noble parents, hidalgos of pure blood.[2] Since her parents were not as rich as would be expected considering the nobility of their lineage, they had their house in a place called Tordillos, which is two leagues from the said town of Alba. It is a great pity that the world is so influenced by vanity that people would

prefer to remain in these little villages where there is a lack of Christian doctrine and of many other things that are means to the enlightenment of souls, than to fail even one iota in those punctilios that accompany what they call honor. Since the parents already had four daughters when Teresa de Layz was born, they were much distressed to see that she also was a daughter.

3. Certainly, it is something to be much wept over that human beings do not know what is best for them and are totally ignorant of the judgments of God and of the great blessings that can come to them through daughters or of the great sufferings that can come from sons. It doesn't seem they want to leave this matter to the One who creates their children and understands everything, but they kill themselves over what should be making them happy. As people whose faith is asleep, they do not reflect or recall that it is God who thus ordains, and so they do not leave everything in His hands. And being so blind that they do not do this, they suffer great ignorance in not understanding how little these afflictions help them. Oh, God help me! How differently will we understand these ignorances on the day when the truth about all things shall be understood. And how many fathers and mothers will be seen going to hell because they had sons and also how many will be seen in heaven because of their daughters.

4. Well, to return to what I was saying, things came to the point that on the third day after her birth they left their baby girl alone and forgot about her for the entire day, from morning until night, as though she mattered little to them. One thing they had done well was to have her baptized by a priest as soon as she was born. When at night, a woman came who

was taking care of the baby and knew what was going on, she hastened to see if the child was dead. Some other persons who had gone there to visit the mother were also witnesses to what I shall now tell. Weeping, the woman took the baby into her arms and complaining of the cruelty said: "How is it, my daughter, are you not a Christian?" The baby girl lifted her head and answered, "Yes, I am," and spoke no more until reaching that age at which all children begin to speak. Those who heard her were amazed, and her mother began to love and cherish her from then on, and she often said that she would like to live to see what God would do with this child. She reared her daughter in keeping with high moral standards and taught her everything about virtue.

5. When the time came that her parents wanted her to marry, she refused, nor did she have any desire at all to get married. She happened to find out that Francisco Valazquez, now her husband, who is also the founder of this house, was seeking her. In hearing his name, she decided to marry if she could marry him, never having seen him in her life. But His Majesty saw that this was fitting so that the good work both of them did in order to serve Him could be done. Besides being a virtuous and rich man, Francisco Velázquez loves his wife so much that he seeks to please her in everything. And rightly so, for all that one can seek in a married woman the Lord gave to him in great abundance. Along with the diligent care she takes of her household, her goodness is so great that when her husband brought her to his native town of Alba and the duke's housing administrators happened to arrange that lodging be given in her house to a young gentleman, she was very upset and began to abhor the town.

For being youthful and attractive in appearance, she could have been the victim of some evil deed since the devil began to put bad thoughts in that gentleman's mind.

6. Aware of this, but without saying anything to her husband, she asked him to take her away from there. He did so and brought her to Salamanca where she lived very happily, surrounded by much of the world's goods, since he held a position that made others want to please and flatter him.[3] They had but one sorrow, that God had not given them children. That He might give them, she offered many devotions and prayers. And she never begged the Lord for anything else but that He give her offspring so that after her death her children could continue the praise of His Majesty, for it seemed to her unfortunate that this praise would end with her and that there would be no one after her days to praise Him. And she told me that there wasn't any other desire that came to her mind. And she is a woman who is so truthful and good a Christian and virtuous, as I have said, that it often makes me praise our Lord to see her works and her great desires never to fail to use her time well and to please Him always.

7. Well, then, living many years with this desire and recommending it to St. Andrew, who, she was informed, is a patron of such causes, and after many other devotions that she had offered, she was told one night while lying down: "Do not desire children, for you will be condemned." She was left frightened and fearful. But not for this reason did the desire leave her, for it seemed to her that since her purpose was so good there would be no reason for her to be condemned. So she continued to beg our Lord. Especially, she carried out a particular devotion to St. Andrew. Once, while experiencing

this desire, though she doesn't know whether she was awake or asleep (whatever may be the case, it is clear that the vision was true from what followed), it seemed to her that she was in a house where on the patio beneath the gallery was a well. And she saw in that place a green meadow with white flowers, so beautiful she wouldn't be able to describe what she saw. Near the well, St. Andrew appeared in the form of a very venerable and handsome person, for it gave her great delight to look on him, and he said to her: "These are children other than those you desire." She did not want the great consolation she felt in that place to end; but it did not last. And she understood clearly that the vision was of St. Andrew, without anyone telling her; and also that our Lord willed that she found a monastery. Hence it can be understood that the vision was an intellectual as well as an imaginative one, nor could it have been either a whim or an illusion caused by the devil.

8. First, the vision was not a whim; this can be deduced from its great effect, for from that point on she never more desired children. She remained so convinced in her heart that this was God's will that she no longer asked for or desired them. Thus she began to think about the way in which she could do what the Lord wanted. Nor was it an illusion caused by the devil. This can be discerned from the fact that a monastery is now founded where our Lord is much served, for the devil of himself cannot do good. In addition, this took place more than six years before the monastery was founded, and the devil cannot know the future.

9. Very surprised by this vision, she told her husband that since God did not desire to give them children they should found a monastery of nuns. Being so good and loving her so

much, he husband was happy with the idea and began to consider where they might found one. She wanted it in the town where she had been born. He put up legitimate objections to convince her that her own town would not be a good place for it.

10. While they were discussing this, the Duchess of Alba called for him. When he arrived, she ordered him to return to Alba to undertake duties in her house, and he accepted the office even though it was a less important one than the office he had held in Salamanca.[4] When his wife heard about it, she was very distressed because, as I said, she abhorred Alba. Being assured by her husband that they would not accept guests any more, she was somewhat appeased; although she was still very troubled since Salamanca was more to her liking. He bought a house and sent for her. She came with great weariness and felt wearier when she saw the house. For although the location was very good and the property extensive, the house did not have enough rooms; thus she was very troubled that night. The next morning, when she walked onto the patio, she saw on the same side the well where she had seen St. Andrew. And she saw everything else, no more nor less than what had been shown to her—I mean the place, not the saint or the flowers or the meadow, although she did have and still has them well imprinted in her imagination.

11. When she saw these things, she became troubled and resolved to found the monastery there. She did this now with great consolation and tranquility, without wanting to go somewhere else, and they began to buy more houses nearby until they had ample land. She was concerned about which order they would ask, for she wanted the nuns to be few and strictly

enclosed. In discussing the matter with two religious from different orders, who were very good and learned men, she was told by both that it would be better to do some other good works because nuns are usually unhappy. And she was told many other things, for since the project saddened the devil he wanted to prevent it, and thus he made them think that the reasons they gave her were very sound. Since they presented so many as to why it wouldn't be good, and the devil presented more in order to hinder it, she became fearful and disturbed and decided not to go ahead. This she told to her husband, and the two of them felt that since such men had told her that it would not be good and her intention was to serve our Lord they should forget about it. Thus they agreed to arrange for a marriage between a niece on her husband's side and a nephew of hers, who was very virtuous and still young and whom she loved very much, and give them a great part of their estate, keeping the rest for their own spiritual well-being. They were both left feeling certain and serene about this decision.

12. But since our Lord had ordained something else, their agreement was of little benefit. In less than fifteen days, the nephew became so seriously ill that within a very few days our Lord brought him to Himself. She became so convinced that the cause of her nephew's death had been her decision to set aside what God wanted her to do, in order to leave the estate to him, that she felt great fear. She recalled what happened to Jonah the prophet for not having wanted to obey God,[5] and it seemed to her that God had punished her by taking away that nephew whom she loved so much. From that day on she was determined not to let anything make her fail to found the monastery, and her husband was also; although they didn't

know how to go about it. It seemed to her that God had put into her heart what has now been accomplished. Those whom she told about the monastery, and to whom she described how she wanted it, laughed over the matter since they thought she would not find the things she was looking for; this was true especially of a confessor of hers, a Franciscan friar, a distinguished man of learning. She was very dejected.

13. At that time, this friar happened to go to a certain town where he was told about these monasteries of Our Lady of Mt. Carmel that were now being founded. Very well informed about them, he returned and told her he had now discovered how she could found the monastery she desired. He told what had happened and that she should try to speak with me about it. This she did. We underwent much difficulty in trying to come to an agreement. For in the case of monasteries founded with an income, my goal always was that they have enough to keep the nuns from dependence on relatives, or on anyone, and that food and clothing and everything necessary be given to them in the house, and that the sick be very well cared for. For when necessities are lacking, many troubles arise. In founding many monasteries in poverty, without an income, I never lack courage or confidence; I am certain that God will not fail them. In founding them with an income that is small, everything fails me; I find it better that they not be founded.

14. She and her husband finally became reasonable and offered enough revenue to provide for the number of nuns. And what I highly appreciated, they left their own house in order to give it to us and moved into one that was in a dilapidated condition. The Blessed Sacrament was reserved and the foundation was made on the feast of the Conversion of St. Paul,

in the year 1571,[6] for the glory and honor of God. In this foundation, in my opinion, His Majesty is very much served. May it please Him to protect it always.

15. I began to say some particular things about some of the Sisters in these monasteries thinking that when this would be read those now living in them would not be alive and that those who come after would be inspired to carry on in the tradition of such a good beginning. Afterward, it has seemed to me, there will be someone who will tell these things better and in more detail and without having the fear that I have had of giving the impression of being partial.[7] And so I have left out many things considered miraculous by those who had seen or known of them, for such things are supernatural. I have not wanted to say anything about them or of what our Lord has been clearly seen to do through the nuns' prayers.

In the account of the dates on which these monasteries were founded I suspect that I am sometimes mistaken, although I try diligently to remember.[8] Since these dates are not of great importance, because they can be corrected afterward, I put them down according to what I can remember; it makes little difference if there is some error.

ALBA DE TORMES,
(DOÑA TERESA DE LAYZ) (1571)

Summary and Background: Chapter 20

After only two months in Salamanca, Teresa received a request from Francisco Valázquez (the financial manager of the Duke of Alba de Tormes) and his wife, Teresa de Layz. They asked Teresa to come to Alba de Tormes to found a monastery. Teresa tells us that she "was not too keen about the idea because the town was a small one, which would make it necessary to have an income" (F. 20. 1.). Teresa decided to make the foundation only after consulting with Domingo Báñez, O.P., her former confessor.

> Father Master Fray Domingo Báñez (who had been my confessor, whom I consulted when beginning these monasteries) happened to be in Salamanca, and he reprimanded me and told me that since the Council [of Trent] had given permission it would not be right to forego the foundation of a monastery because of a need for an income. He said further that I failed to understand that whether the monastery had an income or not made little difference in regard to nuns being poor and very perfect." (F. 20. 1.)

Three years previous, Teresa had struggled with the same issue. Should she found the monastery at Malagón with a fixed income? At that time, Báñez, using the same argument, persuaded Teresa that she should not have any scruples about doing so. "Both my confessor [Banez] and other learned men with whom I discussed the matter told me that I was doing wrong, that since the holy Council had given permission to have an income, I shouldn't, because of my own opinion, fail to found a monastery where God could be so much served" (F. 9. 3.). For the rest of the chapter, Teresa recounts the story of Doña Teresa de Layz.

Doña Teresa de Layz was the daughter of noble parents, "*hidalgos* of pure blood," that is, Spaniards who are free from any taint of either Jewish or Moorish blood (F. 20. 2.). In Teresa's time, having "pure blood" was considered an essential component of a noble lineage. Therefore, at first glance, it would seem that Teresa is praising the pedigree of the Layz family. However, as she continues, Teresa exposes a dark side of this "noble" family.

When Doña Teresa was born, her parents already had four daughters. Her parents were so overly distressed at not having a male heir that they neglected Doña Teresa, almost to the point of death. Though she does not say this explicitly, St. Teresa gives the impression that the neglect was deliberate and that Doña Teresa's parents were *hoping* that their daughter would die. As a commentary on the obsession that the nobility had with obtaining a male heir, St. Teresa writes,

> Certainly, it is something to be much wept over that human beings do not know what is best for them and are totally ignorant of the judgments of God and of the

great blessings that can come to them through daughters or of the great sufferings that can come from sons. It doesn't seem they want to leave this matter to the One who creates their children and understands everything, but they kill themselves over what should be making them happy. (F. 20. 3.)

Fortunately, through the intervention of a nurse, Doña Teresa did not die but grew into womanhood and married Francisco Valázquez, the bursar of the University of Salamanca. Doña Teresa and Francisco had a happy marriage though they were not blessed with children.

One night as Doña Teresa was praying that God would grant her children, she heard a voice saying, "Do not desire children, for you will be condemned." Though she was shaken by what she had heard, Doña Teresa continued to pray for children. However, one night in a dream, she saw a house with a patio and a courtyard that had a well. Surrounding the house was a beautiful meadow carpeted with white flowers. A figure, whom she recognized as St. Andrew, approached her and said, "These are children other than those you desire" (F. 20. 7.). Upon awaking, Doña Teresa felt that her dream was God's way of telling her that she should found a monastery. However, she did not know how to proceed.

Shortly after the dream, Doña Teresa's husband accepted the position of financial manager of the Duke and Duchess of Alba (a town situated only fifteen miles from Salamanca). In consequence, Doña Teresa and Francisco moved to Alba de Tormes. The day after they moved into their new house, Doña Teresa walked out onto the patio. To her astonishment, she recognized the place that had been depicted in her dream.

She told Francisco and they decided to endow a monastery of cloistered nuns, but only after they had provided for the marriage of a nephew and niece, to whom they would give "a great part of their estate" (F. 20. 11.). Unexpectedly, their nephew died fifteen days later. Doña Teresa became afraid. "She became so convinced that the cause of her nephew's death had been her decision to set aside what God wanted her to do . . . [that] it seemed to her that God had punished her by taking away that nephew whom she loved so much" (F. 20. 12.).

In consequence of this belief, Doña Teresa consulted a Franciscan friar and asked his advice regarding how she should proceed in endowing a monastery of cloistered nuns. He recommended that she contact a nun named Teresa who was presently living close by in Salamanca. Teresa was reluctant to accept Doña Teresa's offer because she did not want another monastery endowed with an income. Since Alba de Tormes was a small, poor village, a convent founded in poverty was also out of the question. In the end, Teresa accepted Doña Teresa's offer, having remembered Domingo Báñez words "that whether the monastery had an income or not made little difference in regard to nuns being poor and very perfect" (F. 20. 1.).

However, Teresa felt that the endowment being offered was inadequate. In consequence, she entered into negotiations with Doña Teresa to ensure that her nuns would be adequately provided for.

> We underwent much difficulty in trying to come to an agreement. For in the case of monasteries founded with an income, my goal always was that they have enough to keep the nuns from dependence on relatives, or on anyone, and that food and clothing and everything necessary be given to them in the house, and that the sick be very well cared for. For when necessities are lacking, many troubles arise. In founding many monasteries in poverty, without an income, I never lack courage or confidence; I am certain that God will not fail them. In founding them with an income that is small, everything fails me; I find it better that they not be founded. [Doña Teresa] and her husband finally became reasonable and offered enough revenue to provide for the number of nuns. (F. 20. 13–14.)

Teresa had an aversion to dealing with financial matters. However, as the above passage indicates, she did so because of her concern for her sisters. It is also worth noting that as a result of founding several monasteries, Teresa became very knowledgeable in the ways of the world. This is indicated in a letter that she wrote to her brother Lorenzo, a year before Alba de Tormes was founded. "I have become so adept at bargaining and managing business affairs for these houses of God and of the order that I am abreast of everything" (LE. 1. 24. 5). The convent at Alba de Tormes was founded "on the Conversion of St. Paul [January 25], in the year 1571" (F. 20. 14.).

Reflection. Charles Dickens' novel, *Dombey and Son*, begins with the birth of Paul Dombey, Jr., and the death of his mother in childbirth. Paul Dombey, Sr., is not overly distraught by the death of his wife because in the process he has obtained what he has so desperately desired, a *son* who will ensure that the firm of *Dombey and Son* will continue. Paul Dombey, Sr., also has a daughter Florence, who is seven years old. However, she is of no account to him, for she was of no use to him in perpetuating the family's commercial dynasty. "Dombey's feelings toward Florence had been negative from her birth. He had never conceived an aversion to her: it had not been worth his while or his humour."[9]

Florence was such a nonentity to her father that at the funeral of Paul, Jr. (who died in childhood), when the undertaker asked Paul, Sr., what he wished to have inscribed upon his son's tombstone, he responded, "Beloved and *only child.*"[10]

Teresa de Layz and Florence Dombey were born into families that had an obsession for a male heir. In consequence, both became victims of neglect. Such examples of neglect should give us pause. For though we may not be guilty of what Dickens calls the monstrous neglect of children, negligence is a sin of which we are all guilty.

In Dante's *Purgatorio*, the sin of negligence is summed up as that which "in life was left undone that should have been done" (*Pur.* canto 7. li. 93). In this regard, all of us can look back over our lives and see duties and responsibilities that we have shirked, some of which have had a very negative impact upon the lives of others.

The Latin word for neglect, *neglegere*, is derived from *neg* meaning "not" and *legere* meaning "to choose, to pick up." How accurately the root meaning of neglect describes the consequences of negligence. When we don't pick up after ourselves, other people have to pick up the pieces.

Questions. Both Paul Dombey, Sr., and the parents of Doña Teresa were so obsessed with having a male heir that they neglected their other children. In both cases, we see an intrinsic relationship between an obsession and neglect. For when we are obsessed with a desire to obtain something, we neglect important aspects of our lives—family, friends, obligations, and responsibilities. Have you ever allowed an obsession to so consume you that you neglected someone you love?

Reflection. Doña Teresa had decided to use her money to establish a convent but changed her mind after consulting some "good and learned men" (F. 20. 11.). They told her that it would be better to use her money for other good works. In consequence of this advice, she and her husband decided to finance the marriages of a niece and nephew on her husband's side. Doña Teresa and her husband were "left feeling certain and serene about this decision" (F. 20. 11.). However, their peace was shattered two weeks later when their nephew died suddenly. Doña Teresa was filled with a profound sense of guilt. She believed that God was punishing her. "She became so convinced that the cause of her nephew's death had been her decision to set aside what God wanted her to do . . . [that] it seemed to her that God had punished her by taking away that nephew whom she loved so much" (F. 20. 12.).

When tragedy strikes, we can believe that God is punishing us. Like Doña Teresa, we become convinced that the cause of the tragedy is the result of a choice that we have made. We can almost hear Doña Teresa saying to herself, "If I had only listened to my original instinct about my dream; if I had not consulted those men, none of this would have happened." But what Doña Teresa forgot was both the certitude and the deep sense of peace that she had felt after she had made her decision—she was "left feeling certain and serene about this decision" (F. 20. 11.). However, the grief that overcame Doña Teresa was so powerful that it distorted her reason to such an extent that she not only doubted her decision, but she actually believed that she was the cause of her nephew's death.

Questions. Has either grief or false guilt ever caused you to believe that God was punishing you for a decision or choice that you have made? What have you found helpful in restoring peace to your soul?

Chapter 21

Treats of the foundation in Segovia of the Carmel of the glorious
St. Joseph. It was founded on the very feast of St. Joseph in 1574.

1. I have already mentioned how after I founded the monasteries of Salamanca and Alba and before we had our own house in Salamanca, the Father Maestro Fray Pedro Fernández, who was then the apostolic commissary, ordered me to go to the Incarnation in Avila for three years.[1] I also mentioned that when he saw the need of the nuns in Salamanca for a house, he ordered me to go there so that they could move into one of their own.[2] One day while I was there in prayer, our Lord told me to go to Segovia and make a foundation. This seemed impossible to me, for I could not go unless ordered to do so, and I had learned from the apostolic commissary, the Father Maestro Fray Pedro Fernández, that he did not want me to make any more foundations. I also saw clearly that since the three years I was to stay in the Incarnation were not over, he had great reason for not wanting any more foundations. While I was thinking about this, the Lord told me to tell him and that He Himself would bring this foundation about.

2. At the time, I was in Salamanca. From there I wrote to His Paternity reminding him that he already knew I had a command from our most Reverend Father General to make a foundation when I saw that there was an opportunity for doing so. I mentioned that one of these monasteries had been accepted in Segovia by both the city and the bishop, that if His Paternity would give the order I would found it, that I was pointing this out to him to satisfy my conscience, and that I

would feel confident and content with whatever he ordered. I believe these were the words, more or less, and I added that it seemed to me the monastery would render service to God. I think, indeed, that His Majesty wanted it, because the apostolic commissary said immediately that I should found it, and he gave me permission. From what I had known about him in regard to these matters, I was very much amazed. And from Salamanca I arranged that they rent me a house, for after the experience in Toledo and Valladolid I had learned that it was better to rent a house and take possession first and then look for one to buy. This was so for many reason, the principal one being that I didn't have a cent to buy one with. Once the monastery was founded, the Lord would then provide; also, a more appropriate site could be chosen.

3. There was a lady there who had been the wife of the owner of an entailed estate. Her name was Doña Ana de Jimena. She had once come to see me in Avila. She was a good servant of God, and her calling had always been to be a nun. Thus after the founding of the monastery, she and one of her daughters, who was living a devout life, entered it. And the Lord took away the unhappiness she had experienced both while married and as a widow and gave her a double measure of happiness in the religious life. Both mother and daughter had always been very recollected and faithful servants of God.[3]

4. This good lady acquired the house and provided for everything she saw we needed, both for the church and for ourselves. As a result, I had little work to do. But there is never a foundation in which there is not some trial. And the trial came in addition to the fact that I went there while suffering from a high fever and nausea, and from interior ills of very great dryness and darkness of soul, and from bodily complaints of

many kinds, the intensity of which lasted three months. And for the half year that I was there, I was always sick.

5. On the feast of St. Joseph, we reserved the Blessed Sacrament. Although we had permission from both the bishop and the city, I did not want to enter except on the eve of the feast, secretly, and at night. Much time had passed since the permission had been given, but because I had been at the Incarnation and did not have our Father General for superior, but someone else,[4] I had not been able to make the foundation. The permission I had received from the bishop of the place—when agreed—was in word. He gave it through a gentleman named Andrés de Jimena who was looking for a house for us. But this gentleman didn't bother about getting the permission in writing, nor did this seem to me to matter. I was mistaken, for when the vicar general learned that the monastery had been founded, he came at once, very angry, and did not allow Mass to be said any more and wanted to take prisoner the one who said it, a discalced friar, who came with both Father Julián de Avila and another servant of God, who came with me, named Antonio Gaytán.[5]

6. This latter was a gentleman from Alba. He was called by the Lord some years before while very much involved in the world. He so trampled it under foot that all he thought about was how to serve the Lord more. In the foundations that will be dealt with from here on, mention will have to be made of him, for he helped me much and did a great deal of work for me. I have told who he is, and if I should have to tell of his virtues, I would not finish very quickly. What mattered most to us was that he was so mortified, for there was no servant from among those who came with us who was as ready as he was to do all the necessary things. He is a man of deep prayer, and God has granted him so many favors that everything

others would consider a burden made him happy and was easy for him to accept. This is the way he is in all the work that he has done for these foundations. For it indeed seems that God called both him and Father Julián de Avila for this purpose, although Father Julián de Avila was with us from the first foundation. By giving me company like this, our Lord must have desired that everything turn out well for me. It was Father Julián's characteristic while traveling to speak of God and to teach those who traveled with us or whom we met, and thus in every way he served His Majesty.

7. It is only right, my daughters, that those of you who read these foundations should know what you owe to these two (for without any self-interest they labored so much for this good that you enjoy, of being in these monasteries) in order that you might recommended them to our Lord and they might receive some benefit from your prayers. For if you knew the bad nights and days they suffered, and the trials on the roads, you would do so very willingly.

8. The vicar general did not want to go away without leaving a guard at the door of the church. I don't know why; it served to frighten a little those who were there. As for me, I was never much bothered by what happened once possession of the foundation had taken place; all my fears came before. I sent for some persons, relatives of a companion I brought from among my sisters,[6] who were renowned in that place that they might speak to the vicar general and explain to him that I had permission from the bishop. He knew this very well, as he said afterward, but he thought we should have informed him. I believe that had we done so, things would have been much worse. Finally, they got him to agree to let us stay in

the monastery, but he removed the Blessed Sacrament. This didn't matter to us. We remained thus for some months until a house was bought;[7] along with it came many lawsuits. We had lawsuits with the Mercedarians and, because the house had an annuity attached to it, with the cathedral chapter. Before this we had many difficulties with the Franciscan friars because of a house we tried to buy near them.

9. O Jesus! What a trial it is to have to contend with many opinions. When the litigation would seem to be over, it would begin anew because it wasn't enough to give them what they asked for; there was at once some other difficulty. Explained in this way, it all seems like nothing; but going through it was much different.

10. A nephew of the bishop did all that he could for us, for he was the prior and canon of that church;[8] and so, too, did the licentiate Herrera, a very great servant of God. Finally, after we gave much money, the lawsuit came to an end. We were left with the lawsuit of the Mercedarians, for in order to move to the new house great secrecy was necessary. When they found out that we were there, for we had moved a day or two before the feast of St. Michael,[9] they thought it would be good to settle for a sum of money. The greatest suffering that these obstacles caused me was that in no more than seven or eight days my three years as prioress at the Incarnation were to come to an end, and I necessarily had to be there.

11. Our Lord was pleased that everything should turn out so well that no contention remained, and within two or three days I was at the Incarnation.[10] May His name be ever blessed who has always granted me so many favors, and may all creatures praise Him. Amen.

SEGOVIA (1574)

Summary and Background: Chapter 21

Between the foundations of Alba de Tormes (1571) and Segovia (1574), Teresa was ordered back to the Incarnation in Avila to serve as prioress for three years "in the midst of this whole Babylon," as she called the convent (LE. 1. 38. 4.). Teresa had to put some strictures on the nuns' behavior. Her actions were met with fierce resistance, for as Teresa puts it, "changing a habit is like death" (LE. 1. 38. 4.). However, over time, she gained the respect of the community.

During her term of office, she wanted to visit some of her foundations in order to deal with various issues. However, there was a twofold problem. First, Teresa began to doubt whether or not she should leave the cloister because certain people had told her that it was wrong for her to do so. At this time, Teresa received a locution from God that eradicated her doubts. "I thought that their recommendation would be God's will because of what St. Paul said about the enclosure of women, of which I was recently told and had even heard before. The Lord said to me: 'Tell them they shouldn't follow just one part of Scripture but that they should look at other parts, and ask them if they can by chance tie my hands," (ST. 15.).

Now that she had assurance from God that she could leave the cloister with impunity, another obstacle lay in her path. The Carmelite provincial refused her request.

However, Teresa circumvented this roadblock by writing directly to King Phillip II, who granted her permission. It is worth noting *how* Teresa obtained permission, for it demonstrates her worldly astuteness.

In her letter to the King, Teresa never directly asked for permission to leave the Incarnation. She simply told the King (who was an advocate of reformed orders) that her monasteries were a great service to the Church. She sent the letter by way of Juan de Padilla, a very zealous priest who was held in high esteem by King Philip. Like the king, Padilla advocated the founding of reformed monasteries. Thus, Teresa knew that Padilla would appeal to the King to allow her to leave the Incarnation. King Philip granted his permission.

Because she had obtained permission *indirectly*, if Teresa were ever confronted by her provincial for circumventing his authority, she could tell him that she had *never asked* the King for permission. He simply had *given* it to her. And who was she, a poor, humble, simple nun not to respect the wishes of the king.

With royal approbation in hand, Teresa set forth to Alba de Tormes and then on to Salamanca. During her stay in Salamanca, Teresa began writing the book of her *Foundations* and was told by the Lord in prayer to make a foundation in Segovia. Obedient to the Lord's command, Teresa obtained permission from the bishop and the city authorities of Segovia to establish a monastery. She then rented a house in which the convent was to be established. Everything seemed too good to be true. And it was.

In March 1574 Teresa set out for Segovia, accompanied by four nuns, Julián of Avila, the convent's chaplain, Antonio Gaytán (a gentleman from Alba de Tormes), and St. John of the Cross. They arrived at night, set up the monastery, and the next morning celebrated the Eucharist and reserved the Blessed Sacrament. All seemed well, but the permission that Teresa had received from the bishop was *not in writing*; it had been given *verbally* through a benefactor. Unfortunately, the bishop was out of town.

During the bishop's absence, a very prickly, choleric cleric was appointed as the vicar general. "When the vicar general learned that the monastery had been founded, he came at once, very angry, and did not allow Mass to be said any more and wanted to take prisoner the one who said it" (F. 21. 5.). He said that we had no permission to make a foundation.

Teresa contacted some influential people in Segovia and asked them to inform the vicar general that permission had been granted by the bishop. When they did so, Teresa discovered that "[the vicar general] *knew this very well, as he said afterward, but he thought we should have informed him. I believe that had we done so, things would have been much worse*" (F. 21. 8.) (italics added). The townsfolk finally persuaded the vicar general to let the nuns stay in the monastery. However, as a last gasp to exert his brief authority, "he removed the Blessed Sacrament" (F. 21. 8.). The foundation was established on March 19, 1574.

One of the reasons that Teresa wanted to have a foundation in Segovia was because of its proximity to Pastrana.

Less than a month after Segovia was founded, Julián of Avila and Antonio Gaytán rescued the nuns of Pastrana from the clutches of the Princess of Eboli. The foundation of Pastrana existed for fewer than five years. It was the only convent that failed during Teresa's lifetime.

Teresa stayed on in Segovia for several months before returning to Avila. During this time, she bought a house to serve as a convent. This resulted in two lawsuits, one from the Franciscans and the other from Mercedarians. The disputes were interminable. "When the litigation would seem to be over, it would begin anew because it wasn't enough to give them what they asked for; there was at once some other difficulty" (F. 21. 9.).

Reflection. At the beginning of Shakespeare's play, *Measure for Measure*, the Duke of Vienna, who is also the city's governor, is preparing to take a journey. He appoints Angelo, his deputy, to be in charge of governing the city in his absence. As the play unfolds, Angelo is unmasked as a devil. He is a strict moralist who executes the law without mercy. The basic truth that *Measure for Measure* sets before us is that if you want to truly know someone, give him power. In the case of Angelo, power disclosed him to be a petty tyrant. "Proud man, dressed in a little brief authority . . . is like an angry ape" (Act 2, Sc. 2, li. 117).

This chapter of the *Foundations* sets before us a situation similar to the one we find in *Measure for Measure*. The bishop of Segovia is out of town. In his absence, he appoints someone similar to Angelo to be his vicar general, a man who once dressed in his brief authority, acts like an angry ape.

The vicar general strikes us as a man who throws his weight around and tries to make his authority felt. He justifies his threats and angry outbursts by accusing Teresa of founding a monastery without obtaining permission. But he *did* know that Teresa had received permission from the bishop and eventually admits this fact. "He knew very well, as he said afterward, but he thought we should have informed him" (F. 21. 8.). Let us explore what might have been the source of the vicar's indignation.

Consider the following scenario. The vicar is a priest who has always aspired to be a bishop but knows that most probably he will never be appointed. He has always wanted to be in a position of power and importance in which he would be both respected and feared. He feels insecure in his temporary role. He is both afraid and angry that people will not take him seriously. And now, during his one shining moment, dressed in his brief authority, he feels slighted and demeaned. "How dare this group of nuns set up a convent in my domain without first consulting me? What disrespect! I will show them that I am a person to be reckoned with, not some figurehead. I will show them that I have real power and authority. I will prohibit them from saying Mass, arrest them, and throw them into jail."

In how many ways does this scenario play itself out in daily life? Take the petty bureaucrat or frustrated low-level executive who tyrannizes his or her subordinates. Or how many times, when the boss goes on vacation, does the person who is left in charge make everyone's life a living hell? And isn't it ironic that it is often the "submissive" person who humbly takes orders from the boss who is transformed into an autocrat the moment that he or she is in control?

Questions. One of the main attractions of having power or being in charge is that it puts us in a position to work our own will, get our way, and have things done the way we want. However, have you ever considered the type of person that you are becoming as you exert your brief authority?

Reflection. In light of our last reflection, the question arises, "What if Teresa *had* informed the vicar general?" Would he have acted any differently? Perhaps, he would not have stormed into the convent and ranted and raved. However, this does not mean that he would have been placated. Most probably he would have exerted his authority in some shape or form. Perhaps this is what was behind Teresa's statement, "I believe that had we done so [that is, informed him], things *would have been much worse*" (F. 21. 8.) (italics added).

We don't know what Teresa meant by these words, but we can speculate. Teresa knew that ultimately the vicar general could not prevent her from founding a convent in Segovia because she had permission from the bishop. However, she also knew that since he was in authority, he could make life miserable for her. He could make her wait before she took possession of the house by tying her up in ecclesiastical and civil red tape. In short, the vicar general could have dragged his feet. By doing so, he could exert his authority and avoid getting in hot water with his boss. He is not rescinding the bishop's permission; he is carrying it out but *in his own way.*

Questions. Have you ever punished people by making them wait? Or have you ever punished someone by being an obstructionist?

Chapter 22

Treats of the foundation named after the glorious St. Joseph of the Savior and made in the town of Beas on the feast of St. Matthias in the year 1575.[1]

1. When I was sent, as mentioned, from the Incarnation to Salamanca,[2] a messenger came there from the town of Beas with letters for me from a lady in that area and from the curate beneficiary there. The letters contained both the offer of a benefice from that town and requests from other persons asking me to come and found a monastery. They already had a house; all that was needed was to go and make the foundation.

2. When questioned by me, the man recounted wonderful things about the land, and rightly so, for it is very delightful and has a good climate. But in considering the distance, many leagues from here, the notion of making a foundation there seemed to me foolish. Especially so, since I was under the orders of the apostolic commissary, who, as I mentioned,[3] was opposed to, or at least not in favor of, my making foundations. So I wanted to answer that I was unable, and avoid asking permission of the apostolic commissary about it. Afterward, it seemed to me that since he was present at that time in Salamanca and I had received the order from our Reverend Father General not to fail to make foundations,[4] it would be unwise to refuse without getting his opinion.

3. When he saw the letters brought to me by the messenger, he sent word that he didn't think it would be good to disappoint them, that he had been edified by their devotion, that I should write telling them that when they had permission from

the Order of Knights of that town, provisions would be made for the foundation.[5] He was certain that the council of the Order of Knights would not give the permission, for he had known from elsewhere that in many years no one had been able to receive such a permission from it, and he did not want my answer to sound like a refusal. Sometimes I think about this and how that which our Lord wants, even though we may not want it, comes about in such a way that without our being aware we are the instruments of it. In this case the instrument was the Father Maestro Fray Pedro Fernández, who was the commissary. And so when they received the permission from the council, he couldn't refuse. The foundation was made in this way.

4. This monastery of the blessed St. Joseph was founded in the town of Beas on the feast of St. Matthias in the year 1575. It came about for the honor and glory of God in the following way.

There was in this town a gentleman named Sancho Rodríguez de Sandoval, of noble lineage and having many temporal possessions. He was married to a lady named Doña Catalina Godínez. Among the children that our Lord gave them were two daughters, those who founded this monastery. The older[6] was fourteen when our Lord called her to His service. Up to this age she was far from ready to leave the world; on the contrary, she had such a high estimation of herself that all that her father sought for her in marriages seemed of small account.

5. One day while in a room next to the one in which her father was lying down, she happened to read on a crucifix the inscription that is placed over the cross. Suddenly when she

read it, the Lord worked a complete change in her: She had been thinking of a marriage that was being sought for her, which was better than she could have hoped for, and saying to herself: "With what little my father is content, that I become connected with an entailed estate; I am thinking of becoming the origin of a new line of descendants." She was not inclined toward marriage, for she considered it demeaning to be subject to someone; nor did she know where this pride came from. The Lord knew how it could be remedied. Blessed be His mercy.

6. The moment she read the inscription, it seemed to her that just as sunshine enters a dark room, a light came into her soul by which she understood the truth. With this light she set her eyes on the Lord who was on the cross shedding blood, and she thought about how badly He was treated and of His great humility and about how different the road of pride was that she was following. There must have been some space of time in which the Lord suspended her. There His Majesty gave her a deep knowledge of her own misery, and she desired that all might know of it. He gave her so great a desire to suffer for God that all that the martyrs suffered she desired to suffer with them. She experienced such profound humiliation and self-abhorrence that were it not an offense against God, she would have wanted to be a very dissolute woman so that all might abhor her. Thus she began to despise herself with great desires for penance, which afterward she put into effect. She at once promised chastity and poverty and wanted to see herself so subject that she would have rejoiced to be carried off then to the land of the Moors and remain there. All of these virtues lasted in her in such a way that the experience was clearly

seen to be a supernatural favor from our Lord, as will be said later, so that all might praise Him.

7. May You be blessed forever and ever, my God, for within a moment You undo a soul and remake it. What is this, Lord? I would want to ask here what the apostles asked You when You cured the blindman, whether it was his parents who had sinned.[7] I mean, who could have merited so sublime a favor? She certainly did not, for it was already mentioned what thoughts You took away from her when You granted that favor. Oh, great are Your judgments, Lord! You know what You are doing, but I do not know what I am saying since Your works and judgments are incomprehensible. May You be ever glorified, for You have the power to do even more. What would become of me if this were not so? But, did the merit in some way come from her mother? For so great was her mother's practice of Christianity that it would be possible that Your goodness, being merciful, would desire that she see within her lifetime this great virtue in her daughters. Sometimes I think You grant similar favors to those who love You, and You do them so much good that You give them that by which they may serve You.

8. While she was in this state, such a loud noise came from the room above that it seemed everything was falling down. It seemed that all of that noise was coming down in the corner where she was, and she heard some roars that lasted quite a while. They were such that her father who although he had not yet got up, as was mentioned,[8] became so frightened he began to tremble. As though beside himself, he took a robe and his sword and entered there and very much shaken asked her what that noise was. She told him that she hadn't seen

anything. He looked in the next room further and since he saw nothing told her to go stay with her mother and informed her mother about what he had heard and not to let their daughter be alone.

9. This indeed explains what the devil must feel when he sees a soul already considered to be his own loosed from his power. Since he is so hostile toward what is good for us, I am not surprised that in seeing our merciful Lord grant so many favors all at once he should become frightened and make such a show of his feeling. This was especially so, because he understood that on account of the riches that were left in that soul he had to remain without any that could be considered his. For I hold that our Lord never grants so great a favor to a person without allowing others to share in it as well. She never said anything about this. But she was left with the strongest desire to embrace religious life and frequently sought permission from her parents to do so. They would never give their consent.

10. After three years had gone by in which she frequently sought permission, she began, on the feast of St. Joseph,[9] to dress in a simple manner since she saw that they did not want her to be a religious. She told only her mother from whom it would have been easy to obtain the permission to be a nun. As for her father, she did not dare ask, but she went to the church so that once the townspeople had seen her in this dress, she could be sure her parents would not take it away. And this is what happened, for they let the matter go. During those three years, she observed hours of prayer and mortified herself in every way she could, for the Lord taught her. She used to enter the courtyard and throw water on her face and then expose it

to the sun so that because of the resulting ugly appearance her parents would give up the idea of a marriage for her, for she was still being urged to marry.

11. She no longer had any desire to give orders to anyone. Since she had charge of her father's house, it happened that when she realized that she had given orders to the house-maids, for she couldn't do otherwise, she would wait until they were asleep and kiss their feet, anxious because they, though better than she, were serving her. Since during the day she was busy with her parents, when it was time for sleep, she would spend the whole night in prayer. Thus, she often went with so little sleep that it would have been impossible for her to do so without supernatural aid. The penance and the dis-ciplines were many because she had no one to guide her nor did she speak with anyone. Among other things, one Lent she wore her father's coat of mail next to her flesh. She used to go to a secluded place to pray, where the devil heaped ridicule on her. Often she began prayer at ten at night and was absorbed in it until daylight.

12. She spent about four years in these exercises. Then, desiring that she serve Him through other greater ones the Lord gave her most serious and painful illnesses. Thus she suffered from continual fever, dropsy, heart trouble, and a breast tumor which was removed. In sum, these illnesses lasted almost seventeen years; there were but few days in which she felt well. Five years after she had received the above favor from God, her father died.[10] Her sister, when fourteen (one year after Doña Catalina had made this change) also put on a simple garb, for she had been fond of fine clothes, and began as well to practice prayer. Her mother helped them in

all their good practices and desires. She thought that it was good for them to become occupied in a very virtuous work, one that was far out of harmony with their status: teaching girls needlework and reading, without any fee, but only for the opportunity to instruct the girls in prayer and doctrine. Their work was very fruitful because many girls were helped, and even now the good habits these girls learned when small are visible. The good work didn't continue for long because the devil, saddened by it, made the parents of the little girls feel that it was an affront for their daughters to be taught free of charge. This along with the beginning of the illnesses that afflicted her caused her to discontinue the work.

13. Five years after the father of these young ladies died, their mother died. Doña Catalina had always felt called to be a nun, but she could not get her parents' consent. She now wanted to go away at once to be a nun. Since there was no monastery in Beas, her relatives counselled her that since they had the sufficient means they should strive to found a monastery in their own town, that this would be of greater service to our Lord. Since the town is a commandery of the Order of the Knights of Santiago, permission was necessary from the council of this order, and so she diligently sought to obtain it.

14. It was so difficult to obtain that they spent four years in which they underwent many trials and expenses; and until a petition was sent to the king himself, nothing proved helpful. And it happened that because the difficulty became so great, her relatives began to tell her that the idea was foolish and that she should forget about it. Since she was almost always in bed with such serious illnesses, as was mentioned, they said that no monastery would accept her as a nun. She answered

that if within a month our Lord gave her health they should understand thereby that He would be served by the monastery and that she would go to the royal court herself to obtain the license. When she said this, it had been more than half a year that she had not got out of bed; and for almost eight years she had hardly moved from it. During those eight years she suffered from a continual fever, consumption, tuberculosis, dropsy, and an inflammation of the liver. This latter could be felt, and it so burned that even her clothes were affected by it and her chemise scorched. This seems incredible, and I myself inquired of the doctor about these illnesses that she had at that time, for I was amazed. She also suffered from gout and sciatica.

15. On the eve of the feast of St. Sebastian, which was a Saturday,[11] our Lord gave her such complete health that she didn't know how to conceal it and prevent the miracle from being known. She says that when our Lord desired to cure her He gave her an interior trembling that made her sister think that her life was coming to an end. And she saw within herself the greatest change, and in her soul, she says, she felt another change which was beneficial to her. Because of her health she was able to attend to the business of the monastery, and this made her happier than did her feeling of good health. From the beginning when God called her, He gave an abhorrence of self, for she made little of all. She says she was left with so powerful a desire to suffer that she begged God earnestly to exercise her in suffering in every way.

16. His Majesty did not fail to fulfill this desire. During those eight years they bled her more than five hundred times, without counting the many cuppings; the body shows them

clearly. They put salt in the wounds, for the doctor said it was good for drawing the poison from a sore of her side; they did this more than twenty times. What is more amazing is that as soon as she was told that the doctor prescribed one of these remedies, she fearlessly longed for the time to come in which they would carry it out, and she encouraged the doctors to apply the cauteries, which were used often for a breast cancer and other purposes. She says that what made her want this was the desire to prove whether or not the longings she had for martyrdom were authentic.

17. Since she found that she had suddenly become well she discussed with both her confessor and doctor the possibility of being brought to another town so that they could say the change of environment had caused the cure. They did not want to do so; on the contrary, they spread the news. They had already judged her to be incurable because the blood she was spitting up was so putrefied that they said it contained part of the lungs. She remained in bed for three days, not daring to get up lest the miracles of her health become known. But since it could be no more disguised than could her illness, the attempt to hide it was of little benefit.

18. She told me that the previous August while begging our Lord either to take away her great desire both to be a nun and to found a monastery or give her the means to do so she was convincingly assured that she would be well in time to go, during Lent, to obtain the license. Thus, she says that at that time even though the illnesses weighed more heavily on her, she never lost the hope that our Lord was going to grant her this favor. Even though she was anointed twice (one time she was so close to the end that the doctor said there would

be no reason to go for the oils, that she would be dead before they arrived), she never stopped trusting in the Lord that she would die a nun. I don't mean that they anointed her twice between August and the feast of St. Sebastian, but before that. When her brothers and relatives saw the favor and miracle that the Lord had performed in giving her health so suddenly, they did not dare prevent her from going, although it seemed foolish. She was at the royal court for three months, and in the end the license was not given. When she presented this petition to the king and he learned that it was for discalced Carmelite nuns, he ordered that it be given at once.[12]

19. When the time came to found the monastery, it seemed obvious that she had obtained this from God, for the superiors accepted it even though the town was so far away and the income small. What His Majesty desires cannot be set aside. Thus the nuns came at the beginning of Lent in 1575. The people of the town received them with a solemn procession and great joy. The happiness was so universal that even the children showed that our Lord would be served by this work. The monastery was founded under the patronage of St. Joseph of the Savior this same Lent on the feast of St. Matthias.[13]

20. On the same day the two sisters received the habit with much joy.[14] The health of Doña Catalina continued to improve. Her humility, obedience, and wish to be despised show clearly that her desires had been authentic and for the service of our Lord. May He be glorified forever and ever, amen.[15]

21. This Sister told me, among other things, that almost twenty years ago she went to bed one night longing to find the most perfect religious order there was on earth so as to be a nun in it. She began to dream, in her opinion, that she was walking

along a very straight and narrow road, very dangerous in that one could fall into some deep ravines that appeared. She met a discalced friar. (Seeing Fray Juan de la Miseria,[16] a little friar, lay brother of the order who was in Beas while I was there, she said that he seemed to be the same one she had seen in the dream). He said to her, "Come with me, sister," and brought her to a house with a great number of nuns in which there was no other light than that coming from some candles they were carrying. She asked what order this was; all remained silent, and then they lifted their veils and their faces were joyous and they were laughing. And she declares that she saw the faces of the same Sisters she now sees, and that the prioress took her by the hand and said to her, "Daughter, I want you here," and showed her the constitutions and the rule. When she awoke from this sleep, she felt a happiness that made her think she had been in heaven, and she wrote down what she remembered from the rule. Much time passed in which she didn't tell her confessor or anyone, and no one knew anything about this religious order.

22. When a Father from the Society[17] who knew of her desires came there, she showed him the paper and told him that if he found that religious order she would like to enter it. He knew of these monasteries and told her how what was written was taken from the rule of the order of Our Lady of Mount Carmel; although he didn't explain things to her so clearly, but just spoke of the monasteries that I was founding. Thus she arranged to send me a messenger as was mentioned.[18]

23. When they brought her the reply, she was so sick that her confessor told her to be calm and that even if she were in the monastery they would dismiss her, how much less would

they accept her now. She was terribly distressed and turned to our Lord with great anxieties and said to Him: "My Lord and my God, I know through faith that You are He who can do all things; well, then, Life of my soul, either take away these desires or give me the means to carry them out." She said this with extreme confidence, begging our Lady through the sorrow she felt when she beheld her dead Son in her arms, to intercede for her. She heard a voice within her say: "Believe and hope for I am He who can do all things; you will be healthy, for He who had the power to prevent so many illnesses, each deadly in itself, from bringing about their effect will more easily take them away." She says that these words came with such force and certitude that she couldn't doubt that her desire would be granted, even though many more illnesses weighed her down until the Lord gave her the health we have mentioned. Certainly, what she has suffered seems incredible. Had I not been informed by the doctor and those who were in the house, or by other persons, being as wretched as I am, it would not have been unusual for me to think that some of this was exaggerated.

24. Although she is weak, she is now healthy enough to keep the rule. She is a good subject and has a very happy disposition and, as I have said,[19] is humble in everything, which makes us all praise our Lord. The inheritance of each of them was given to the order without any conditions, so that even if they were not admitted to profession the money would still belong to the order. The detachment she has from both her relatives and property is great. And she always has the strong desire to move far away, and thus she begs this of her major superiors very much, although her obedience is so great that

she is happily willing to remain there. And in this same spirit she received the white veil; for there was no way of getting her to become a choir Sister, but she wanted to be a lay Sister. This was so until I wrote to her telling her many things, scolding her because she wanted something other than what was her Father Provincial's will.[20] I told her that wanting to be a lay sister was not more meritorious, and I mentioned other things, and dealt with her harshly. And this is her greatest happiness, to be spoken to harshly. As a result she submitted, very much against her will, to becoming to choir Sister. I don't know anything about this soul that does not have to do with her trying to be more pleasing to God, and all the nuns feel the same way. May it please His Majesty to keep her in His hands and increase the grace and virtues He has given her for His greater service and honor. Amen.

BEAS, CATALINA SANDOVAL Y GODÍNEZ (1575)

Summary and Background: Chapter 22

Around the time that Teresa founded Segovia, she received a request from the citizens of Beas to found a monastery in their city. They offered Teresa both a benefice and a house. In theory, Teresa was in favor of the idea, but she didn't feel that it was practical. "But in considering the distance [about 370 miles] . . . the notion of making a foundation there seemed to me foolish" (F. 22. 2.). If one considers the travel conditions in Teresa's day, Beas may as well have been on the far side of the Moon.

Besides the great distance to Beas, Teresa had to contend with the opposition of the apostolic visitator, Pedro Fernández. He disapproved of Teresa's establishing any more monasteries; however, he did not want to offend the people of Beas. The solution to his dilemma was very simple. He granted Teresa his consent on the condition that she obtain permission from the Order of Santiago in Beas. The Order was a military, quasi-religious group that governed certain cities in Spain.

Fernandez's consent was bogus. He was confident that Teresa's request would be refused, for the Order had never granted permission for any convent to be established in its territories. However, to his chagrin, Teresa obtained permission. As a result, "[H]e couldn't refuse" (F. 22. 3.).

At the end of September 1574, Teresa was ordered back to the Incarnation by Fernández to make preparations for the new foundation of Beas. This was fortuitous, for Teresa's term as prioress was coming to an end (October 6). This would allow her the opportunity to make a smooth transition from the Incarnation back to St. Joseph's.

When we read Teresa's letters, dated September 1574, which were written while she was still in Segovia making preparations to return to the Incarnation, we get a glimpse into the nitty-gritty of her daily life. She was dealing with a wide variety of issues: answering the question of a prioress regarding how many lay sisters a convent should accept trying to borrow money for the financially strapped convent of the Incarnation, and handling a dispute with the canons of the Cathedral of Segovia who were attempting to charge Teresa rent because her convent abutted the Cathedral. "How these canons weary me" (LE. 1. 70. 4.). This dispute dragged on for five years. In addition, Teresa had health problems. "[I suffered] from a high fever and nausea, and from interior ills of very great dryness and darkness of soul and from bodily complaints of many kinds, the intensity of which lasted three months. And for the half year that I was there, I was always sick" (F. 21. 4.). In commenting upon the severity of her ailments, she writes to a friend. "If I knew how to complain as well as you do, you would consider your sufferings a trifle" (LE. 1. 67. 2.).

In December, after a two-month stay at St. Joseph's in Avila, Teresa began her long journey to Beas. On route, she stopped at Valladolid to help the prioress (Maria Bautista) settle the ongoing dispute between Casilda de Padilla and her family regarding Casilla's inheritance (see chapter 11).

In January 1575, Teresa left Valladolid and arrived in Beas on February 16. In chapter twenty-two, Teresa does not provide us with any of the incidences that took place on her long journey to Beas. Instead, she devotes the entire chapter to the conversion of Catalina Sandoval y Godínez, who was instrumental in the foundation of Beas.

Catalina was the haughty daughter of a nobleman. She never felt that there was any man worthy of her hand in marriage. "She considered it demeaning to be subject to someone; nor did she know where this pride came from" (F. 22. 5.).

One day, however, her whole view of herself changed when she happened to be reading the inscription on a crucifix.

> The moment she read the inscription, it seemed to her that just as sunshine enters a dark room, a light came into her soul by which she understood the truth . . . His Majesty gave her a deep knowledge of her own misery, and she desired that all might know it . . . She experienced such a profound humiliation and self-abhorrence that were it not an offense against God, she would have wanted to be a very dissolute woman so that all might abhor her. Thus she began to despise herself with great desires for penance, which afterward she put into effect. (F. 22. 6.)

Catalina began to have a strong desire to enter religious life, but her parents would not give their consent. After three years, Catalina began to dress in a simple manner, observe hours of prayer every day, and perform acts of mortification. In due time, her health was affected by "serious and painful illnesses" (F. 22. 12.).

Catalina's sister Maria saw the change that had happened in Catalina and likewise donned a simple garb and began to practice prayer. When their father died, their mother encouraged her daughters to practice good works—teaching poor girls reading and needlework. However, such behavior was considered unbecoming of these two sisters because it "was far out of harmony with their status" (F. 22. 12.).

When their mother died, the two sisters desired to use their inheritance to found a monastery, which they hoped to enter. However, their plan was prevented from being actualized because of severe illnesses that continued to plague Catalina and opposition from their relatives. Both barriers were removed when Catalina was miraculously cured. Witnessing Catalina's miraculous recovery, her relatives "did not dare prevent her from [going forward with her plans], although it seemed foolish" (F. 22. 18.). When Catalina asked King Philip to grant permission to found a convent of "discalced Carmelite nuns, he ordered that it be given at once" (F. 22. 18.).

Unlike Teresa's other foundations, she was received in Beas with open arms. Her party was escorted into town by an entourage of the Knights of the Order of Santiago. She was greeted by cheering townsfolk and led ceremoniously to her new convent by a procession of the clergy dressed in surplices, led by a crossbearer. This stood in stark contrast to her other foundations, when Teresa had to sneak into town stealthily under the cover of darkness in order to avoid detection. Beas was founded on February 24, 1575, the same day on which Catalina and Maria received the habit. Unfortunately, the foundation of Beas proved to be the source of trouble for Teresa for a reason that she had never suspected.

Reflection. Months before Teresa traveled from Avila to Valladolid (May 1574) and while she was embroiled in lawsuits regarding the house she had purchased in Segovia, she wrote to Maria Bautista about the stress that Maria was experiencing as a result of dealing with the protracted quarrel with the family of Casilda de Padilla.

> I am sorry about the great trial you have had and still must endure with so many business affairs and such important ones, for I know what it is. But I don't think you would feel any better if you had the quiet you speak of, but worse. Of this I am very certain, for I know your temperament and I accept the fact that you will have to suffer trials because in one way or another you must become a saint; and this desire you have for solitude is better than having solitude. (LE. 1. 63. 2.)

This passage testifies not only to Teresa's capacity to empathize with a fellow sufferer but her ability to interpret the stress of daily life from a spiritual perspective. Teresa knows the burden of having to deal with the affairs of the world, be it lawsuits, the purchasing of houses, or enduring the prickly personalities of the nobility. Teresa also shares Maria Bautista's desire for silence and solitude. However, she has come to realize that there are few things more beneficial to our souls than *having* a desire and being willing to forego its fulfillment for the sake of doing God's will. This is why Teresa says to Maria "this *desire* you have for solitude is better than *having* solitude."

What determines that which makes an activity sacred or secular is not the *outer form* of the action but *our relationship* to it. For example, praying in church is not a spiritual exercise if, in doing so, you are neglecting your duties. Conversely, doing a monthly financial statement and attending to necessary business affairs can be the means by which you grow spiritually. It all depends upon what God is asking you to do.

Teresa is telling Maria Bautista that her willingness to be involved in dealing with Casilda de Padilla's family is beneficial for her spiritual growth because in the process, she is growing in detachment from what she desires.

Questions. What differentiates the spiritual from the worldly is not the outer form of the activity but rather the spirit in which we do it. Have you ever considered that the most "secular" tasks that you perform are really the most spiritual?

Reflection. Catalina Sandoval y Godínez died in 1586, only eleven years after she entered Carmel whereas her sister Maria died in 1604, outliving St. Teresa by twenty-two years and St. John of the Cross by thirteen years. In 1589, Maria became prioress of Córdoba. We have three letters written to her by John of the Cross, while she was prioress. In one of them, just as Teresa had warned Maria Bautista (prioress of Valladolid) about the danger of succumbing to the stress of business affairs by fleeing into solitude, so John warns Maria Sandoval y Godínez (prioress of Córdoba) of the danger of becoming consumed by her worry over the material welfare of her community.

> I would desire that you not be so solicitous for the temporal things of the house because God will gradually forget you and you will come to a state of spiritual and temporal need; for it is our anxiety that creates our needs. Cast your care on the Lord, daughter, and he will sustain you [Ps 55:22], for he who gives, and wants to give, the highest cannot fail to give the least. Be careful that you do not lack the desire to be poor and in want; for if you do, at that very hour devotion will fail you and you will gradually weaken in the practice of virtue. If previous you desired poverty, now that you are superior you ought to desire and love it much more. You ought to govern and provide the house with virtues and ardent desires for heaven rather than with worries and plans about temporal and earthly things. The Lord tells us not to be thinking about food and clothing or tomorrow [Mt 6:31–34].[21]

John of the Cross, having been a prior many times over, knew how important it is for a religious superior to attend to the temporal welfare of the community. On the other hand, he also knew how easy it was to become *"so solicitous* for the temporal things of the house" that one forgets the reason that one has entered religious life. Thomas à Kempis in *The Imitation of Christ*, addressing religious, admonishes them to *frequently* remind themselves *why* they entered the monastery. The reason behind this admonition is that they *frequently forget*.

This is true for all of us. We can become so mentally absorbed in the tasks of daily life that we *forget* the reason why God created us. St. Augustine, in his work *On Music*, says that the art of living "lies in learning how to perform the rhythms of one's life without getting entangled in them."[22] John tells Maria that because she has become entangled in temporal and earthly things, she is in danger of forgetting the purpose of her calling.

Questions. St. Augustine's statement that the art of living requires that we *perform* the rhythms of life without becoming *entangled* in them is at the heart of John's admonition to Maria—*attend* to the needs of the community but do not become *consumed* by them. Like Maria we are called to attend to the needs of our families, friends, and coworkers. How do you attend to these responsibilities without becoming enmeshed in them? How can you avoid becoming so mentally absorbed in the tasks of daily life that you forget the reason why God created you?

Chapter 23

Treats of the foundation of the monastery of the glorious St. Joseph of Carmel in Seville. The first Mass was said on the feast of the most Blessed Trinity in 1575.[1]

1. While I was in this town of Beas waiting for the license from the Council of the Order of Knights for the foundation of Caravaca, a Father from the discalced of our order named Maestro Jerónimo Gracián de la Madre de Dios came to see me.[2] A few years before he had received our religious habit while in Alcalá. Throughout his life he has been a man of much learning, intelligence, and modesty along with other great virtues. It seems, while he was in Alcalá, that he was chosen by our Lady for the good of this primitive order without his having the remotest idea of receiving our habit, although he had considered entering the religious life. His parents had other intentions because of his great talent and their good standing with the king,[3] but he was far from being inclined toward their plans for him. From the time he began school, he was urged by his father to take up the study of law. Yet, while still very young, he felt so strongly the desire to study theology that by force of tears he got his father to allow him to do so.

2. After graduating with a master's degree, he took steps to enter the Society of Jesus, and they had accepted him. But for a certain reason they told him to wait several days. He tells me that he was tormented by all the enjoyments in his life and that he didn't think they constituted a safe path to heaven. He always set aside the hours for prayer and was extremely recollected and upright.

3. At this time a close friend of his entered the monastery in Pastrana to become a friar in our order. This friend's name was Fray Juan de Jesús, and he, too, had a master's degree.[4] I don't know how the interest began, whether it did so because of a letter Fray Juan wrote about the greatness and antiquity of our order or in some other way; for Father Gracián enjoyed very much reading everything about the order and verifying, through important authors, what was asserted. He says that he often had scruples about failing to study other things because he was unable to set these studies aside, and he occupied his hours of recreation in this way. O wisdom and power of God! How impossible for us to flee from His will! Our Lord truly saw the great need there was for a person like this to carry on the work that He had begun. I often praise Him for the favor He granted us in this matter. Had I very much desired to ask His Majesty for a person to organize all the things pertaining to the order in these initial stages, I would not have succeeded in asking for all that He in fact gave in Father Gracián. May the Lord be blessed forever.

4. Well then, while not having the slightest thought of taking the habit of this order, he was asked to go to Pastrana to speak to the prioress of our monastery there—for it had not yet been abandoned—that she might accept a nun.[5] What means the divine Majesty takes! For had Father Gracián decided to go there to take the habit, he would perhaps have met with so much opposition that he might never have done so. But the Blessed Virgin, our Lady, to whom he is extremely devoted, wanted to repay him by giving him her habit. So I think she was the mediatrix through whom God granted him this favor. And this glorious Virgin was the reason he received

it and became so fond of the order. She did not want one who desired to serve her so much to lack the occasion for putting this desire into practice. It is her custom to favor those who want to be protected by her.

5. While still a boy in Madrid, he often went to pray before an image of our Lady to whom he had great devotion. I don't remember where it was; he called her "his love," and his visits were very frequent.[6] She must have obtained for him from her Son the purity in which he always lived. He says that sometimes it seemed to him his eyes were swollen from weeping over the many offenses committed against her Son. As a result there arose in him a strong impulse and desire to help souls, and he felt it very deeply when he saw offenses committed against God. He has so great an inclination toward the good of souls that any hardship becomes small to him if he thinks that through it he can produce some fruit. I have seen this myself in the many trials that he has undergone.

6. Well, the Virgin brought him to Pastrana as though by tricking him into the thought that he was going there in order to request the habit for a nun. And God brought him there in order to give him the habit. Oh, secrets of God! But how true that without our desiring it, He disposes us so as to give us favors. And this soul was repaid for the good deeds that he did, for the good example that he had always given, and for his great desire to serve the Lord's glorious Mother. His Majesty must always repay this latter with wonderful rewards.

7. Well, when he arrived in Pastrana, he went to speak to the prioress that she might accept the nun; and it seemed as though he had asked her to pray to the Lord that he himself might enter. For he is a very pleasant person so that generally

he is loved by those who have dealings with him—it is a grace
our Lord gives—and thus he is extremely loved by all his subjects, both friars and nuns. Yet he doesn't let any fault go by,
for he is extraordinarily careful in looking out for the welfare
of the religious life. In his actions he is so gentle and pleasant
that it seems no one is able to complain about him.

8. Well, when this prioress saw him, that which happened
to others happened to her; she felt a strong desire that he enter
the order and told the Sisters how important it was to get him
to join, for at the time there were very few, or almost none like
him.[7]And she told them all to beseech our Lord not to let him
go without his receiving the habit.

This prioress is a very great servant of God. By her prayer
alone I think she would have been heard by His Majesty; how
much more would the prayers of nuns as good as those that
were there be heard. All of them took the matter very much to
heart and with fasts, disciplines, and prayer begged His Majesty continually. Thus He was pleased to grant us this favor.
For since Father Gracián went to the monastery of the friars
and saw so much religious observance and opportunity to
serve our Lord and above all that it was the order of the Lord's
glorious Mother whom he so much desired to serve, his heart
was moved not to return to the world. The devil set before
him many difficulties, especially the pain this would bring his
parents. They loved him very much and had great trust that
he would help provide for their children, for they had many
daughters and sons.[8] He left this care to God for whom he left
all, and decided to be a subject of the Virgin and take her habit.
So they gave it to him amid the great happiness of all, especially of the nuns and the prioress. The nuns gave much praise

to our Lord, thinking that His Majesty had granted them this favor through their prayers.

9. He spent the year of probation with the humility one would find among the youngest novices. His virtue was especially tried at a time when the prior was absent. A very young friar was in charge who had no learning, very little talent, and no prudence for governing. He was without experience since he had only recently entered. The manner in which he guided them was excessive as well as were the mortifications he made them perform. Every time I think of them I am amazed at how Father Gracián was able to suffer them, especially how he could put up with persons like that. The spirituality God gave him was necessary for this suffering. It was clearly seen afterward that the young friar was the victim of much melancholy, and nowhere was he free of it.[9] Even as a subject, he's a source of trouble, how much more so when he governs! The humor has much control over him, for he is a good religious, and God sometimes permits this mistake of putting such persons in office so as to perfect the virtue of obedience in those He loves.

10. So it must have happened that as a reward God has given Father Fray Jerónimo de la Madre de Dios the greatest light in matters of obedience so that as one who had such a good initiation into its practice he might teach it to others. And that he might not lack experience in all the things we need to know about, he underwent the most severe temptations for three months prior to his profession. But as the good captain of the sons of the Virgin that he was to become, he defended himself well against these temptations. For when the devil harassed him most to get him to give up the habit, he defended

himself by promising to make his vows and not give it up. He
gave me a certain work that he wrote while undergoing those
great temptations. It inspired me with much devotion, and the
fortitude the Lord gave him is clearly seen.

11. It will seem inappropriate that he should have informed
me of so many personal matters about his soul. Perhaps the
Lord wanted this that I might record it here, and He might
be praised in His creatures. For I know that neither to any
confessor nor to any other person has this Father manifested
so much about himself. At times he had reason for so doing
because he thought that on account of my age and from what
he had heard about me I had some experience. It was while
we were speaking about other matters that he told me about
these things and additional ones that cannot be suitably put in
writing, for I would be going on at much greater length.

12. Certainly, I have used much restraint so that if this
work should ever get into his hands he won't suffer pain. I
couldn't help it, nor did it seem to me (for if this work is to
be seen, it won't be for a long time yet) that one who did so
much good for the renewal of the observance of the primitive
rule should be forgotten. Although he was not the one who
first began, he came along at the right moment. For sometimes
I would have regretted[10] ever having begun had it not been
for the great confidence I had in the mercy of God. I'm referring to the houses of the friars, for those of the nuns, through
God's goodness, have so far always gone well. Those of the
friars were not going badly, but the basis was there for a very
quick collapse. Since the discalced didn't have their own province, they were governed by the calced. Those who could have
governed, such as Fray Antonio de Jesús, the one who began

the renewal,[11] were not given the power to do so. Nor did the friars have constitutions given by our most Reverend Father General.[12] In each house they did as they saw fit. Until the day comes in which they can govern themselves they will have much trouble because some think one way and others another. At times I found them very tiring.

13. Our Lord provided a remedy through the Father Maestro Fray Jerónimo de la Madre de Dios, because they made him apostolic commissary and gave him authority and rule over the discalced friars and nuns.[13] He drafted constitutions for the friars, for we already had ours from our most Reverend Father General, and so he did not draw up any for us. But he did draw them up for the friars through the apostolic power he had and the talents that the Lord has given him as I have mentioned. In his first visitation of the friars, he arranged everything with such moderation and harmony that it indeed seemed he was helped by the Divine Majesty and that our Lady had chosen him to help her order. I begged her very much to intercede that her Son always favor this Father and give him grace to advance far in His service. Amen.

SEVILLE (1575)

Summary and Background: Chapter 23

While Teresa was in Beas preparing to found her next monastery in the city of Caravaca, she was introduced to Jerónimo Gracián. Gracián had been ordained a diocesan priest in 1571 in Alcalá. That year he went to celebrate the Eucharist on the feast of St. Francis at a convent of Franciscan nuns. He lost his way and ended up at the Carmelite convent founded by María of Jesus (see chapter 9). After Mass, Gracián talked with María. She told him about Teresa's reform and gave him a copy of Teresa's constitutions. Gracián was enthused by what he read. He began to take an interest in Carmelite spirituality and even wrote to Teresa.

The following year, Gracián traveled to Pastrana on behalf of a nun (Bárbara del Espíritu Santo). She had asked Gracián if he would talk to the prioress of the Carmelite convent on her behalf, requesting permission to enter the community. However, before Gracián left Pastrana, the prioress persuaded him to become a Carmelite himself. "Well, the Virgin brought him to Pastrana as though by tricking him into the thought that he was going there in order to request a habit for a nun. And God brought him there in order to give him the habit. Oh, secrets of God! But how true that without our desiring it, he disposes us so as to give us favors" (F. 23. 6.).

Gracián entered the Carmelite novitiate in Pastrana in 1572. Unfortunately, his novice master lacked experience and was mentally unbalanced. "He had no learning, very little talent and no prudence in governing . . . The manner in which he guided [the novices] was excessive as well as were the mortifications he made them perform . . . He was a victim of much melancholy and nowhere was he free of it" (F. 23. 9.).

Teresa was not only amazed that Gracián survived his novitiate unscathed but marveled at the fact that it actually proved to be beneficial. Teresa believed that his novice master taught him how *not* to govern others. She believed that one of the reasons Gracián was never tyrannical when placed in a position of power was that he had learned by experience the damage caused by harsh superiors.

Gracián was a highly intelligent, refined, educated, diplomatic man. As a result of these qualities, he was placed in positions of responsibility shortly after he made his profession in 1573.

In 1573, he was appointed apostolic visitator of the Carmelites of the Ancient Observance in Andalusia. The following year, he was appointed as their vicar provincial. Finally, in 1575, Gracián's authority was extended to the Carmelite nuns. It was during this time that Teresa first met Gracián. Teresa was sixty; Gracián was twenty-eight.

They met in Beas in April 1575, scarcely two months after the Beas community had been founded. There was an immediate affinity between them. Besides being intelligent, gentle, diplomatic, and charming, Gracián was a deeply religious man who had a great love for the Carmelite Order. Teresa found these qualities very attractive. In Gracián, she felt that she had found someone to whom she could entrust her soul.

Teresa was intoxicated by Gracián, and when she spoke of him, she sounded like a schoolgirl who had fallen in love for the first time. "So during those days [when Gracián was in Beas] I went about with such excessive consolation and happiness that indeed I was surprised at myself" (F. 24. 2.). Teresa idealized Gracián. Shortly after her initial meeting with Gracián, Teresa wrote enthusiastically to the prioress of Segovia. "He is without fault in my eyes, and for us better than what we would have asked God for. What you must do now, and all the nuns, is to beseech His Majesty to give him to us for our superior" (LE. 1. 81. 2.). In addition, Teresa became defensive when there was any hint of criticism regarding Gracián. She wrote to Maria Bautista, the prioress of Valladolid, who obviously did not share Teresa's exulted view of Gracián. "If you find faults in him, it will be because you have not spoken much with him and do not know him well. I tell you he is a saint and not at all impetuous, but very cautious. I already have experience of that, and one can trust in him more than in books" (LE. 1. 88. 9.).

On May 24, 1575, less than a month after she had met Gracián, Teresa had a vision, after which she made a vow of obedience to him.

It seemed to me our Lord Jesus Christ was next to me in the form in which He usually appears, and at His right side stood Master Gracián himself, and I at His left. The Lord took our right hands and joined them and told me He desired that I take this master to represent Him as long as I live, and that we both agree to everything because it was thus fitting. (ST. 36. 2.)

Reflection. In *The Way of Perfection* (chapters four through seven), Teresa deals with three types of love. The first type Teresa refers to as "sensual love," which is desire that leads us away from God. It includes everything from illicit carnal love to an excessive emotional attachment to others. The second type of love Teresa calls "spiritual love" or "perfect love." This love is purely spiritual because its sole desire is that its friend grows in the love of God. "It is not happy unless it sees the loved one make progress" (W. 7. 1.).

The third type of love Teresa calls "love that is mixed with sensuality." It encompasses friendships between siblings, relatives, and any person with whom we share common values. "[I]t seems to be licit, as it is love for our relatives and friends" (W. 4. 12.). When this love is healthy between two people "their spiritual bonds are engrafted in natural sympathies."[14] Teresa's relationship with Gracián fits this definition, for her attraction to Gracián was both natural and spiritual.

However, in spite of the healthiness of Teresa's relationship with Gracián, her initial reaction to Gracián is worth pondering, for it places before us a danger inherent in the early stage of all intense relationships. When we idealize someone, when someone "is without fault in [our] eyes," we lose objectivity (LE. 1. 81. 2.). We become blind by seeing everything the other person does in the best light. We excuse behaviors that ordinarily we would criticize in others. We gloss over negative qualities and transform them into positive ones. We become deaf to the warnings of others. These dynamics manifest themselves in various relationships: a teacher whom we worship, our first love, a friend or trusted authority figure whom we idolize. While this phenomenon is both common and natural, it can also have tragic consequences.

Questions. Have you ever idealized someone in your life? What were the consequences of your loss of objectivity?

Reflection. When Charles Dickens was twenty, he aspired to be an actor. He scheduled an audition with Mr. Bartley, the stage manager of Covent Garden, a private theatre in London. However, Dickens had to cancel his audition because of sickness. He planned to reschedule another audition but never did so because he discovered that he had a gift for writing. The rest is history.

What if Dickens had not become sick on the day of his audition? Would he have ever become a writer? *What if* Gracián had not lost his way to the Franciscan convent to say Mass on the feast of St. Francis? Would he have ever heard of Teresa's reform? Would he have ever become a Carmelite?

Are our lives any different? If one day was struck out of it, a day filled with *seemingly* insignificant events, it's possible that the whole course of our life would be different.

All of our lives have *what if* events, events that *at the time* they happen seem unimportant. However, when we look back at these events, they reveal themselves as major crossroads in our lives.

Questions. How should we interpret such events? Some people regard them as accidents, coincidences, or moments of fate. But seen through the eyes of faith, they can be interpreted as experiences of Divine Providence. Have you ever looked back upon a *what if* event in your life and seen the hand of God?

Chapter 24

Continues with the foundation of St. Joseph of Carmel in the city of Seville.

1. When, as I mentioned,[1] the Father Maestro Fray Jerónimo Gracián came to see me at Beas, we had never previously met although I had very much desired to meet him. (Yes, at times, we had corresponded.) I was extremely delighted when I learned he was there, for I greatly desired to meet him on account of the good reports given me concerning him. But much greater was my happiness when I began speaking with him, for it seemed from the way he pleased me that those who had praised him had hardly known him at all.

2. Since at that time I had so many difficulties, it seems that when I saw him the Lord showed me the good that was going to come to us through him. So during those days I went about with such excessive consolation and happiness that indeed I was surprised at myself. At that time he did not have authority outside Andalusia. It was when he was in Beas that the nuncio sent to see him and then gave him authority over the discalced friars and nuns of Castile.[2] So much joy did my spirit feel that I couldn't thank our Lord enough those days, nor did I want to do anything else.

3. At this time they had brought the license for the foundation in Caravaca. The permission granted did not correspond with my proposal, and so it was necessary to petition the royal court again. For I had written to the foundresses that the foundation would in no way be made unless a certain missing detail were asked for, and so it was necessary to appeal again

to the court.[3] It cost me a great deal to wait there so long, and I wanted to return to Castile. But since Father Fray Jerónimo was there, to whom that monastery was subject, and since he was the commissary for the whole province of Castile,[4] nothing could be done without his approval; so I talked to him about it.

4. He thought that if I were to leave, the foundation in Caravaca would fail, and also that a foundation in Seville would render great service to God. It seemed to him this latter would be very easy, for some well-to-do people had asked him and were able and wealthy enough to provide a house at once. The archbishop of Seville[5] so favored the order that Father Fray Jerónimo believed a foundation would render the order a great service. So it was arranged that the prioress and the nuns who were to go to Caravaca would instead go to Seville, although for certain reasons I had always strongly refused to found these monasteries in Andalusia. If when I went to Beas I had known that it was in Andalusia, I would by no means have gone. The mistake was that although the land was not yet within Andalusia, which I believe begins five or six leagues further, the ecclesiastical province was.[6] Since I saw that a foundation in Seville was the resolve of my major superior, I immediately submitted, although I had decided on another foundation and had some very serious reasons against going to Seville. (This is a favor our Lord grants me, to have the opinion that these superiors are right in everything).

5. Preparations were immediately begun for the journey because it was beginning to get very hot. Father Apostolic Commissary, Gracián, responding to a call from the nuncio left for a meeting with him,[7] and we for a journey to Seville with

my good companions, Father Julián de Avila, Antonio Gaytán, and a discalced friar.[8] We journeyed in wagons well covered, which was our mode of traveling, and when we reached an inn we took whatever room was available, good or bad. And one Sister received what we needed at the door, for not even those who journeyed with us entered the room.

6. Although we hurried along on our journey, we did not reach Seville until the Thursday before Trinity Sunday,[9] after having endured scorching heat. Even though we did not travel during siesta time, I tell you, Sisters, that since the sun was beating on the wagons, getting into them was like stepping into purgatory. Sometimes by thinking of hell, at other times by thinking that something was being done and suffered for God, those Sisters journeyed with much happiness and joy. The six souls who were with me were of the kind that made me think I was daring enough to go off with them to the land of the Turks and that they had the fortitude, or better, our Lord gave them the fortitude, to suffer for Him; for this was the subject of their desires and conversations. They were very experienced in prayer and mortification. Since they had to remain so far away, I chose those who seemed to me to be the most apt.[10] And this was all necessary because of the trials that were suffered. Some of the hardships and the greatest, I won't mention because another person might be involved.

7. One day before Pentecost, God gave them a severe trial by sending me a very high fever. I believed that their cries to God were enough to prevent the sickness from getting worse. Never before in my life had I experienced a fever like this without its growing worse. It made me think I had sleeping sickness so withdrawn did it make me. They threw water on

my face, but being so hot from the sun, the water provided little refreshment.

8. I don't want to fail to mention the bad inn at which we stayed when I was in this condition. We were given a small room with just a bare tile roof. It had no window, and when the door was opened, the sun poured in everywhere. You must remember that the sun in that region is not like it is in Castile, but much more annoying. The bed on which they made me lie down was such that I would have fared better on the ground. One part was so high and the other so low that one didn't know how to stay in it; it was like lying on sharp stones. What a thing sickness is! For when we're healthy, it's easy to put up with all kinds of inconveniences. Finally I decided it would be better if I got up and we left. It seemed better to me to suffer the sun in the field than in that little room.

9. What will it be like for the poor ones who are in hell? Never will there be any change at all, for even a change from one trial to another brings with it some relief. It has happened to me that when after suffering from very severe pain in one place I experienced other pain elsewhere, the change seemed to provide some relief even though the pain was just as great; so it was in this instance. As for me, insofar as I remember, it didn't cause me any distress that I was sick; the Sisters suffered much more than I. The Lord was pleased that the severity of the fever did not last beyond that day.

10. A little before this—I don't know whether it was two days—something else happened to us which got us into a tight spot while we were crossing the Guadalquivir on a barge. When it was time for the wagon to cross, it was not possible to make a straight crossing where the rope was, but they had

to wind their way across; the rope from the other shore was of some help by flowing with the barge. However, it happened that those who were holding the rope let it go, or I don't know what happened, for the barge went off with the wagon and without rope or oars. I felt much more concern in seeing the anxiety of the boatman than I did about the danger. We were all praying; the others were all screaming.

11. A gentleman watching us from a nearby castle was moved with pity and sent someone to help, for the barge then had not yet broken loose and our brothers[11] were pulling, using all their strength; but the force of the water dragged them along to the point that some fell to the ground. Indeed, the boatman's son caused in me feelings of great devotion, which I never forget—he must have been ten or eleven years old—for the way he was working so hard upon seeing his father in this difficulty made me praise our Lord. But as His Majesty always gives trials in a compassionate way, so He did here. It happened that the boat got stuck on part of a sand bar where there was not much water; thus a rescue was made possible. Since nightfall had come, we would not have known how to continue our journey if someone from the castle had not come to guide us.

I had not thought of dealing with these things because they are of little importance, and I could have mentioned many bad incidents that occurred on our journeys. But I have been urged to enlarge on my account of this trip.

12. A much greater trial for me than those mentioned was what happened to us on the second day after Pentecost. We were hurrying to reach Córdoba in the morning so as to hear Mass without being seen by anyone. For the sake of greater

solitude, they led us to a church located on the other side of a bridge. When we were about to cross the bridge, we found that on account of the wagons we needed a license which is issued by the magistrate. This took more than two hours since he was not up yet, and many people approached to find out who we were. This didn't bother us much because, since the wagons were well covered, the people were unable to do so. When the license finally came, we found that the wagons wouldn't fit through the gate of the bridge. It was necessary to saw them, or I don't know what, which took another while. When we finally reached the church where Father Julián de Avila was to say Mass, it was filled with people. The church was dedicated to the Holy Spirit, which we had not known, and thus they were celebrating an important feast in which a sermon was to be preached.

13. When I saw this I was very sorry. It seemed to me better to go without hearing Mass than to enter such turmoil. It didn't seem so to Father Julián de Avila. And since he was a theologian, we all had to follow his opinion. My other companions perhaps would have followed mine, and it would have been ill-advised, although I don't know if I would have trusted only in my opinion. We got out near the church, and although no one was able to see our faces, since we always wore large veils in front of them, it was enough for the people to see us with the veils, the white coarse woolen mantles we wore, and our sandals of hemp for them to get all stirred up; and that's what happened. The shock was certainly a great one for me and for all, and it must have taken away my fever completely.

14. As we entered the church, a friendly man approached me so as to hold off the people. I pleaded with him to bring

us to some chapel. He did so and closed it and did not leave us until we left the church. After a few days, he came to Seville and told a Father of our order that he thought God had rewarded him for the good deed he had performed, for the Lord had provided him with, or given him, a large estate about which he had forgotten.

I tell you, daughters, although it may perhaps seem to you to be nothing, this incident was for me one of the really bad moments I went through. From the uproar of the people you would think that a herd of bulls had come into the church. Thus, I couldn't wait to get out of that place. Since there was nowhere nearby to take siesta, we took it under a bridge.

15. When we reached Seville and the house that Father Fray Mariano had rented for us, which he had been told about, I figured that everything was done. As I say, the archbishop favored the discalced and had at times written to me manifesting much love.[12] That wasn't enough to keep him from causing me much trouble, for God so desired it. The archbishop is very much opposed to monasteries of nuns founded in poverty, and he is right. The trouble was that he hadn't been told; or rather, that was to the advantage of this foundation, for had he been told I am certain he would not have agreed to it. Since Father Commissary and Father Mariano (for whom also my arrival had been the source of the greatest happiness) were most certain that by my coming I would be doing the archbishop an enormous favor, they did not tell him beforehand. And, as I say, while thinking they were right, they could have been making a great mistake. With the other monasteries, the first thing I did was to obtain the license from the ordinary of the place as the holy Council requires.[13] In this case,

not only did we consider the license as given, but also, as I say, we thought the monastery would be a great favor to him, as it truly was, and this he came to understand afterward. But the Lord desired that no foundation be made without some trial in one way or another.[14]

16. Well, when we arrived at the house which, as I say, they had rented for us, I thought we could immediately take possession, as was my custom, so that we could say the Divine Office. But Father Mariano began to procrastinate—he was the one who was there—and so as not to cause me any grief, he did not want to tell me everything. Since he didn't have sufficient reasons, I understood where the difficulty lay, which was that the license had not been granted. The archbishop told me that it would be good if the monastery were founded with an income, or something like that, for I don't remember. Finally, he told me that he didn't like to grant permission for monasteries of nuns, and that since he had been archbishop he had never done so for any. He had been there many years, as well as in Córdoba, and he is a great servant of God. Especially, he didn't like giving a license for a monastery to be founded in poverty and said that he would not do so.

17. This amounted to saying that the monastery must not be founded. First, it would have seemed to me wrong to found in the city of Seville a monastery with an established income even though I could have done so. The places where I did agree to make foundations with an income were small and required that either I found the monastery with an income or not at all since without one there would be no means of sustenance. Secondly, not a cent was left from the expenses of the journey, and we hadn't brought anything with us except what

we were wearing and some tunics and toques, and what was necessary in order to cover the wagons and travel comfortably in them. In order that those who came with us could return, they had to look for a way of borrowing. One of Antonio Gaytán's friends who was there lent them what they needed. And Father Mariano looked for what was necessary to furnish the house; nor did we have a house of our own. Thus, it was an impossible situation.

18. Through what must have been persistent pleading on the part of the said Father we were allowed to have Mass, which was the first, on the feast of the most Blessed Trinity.[15] But word was sent that the bell should not be rung; neither was it to be put up, although it had already been put up. We were in this situation more than fifteen days. I know that if it had not been for Father Commissary and Father Mariano, I would definitely have returned with my nuns, and with very little regret, to Beas for the foundation in Caravaca. Much greater was the regret I actually experienced those days; since I have a bad memory, I do not remember, but I believe this lasted more than a month. For it was more difficult to return now after the monastery was known than it would have been immediately after our arrival. Father Mariano never allowed me to write to the archbishop, but instead went about gradually trying himself to convince him, making use also of letters from Father Commissary who was in Madrid.

19. As for me, one thing was calming and prevented me from feeling great scruple; it was that Mass had been said with the archbishop's permission, and we always said the Divine Office in choir. The archbishop did not fail to send a visitor with the message that he would see me soon, and an assistant

was sent to say the first Mass. Hence I saw clearly that there was no point in my being disturbed. Yet, I felt distressed, not because of me or my nuns, but because of the anxiety Father Commissary experienced. Since he had ordered me to come, he felt very bad and would have been pained were something unfortunate to have happened, and he had many reasons for worrying about that.

20. At this time the calced Fathers came in order to inquire concerning the authority by which the foundation had been made. I showed them the patents I had from our most Reverend Father General.[16] With this they were calmed. But if they had known what the archbishop was doing, I don't think the documents I showed them would have sufficed. However, this was not known, and everyone thought the foundation pleased the archbishop very much and made him happy. Finally, God was pleased that he come to see us. I told him about the harm he was doing us. In the end, he told me that the monastery could remain and in the way I wanted it. From then on, he always favored and supported us in everything that occurred.

SEVILLE CONTINUED

Summary and Background: Chapter 24

While Teresa was in Beas, she planned to establish her next foundation in Caravaca. However, these plans were put on hold because the license that she had received to make the foundation "contained so many unsuitable requirements that [she] did not want to proceed with [the foundation]" (LE. 1. 83. 2.). The specific stipulation that Teresa found completely unacceptable was that the convent would be subject to the Order of Santiago. Undeterred as ever, Teresa wrote to King Philip to ask if he could exempt her foundation from the Order's subjection.

While Teresa was waiting for a response, she received offers to found two other monasteries, one in Madrid and the other in Seville. Teresa asked Gracián which one she should choose. He said, ". . . discuss it with our Lord God."[17] Teresa did as Gracián advised.

In prayer, God told Teresa that she should found the monastery in Madrid. She informed Gracián about what God had told her. However, this was not the answer that Gracián wanted to hear. He had a very strong preference that the next foundation be in Seville and when he expressed his desire to Teresa, she felt that she would be disobedient if she went against his wishes. "I truly believe that [Gracián] would not have placed me under any obligation, but his desire for this was so great that if I hadn't complied, I would have been left with a disturbing scruple that I wasn't being obedient" (LE. 1. 80. 3.).

Gracián painted a rosy scenario for Teresa. He told her that the foundation in Seville "would be easy" (F. 24. 4.) because some rich benefactors had promised him enough money "to provide a house at once" (F. 24. 4.). In addition, he told Teresa that the Archbishop of Seville was in favor of the foundation. With these assurances, Teresa set out on what would prove to be the most arduous journey and one of the most troublesome foundations of her life.

On May 18, 1575, Teresa's caravan of four covered wagons began its journey to Seville. Teresa's troupe considered of six nuns, several mule drivers and mule boys, "Fr. Julián of Avila, Antonio Gaytán and a discalced friar [Fr. Gregorio Nacianzeno]" (F. 24. 5.). Julián's account of the journey fills in many events and details that were not recorded by Teresa. For example, he tells us that after the first day of their journey, their food went bad because of the sweltering heat. The next day, when they stopped to rest at a roadside inn, they encountered a band of ill-tempered, violent men.

> We came to an inn by the roadside. There were some men there, and I have never seen such a depraved lot in all my life . . . They shouted all sorts of vile things at Fr. Gregorio Nacianzeno and there was no way we could prevail on them to stop it . . . In the end, they drew knives and began fighting among themselves . . . While all this was going on the Mother and sisters remained in their covered wagons, and were not seen. Had the men

seen them, they would have treated them as they had treated Father Gregorio.[18]

Leaving the inn, shaken but unharmed, they continued their journey. The next trial that awaited them was the fording of the Guadalquivir river. When the wagons reached the river, an unscrupulous boatman told the party that he would take them across the river, even though he knew that his barge was incapable of doing so. The boatman's scheme to make a few extra pesos almost ended in disaster when the barge broke loose from its pull-ropes and was carried down stream by the river's swift current. Fortunately, it ran ashore on a sandbank and no one was hurt.

The next day, amid the scorching heat, the party traveled on without mishap. However, Teresa came down with a high fever so they had to stop at an inn. The accommodations were deplorable. The room they were given, recounts Julián, was one "in which the pigs used to be kept."[19] Teresa recounts.

> I don't want to fail to mention the bad inn at which we stayed when I was in this condition. We were given a small room with just a bare tile roof. It had no window, and when the door was opened, the sun poured in everywhere. You must remember that the sun in that region is not like it is in Castile, but much more annoying. The bed on which they made me lie down was such that I would have fared better on the ground. One part was so high and the other so low that one didn't know how to stay in it; it was like lying on sharp stones . . . Finally

I decided it would be better if I got up and we left. It seemed better to me to suffer the sun in the field than in that little room. (F. 24. 8.)

"Life is like a night in a bad inn," Teresa once quipped. Perhaps, when she mouthed these words, this was the place that she had in mind. The following day, they arrived at Córdoba; it was Pentecost Sunday. In light of the trials that they had endured for the previous two days (the cursing, abusive, knife-fighting men, the fording of the Guadalquivir river, and the wretched inn), all they wanted was a quiet little church in which they could celebrate the Eucharist. They were directed to an out-of-the-way church "located on the other side of the bridge" (F. 24. 12.). Unfortunately, both the location of the church and the specific church itself proved to be the cause of what Teresa said was "a much greater trial for me than those mentioned [so far]" (F. 24. 12.).

The trial unfolded in stages. First, they had to wait at the bridge for two hours in the sweltering heat because of bureaucratic red tape. A license was required for wagons to cross the bridge, a license that only the local magistrate (who was still asleep) could issue. During these two hours, curious onlookers began to congregate around the wagons "to find out who we were" (F. 24. 12.). However, since "the wagons were well covered" (F. 24. 12.), the nuns were protected from prying eyes. But this meant that the nuns had to sit in an oven with no ventilation for two hours. We need to remember that Teresa was still suffering from a fever.

Second, once the license arrived, it was discovered that "the wagons wouldn't fit through the gate of the bridge" (F. 24. 12.). This resulted in another delay. A saw had to be obtained in order to cut off the protruding ends of the wagon.

Third, the greatest trial began when they arrived at the church. Because it was Pentecost and the church was dedicated to the Holy Spirit, it was overflowing with people. When Teresa saw the situation, she felt that it would be "better to go without hearing Mass than to enter such turmoil" (F. 24. 13.). She expressed this opinion to Fr. Julián, who disagreed with Teresa. In the end, Teresa conceded to Julián's viewpoint.

When the nuns entered the church, dressed as they were with large veils covering their faces, coarse woolen mantles draped over their shoulders, and hemp sandals on their feet, the congregation got so "stirred up . . . [that] from the uproar of the people you would [have thought] that a herd of bulls had come into the church" (F. 24. 14.).

The next day, the party arrived at Ecija, a fairly large town with a population of nearly 7,000 inhabitants. They were able to spend a peaceful morning in prayer at the hermitage of St. Anne. It was here that Teresa made her private vow of obedience to Gracián. However, the afternoon was in stark contrast to this peaceful morn.

One of Teresa's companions, Sr. Leonor de San Gabriel, tells the following incident. "Near an inn they call Andino Inn, we came on a group of soldiers and muleteers fighting with knives. There was complete disorder and nobody could make them stop. Mother (Teresa) stuck her head out of the wagon and with one word calmed them down."[20]

When Teresa's weary caravan finally rolled into Seville, they did not find what they had been led to expect. The rich people whom Gracián had told Teresa would "provide a house at once" (F. 24. 4.) were not to be found; neither was Gracián to be found. He was in Castile on business. In his absence, he put Fr. Mariano, a discalced friar, in charge of finding lodgings for Teresa. He rented a cramped, damp house. However, on the positive side, the house was furnished. Unfortunately, the furniture was on loan and was taken back by its owners shortly after Teresa arrived. Because of a lack of funds, the prospect of procuring a house was not favorable.

However, the lack of a permanent residence was the least of Teresa's worries. Contrary to what Gracián had told Teresa, the archbishop was opposed to monasteries being founded in poverty. And what complicated the situation was that "[the archbishop] hadn't been told" (F. 24. 15.) that Teresa was planning to found her monastery in poverty. Gracián and Mariano had deliberately concealed this from the archbishop because "had he been told . . . he would not have agreed to it" (F. 24. 15.).

At best, Gracián and Mariano were presumptuous. "Since [they] were most certain that by my coming I would be doing the archbishop an enormous favor, they did not tell him beforehand" (F. 24. 15). In short, Teresa had come to Seville under a misconception. "[N]ot only did we consider the license [to found the monastery] as given, but also, as I say, we thought the monastery would be a great favor to [the archbishop]" (F. 24. 15.). Furthermore, Teresa discovered that the archbishop had wanted her to come to Seville to reform a *preexisting* monastery, rather than to found a convent of her own.

Teresa's situation in Seville was further complicated when she became aware that her monastery in Beas may have been founded illegally. To understand this we need to recall that Rossi, the Carmelite General, had restricted the foundations of Teresa's convents to Castille. Under no condition was she to establish foundations in the province of Andalusia.

When Teresa founded Beas, she believed that she was not violating this stipulation. "You should know that Beas is not in Andalusia, but five leagues this side, for I know that I cannot make foundations in Andalusia" (LE. 1. 73. 3.). In one sense, Teresa was correct. Beas was not within the *civil* boundaries of Andalusia, but it was within the *ecclesiastical* jurisdiction of Andalusia. There's the rub.

The illegality of the foundation of Beas was a part of a bigger jurisdictional fracas between the Discalced and Calced friars, which had began eight years previous. After Rossi, the Carmelite General, returned to Rome in 1567 from his disastrous attempt to reform the Carmelite friars of Andalusia, Pope Pius V appointed two Dominicans to be apostolic visitators (reformers) of Spain (Fernández for Castille and Vargas for Andalusia).

Vargas, knowing that trying to reform the friars of Andalusia would be a herculean task, wrote to King Phillip suggesting that the task would be better served if it were done by Carmelite friars themselves. The King agreed. Vargas first asked Fr. Baltasar Nieto (the Discalced prior of Pastrana) to act as the apostolic visitator of Andalusia. He agreed, but soon was removed from his office because of his incompetence. However, before he was dismissed, Baltasar had created bad blood with the Calced Carmelites of Andalusia because he founded a monastery of Discalced Friars in Granada. After Baltasar left office in September 1573, Vargas appointed Gracián as the apostolic visitator. Gracián traveled to Andalusia with plans to found more monasteries of Discalced friars. The Calced Carmelites were justifiably indignant because neither Baltasar nor Gracián had any authority to found a monastery in Andalusia. Besides, even if they had the authority, they had been sent to Andalusia to *reform* monasteries, not to *make* new foundations.

When all this became known to Rossi in Rome, he became enraged. He called a meeting of the Order, which approved a series of edicts against the Discalced Friars. The chapter was convened on May 22, 1575. Three days later, Teresa, like a trusting lamb arrived in Seville, which like Beas was in Andalusia. Since Gracián who was Teresa's superior, had initiated the idea of founding a monastery in Seville, Teresa may have believed that there was no jurisdictional impediment.

Chapter 24 of the *Foundations* ends with the Calced Carmelite Friars of Seville coming to Teresa "to inquire concerning the authority by which [her] foundation had been made" (F. 24. 20.). Fr. Mariano, who had long been aware of the brewing storm between the Calced and Discalced friars, fled to Madrid, leaving Teresa to continue to look for a house and to face the displeasure of the Calced Carmelite Friars alone. Teresa, writing to Mariano who was safely in Madrid, expressed her outrage. "When I consider the embroilment you left me with . . . I don't know what to think except *accursed be the man*, et cetera" (LE. 1. 106. 2.). Teresa was referring to Jer 17:5: "Cursed is the man *who trusts* in human beings."(italics added). The implication is clear. Teresa's curse was that she had put her trust in someone who proved to be untrustworthy.

Reflection. In the months just prior to the foundation of the convent in Pastrana, Teresa lived at the palace of the Princess of Eboli. During her stay, the princess tried to persuade Teresa to adopt changes in the life of the nuns. They were so completely unacceptable that Teresa decided not to make the foundation. Teresa became so infuriated that she tells us "I decided, rather than make the foundation, to leave" (F. 17. 13.). However, Teresa did not act upon her initial reaction but decided to stay for the sake of a greater good. "And I bore with some things because I was more desirous that the monastery of friars be founded" (F. 17. 13.).

It is worth asking the question. Was there ever a time when Teresa considered leaving Seville without making the foundation, as was the case in Pastrana?[21] Teresa had been mislead and must have been furious when she found out the truth. Considering the pack of falsehoods that greeted Teresa when she arrived at Seville (the promised house that never materialized, the rich benefactors that didn't exist, the consent of the Archbishop), not to mention the concealment of information and abandonment by Mariano, it is not hard to imagine Teresa packing her bags and buying a ticket for the next ox cart heading north to Castille. Yet, she decided to stay.

How hard it is to refrain from making choices based upon our emotional reactions. How hard it is to choose to continue to work for a greater good when we are battling with feelings of betrayal, anger, bitterness, or resentment. Who of us hasn't been misled into believing things that were not true? Who of us hasn't worked with people who either never followed through on what they promised that they would do or bailed out on us at the last minute? It is only Divine Grace that gives us the strength to continue to do the task that God has assigned to us when everything seems to turn out wrong.

Questions. Have you ever found yourself in a situation similar to Teresa's? What were you *tempted* to do? What *did* you do?

Reflection. Many stories were woven out of Teresa's long journeys to Beas and Seville. Whether they are fact or fiction, one is worth recounting because it captures Teresa's spirit. It has been said that one night, Teresa and her companions stopped at the house of a nobleman. When he served partridge for dinner, Teresa's companions were thrown into confusion. How could they, a group of poor nuns, partake of a meal that was the exclusive domain of the rich? Teresa smiled and said, "There is a time for penance and there is a time for partridge."

What is the time for eating partridge? When it is served by your host. In The Rule of St. Albert (The Primitive Carmelite Rule) the hermits on Mount Carmel were to abstain from eating meat, except when they were the guests of others. The reason for this exception is "to avoid giving trouble to your hosts."

Hospitality, which Teresa considered an important aspect of charity, involves more than being a *good host*. It also includes being a *gracious guest*. How ungracious it would have been for Teresa to tell her host that she and her companions could not eat the meal that he had prepared for them because they had to mortify themselves.

One of the great dangers of overvaluing any one particular virtue is that we can become blind to the demands of charity. Charity must be the rule or measure of all of our actions; it is the *form* of all the virtues, as St. Thomas teaches. Charity *informs* us how we are to practice all the other virtues.

Questions. Is there a spiritual discipline in your life which you practice with such rigidity that you are insensitive to the needs and considerations of others? How can charity inform you when it is time for penance and when it is time for partridge?

Chapter 25

Continues telling about the foundation named after the glorious
St. Joseph in Seville and about what we suffered in order to get our
own house.

1. No one would have thought that in a city as wealthy as
Seville and with so many rich people there would be fewer
opportunities for a foundation than in any of the other places
I had gone to. There was so much less help that I sometimes
thought that it would not be good for us to have a monastery
in that place. I don't know if the climate itself of that territory
is the reason. I have always heard it said that the devils have
greater leeway there to tempt souls, for God must grant it to
them. They certainly afflicted me there, for I never felt more
pusillanimous or cowardly in my life. Indeed, I didn't recognize myself, although the confidence I usually have in our
Lord did not leave me. But in my human nature I felt very
different from the way I usually do after taking part in these
things. I figured that the Lord partly withdrew His hand so
that my human nature might be left to itself and I might see
that my courage did not come from me.

2. Well then, I stayed there from this time of which I am
speaking until a little after Lent.[1] There was not a chance of
buying a house, nothing either with which to buy one, nor even
anyone who would lend to us as there were in other places.
Those women who had often told Father Apostolic Visitator[2]
that they would enter our community and had asked him to
bring nuns there, afterward thought we were too strict and
that they would not be able to endure the life. Only one person,

about whom I shall speak later, entered.[3] The time, then, came in which I received orders to leave Andalusia because there were other business matters for me to attend to up here.[4] It distressed me deeply to have to leave the nuns without a house, although I saw clearly that I wasn't accomplishing anything there. For the favor God grants me up here of having people to help me in these works, I did not have there.

3. God was pleased at that time that my brother, Lorenzo de Cepeda, return from the Indies where he had been for more than thirty-four years.[5] Feeling worse than I that the nuns would be staying there without having their own house, he helped us a great deal, especially in procuring the house in which they now live. For my part, I pleaded with our Lord, begging Him that I not have to go away and leave the nuns without a house. I had the Sisters ask Him as well as the glorious St. Joseph for this favor and we offered many processions and prayers to our Lady. Along with this, seeing my brother determined to help us, I began discussing the purchase of some houses. Just when it seemed that everything was starting to work out, it all came to naught.

4. One day, while I was in prayer beseeching our Lord to give them a house since they were His brides and had such desire to please Him, He told me: "I have already heard you; leave it to Me." I was left feeling very happy since it seemed I already had the house. And this was so. His Majesty prevented us from buying one that because of its nice location was pleasing to all. But the house itself was so old and run down that only the site was being bought and for not much less than was paid for the house we have now. Though all was agreed upon and only the contract remained to be drawn up, I was by

no means satisfied. This didn't seem to be in accord with the words I had heard in prayer; for those words, I believed, were a sign that a good house would be given to us. And thus the Lord was pleased that the owner, even though he was making a great profit, should raise a difficulty about signing the contract at the established time, and we were able, without any fault, to get out of the agreement. This was a great favor from our Lord, for there was so much work to be done on the house that the Sisters living there would never in all their lives have been able to do it; and their means were few.

5. Much help was given to us by a servant of God who, from almost as soon as we arrived, began to come each day to say Mass, since he knew that we did not have a celebrant, even though his house was far away and the weather was extremely hot. His name is Garciálvarez.⁶ Highly esteemed in the city on account of his good works, he is never occupied with anything but them. And had he been wealthy, we would not have lacked anything. Knowing all about the house, he thought it would be very foolish to give so much for it. Thus, each day he told us so and managed to get us to speak of it no more. He and my brother went to see the house in which the nuns now live. They got to like it so much, and rightly so—and our Lord wanted this—that in two or three days the contract was signed.⁷

6. What we had to go through before moving in was no trifle. The occupant did not want to leave, and the Franciscan friars, since they were nearby, came at once trying to persuade us that we should by no means move in. If the contract had not been so firmly signed, I would have praised God that it could be broken, because we found ourselves in danger of paying

six thousand ducats for a house we were unable to move into.
This was not how the prioress viewed the matter.[8] She praised
God that the contract could not be broken, for in regard to that
house, His Majesty gave her more faith in Him and courage
than He did me; just as in everything else, for she is much
better than I.

7. This trouble lasted more than a month. God was finally
pleased that we move, the prioress with myself and two other
nuns, in great fear, at night so that the friars would not be
aware until we took possession. Those who came with us said
that every shadow they saw seemed to be a friar. When morning came, the good Garciálvarez, who was with us, said the
first Mass, and then our fears left us.

8. O Jesus! How many fears I have suffered before taking
possession of these foundations! I reflect on the fact that if one
can feel so much fear in doing something good, for the service
of God, what must be the fear of those who do evil deeds that
are against God and against neighbor? I don't know what they
can gain or what satisfaction they can find as a counterbalance
to all that fear.

9. My brother was not there yet since he had sought sanctuary on account of a certain error made in the contract which
was drawn up so hastily. The error was very harmful to the
monastery, and since he was the guarantor of the loan they
wanted to arrest him.[9] And because he was an outsider, there
was the possibility that they would harass us, and in fact they
did, for until he put up collateral there was trouble. Afterward
the negotiations went well, although there was some contention at times so that we might suffer greater trial. We were
enclosed in some rooms on the ground floor, and he was there

all day with the workers, and he provided us with food as he
had been doing before. Since we were in what had been a private home, not everyone knew it was a monastery, and thus
there were few alms save for those of the saintly old prior of
Las Cuevas, a Carthusian monk and very great servant of God
from the Pantoja family in Avila.[10] God gave him so much love
for us that from the time we arrived he did not cease helping
in every way, and I think he will continue doing so until he
dies. We owe a great deal to this saint. I put this down here,
daughters, so that if you read it you will pray for the one who
helped us so much, and it is right that you pray for him and
for all those, living or dead, who have helped us.

10. My brother stayed with us more than a month, I think.
(On this subject of time, I have a poor memory and so I could
be mistaken; always understand me to be saying "more or
less" since it doesn't matter.) During this month he worked
a great deal in constructing the church out of some rooms in
the house and adapting everything so that we didn't have to
do anything.

11. After all the work was finished, I wanted to have
the Blessed Sacrament reserved without any noisy display,
for I am much opposed to causing any bother if it can be
avoided, and so I mentioned this to Father Garciálvarez. He
spoke about it with the Father Prior of Las Cuevas, for they
were looking after our affairs as they would their own. Their
opinion was that in order to make the monastery known in
Seville the Blessed Sacrament would have to be reserved
with solemnity, and they went to the archbishop. All agreed
that the Blessed Sacrament should be brought with much
solemnity from a parish, and the archbishop ordered that the

clerics and confraternities gather for the occasion and that the streets be decorated.

12. The good Garciálvarez decorated our cloister which then, as I mentioned, looked on to the street. And in decorating the church he went to every extreme with many very nice altars and some other contrivances. Among these latter was a fount having orange-flower water which we neither requested nor even wanted; although afterward it did give us much devotion. And we were consoled to see that our festival was celebrated with such solemnity, with the streets highly decorated, and a great deal of music and many musical instruments. The saintly prior of Las Cuevas told me that he had never seen anything like this before in Seville, that it was evidently the work of God. He himself walked in the procession, which he was not accustomed to doing. The archbishop reserved the Blessed Sacrament.[11]

Here you see, daughters, the poor discalced nuns honored by all. A little earlier it didn't seem that there would even be any water for them, although there is a great deal in the river. The number of people that came was extraordinary.

13. One thing that happened, according to all who saw it, is worth noting. Since after the procession there was much shooting of artillery and firecrackers, the people had the urge to continue, for it was almost night. And I don't know how, but some powder caught fire, and it was a great wonder that the person who had it didn't get killed. A huge flame leaped up as high as the cloister. The people thought that the taffeta hangings covering the arches would all be reduced to ashes. But no damage was done to them at all, though they were yellow and bright red. What was frightening is that the stone of

the arches, under the hangings, was blackened by the smoke, but the taffeta hangings were left unmarred as if the fire had not reached them.

14. All were amazed when they saw it. The nuns praised the Lord that they didn't have to pay for new taffeta. The devil must have been so angry at seeing another house of God and the solemnity that was demonstrated that he wanted somehow to get revenge. But His Majesty did not allow this; may He be blessed forever, amen.

SEVILLE CONTINUED

Summary and Background: Chapter 25

Teresa begins this chapter by enumerating her problems—
no benefactors, no money, no credit, no vocations.

> No one would have thought that in a city as wealthy as
> Seville and with so many rich people there would be
> fewer opportunities for a foundation than in any of the
> other places I had gone to . . . There was not a chance
> of buying a house, nothing either with which to buy one,
> nor even anyone who would lend money to us as there
> were in other places. Those women who had often told
> [Gracián] that they would enter our community and had
> asked him to bring nuns there, afterward thought we
> were too strict and that they would not be able to endure
> the life. (F. 25. 1–2.)

In spite of all of these problems, Teresa was anxious
that the house be founded as soon as possible because
she had "received orders to leave Andalusia" (F. 25. 2.). In
her urgency to find a house, Teresa almost purchased one
based solely upon its good location, without taking into
consideration that it was old and in much need of repair.
With the help of Fr. Garciálvarez, a secular priest, Teresa
avoided signing a contract with the owner, who stood to
make a great profit from the sale. Garciálvarez must have
discovered deceit on the owner's part because he alerted
Teresa to his suspicions. "I remember when others wanted

to deceive us about a house they were selling, [Garciálva-rez] alerted us to their deceit" (LE. 2. 264. 1.). Having saved Teresa from purchasing a bad house, Garciálvarez helped her to find a suitable one. And with the financial help of her wealthy brother Lorenzo (who would soon arrive from Ecuador), Teresa was able to purchase the house. However, just as the Augustinian friars had opposed Teresa's foundation in Medina del Campo, so the Franciscan friars tried to thwart Teresa's foundation in Seville, but to no avail.

In the end, the archbishop "told [Teresa] that the monastery could remain and in the way [she] wanted it [that is, founded in poverty]" (F. 24. 20.). So, on May 27, 1576, amid much fanfare (see F. 25. 12–13.) and over a year after they had arrived in Seville, the nuns were able to move into their new home.

Reflection. Teresa tells us that in preparation for the dedication of their new house, Fr. Garciálvarez decorated the convent's cloister and church. "[H]e went to every extreme with many very nice altars and some other contrivances . . . which we neither *requested nor even wanted*" (F. 25. 12.) (italics added). This is the first indication that Garciálvarez, who became the monastery's chaplain, was becoming so problematic to the community that eventually he would be dismissed. Garciálvarez was a well-meaning, charitable man but was scrupulous, often indiscreet and of very limited intelligence.

Shortly after Seville was founded, Teresa moved to the Carmelite monastery in Toledo. During her stay in Toledo, Teresa carried on a lengthy correspondence with Madre María de San José, the prioress of Seville. Several times in her letters, Teresa responded to Madre María's concerns about the problems that Garciálvarez was causing the community at Seville. For example, referring to his scrupulosity (being "so perfect") and his emotional instability, Teresa wrote, "I am delighted that [Fr. Garciálvarez] is in the present mood. Nonetheless, you should all be careful, for he is so perfect that what we might think is edifying will scandalize him" (LE. 1. 122. 9.).

In addition, because he lacked learning and discretion, Garciálvarez was frightening many of the nuns by telling them that their spiritual experiences were from the devil. Teresa, in a letter to Madre María, writes: "I had thought of writing to Garciálvarez to ask him that when he needs counsel he should . . . search out some truly learned men, for these have rescued me from many troubles. I am not surprised about the sufferings of which you speak, for I have suffered much because [unlearned men] told me the devil was behind my experiences" (LE. 1. 152. 3.).

After two years of correspondence, Madre María told Teresa that Garciálvarez had to go. Teresa knew that Madre María was right. However, Teresa felt guilty about having to confront Garciálvarez because he had been so helpful to the Seville community at its inception. Therefore, she begged María not to send him away.

For love of our Lord I beg you, daughter, to suffer and to be silent and not try to send that *padre* away from there, no matter how many trials and troubles he causes, unless something amounts to an offense against God. I cannot bear our seeming to be ungrateful to someone who has helped us. For I remember when others wanted to deceive us about a house they were selling, he alerted us to their deceit. I can never forget the good he did us in that instance and the trouble he saved us from . . . I see clearly that this need in me to show gratitude is not a sign of perfection. It must be a natural trait, for I could be bribed with a sardine." (LE. 2. 264. 1.)

At first, Gracián, as the religious superior, had to put restrictions on Garciálvarez's powers as a confessor. Eventually, a more drastic measure had to be taken. Three years after Garciálvarez joyously decorated the convent of Seville in celebration of its foundation, his role as its chaplain was terminated.

Questions. Teresa's gratitude toward Garciálvarez is understandable. However, it obscured her judgment. She allowed an intolerable situation in the Seville community to continue, causing the nuns much suffering. Like Teresa, have you ever been in a situation where your fear of hurting someone's feelings or the fear of seeming ungrateful prevented you from doing what needed to be done?

Reflection. Teresa's account of both the long and grueling journey from Beas to Seville and all the problems that she encountered in the establishment of the Seville community can easily overshadow what she tells us was one of her greatest sufferings—*the heat*, what she refers to in her letters as "the sizzling heat of Seville" (LE. 1. 81. 5.), "the scorching heat [of Seville]" (LE. 1. 81. 3.). Teresa tells us that the heat affected her to such a degree that she became so faint-hearted that she was beside herself. "I don't know if the climate itself of that territory is the reason . . . I never felt more pusillanimous or cowardly in my life. *Indeed I didn't recognize myself*" (F. 25. 1.) (italics added).

If even the saints are so affected by something so ordinary as a change in the weather that they do not even recognize themselves, how much more so are we impacted by the common vicissitudes of daily life? How often are we spun around or sent into an emotional tailspin when some little inconvenience comes our way? How often does a minor ailment like a headache put us so out of sorts that we begin biting people's heads off? In such moments, we watch our "solid virtue" crumble before our eyes. It is mortifying to realize that a slight change in circumstance or alteration in fortune can so bend us out of shape that we are unable to muster enough strength even to be courteous or exercise common decency. Such a realization contains an invitation to humility.

Reflecting upon how the heat affected her, Teresa writes, "I figured that the Lord partly withdrew His hand so that my human nature might be left to itself and I might see that my courage did not come from me" (F. 25. 1.). This perspective contains a great lesson in humility, namely, that our strength and determination to do God's will is very fragile. It often waxes and wanes because of circumstances. For Teresa, this was true not only in regard to the heat but also sickness. Reflecting upon how a fever affected her, Teresa writes, "What a thing sickness is! For when we're healthy, its easy to put up with all kinds of inconveniences" (F. 24. 8.).

All of us know the truth of these words. When we are sick or worried, every small task, every little annoyance, and every minor upset become difficult to bear. They throw us off balance or so put us on edge that daily aggravations, which we usually take in stride, set us off. There are some days when a jammed printer or a nasty checkout cashier is enough to make us cry. If we can accept ourselves with gentleness in the midst of being frazzled, we are practicing a rare form of humility. It takes great strength to accept that we are weak and great virtue to admit that we are not so virtuous after all.

Questions. All of us are like Teresa. Little things such as a change in the weather or a slight illness can make the practice of virtue very difficult. What specific vicissitudes of life throw you off balance or put you on edge? Have you ever thought that during these times, when the practice of patience and charity are extremely difficult, you are being offered an opportunity to practice humility—the humility that recognizes and accepts the fragileness of your virtue?

Chapter 26

Continues the account of the foundation of the monastery of St. Joseph in the city of Seville. Tells some very noteworthy things about the first nun who entered there.

1. You can easily understand, my daughters, the consolation we had that day. For my part, I can tell you that it was very great. I was especially consoled to see that I was leaving the Sisters in a house that was so good and well located, and that the monastery was known, and that there were enough new nuns to pay for the greater part of the cost of the house. Thus, those who in the future, before the established number is reached, may want to enter can do so no matter how little the dowry they bring with them, and the debt can still be paid off. Above all, I was happy for having shared in the trials, and when there was opportunity for a little rest, I left. This festival took place the Sunday before Pentecost in the year 1576, and immediately on Monday, the following day, I departed,[1] for the extremely hot weather was beginning to come and I wanted to be in Malagón before Pentecost and not have to travel on that day. I would have liked to have delayed a day or so, but for the above reason I left in a hurry.

2. The Lord was not pleased that I be there even one day to hear Mass in the chapel. The nuns' happiness was greatly spoiled by my departure.[2] They felt it very keenly, for we had gone through so many trials together in that year. As I have said,[3] I am not recording the worst ones here. In my opinion, aside from the first foundation in Avila (for with that one there is no comparison), none of the other foundations cost me as

much as this one did in which the trials were for the most part interior ones. May it please the Divine Majesty that He always be served there, as I hope He will be, for then everything else is of little importance. His Majesty began to draw good souls to that house. As for the five who remained out of the six I brought with me, I have already told you how good they were; that is, something of what can be told, which is the least. I wish to speak now of the first nun who entered there since her story is something you will enjoy hearing about.

3. She was the young daughter of very Christian parents. Her father was from the mountain region. She was still young, around seven, when her aunt, who had no children, begged her mother to allow her to stay with her. When she was brought to the house, her aunt must have shown her much love and affection as was natural. The maids had been hoping they would get the aunt's inheritance, but now it was clear that since the aunt loved the child she would leave it to her. The maids decided together to remove that obstacle through a diabolical plot, inventing a calumny against the child, saying that she wanted to kill her aunt. And in order to carry this out they gave one from among them I don't know how much money to buy some corrosive sublimate. When they told the aunt, she believed them at once because they all said the same thing. And the child's mother did too, for she is a very virtuous woman.

4. She took the child and brought her home thinking that she might turn out to be a very bad woman. Beatriz de la Madre de Dios,[4] for that is her name, tells me that for more than a year they spanked, punished, and made her sleep on the floor so that she would confess that she had planned to do

something so evil. Since the girl denied that she had done it and said that she didn't know what corrosive sublimate was, her mother thought she was much worse since she was stubborn enough to deny it. The poor mother was so afflicted to see her daughter so headstrong in her refusal to admit she had done anything that she thought her daughter would never make amends. It's amazing that the girl didn't admit she was guilty just to free herself from so much punishment. But since she was innocent, God sustained her so that she continued to uphold the truth. And since His Majesty defends those who are without fault, He sent two of those maids an illness so bad that it seemed they had caught the rabies. Secretly they sent for both the little girl and her aunt and begged pardon from them, and finding themselves at the point of death they retracted. The other maid did likewise before dying in childbirth. In sum, all three of them died agonizing deaths in payment for what they had made that innocent girl suffer.

5. I did not learn this solely from her, for her mother, after she saw that her daughter had become a nun, grieved over the bad treatment they had given her, and told me about it along with other things, for the girl's martyrdoms were many. And God permitted that, without it being her fault, the mother, who was a good Christian and loved her daughter, become her daughter's executioner. This mother is a woman of great honesty and deep Christian spirit.

6. While reading a book on the life of St. Anne, the child, when a little more than twelve years old, became very devoted to the saints of Carmel. For the author of the book says that St. Anne's mother — I believe her name is Merenciana — often went to speak to those saints. The effect this reading had on

the girl was one of great devotion to the order of our Lady, for she then promised to become a nun in that order and also made a promise of chastity. When she could, she gave much time to solitude and prayer. In this solitude God and our Lady granted her many great and special favors. She would have liked to become a nun at once but she didn't dare because of her parents. Nor did she know where to find this order; which is surprising, for there was a monastery of the mitigated rule in Seville. But she had never heard of it until she heard of our monasteries many years later.

7. When she reached the marriageable age, though she was still but a girl, her parents came to an agreement on whom she should marry. She was their only child. Although she had had other brothers, they had all died, and she, the less loved by her parents, was left. (When what I mentioned[5] happened one of her brothers was alive, and he defended her saying that the calumny should not be believed.) Once the marriage was arranged, her parents didn't think she would have any objection, but when they told her she answered that she had made a vow not to get married and that no scheme whatever on their part, even if they were to kill her, would get her to do so.

8. Because either the devil blinded the parents or God permitted this so that she would be a martyr, they thought she had done something wicked and that for that reason she did not want to get married. Since they had already given their word and their not following through on it would have been taken as an affront by the other party, they gave her so many whippings, inflicted on her so many punishments, even to the point of wanting to hang her, for they were choking her,

that it was fortunate they didn't kill her. God who desired her for greater things saved her. She tells me that in the end she hardly felt anything because she recalled what St. Agnes had suffered, that the Lord had brought it to her mind, that she was pleased to suffer something for Him, and that she did nothing but offer herself to Him. They thought she would die, for she was in bed three months, unable to stir.

9. It seems very strange that the parents of this young maiden, a girl who never left her mother's side and whose father was very circumspect, should think so much evil of their daughter. She was always holy and virtuous, and very dedicated to almsgiving; all that she could obtain she gave away in alms. If our Lord wishes to grant someone the favor of suffering, He has many means; although, for some years our Lord had been revealing to her parents the virtue of their daughter so that they gave her all she wanted for distributing alms, and the former persecutions were changed into tokens of affection. Nonetheless, because of her longing to be a nun everything was a hardship for her; thus, according to what she told me, she went about dejected and troubled.

10. It happened that thirteen or fourteen years before Father Gracián went to Seville (when nobody had even heard of discalced Carmelites), while she was with her father and mother and two other women who were neighbors, a discalced friar of our order dressed in the coarse wool habits these friars now wear entered their house. They say his face was both fresh and venerable, although he was so old that his beard seemed made of silver threads, and it was long. He approached her and began to speak to her a little in a language that neither she nor anyone else understood. When he finished, he blessed

her three times saying: "Beatriz, may God make you strong."
And then he went away. No one stirred while he was there,
but all remained as though stupefied. Her father asked her
who he was. She had thought that her father had known him.
They got up at once to go and look for him, but he was seen
no more. She remained very consoled, and all the others very
amazed, for they considered this to be something from God,
and so they then began to esteem her highly as was said.[6]
After this, all those years passed, I believe they were fourteen,
while she was ever serving our Lord, beseeching Him to fulfill
her desire.

   11. She was very weary by the time Father Maestro Fray
Jerónimo Gracián arrived there. Going one day to hear a sermon in a church in Triana, which is where her father was living, without knowing who the preacher would be—it was the
Father Maestro Gracián—she saw him go up to receive the
blessing. When she saw the habit and that he was discalced,
she at once recalled the one who she had seen, for the habit
was the same; although the face and the age were different, for
Father Gracián was not yet thirty years old. She tells me that
her joy was so great she almost fainted, for although she had
heard that a monastery was founded there in Triana she had
not known to which order it belonged.[7] Immediately, from
that day she began to try to confess to Father Gracián. Yet
God desired that even that would cost her much, for she tried
more than, or at least as many as, twelve times, but the Father
never wanted to hear her confession. Since she was young and
attractive in appearance—for she must have been no more
than twenty-seven—he avoided conversation with her; he is
very circumspect.[8]

12. Finally, one day while she was in the church weeping (being also very reserved), a lady asked her what the trouble was. She told her that she had been trying for a long time to speak with that Father who was then in the confessional and that she had not succeeded. The lady brought her to the confessional and begged him to hear the young girl's confession, and thus this girl was able to make a general confession to him. When he saw what a virtuous soul she was, he was greatly consoled, and he consoled her, telling her that perhaps discalced nuns would come there and that he would arrange that they accept her immediately. And that is what happened. The first command he gave me was that she be the first to be admitted, for he was satisfied with her soul. And he informed her of this after we had arrived there. He insisted that she not let her parents know because otherwise there would be no possibility of her entering. And thus on the feastday of the Holy Trinity[9] she took leave from some women who accompanied her to the church. (Her mother did not go with her when she went to the monastery of the discalced friars for confession, which is where she always went, for it was far away. And she, and her parents through her, gave many alms to the monastery.) She had arranged with a woman who was a very good servant of God to bring her and told the women who were accompanying her that she would soon return. And they allowed her to go since the woman companion was very well known in Seville as a servant of God who did great works of mercy. She put on her habit and mantle of coarse wool; I don't know how she was able to move, except that the happiness she felt made everything seem easy. Her only fear was that someone might recognize her behind this

heavy habit, so different from her usual mode of dress, and stop her. What wonders the love of God works! Since she was no longer concerned about her honor and thought of nothing but how to realize her desire, we opened the door at once. I sent word of this to her mother. Her mother came to the monastery as though out of her mind; but she said that she already saw the favor God was granting her daughter. And although she was grieved, she overcame it courageously and did not go to the extreme of not speaking to her daughter as others do. She gave us many alms.

13. This bride of Christ began to enjoy the happiness she had so much longed for and was so humble and fond of doing all there was to do that we could hardly get the broom away from her. Whereas in her own home she had been so pampered, here she found all her rest in working. In her great happiness she began to put on weight. This pleased her relatives so much that they were now content to see her there.

14. In order that she would not enjoy so much good without suffering, she experienced very severe temptations two or three months before the time in which she was to make her profession;[10] not because she had decided against making it, but because it seemed to her a very serious step to take. The devil, making her forget all those years in which she had suffered to attain this blessing, was so tormenting her that she could not overcome the temptation. Nevertheless, by absolutely forcing herself, she defeated him in such a way that in the midst of these torments she made the plans for her profession. Our Lord, who must not have been waiting for anything more than the testing of her fortitude, visited and consoled her in a very special way three days before the profession and put

the devil to flight. She remained so consoled that during those three days it seemed as though she was outside herself with happiness; and rightly so because the favor had been great.

15. A few days after she entered the monastery, her father died. Her mother took the habit in the same monastery and gave all she possessed in alms.[11] Both mother and daughter experience the greatest happiness, edifying all the nuns and serving Him who granted them so wonderful a favor.

16. A year had not passed before another young lady, against the will of her parents, entered. And thus the Lord continues to fill this house of His with souls so desirous of serving Him, for neither austerity nor enclosure deters them. May He be blessed and praised forever and ever, amen.

SEVILLE CONTINUED

Summary and Background: Chapter 26

Teresa begins this chapter by alluding to trials that she does not expound upon. "None of the other foundations cost me as much as this one did in which the trials were for the most part interior ones . . . I'm not recording the worst ones here" (F. 26. 2.). Two of the worst trials that Teresa had to bear in the year between the day she arrived in Seville on May 26, 1575, and the day the community moved into their new house on May 27, 1576, came from within her own ranks. First, Sr. Isabel de San Jerónimo, one of the six handpicked nuns that Teresa had brought to Seville, began to deteriorate mentally. For many years there had been indications of mental imbalance. At first, it was thought that she was possessed by the devil. However, when John of the Cross was asked for his opinion, he said that he believed that Sr. Isabel was exhibiting the beginning stages of a mental illness. The year was 1573. Three years later, shortly after Teresa had left Seville, she wrote to Gracián about Sr. Isabel's hallucinations. "Her imagination is weak and what she meditates on she thinks she sees or hears" (LE. 1. 136. 9.). How painful it must have been for Teresa to witness the gradual mental deterioration of someone whom she had known and loved over the years.

The second interior trial also had to do with a member of the Seville community, not one whom Teresa had brought from Castille, but a native Andalusian vocation,

a self-proclaimed *beata* who liked to exhibit her "raptures." Teresa may have had such people in mind when,
shortly after she left Seville, she wrote, "[they] let themselves be absorbed . . . who fancy that they are being
carried away in rapture. I call it being carried away in
foolishness" (IC. 4. 3. 11.).

This nun was in love with the *idea* of religious life and
the mystique of the cloister. However, she soon discovered that the reality of convent life was not what she had
envisioned. She felt hemmed in by the cloister, was disgusted by the simple fare the community ate, and had frequent conflicts with the prioress. She, along with another
nun, left the convent feeling misunderstood, unappreci-
ated, indignant, and full of resentment. In retaliation, she
spread vicious rumors about the community. For example,
she claimed that the nuns were flogged after their hands
and feet were tied (LE. 1. 105. 6.). These rumors led the
Inquisition to interrogate Teresa and the entire community
of Seville; however, no evidence was found to substantiate
these wild accusations.

After alluding to the above trials, Teresa, almost as if
she needs a breather, turns her attention to a nun who was
a source of happiness for her (at least for a while). "I wish
to speak now of the first nun who entered there [Seville]
since her [Beatriz de la Madre de Dios] story is something
you will enjoy hearing about" (F. 26. 2.).

Beatriz had been abused as a child. When she was
seven, her mother gave her to a childless aunt to raise.
The aunt adored Beatriz; however, the aunt's maids did

not. Knowing that their employer had no children of her own, the maids were hoping to receive her inheritance. But when they saw how much the woman loved her niece, they became afraid that all of the inheritance would be given to Beatriz. As a result, the maids bought some poison and told the aunt that they had discovered that Beatriz was planning to kill her. Both Beatriz's aunt and mother believed the maids.

As a result, Beatriz's mother brought her home and "for more than a year spanked, punished, and made [Beatriz] sleep on the floor so that she would confess that she had planned to do something evil" (F. 26. 4.). Beatriz did not confess. In fact, she denied the allegation. The more Beatriz denied that she planned to do something evil, the more her mother thought that she was evil. "It's amazing that the girl didn't admit she was guilty just to free herself from so much punishment . . . But God sustained her to uphold the truth" (F. 26. 4.). In the end, Beatriz was vindicated when the three maids confessed to the plot that they had hatched against her.

As Beatriz grew, she became devoted to the saints of Carmel and longed to enter the cloister, but her parents had arranged to have her marry. They especially wanted her to marry because all of their other children had died, and thus she was the sole survivor who would inherit the family's wealth. However, Beatriz had made a private vow of virginity. This caused a problem for her parents because they "had already given their word [to give Beatriz's hand to the fiancée's parents] and their not following through on it would have been taken as an affront by the other party. They gave Beatriz so many whippings, inflicted on her so many punishments, even to the point of wanting to hang her, for they were choking her, that it was fortunate that they didn't kill her" (F. 26. 8.).

Years passed and Beatriz continued to remain faithful to her private vow. One day, she heard Gracián preach in a church and after persuading him to hear her confession, he felt that Beatriz was very holy and had a vocation to Carmel. Gracián told Teresa to admit her to the Seville Carmel. "The first command [Gracián] gave me was that [Beatriz] be the first to be admitted, for he was satisfied with her soul" (F. 26. 12.).

Beatriz's entrance into religious life was similar to Doña Teresa de Layz's entrance (see chapter 20). One day, Beatriz walked to the convent and asked for admittance without either her parents' knowledge or permission. After Beatriz was admitted, Teresa sent word to Beatriz's mother. At first, she was "as though out of her mind" (F. 26. 12.), but over time she accepted her daughter's entrance as the will of God.

Teresa ends her account with a description of Beatriz as a picture of happiness in her new found vocation. "This bride of Christ began to enjoy the happiness she had so much longed for and was so humble and fond of doing all there was to do that we could hardly get the broom away from her. Whereas in her own home she had been so pampered, here she found all her rest in working" (F. 26. 13.). This passage echoes Teresa's description of Fr. Antonio at

Duruelo "sweeping the doorway to the church with a joyful expression on his face" and cursing the day that he had any honor (F. 14. 6.). And just like Antonio, whom we discovered was a very complex and wounded human being, so too was Beatriz.

Shortly after Beatriz entered religious life, she began to have "mystical experiences" that were, in fact, false visions and ecstasies. Fr. Garciálvarez believed that Beatriz's experiences were from God. He began to counsel her for several hours each day over a period of three months. Beatriz told Garciálvarez of strange and scandalous things that were happening in the cloister.

She told Garciálvarez that Teresa and her lover Gracián had initiated the nuns into their perverse sexual practices and that Gracián danced naked in front of the community as a means of promoting a type of mystical prayer. Garciálvarez circulated these rumors and, in consequence, the prioress dismissed him as the community's confessor.

"Oh, the lies that circulate down here! It's enough to make you faint" (LE. 1. 106. 9.). Yes, but often unbelievable lies are *believed*, which is exactly what happened in this case. These allegations were believed by Diego de Cárdenas, a Carmelite of the Observance, who recently had been appointed provincial over both the Discalced friars and nuns. After making a visitation to the community, he reinstated Garciálvarez as the confessor, removed Mária de San José as prioress, and installed Beatriz as the new prioress. This intolerable situation lasted about a year, when Diego de Cárdenas was removed from office and replaced by

Angel de Salazar, who had Garciálvarez dismissed as the community's confessor and removed Beatriz from office.

Reflection. Edwin Arlington Robinson's poem, "Isaac and Archibald," relates a man's reminiscence about an event from his childhood. When the man was a young boy, he used to visit Isaac and Archibald, two old men who lived on adjoining farms. One day as the young boy is walking with Isaac to Arbhibald's farm, Isaac tells the boy that he has noticed a "a slackening" in Archibald's speech and a slight alteration in the way that Archibald says certain words. Furthermore, Isaac shares the pain that he feels upon noticing these incremental changes in his dear friend.

> Now in a common word that would have passed
> Uncaught from any other lips than his,
> Now in some trivial act of every day
> Done as he might have done it all along
> But for a twinging little difference
> That nips you like a squirrel's teeth.[12]

We all have experienced the truth that Robinson relates. How often have we noticed a slight change in the speech, gait, or memory of an aging parent or friend that shocks us into a recognition that they are failing? It's a sharp and piercing awareness that nips us like a squirrel's teeth. It is the biting realization that our parent or friend is deteriorating, and the change is progressive and irreversible.

There are two basic types of suffering in life. The first is symbolized by Jesus *on* the cross; the second is symbolized by Mary *at the foot* of the cross as she stands by and *watches* a loved one suffer. In a certain sense, Mary's suffering was the greater, for to *watch* a loved one suffer is a far greater agony than to undergo pain itself. This is the type of suffering that Robinson's poem addresses, the suffering that exists within the context of a long enduring relationship. This is the suffering that Teresa must have endured in witnessing the gradual mental deterioration of her friend Sr. Isabel de San Jerónimo. This was one of the "interior [trials]," one of the "worst ones" that Teresa had to bear (F. 26. 2.).

As we witness the gradual deterioration of a loved one whom we have known for years, there is a form of double exposure. We see his or her deteriorating state against the backdrop of how we remember the person in his or her youth. It is the sharp contrast between *what is* and *what was* that is so biting. Add to this the cold fear of what *will be.*

Questions. All of us, like Mary, have stood at "the foot of the Cross," that is, watched a loved one suffer or die. Have you ever considered that your suffering, like hers, can be redemptive if, like Mary, you unite it to Jesus on the Cross?

Reflection. In one of his sermons, St. Augustine says that there are many candidates for community life who seem promising before they enter. However, under the pressure of communal living, they crack. "There have been many who have promised themselves that they would faithfully live a holy life . . . yet when such aspirants were put into the kiln, they cracked."[13]

People who seem to be excellent candidates for religious life *before* they enter sometimes turn out to be nightmares once they do. Such was the case of Beatriz. She seemed promising. She was a very pious woman. Gracián was impressed by her holiness; he "was satisfied with her soul" (F. 26. 12.). However, under the pressure of living a cloistered existence, the cracks of Beatriz's personality began to manifest themselves.

As a child, everything that Beatriz did was interpreted by her parents in the worst light. Teresa writes, "It seems very strange that the parents of this young maiden, a girl who never left her mother's side and whose father was very circumspect, *should think so much evil of their daughter*" (F. 26. 9.) (italics added). Beatriz's parents raised her in an atmosphere of distrust, suspicion, and punishment. Considering the pathological effect that this environment must have had upon Beatriz's personality, we can understand that when she cracked under the pressure of community life, it manifested itself in bizarre and twisted interpretations of Teresa's affection toward Gracián.

Questions. Like Beatriz, the fissures of our personalities are formed in childhood. Have you ever considered that when you are under pressure and are tempted to act out in bizarre ways, that they are understandable in the light of your childhood? Can you be both understanding and compassionate toward yourself during these times of stress?

Chapter 27

Treats of the foundation made in the town of Caravaca. The Blessed Sacrament was reserved on New Year's Day, 1576. The monastery is under the patronage of the glorious St. Joseph.

1. While I was at St. Joseph's in Avila about to leave for the foundation in Beas that was mentioned[1]—for the only thing we had still to prepare was the means of transportation—a private messenger arrived from a lady in Caravaca named Doña Catalina.[2] After hearing a sermon preached by a Father from the Society of Jesus, three young ladies went to her house determined not to leave until a monastery was founded in that town.[3] This action must have been something they had already discussed with this lady who is the one who helped them make the foundation. They belonged to the most important families of that town. The father of one of them was Rodrigo Moya, a very great servant of God and a man of much prudence.[4] Among the three of them they had enough resources to seek to accomplish a project like this. They learned from the Fathers of the Society of Jesus, who have always favored and helped this work, of what our Lord has done in founding these monasteries.

2. Since I saw the desire and fervor of those souls and that they went so far looking for the order of our Lady, I was moved with devotion and there arose in me the desire to help them carry out their good intention. Learning that Caravaca was close to Beas, I took with me a greater number of nuns than I usually do. My intention was to go there after completing the foundation in Beas. According to the letters these ladies sent,

it seemed to me we could come to an agreement. But since the Lord had disposed otherwise, my plans were of little help, as was said when speaking of the foundation in Seville. For they had obtained the license from the council of the Order of Knights in such a way that even though I had made up my mind to go, I had to give up the idea.[5]

3. The truth of the matter is that when I learned in Beas where Caravaca is and saw that it was so out of the way and the road for those who would have to visit the nuns was so bad and that the superiors would be displeased, I had little enthusiasm for making the foundation. But since I had raised the hopes of those ladies, I asked Father Julián de Avila and Antonio Gaytán to go there to see what the place was like and, if they so decided, to cancel the plans. They felt lukewarm toward the project not because of the three who wanted to be nuns but because Doña Catalina who was mainly responsible for the foundation, for she kept these ladies in a separate room by themselves as though they were already enclosed.

4. These nuns, or better, these who were about to become nuns, especially two of them, were so convinced of their vocation that they knew how to gain the goodwill of Father Julián de Avila and Antonio Gaytán. Before returning, these latter two signed the documents of agreement[6] and returned leaving the young ladies very happy. They came back so enthused about these women and the place that they never stopped talking about it, nor did they stop talking about the bad road. Since I saw that the agreement had been reached but that the license was delayed in coming, I sent the good Antonio Gaytán there again who for love of me underwent all the hardship willingly. He and Father Julián de Avila were eager

that the foundation be made. The truth of the matter is that they are the ones who should be thanked for this foundation. If they hadn't gone there and reached an agreement, I would not have bothered about it.

5. I sent Antonio Gaytán to put up the turn and the grille in the house where the nuns were going to live until finding another suitable one. This was the house of Rodrigo de Moya, who, as I mentioned, [7] was the father of one of these ladies, and very willingly allowed them to use a part of his house. Antonio Gaytán remained there doing this work for many days.

6. When they brought the license and I was about ready to depart for Caravaca, I learned from the license that the house would have to be subject to the council of the Order of Knights and obedience given to them, which is something I could not do because we belonged to the Order of Our Lady of Mount Carmel.

And thus, another license was asked for that would not have this condition, for otherwise neither there nor in Beas would a foundation be possible. When I wrote to the king, who at present is Don Philip, he granted me the great favor of issuing orders that the license be granted. [8] The king is so fond of favoring religious who he knows are faithful to their profession that once he had learned of the manner of life in these monasteries and that we follow the primitive rule, he favored us in everything. And thus, daughters, I beg you that special prayer be always offered for his majesty, as is done by us now.

7. Since they had to petition again for the license, I departed for Seville by order of Father Provincial, who was then, and still is, Father Fray Jerónimo Gracián de la Madre de Dios, as was said. [9] And the poor young ladies were enclosed

there until the following New Year's Day. It had been around February when they had sent me a messenger in Avila. The license, then, was obtained in a short time, without delay. But since I was so far away and involved in so many troubles, I was not able to help them. And I felt most sorry for them, for they wrote to me frequently very distressed, and so I could not bear making them wait any longer.

8. Since it was impossible for me to go because I was so far away and the foundation in Seville was not completed, Father Maestro Fray Jerónimo Gracián, who was the apostolic visitator, as was mentioned, ordered those nuns to go, even though I could not go with them, who had been chosen for the foundation and who were waiting at St. Joseph's in Malagón. I arranged for someone to be prioress who I trusted would fulfill the office very well, for she is far better than I.[10] And taking with them all the provisions, they left with two discalced Fathers of our order.[11] Father Julián de Avila and Antonio Gaytán had already returned home some time before, so I did not want them to accompany the Sisters because they were too far away and the weather was so bad, for it was the end of December.

9. When the nuns arrived in the town, they were received with great joy by the people and especially by those women who had been living an enclosed life. They founded the monastery, reserving the Blessed Sacrament, on the feast of the Holy Name of Jesus, in the year 1576.[12] Two of the women immediately took the habit. The other one suffered very much from melancholy. It must have been bad for her to live an enclosed life, and how much more so when it was so strict and penitential. She decided to return home to live with one of her sisters.[13]

10. Reflect, my daughters, on the judgments of God and on our obligation to serve Him who has allowed us to persevere until making profession and to live always in the house of God and be daughters of the Virgin. For His Majesty benefited by the good will of this young lady and by her property so that the monastery could be founded, and when the time came for her to be able to enjoy what she had so desired, she was lacking in fortitude and became subject to the melancholic humor. This latter, daughters, we often blame for our imperfections and inconstancy.

11. May it please His Majesty to give us abundant grace, for with this, nothing will prevent us from advancing ever in His service. And may He protect and favor all of us so that this excellent beginning, which He was pleased to initiate in women as miserable as we, may not be lost through our weakness. In His name I beg you, my daughters and Sisters, that you always ask our Lord for this and that each one who enters in the future bear in mind that with her the observance of the primitive rule of the order of the Virgin, our Lady, begins again and that she must in no way consent to any mitigation. Consider that through very little things the door is opened to very big things, and that without your realizing it the world will start entering your lives. Remember the poverty and hardship that was undergone in obtaining what you now quietly enjoy. If you note carefully, you will see that in part these houses, most of them, have not been founded by men but by the powerful hand of God and that His Majesty is very fond of advancing the works He accomplishes provided we cooperate. From where do you think a useless woman like me, subject to obedience, without even a maravedi, with no one to

help me in any way, could get the power for such great works? For this brother of mine, who helped with the foundation in Seville and had the means, courage, and goodness of soul to help, was in the Indies.[14]

12. See, my daughters, see the hand of God. Well, it could not be because I am from the nobility that He has given me such honor. In whatever way you want to look at this you will recognize that it is His work. It would not be right for us to undermine it in any way. We must not do so even if it cost us our life, honor, and tranquility. Moreover, we have everything here, for to have life is to live in such a way that there is no fear of death or of any of life's happenings, to have an habitual happiness, as you now all have, and to enjoy this prosperity that cannot be surpassed when there is no fear of poverty, but on the contrary desire for it. Well, to what can the interior and exterior peace that you always enjoy be compared? It is in your power to live and to die with this peace, as you have witnessed in those you have seen die in these houses. For if you always ask God to foster this way of life and you trust not at all in yourselves, He will not deny you His mercy. And if you have confidence in Him and have courageous spirits—for His Majesty is very fond of these—you need not fear that He will fail you in anything. Never refuse to accept because they are not wealthy those who ask to become nuns provided they are virtuous and you are pleased with their desires and talents, and they do not come merely as a remedy for their social situation but come to serve God with greater perfection. God in other ways will provide doubly for that which you might lack because of doing this.

13. I have much experience of this. His Majesty knows well that insofar as I can remember I have never refused to

accept anyone because of lack of money, provided I was satisfied with all the rest. The witnesses of this are the many who have been received only for God, as you know. And I can certify that when I received those who brought much wealth I did not feel as great a joy as I did with those I accepted only for God. On the contrary, I had fear about those with wealth, but the poor filled and enlarged my spirit with a happiness so great I wept for joy. This is the truth.

14. Well, if when we had to buy and build houses we got along so well following this procedure, why shouldn't we do so now that we have a place to live? Believe me, daughters, the means by which you think you are accumulating are those by which you will be losing. When the person about to enter has wealth, without any other obligation, it is good that she give it to you as alms instead of giving it to others who have no need of it. For I confess that it would seem to me a lack of love if she didn't do this. But always bear in mind that the one who is about to enter should dispose of her possessions in conformity with what learned men advise her is for the greater service of God. It would be very bad if we were to look for any other good from those who enter this service. We gain much more when she does what she ought for God—I mean with greater perfection—than from all that she brings with her, for none of us is aiming after anything else. Nor may God allow this to happen, but only that His Majesty be served in all and through all.

15. And although I am wretched and miserable, I say this for the honor and glory of God and so that you may rejoice in how these houses of His were founded. Never in any business related to these foundations, nor in anything that happened

relative to them, did I do anything or would I have done anything—I mean with regard to these foundations—that I understood to go contrary to the will of God in even one point, and this, too, when I thought that in order to succeed I would have to cover up my intentions. I proceeded according to what my confessors advised me, for since I have been working on these foundations, my confessors have always been very learned men and great servants of God, as you know. Nor, insofar as I remember, did anything else pass through my mind than to proceed in this way.

16. Perhaps I am mistaken and have done many things wrong without realizing it; and the imperfections are countless. Our Lord who is the true judge knows that my intentions were good, insofar as I could discern concerning myself, I mean. Also, I see clearly that this good did not come from me but from God who willed that this work be done, and because it was His work He favored me and granted this gift. The reason why I'm telling you this, my daughters, is that you may understand how obliged you are and know that so far nothing offensive has been done to anyone. May He who has done everything be blessed and may charity be awakened in the persons who have helped us. May it please His Majesty to protect us always and give us His grace so that we will not be ungrateful for so many favors, amen.[15]

17. You have seen, daughters, that we have undergone some trials, although I believe I have written about the least part of them. For it would be tiresome if I had to describe in detail the roads, the rain and snow, and getting lost and, above all, frequently, my very poor health. With regard to this latter it happened to me—I don't know if I mentioned

it—that on the first day of our journey from Malagón to Beas I was traveling with a fever and so many illnesses all together that while considering the distance we still had to travel and seeing myself in this condition I remembered our Father Elijah when he was fleeing from Jezebel, and said, "Lord, how can I suffer this? You take care."[16] The truth is that when His Majesty saw me so weak, He suddenly took away my fever and illness. This so happened that afterward when I thought about it I figured that perhaps it was because a priest, a servant of God, was going to enter the order there;[17] at least the exterior and interior illnesses were suddenly taken away. When I had good health, I underwent the bodily hardships with joy.

18. Well, putting up with the many different personalities one necessarily finds in every town caused no small amount of trouble. And to leave my daughters and Sisters when going from one place to another, was not the smallest cross, I tell you, since I love them so much; especially when I thought I was not going to return to see them again and I saw their great sadness and tears. Even though they are detached from other things, God has not given them the gift to be detached from me, perhaps so that it might be a greater torment to me, for I am not detached from them either, even though I forced myself as much as I could so as not to show it and I reprimanded them. But this was of little help since their love for me is great, and in many ways it is obvious that this love is true.

19. You have heard how it was not just with the permission of our Most Reverend Father General that these foundations were made but that I was ordered under obedience by him afterward to do so.[18] And not only this, but he used to write to me about the great joy each new house that was founded gave

him. Assuredly, the greatest relief I experienced in the midst of the trials was to see the happiness this work gave to him, for it seemed to me that by giving him this happiness I was serving our Lord since he is my major superior, and besides this I love him much.

20. That which came about next did so either because His Majesty desired to give me some rest or because the devil was displeased that so many houses were being founded where our Lord was being served. (It was easy to understand that what came about was not the will of our Father General because he had written me not many years before in answer to my request not to found any more houses that he would not stop ordering me to do so because he wanted me to make as many foundations as I had hairs on my head.) Before I came back from Seville, a general chapter was held. In a general chapter one would think they would be concerned about the expansion of the order, but instead the definitory gave me a command not merely to make no more foundations but not to leave the house in which I chose to reside, which would be a kind of prison, for there is no nun who for necessary matters pertaining to the good of the order cannot be ordered by the provincial to go from one place to another, I mean from one monastery to another. And what was worse and what made me sad was that our Father General was displeased with me, without any reason at all, because of information given by biased persons.[19]

Along with this I was told of two other serious calumnies that were raised against me. I tell you, Sisters, so that you will see the mercy of our Lord and how His Majesty does not abandon the one who desires to serve Him. For these calumnies not only failed to make me sad but gave me so great an accidental joy[20] that I could not restrain myself. As a result, I'm not surprised at what David did when he went before the ark of the Lord,[21] for because of my joy which I didn't know how to conceal I wanted to do nothing else at the time. I don't know the reason, for this has never happened to me in all the other great criticism and opposition I have received. Moreover, one of these two calumnies spoken against me was most serious. But the command not to make foundations—aside from the displeasure of our Most Reverend Father General—brought me great tranquility and was what I was often desiring: to end my days in quiet. But this was not what those who devised this were intending. They wanted to inflict on me the greatest sorrow in the world, and perhaps they may have had other good intentions.

21. On occasion, also, the strong opposition and criticism (sometimes offered with good intentions and at other times for other purposes) that I received in making these foundations gave me great joy. But I don't ever remember, no matter how much the hardship, experiencing happiness as great as I did in this instance. For I confess that at other times any one of these three things that came all together would have been a severe trial for me. I believe that my main joy came from my thinking that since creatures repaid me like this I was pleasing the Creator. For I am convinced that he who looks for joy in earthly things or in words of praise from men is very much mistaken, without mentioning the little advantage there is in them. Today people will think one thing, tomorrow another; at one time they will speak well of something; soon they will speak badly of it. May You be blessed, my Lord and my God,

for You are unchangeable forever and ever, amen. The one who serves unto the end will live without end in Your eternity.[22]

22. I began to write about these foundations by order of Father Maestro Ripalda of the Society of Jesus, as I said at the beginning,[23] for he was then the rector of the College in Salamanca and my confessor. While I was in the monastery of St. Joseph in that city in 1573, I wrote about some of these foundations. But because of my many duties I set the work aside. I did not want to continue, for Father Ripalda was no longer my confessor, and we lived in different places, and also because of the great hardship and trials that what I have written cost me; although since I was always ordered to do so under obedience, I consider them well worthwhile. Though I was determined to write no more, the apostolic commissary, who is now Maestro Fray Jerónimo Gracián de la Madre de Dios, ordered me to finish the account of these foundations. Being wretched in the practice of obedience, I told him of the little opportunity I had and other things that came to my mind and also that the task was very tiring for me on top of all the other things I had to do. Nonetheless, he ordered me to finish them little by little as best I could. This I did submitting in everything to what those who know about these things might want to delete. What is poorly expressed, let them delete, for perhaps what seems to me better will sound bad to them.

I have finished today, the vigil of St. Eugene, the fourteenth day of the month of November in the year 1576 in the monastery of St. Joseph in Toledo. This is where I now reside by order of Father Apostolic Commissary, Maestro Fray Jerónimo Gracián de la Madre de Dios, who we now have as superior for the discalced friars and nuns of the primitive rule, and who is also visitator for those of the mitigated rule living in Andalusia. May this work contribute to the honor and glory of our Lord Jesus Christ who reigns and will reign forever, amen.

For the love of our Lord, I beg the Sisters and Brothers who might read this to recommend me to our Lord that He might have mercy on me and free me from the pains of purgatory, if I should be there, and let me enjoy Him. Since you will not see this while I am living, may the weariness I experienced in writing it as well as the great desire I had to say something that would be consoling to you, if you are allowed to read it, be of some benefit to me after my death.[24]

CARAVACA

Summary and Background: Chapter 27

When Teresa was in Avila making preparations for the foundation in Beas, she received a request from a wealthy widow named Doña Catalina de Otalora to come to Caravaca to make a foundation. Doña Catalina made this request at the entreaty of three young ladies, who after hearing an inspiring sermon, determined to enter a convent. Since Caravaca had no convent, Doña Catalina was eager to provide one for her three supplicants.

Teresa accepted the request. "Learning that Caravaca was close to Beas, I took with me a greater number of nuns than I usually do. My intention was to go there after completing the foundation in Beas" (F. 27. 2.). However, as we said earlier, Teresa's plans to go to Caravaca were put on hold because the license that she had received to make the foundation "contained so many unsuitable requirements that [she] did not want to proceed with [the foundation]" (LE. 1. 83. 2.). One condition that was unacceptable to Teresa was that the convent be subject to the Order of Santiago. Teresa wrote to King Philip concerning this matter and was granted an exemption on June 9, 1575, two weeks *after* she had arrived in Seville.

Since Teresa was personally involved in establishing the monastery in Seville, she made the foundation in Caravaca by proxy. From Seville, she sent to Caravaca a contingent of nuns, accompanied by Julián of Avila and

Antonio Gaytán. Even though the nuns were "received with great joy by the people" (F. 27. 9.), things did not turn out as originally expected.

First, of the three women who had asked Doña Catalina de Otalora to establish a convent in Caravaca, only two entered. The third person [Francisca de Saojosa] changed her mind because she "suffered very much from melancholy" (F. 27. 9.). However, she reapplied and through the intercession of Gracián was admitted a year later.

Second, Doña Catalina de Otalora, who promised that she would underwrite the cost of the foundation, wasn't able to provide adequate funds for the project. In addition, even though King Philip had exempted the Caravaca foundation from being under the jurisdiction of the Knights of Santiago, the convent was required to pay tithes to the Knights. It was within the context of these two financial factors that, in this chapter, Teresa writes about poverty, finances, and the whole issue of accepting candidates without a dowry (F. 27. 11–14.).

Teresa tells her nuns that they should "[n]ever refuse to accept because they are not wealthy those who ask to become nuns provided that they are virtuous . . . insofar as I can remember I have never refused to accept anyone because of lack of money, provided I was satisfied with all the rest" (F. 27. 12–13.). This is Teresa's ideal. Nevertheless, she also knew that a dowry or lack of one often meant the difference between having a roof over one's head and being out in the cold. For example, while Teresa was in Seville, scrambling to obtain funds to purchase a house, she wrote to María Bautista, the prioress of Valladolid, "A candidate wants to enter who is rich and good. If she enters, we will at once look for a house" (LE. 1. 88. 15.).

Beginning with paragraph fifteen, Teresa shifts her focus from the financial concerns of the Caravaca foundation to her justification for founding convents in Andalusia. She writes in such an apologetic tone that one gets the impression that she is standing in the dock giving testimony under oath. "And although I am wretched and miserable . . . I have never in any business related to these foundations, nor in anything that happened relative to them . . . done anything contrary to the will of God in even one point" (F. 27. 15.).

What Teresa is "testifying" to is that she was ignorant of the fact that the foundations of Beas and Seville were in the jurisdiction of Andalusia, a province in which she did not have permission to found convents. This violation of territorial jurisdiction caused an uproar among the Calced Carmelties of Andalusia. As a result, the general chapter of the Carmelite order that was held in Piacenza, Italy, in May and June of 1575, decreed that Teresa retire to one of her monasteries in Castille and cease making new foundations.

"[I was given] a command not merely to make no more foundations but not to leave the house in which I chose to reside [in Castille], which would be a kind of prison" (F. 27. 20.). Teresa welcomed this confinement as a time of rest. "[T]he command not to make foundations . . . brought me great tranquility and was what I was often desiring: to end my days in quiet" (F. 27. 20.). She chose to live in Toledo.

Why Teresa chose to live in the monastery in Toledo is open to speculation. It has been suggested that besides the mild climate, one of the major factors that determined Teresa's choice was her friendship with the local postmaster. Since Teresa knew that she would be confined to quarters for an indeterminate period of time, she wanted to provide a means of staying in contact with her foundations. This she did. In the years that Teresa was in Toledo, she wrote almost one hundred letters, through which she stayed involved with the monasteries that she had established. In addition, during her stay in Toledo, Teresa continued to write the *Foundations* and *The Interior Castle*.

Approximately eight month after Teresa was ordered to retire to a community in Castille, the foundation at Caravaca was established (January 1, 1576). Though Teresa never went to Caravaca, the community held a special place in her heart. For the rest of her life, she carried with her a reproduction of the Cross of Caravaca, which was discovered between the sheets of her deathbed.

Reflection. Teresa headed home to Castille, feeling relief from both the oppressive climate of Andalusia and the Andalusians themselves. In Andalusia, Teresa felt outside of her element. "I do not fare well with these people" (LE. 1. 83. 2.). "I have little in common with the people of Andalusia" (LE. 1. 102. 14.). In addition, Teresa did not have a high opinion of the Andalusians. "The injustices that are the common practices in this area, the deception and the duplicity are a strange thing. I tell you, there is every reason for the reputation this region has" (LE. 1. 105. 2.).

There was a clash of cultures between Teresa and the Andalusians. Teresa's Castilian temperament and the culture in which she had been reared were at odds with the people of Andalusia. Yet, in spite of her feelings, Teresa had to both live and work with Andalusians. Is it any different with us? We live and work with people whose personalities, temperaments, and cultural differences grate on our nerves—people with whom we "have little in common."

Questions. Teresa wrote "I do no fare well with these people." Who are "these people" in your life? Nevertheless, we know that Teresa managed to live and work with "these people." Where do you find the strength to restrain your feelings of irritation or animosity toward "these people"? Have you ever considered that a choice to simply be polite to "these people" may actually be an act of charity, one that demands all your strength? And have you ever considered your effort as your cooperation with divine grace?

Reflection. About six months before she died, Teresa returned to her first foundation, St. Joseph's in Avila, and was brokenhearted at what she saw. Not only was the foundation in financial trouble, but, more importantly, it had deteriorated spiritually. "[T]he nuns at St. Joseph's in Avila are such that there would be no longer a difference between them and the nuns at the Incarnation" (LE. 2. 277. 2.). The poignancy of these words lies in the fact that Teresa feared that her reform of religious life, the very reason why she had left the Incarnation, her whole life's work was crumbling before her eyes.

This was not a new concern for Teresa. In this chapter of the *Foundations*, Teresa prays, "[May God] protect and favor all of us so that this excellent beginning . . . may not be lost through our weakness . . . I beg you my daughters and Sisters, that you always ask our Lord for this . . . and in no way consent to any mitigation. Consider that through very little things the door is opened to very big things, and that without your realizing it the world will start entering into your lives. Remember the poverty and hardship that was undergone in obtaining what you now quietly enjoy" (F. 27. 11.).

Similarly, Teresa wrote to Maria de San José, the prioress of Seville, regarding the mitigation of the lifestyle of the community at Caravaca. "I am writing [Gracián] with much insistence that he not allow anyone to eat in the monastery parlor—see that you don't start something" (LE. 1. 109. 2.). In the same vein, Teresa also wrote to Gracián about the Seville community. "You ought to give orders that the nuns should in no way offer anyone something to eat in the parlor, for this becomes a great disturbance for them" (LE. 1. 108. 11.).

Teresa's concern about the nuns serving food in the front parlor is that it is the first step in the erosion of her reform. It is the crack in the door through which silence and solitude will be lost. It is the beginning of the erosion of the contemplative way of life that Teresa left the Incarnation to establish. It is the loosening of discipline, which in due time will erase any "difference between [Teresa's nuns] and the nuns at the Incarnation" (LE. 2. 277. 2.). In short, Teresa's fears are about the eradication of her life's work.

Is not this a fear that we sometimes experience? Take the example of a man who invested his entire life into building a successful business. When he retires, he hands over the business to his children. Through their mismanagement, the business goes bankrupt within three years. In a similar vein, think of an elderly widow who has moved into an apartment because she cannot take care of the house that she and her husband had lived in all of their lives. She hands over ownership of the house to her son and his family. As time passes, she become sick at heart as she watches the house that she and her beloved husband had taken such pride in and kept up so well fall into disrepair.

Questions. Ultimately, Teresa had to relinquish control and entrust her life's work to others. This required a deep form of detachment. Have you ever invested so much of your self in either your work or your possessions that you were afraid to entrust them to others? What are the spiritual consequences in your life when you cannot relinquish control? Have you ever experienced God's peace when you were able to relinquish control?

Chapter 28

The foundation in Villanueva de la Jara.[1]

1. The foundation in Seville, made more than four years ago,[2] was the last one. It was the last because of the great persecutions that broke out unexpectedly against the discalced friars and nuns. Although there had been many persecutions before, they were not so extreme. Now the whole undertaking was at the point of collapse. It was clearly seen how much the devil resented this holy beginning, which our Lord had initiated, and also that this was the Lord's own work since it was growing. The discalced friars suffered very much, especially the superiors, from serious false testimony and opposition on the part of almost all the calced Fathers.[3]

2. These Fathers informed our Most Reverend Father General[4] in such a way that even though he was a holy man and had given permission for all the monasteries (with the exception of St. Joseph's in Avila, which was the first, for this was founded with the permission of the pope), he was urged to oppose strongly any new foundations among the discalced friars. Toward the monasteries of the nuns, he was always well disposed. And so that I might not be helping the friars make foundations, he was induced into becoming displeased with me, which was the greatest trial I suffered in the work of these foundations, even though I have suffered many. On the one hand, very learned men who were my confessors would not agree that I should stop and counseled me to help toward the growth of the work, pointing out that I clearly rendered service to our Lord and helped toward the increase of our order;

and on the other hand, going against the will of my superior was like a death to me. For apart from the obligation I had toward him because he was my superior, I loved him very tenderly and there were many reasons for obeying him. It is true that even though I wanted to please him by obeying this order, I could not because there were apostolic visitators whom I was obliged to obey.[5]

3. A holy nuncio died who greatly promoted virtue and, as a result, esteemed the discalced. Another nuncio arrived who it seems had been sent by God to test us in suffering. He was a distant relative of the pope, and he must be a servant of God, but he began to take seriously to favoring the calced[6] and in conformity with the information they gave him about us he was convinced that the right thing to do was to put a stop to these foundations. Thus, he began to act with the greatest severity, condemning those he thought could oppose him by imprisoning them or sending them into exile.

4. Those who suffered most were: Father Fray Antonio de Jesús, who was the one who started the first monastery of discalced friars; Fray Jerónimo Gracián, whom the former nuncio made apostolic visitator to the Fathers of the cloth[7] and with whom the new nuncio was greatly displeased; and Father Mariano de San Benito. I have already mentioned who these Fathers are in writing of the preceding foundations. On other friars, among the more outstanding ones, he imposed penances, although not so severe. He issued many censures to prevent them from carrying on any business.

5. It is obvious that all this came from God and that His Majesty permitted it for a greater good and so that the virtue of these Fathers would be better known. The nuncio appointed

a superior from the Fathers of the cloth to visit the monasteries of our friars and nuns,[8] which would have been a great hardship for us if what he thought was going on had been a fact. Still, the hardship that was suffered was very great. This will be recorded in writing by someone who knows better how to write about it. I am only touching on the matter so that the nuns that are to come will know how obliged they are to advance in perfection, since from that which has cost so much to those who are now living they will benefit free of trouble. For some of the nuns now living have suffered very much in these times from serious false testimony, which grieved me far more than what I was undergoing, for this latter was rather a great delight for me. It seemed to me that I was the cause of this storm, and that if they would have thrown me into the sea, as they did Jonah, the tempest would have stopped.[9]

6. May God who favors truth be praised! And this is what happened here, for since our Catholic king, Don Philip, knew of what was going on and was informed of the life and religious observance of the discalced, he took the initiative to favor us. Thus, he did not want our cause to be judged by the nuncio alone but gave him four counselors, responsible persons, three of whom were religious, so that our rights would be carefully looked after.[10] One of these was the Father Maestro Fray Pedro Fernández, a person of very holy life, great learning and intelligence. He had been apostolic commissary and visitator of the Fathers of the cloth in the Castile province, and we discalced had also been subject to him. He knew well the truth about how each group lived, for the desire of us all was nothing other than that this be known. And so when I saw that the king had named him, I considered the matter taken

care of, as by the mercy of God it is. May it please His Majesty that this all be for His honor and glory. Although there were many noblemen and bishops who made haste to inform the nuncio of the truth, all this would have benefited little if God had not chosen the king to intervene.

7. We are all very much obliged in our prayers to our Lord, Sisters, to recommend the king and those who have helped this cause. It is the Lord's cause and our Lady's, the Blessed Virgin's, and so I urge you to do this. Well you can imagine, Sisters, what little possibility there was for making any foundations. We were all occupied unceasingly in prayers and penances so that our Lord would preserve the houses already founded if doing so would be for His service.

8. I was in Toledo when these great trials started, which described so briefly will seem small to you but when suffered for so long a time were very great. I had arrived there from the foundation in Seville in 1576. A priest from Villanueva de la Jara brought me letters from the town council there. He came to negotiate with me and ask that I accept as a monastery a shrine in that town dedicated to the glorious St. Anne where nine women were living together. This shrine has a little house nearby where for some years these women were living with so much recollection and holiness that the whole town was moved to seek to help them attain their desires to become nuns. I also received a letter from a doctor, a priest in this town, named Agustín de Ervías,[11] a learned man of great virtue. Because of his virtue he was moved to help this holy work as much as he could.

9. It seemed to me that for the following reasons it would have been completely unsuitable to accept this foundation:

First, there were so many women, and it seemed to me it would be very difficult for them to adapt to our way of life when they were used to their own. Second, they had almost nothing to live on, and the population of the place is little more than a thousand which is not much help for living on alms. (Although the town council offered to support them, it didn't seem to me to be a stable offer). Third, they didn't have a house. Fourth, the place was far from where these other monasteries were located. Fifth, although I was told that these women were very good, I had not seen them and so could not verify whether they had the qualities we require for these monasteries. Thus I decided to turn down the proposal entirely.

10. Before doing so, I wanted to speak with my confessor who was Doctor Velázquez, a canon and professor in Toledo, a very learned and virtuous man, who is now bishop of Osma.[12] For it is always my custom never to do anything on my own but rather to seek the opinion of persons like him. When he saw the letters and understood the matter he told me not to turn the proposal down but to answer in a friendly manner, for when God has joined so many hearts for the sake of something, one may suppose that He will be served by it. This I did, for I neither accepted it entirely nor turned it down. They continued entreating and getting influential persons to intercede with me until this year 1580. My opinion was always that it would be foolish to agree to this request. When I responded I could never give a completely negative answer.

11. It happened that when Father Fray Antonio de Jesús completed his time of exile at the monastery of our Lady of Succor,[13] he went to preach in Villanueva which is three leagues away. And the present prior of this monastery, Father

Fray Gabriel de la Asunción, a person of very good judgment and a servant of God, also came often to this town,[14] for he and Father Antonio were friends of Doctor Ervías, and they began to converse with these holy Sisters. Becoming admirers of their virtue and persuaded by the townspeople and the doctor, they took this matter upon themselves as their own and through letters tried very hard to persuade me. And while I was at St. Joseph's in Malagón, which is more than twenty-six leagues from Villanueva, this prior came to speak to me about this foundation, giving me an account of what could be done and how after it was made Doctor Ervías would give three hundred ducats income from what he received from his benefice; that permission would be obtained from Rome.

12. This looked very unsure, since it seemed to me that after the foundation was made they would drag their feet saying that the little the Sisters had was quite enough. And then I put forth many reasons, in my opinion sufficient, to convince Father Prior that it would not be suitable to make a foundation, and I said that he and Father Antonio should consider these carefully; and I left the matter on their conscience, thinking that what I had said sufficed for refusing to make the foundation.

13. After he had gone, I considered how much in favor he was of the foundation and that he would persuade the superior we now have, who is Fray Angel de Salazar, to accept it. I wrote to the latter with haste begging him not to give this permission and telling him the reasons. From what he wrote to me afterward, he would not have wanted to give the permission unless the foundation seemed to me a good thing.

14. A month and a half went by, or perhaps a little more. When I thought I had put a stop to the matter, a messenger

came with letters from the town council, which took on the obligation to provide for the needs of the monastery, from Doctor Ervías who obliged himself to what I mentioned, and—very enthusiastic ones—from these two Reverend Fathers. I found myself very confused. On the one hand, I had great fear of admitting so many Sisters thinking that as usually happens they would band together against those others who would join them; and on the other hand, I did not see a sure means for their support, because that which was offered amounted to nothing very impressive. Afterward I understood that my confusion was from the devil, for even though the Lord had given me so much courage, I had become fainthearted to the point that it doesn't seem I was trusting God at all. But the prayers of those good souls in the end prevailed.

15. One day after I received Communion I was recommending this matter to God as I often used to do. For what made me answer them somewhat favorably was the fear of hindering spiritual progress in souls, for my desire is always to be some means by which our Lord may be praised and that there be more to serve Him. While I was praying in this way, His Majesty reprimanded me sternly, asking me with what treasures that which had been done so far had been accomplished and telling me that I should not hesitate to accept this house, that it would be for His great service and the spiritual progress of souls.

16. Since these locutions from God are so powerful, not only does the intellect understand them but it is enlightened so as to understand the truth, and the will is disposed to the desire to carry them out; and this is what happened to me. For not only was I glad to accept the foundation but it seemed to

me that I had been at fault in delaying so long and being tied to human reason when the works I had seen His Majesty do for this sacred religious order were so beyond reason.

17. Having decided to accept this foundation, it seemed to me necessary, for many reasons that occurred to me, that I go with the nuns who were to live there. My human nature resisted very much, for I had arrived in Malagón[15] very sick and have always been so. But since I thought the foundation would serve our Lord, I wrote to my superior to order me to do what he thought best. He sent the license for the foundation and the command that I go personally and bring the nuns of my choice. This latter worried me a great deal since the nuns would have to live with those women who were already there. Praying to our Lord very much over this matter, I took two from the monastery of St. Joseph's in Toledo, one of them for prioress, and two from Malagón, one of them for subprioress.[16] Since we had prayed so much to His Majesty, things turned out very well, which to me was no small matter; for in the foundations that we began by ourselves alone, the nuns adapt to each other well.

18. Father Fray Antonio de Jesús and Father Fray Gabriel de la Asunción came for us. Given an assurance of help from the town, we left Malagón on the Saturday before Lent, the thirteenth of February in 1580. God was pleased to make the weather so good and give me such health that it seemed to me I had never been sick. I was surprised and reflected on how very important it is not to consider our weak state of health or any opposition that occurs when we understand that something serves the Lord since God is powerful enough to make the weak strong and the sick healthy. And when our Lord does

not do this, suffering will be the best thing for our souls; and fixing our eyes on His honor and glory, we should forget ourselves. What is the purpose of life and health save that they be lost for so great a King and Lord? Believe me, Sisters, you will never go astray in following this path.

19. I confess that my wretchedness and weakness have often made me fear and doubt. But I don't remember that from the time the Lord gave me the habit of a discalced nun, and some time before this, He ever failed to grant me the favor, solely out of His mercy, to conquer these temptations and throw myself into what I understood to be for His greater service however difficult it was. I understood clearly that what I did for my part was little, but God wants no more than our determination so that He may do everything Himself. May He be forever blessed and praised, amen.

20. We had to go to the monastery of our Lady of Succor, already mentioned,[17] which is three leagues from Villanueva, and stay there so as to inform the town that we were coming, which had been agreed upon with these Fathers, and it was right that in everything I obey these Fathers with whom we were traveling. This house stood in a delightfully isolated and solitary spot. And as we approached, the friars came out in procession to meet their prior. Since they were discalced and wore their poor, coarse woolen mantles, they inspired us all with devotion and moved me to tender feelings since it seemed to me that I was present in that flourishing time of our holy Fathers of old. In that field, they appeared to be like white fragrant flowers, and indeed I believe that before God they are, for in my opinion He is authentically served there. They entered the church singing the Te Deum with voices

very restrained. The entrance to it is underground, as though through a cave, which represented that of our Father Elijah.[18] Certainly, I was feeling so much interior joy that I would have considered a longer journey well worthwhile. I regretted very much that the saintly woman through whom our Lord founded this house was now dead. I didn't deserve to see her, although I had desired to do so very much.[19]

21. It seems to me that it would not be an idle thing to tell something here about her life and the means by which our Lord desired that this monastery be founded there. It has been of such benefits to souls in the surrounding area, as I have been told. On seeing the penance that was done by this holy woman, may you realize, my Sisters, how far behind we are and may you try harder to serve our Lord. There is no reason that we should do less, for we do not come from such noble and refined family descent. Although this is not important, I am mentioning it because she had lived a comfortable life in keeping with her status in society, for she was a descendant of the dukes of Cardona and thus she was called Doña Catalina de Cardona.[20] After she had written to me a few times, she signed her letter with only the words, "the sinner."

22. Those who will write about her life will recount more in detail the many things that could be said about it before the Lord began to grant her such great favors. But in case you might not come to know of it, I will tell here what some trustworthy persons who knew her told me.

23. While this saintly woman was living among the nobility, she was always very concerned about her soul and did penance. The desire for penance greatly increased in her and also the longing to go where she could be alone to enjoy God

and dedicate herself to doing penance without any hindrance. She spoke of this with her confessors, but they did not give their consent. I am not surprised that this seemed madness to them, since nowadays the world is very rooted in discretion and has almost forgotten the great favors God granted to the many holy men and women who served Him in the desert. But since His Majesty always favors authentic desires, enabling one to carry them out, He ordained that she go for confession to a Franciscan Father whose name is Fray Francisco de Torres. I know him well and consider him a saint. For many years he has been living a life of intense fervor, penance, and prayer, and been suffering many persecutions. He must know well the favors God grants to those who strive to receive them, and thus he told her not to give up but to follow the calling His Majesty granted her. I don't know if these were the exact words, but they must have been something like this since she carried them out at once.

24. She disclosed her plans to a hermit who was living in Alcalá and, without ever telling anyone about them, asked him to accompany her.[21] They arrived at the place where the monastery now stands, and there she found a tiny cave hardly large enough for her; here he left her. But what love must have been hers since she wasn't worried about what there might be to eat or about the dangerous things that could happen to her, or about the bad reputation she would have when it was discovered that she had disappeared. How inebriated must have been this holy soul, so absorbed in not letting anyone prevent her from enjoying her Spouse. And how determined she was not to love the world, since she thus fled from all its satisfactions.

25. Let us consider this well, Sisters, and reflect on how with one blow she conquered everything. For although what you do by entering this holy religious order, offering your will to God, and professing so continual an enclosure may not be less, I wonder whether, in the case of some, a part of this initial fervor does not pass away and out of self-love we make ourselves subject again to some things. May it please the divine Majesty that this not be so, but that since we imitate this holy woman in desiring to flee from the world we may interiorly stay far away from it in all things.

26. I have heard many things about the harsh austerity of her life, and what is known must be the smallest part of it. She must have treated her body terribly because she lived for many years in that solitude with such great desires to do penance and no one to restrain her. I will mention what some persons heard from her directly as well as what the nuns at St. Joseph's in Toledo heard. She went to visit these latter and spoke with them as candidly as with her own sisters. She spoke thus with other persons, too, for her simplicity and humility must have been great. And as one who was convinced that she had nothing of herself, she was far removed from any kind of vainglory and she enjoyed telling about the favors God granted her so that through them His name might be praised and glorified. Doing this would be dangerous for those who have not reached this state, for, at least, it will seem that they are praising themselves. But her candidness and holy simplicity must have freed her from this fault, for I never heard anyone accuse her of it.

27. She said that she had been living in that cave eight years and that on many days she ate only herbs and roots

from the field, for after the three loaves of bread given her by the hermit who accompanied her were gone, she had no more until met by a little shepherd who was passing by. Afterward, he provided her with bread and flour, with which she made small cakes baked over the fire. This was all she ate, and she did so only on each third day. This fact is very certain, for even the friars who are there testify to it, and this went on after she was already very thin and wasted. Sometimes when she went to speak with the friars about how to found a monastery they made her eat a sardine, or other things,[22] and rather than benefit from this she was harmed. She never drank wine as far as I know. She took the discipline with a heavy chain, and it used to last often two hours or an hour and a half. The chains she wore were extremely sharp, for a person told me (a woman)[23] that in going there on pilgrimage she remained for the night and feigning sleep she saw her taking the chains off and cleaning them since they were full of blood. But according to what she told the nuns I mentioned,[24] that which she underwent with the devils was greater, for they appeared to her as huge dogs, and jumped up on her shoulders, and at other times as snakes. She had no fear at all of them.

28. After the monastery was built, she still used to go to her cave, sleep there, and remain there except when she attended the Divine Office. And before the monastery was founded she used to go for Mass to that of the Mercedarians,[25] which was a quarter of a league away; and sometimes she went on her knees. Her garb was made of coarse cloth, and her inner tunic of rough wool,[26] made in such a way that she was thought to be a man.

After these years that she lived there in such solitude, our Lord desired that her way of life become known, and the people began to venerate her so much that she could not get away from them. She spoke to everyone with great charity and love. As time went on, a greater concourse of people came; and those who were able to speak to her considered themselves lucky. She was so worn out from this that she said they were killing her. There were days when the whole field was almost filled with wagons. After the friars came there, there was no other remedy than for them to have her lifted up high so that she could bless all the people, and with that they were freed of them. After eight years in which she lived in the cave (which was now larger, for it had been made so by those who had gone there), she became so sick that she thought she was going to die, and she suffered it all in that cave.

29. She began to have desires that a monastery of friars be founded there, and these persisted for some time without her knowing from which order they would come. Once while praying before a crucifix she always carried with her, our Lord showed her a white mantle, and she understood that they would come from the discalced Carmelites, and she had never known that there were friars like this in the world. At the time only two monasteries of friars had been founded, Mancera and Pastrana. After this experience, she must have inquired. When she learned there was a monastery in Pastrana and since she had been in the past a close friend of the Princess of Eboli, wife of Prince Ruy Gómez, to whom Pastrana belonged, she went there to find out how she might make this foundation which she had been desiring so much.

30. There at the monastery of Pastrana, in the church of St. Peter, for this it is called, she received the habit of our Lady,[27] although not with the intention of being a nun or of

making profession, for she was never inclined toward being a nun since our Lord was leading her by another path. It seemed to her that if she professed obedience her plan to live in harsh austerity and solitude would be frustrated. All the friars were present when she received the habit of our Lady of Mt. Carmel.

31. In their company was Father Mariano, who I mentioned in these foundations.[28] He told me that he himself had experienced at the time a suspension or rapture that carried him completely out of himself and that while in this state he saw many dead friars and nuns. Some were beheaded, some had their arms and feet cut off as though they were martyred, for martyrdom is what this vision was pointing to. And he is not the type of man who would tell what he had not seen, nor has his spirit ever been accustomed to these suspensions, for God does not lead him by such a path. Pray to God, Sisters, that this vision will come true and that we will merit in our times to see so great a blessing and be ourselves among the martyrs.

32. From here, that is, from Pastrana, the holy woman of Cardona began to seek the means to found her monastery and for this purpose she went back to the court which she had so eagerly left before. Doing this must have been no small torment; it was a place where she underwent much criticism and trial. When she left the house where she was staying, she wasn't able to protect herself from the crowd. This happened wherever she went. Some cut pieces from her habit, others from her mantle. She then went to Toledo where she stayed with our nuns. All of them have affirmed to me that the odor of sanctity emanating from her was so great that it permeated

even her cincture and habit, which she exchanged for another given her by the nuns; it was something to praise God for. And the closer they came to her the greater was this fragrance, even though her manner of dress, because of the intense heat, would rather have caused a bad odor. I know that they wouldn't say anything but the complete truth, and thus they were left with great devotion.

33. In the court and elsewhere they gave her the means for the monastery, and once she obtained the license, it was founded. The church was built at the place where her cave was. Another cave was made for her further away in which she had a tomb carved out,[29] and she remained there most of the day and night. She lived this way only a short time, for about five and a half years after the monastery was built. That she lived even as long as she did seemed supernatural because of her harsh, austere life. Insofar as I can remember, she died in 1577. Her funeral services were held with greatest solemnity, for a gentleman named Fray Juan de León[30] had great devotion to her and arranged it all with much care. She is now buried temporarily in a chapel of our Lady, to whom she was extremely devoted, until a church larger than the one they have now will be built to keep her blessed body as is fitting.

34. Great is the devotion they have to her in this monastery, and it seems it remained there and in the surrounding area, especially when they beheld that solitude and cave in which she lived. The friars have testified to me that before she decided to found the monastery, she became so wearied and afflicted at seeing the large number of people coming to see her that she wanted to go to another place where no one would know of her. She sent for the hermit who brought her

there so that he might bring her elsewhere, but he was dead. And our Lord who was resolved that this house of our Lady be founded there did not allow her to leave, for as I have said,[31] I know He is served very much there. The friars have all that is necessary for their way of life, and it is clear that they like to be isolated from people; especially the prior,[32] for God also drew him away from a life of much luxury and has repaid him with special consolation.

35. The prior was very charitable toward us. The friars contributed to our foundation from what they had in the church, for since this holy woman was much loved by so many noble persons, their church was well provided with sacred furnishings. I was very much consoled during the time I was there, although this was accompanied by much shame which continues. I saw that the one who had done such harsh penance there was a woman like me, but more delicate because of her background, and not so great a sinner as I. For in this matter there is no comparison between us, and I have received much greater favors of many kinds from our Lord, and that I am not in hell because of my sins is among the greatest of favors. The desire alone to imitate her, if I could, consoled me; but not much, for all my life has passed in desires, but the deeds I do not perform. May the mercy of God help me. In Him I have always trusted through His most sacred Son and the Virgin, our Lady, whose habit I wear through the goodness of the Lord.

36. One day when I had just received Communion in that holy church, very great recollection came over me with suspension that drew me out of myself. In this suspension, through an intellectual vision, this holy woman appeared in a glorified body and some angels with her. She told me not to

grow weary but that I should strive to go ahead with these foundations. I understood, although she did not indicate this, that she was helping me before God. She also told me something else but there is no reason to put it here in writing. I was left very much consoled and with a great desire to work hard, and I hope in the goodness of the Lord that with help as good as are these prayers of hers I will be able to serve Him in some way.

You can see here, my Sisters, how her trials have now come to an end, but the glory she enjoys will have no end. Let us now force ourselves for love of our Lord, to follow this sister of ours. Holding ourselves in abhorrence as she abhorred herself, we will finish our day's journey, for it goes by so quickly and all comes to an end.

37. We arrived in Villanueva de la Jara on the first Sunday of Lent, the feast of St. Barbaciani,[33] the vigil of the feast of the Chair of St. Peter, in the year 1580. On this same day at the time of the high Mass, the Blessed Sacrament was reserved in the church of the glorious St. Anne.[34] The city council and some others along with Doctor Ervías came out to receive us, and we got down from our wagons at the church in the town, which was quite far from St. Anne's. The joy of the whole town was so great. It gave me much consolation to see the happiness with which they received the order of the Blessed Virgin, our Lady. We had heard from afar the peal of the church bells. Once we were inside the church, they began the Te Deum, one verse sung by the choir and the other played by the organ. When it was finished, they carried the Blessed Sacrament on one portable platform and a statue of our Lady on another, and crosses and banners. The procession proceeded with

much pomp. We were in the middle near the Blessed Sacrament with our white mantles and our veils covering our faces, and next to us were many of our discalced friars from their monastery and Franciscans from the monastery of St. Francis that was located there, and one Dominican who happened to be present (even though he was alone it made me happy to see that habit there). Since the distance was great, there were many altars set up along the way. From time to time the procession stopped and some verses were recited in honor of our order which moved us to great devotion. So did the sight of all of them praising the great God present in our midst and the fact that because of Him they paid so much honor to us seven poor, little discalced nuns who were there. While I was engaged in all these reflections, I became very ashamed in recalling that I was among them and that if they were to do what I deserved they would all turn against me.

38. I have given you so long an account of this honor that was rendered to the habit of the Virgin so that you might praise our Lord and beg Him that he be served in this foundation. I am happier when there is much persecution and many trials, and I tell about them more eagerly. The truth is that these Sisters that were here suffered persecution and trial for almost six years, at least for the five and a half years that they were in this house of the glorious St. Anne. They suffered these in addition to the great poverty and hardship they had in earning their food, for they never wanted to ask for alms. The reason for the latter was that they didn't think the purpose of their being in the monastery was that others might give them to eat. Furthermore, they did great penance, both by fasting often and eating little, and by their uncomfortable beds and

very small house, which was a great hardship because of the strict enclosure that they always observed.

39. Their greatest trial, they told me, came from their intense desire to see themselves clothed with the habit. This was a terrible torment to them day and night since they thought they might never see the desire fulfilled, and thus all their prayers, frequently accompanied by tears, were that God might grant them this favor. And whenever some delay came along, they became extremely distressed and increased their penance. They deprived themselves of food in order to pay from their earnings the messengers sent to me and also for the gifts of gratitude, in their poor way, to those who were able to help them in some way. After having spoken with them and seen their holiness, I well understand that it was through their prayers and tears that they obtained the favor to be admitted into the order. And thus I considered it a far greater treasure to have souls like these in the order than to have a good deal of income, and I hope that the house will prosper.

40. Well when we entered the house, all were inside at the door. Each one was dressed in her individual way, as she was when she entered, and they never wanted to wear the habit of beatas[35] since they were hoping for this foundation, although what they were wearing was very simple. It appeared from their indifferent manner of dress that they took little care of themselves, and almost all were so thin that their life of great penance was evident.

41. They received us with many tears of great joy. It was obvious that these were not feigned, nor were their great virtues, their joy, humility, and obedience to the prioress. They don't know how to please enough those nuns who came to

make the foundation. All their fear was that we might turn around and go back when we saw their poverty and the small size of their house. None of them had acted as superior, but with much sisterly love each of them worked as much as she could. The two oldest took care of business matters when necessary; the others never spoke with anyone, nor did they want to. They had no lock for the door but only a bolt; none of them dared to go to the door; only the oldest answered. They slept very little so as to earn their bread and not lose time for prayer in which they spent many hours—on feast days the whole day.

42. They guided themselves with books by Fray Luis de Granada and Fray Peter of Alcántara. They recited the Divine Office most of the time despite their little ability to read, for only one of them read well. And they did not have identical breviaries. Some used old roman breviaries that were given by priests who no longer used them; others used whatever they could find. And since they did not know how to read, they spent many hours at this. They did not recite the Office in a place where they could be heard by outsiders. God must have accepted their good intention and effort, for they must have said little that was correct. When Father Fray Antonio de Jesús began to guide them, he ordered them to recite only the Office of our Lady. They had their own oven for baking bread. And they did everything with as much harmony as they would have done under a superior.

43. All this made me praise our Lord, and the more I dealt with them the happier I was that I had come. It seems to me that however many the hardships I would have had to go through, I would not have wanted to fail to console these

souls. My companions who remained there told me that on the very first days they experienced some opposition, but as they got to know these new Sisters better and learn of their virtue, they felt very happy to remain with them and loved them very much. Great is the power of holiness and virtue. The truth is that even though they met with many difficulties and trials these Sisters bore them well, with the favor of the Lord, because they desired to suffer in His service. And the Sister that does not feel within herself this desire should not consider herself a true discalced nun, for our desires must not be for rest but for suffering in order to imitate in something our true Spouse. May it please His Majesty to give us grace for this, amen.

44. The origin of this shrine of St. Anne was as follows. There lived in this town of Villanueva de la Jara a priest born in Zamora who had been a friar of our Lady of Mt. Carmel. He was a devotee of the glorious St. Anne. His name was Diego de Guadalajara, and he built near his house this shrine in which Mass could be heard. And in his great devotion he went to Rome and brought back a bull with many indulgences for this church or shrine. He was a virtuous and recollected man. He stipulated in his will that after his death this house and all his possessions be used for a monastery of nuns of our Lady of Mt. Carmel and that if this could not be done a chaplain be appointed to say some Masses each week and that if and when the monastery were built there would be no obligation to say the Masses.

45. The property so remained, with a chaplain, for more than twenty years, and the estate diminished in value. When the women began living in the house, they received only the

house. The chaplain was in another house that belonged to the same chaplaincy which he will now leave to them along with the rest of the estate which amounts to very little. But the mercy of God is so great that He will not fail to favor the house of His glorious grandmother. May it please His Majesty that He be always served in it, and may all creatures praise Him forever and ever, amen.

VILLANUEVA DE LA JARA (1580)

Summary and Background: Chapter 28

Teresa wasted no time leaving Andalusia. At 2 a.m., the day after the nuns were settled in their new home in Seville, Teresa departed with her brother Lorenzo for the cooler climes of Castille (May 28, 1576). However, she did not go directly to Toledo but stopped at the convent of Malagón because the house that Doña Luisa de la Cerda had provided was in desperate need of repairs. "Here the setup of the house is bad" (LE. 1. 108. 5.). Teresa wanted to see the condition of the house for herself before she talked directly to Doña Luisa (who lived in Toledo). While in Malagón, Teresa wrote to Doña Luisa informing her of the situation. However, it doesn't seem that Teresa had too much faith that Doña Luisa would take quick action. She wrote to Gracián, "I sent a messenger at once to Doña Luisa, I am waiting for her and have determined that if she does not do things well, I will arrange to have the nuns transfer to her house in Paracuellos until one is constructed here" (LE. 1. 108. 7.).

After living in Toledo for about a year, Teresa was sent to Avila on business; she had to arrange to have the jurisdiction of St. Joseph's convent transferred from the diocese to the Carmelite order. While she was in Avila, the jurisdictional disputes between the Calced and Discalced friars had so escalated (It was during this time that John of the Cross was abducted and imprisoned by his Calced brethren) that Teresa felt more than ever that the gulf sepa-rating the two factions of the Carmelite family had become so wide that the only solution was to make the Discalced friars an independent province. Years earlier (1575), Teresa had written to King Philip in this regard (LE. 1. 86. 2.). Her pleadings seemed to have fallen on deaf ears.

While in Toledo, Teresa received a request to found a monastery in the village of Villanueva de la Jara. Since she had been forbidden to found any more monasteries, she could not comply. However, in April 1579, when Angel de Salazar was appointed vicar general over the Discalced fri-ars and nuns, he granted Teresa permission to found more monasteries. Now Teresa *had* to decide whether or not to make a foundation in Villanueva de la Jara.

In Villanueva de la Jara, nine women had been living a holy life together in a small house next to a shrine dedi-cated to St. Anne. The townsfolk were so impressed by the piety of these women that they wanted them to become nuns; therefore, they invited Teresa to found a monastery and have these woman as the core members of this new community. Teresa was opposed to this idea. "There were so many women, and it seemed to me it would be very difficult for them to adapt to our way of life when they were used to their own" (F. 28. 9.). However, there were other reasons for Teresa's opposition.

[T]hey had almost nothing to live on, and the popula-tion of the place is little more than a thousand which is not much help for living on alms. (Although the town council offered to support them, it didn't seem to me to be a stable offer). They didn't have a house. And the place was far from where these other monasteries were located. [Finally] although I was told that these women were very good, I had not seen them and so could not verify whether they had the qualities we require for these monasteries. Thus I decided to turn down the proposal entirely. (F. 28. 9.)[36]

Teresa refusal was met with opposition by the village council; Fr. Antonio, prior of the Discalced Carmelite monastery of La Roda, which was located near Villanueva de la Jara; and Doctor Ervías, Antonio's friend, who was a prominent citizen of Villanueva de la Jara. Antonio told Teresa that Doctor Ervías was willing to provide an income of three hundred ducats to support the monastery. Teresa was still very hesitant. She knew by experience that people *promise* to give money but often renege on their offer. "This looked very unsure, since it seemed to me that after the foundation was made they [the benefactors] would drag their feet saying that the little the Sisters had was quite enough" (F. 28. 12.).

However, since it was Teresa's custom never to make a decision without first receiving counsel, she consulted her confessor "Doctor Valázquez, a canon and professor in Toledo, a very learned and virtuous man" (F. 28. 10.). He said, "When God has joined so many hearts for the sake of something, one may suppose that he will be served by it" (F. 28. 10.). Even though Valázquez's opinion had merit,

Teresa vacillated. "I neither accepted [the proposal] entirely nor turned it down . . . My opinion was always that it would be foolish to agree to this request. [However] I could never give a completely negative answer" (F. 28. 10.).

Teresa's reservations were resolved one day in prayer. The Lord told her to found this house for it would be for God's service. She obtained a license for the foundation from Salazar, her religious superior, who directed her to "go personally and *bring nuns of [her] choice*" (F. 28. 17.) (italics added). This directive worried Teresa because ". . . the nuns would have to live with those women *who were already there*" (F. 28. 17.) (italics added). Teresa feared that the preexisting community of nine woman "would band together against those others who would join them" (F. 28. 14.). Teresa's concern was whether two distinct communities (the nine *beatas* of Villanueva de la Jara) and the four Carmelite nuns whom Teresa would bring to Villanueva de la Jara would be able to form a single community without factions being created.

Teresa put her trust in God and decided to make the foundation. On route to Villanueva de la Jara, Teresa stopped at Malagón to oversee the building of the new monastery and to remove from office Sr. Ana de la Madre de Dios, an inexperienced prioress. She had proven to be problematic for the community. "We gave too much leeway in some matters and should not have trusted so much in young people, however holy . . . Since they don't have experience, with good intentions, they cause great havoc . . . It is a terrible thing, the harm that a prioress can cause in one of these houses" (LE. 2. 316. 4–5.). After staying in Malagón for three months, Teresa, accompanied by four nuns, set out for Villanueva de la Jara.

Things turned out well for the two groups (the nine *beatas* and the four Carmelite nuns). They were able to adjust to one another, even though, in the beginning, the nuns whom Teresa had brought with her "experienced some opposition" (F. 28. 43.). But over time "things turned out very well, which to me was no small matter; for in the foundations that we begin by ourselves alone, the nuns adapt to each other well" (F. 28. 17.). Villanueva de la Jara was founded in February 1580.

Reflection. When Fr. Antonio told Teresa that Doctor Ervías and other benefactors were willing to endow the new monastery in Villanueva de la Jara, she was neither happy nor relieved as one might expect. Rather, she was skeptical. "This looked very unsure, since it seemed to me that after the foundation was made they [the benefactors] would drag their feet saying that the little the Sisters had was quite enough" (F. 28. 12.). How are we to interpret Teresa's reaction? Did she mistrust Doctor Ervías? Was she suspicious? Or was she realistic?

Teresa knew from experience that good-hearted people will promise you the moon, but when it comes to delivering the goods, they often "drag their feet" (F. 28. 12.) and offer excuses why they cannot make good on their promises. Teresa knew human nature; she knew that *making* a promise and *keeping* it are two completely different realities.

Questions. Have you ever made a promise in good faith but reneged because you had overextended yourself? Have you ever been on the receiving end of an unfulfilled promise? How did you feel in these situations? What did you learn?

Chapter 29

Treats of the foundation of St. Joseph of Our Lady of the Street in Palencia. It was made in the year 1580 on the feast of King David.[1]

1. Having returned from the foundation of Villanueva de la Jara, the major superior[2] ordered me to go to Valladolid at the request of the bishop of Palencia, Don Alvaro de Mendoza. This was the bishop who had accepted and favored the first monastery, St. Joseph's in Avila,[3] and always favors whatever pertains to this order. Since he was transferred from the diocese of Avila to that of Palencia, our Lord inspired him with the desire to found there another monastery of this sacred order. When I reached Valladolid, I was struck down with so bad an illness that they thought I was going to die.[4] I felt so listless and so unable even to think of doing anything that I could not be persuaded even though the prioress of our monastery in Valladolid who desired this foundation very much was pressing me to go ahead with it.[5] But neither could I find any basis for doing so because the monastery had to be founded in poverty, and they told me that it could not be sustained because the city was very poor.

2. For almost a year this foundation had been a subject of discussion along with that of Burgos. Previously, I had not been so opposed to it, but now, even though I had not come to Valladolid for any other purpose, I found many obstacles. I don't know whether this was due to my severe illness and the resulting weakness or to the devil who wanted to hinder the good that was done afterward. Indeed, I am surprised and saddened. Often I complain to our Lord about how much the

427

poor soul shares in the illness of the body. I seems the soul can do nothing but abide by the laws of the body and all its needs and changes.

3. One of the great trials and miseries of life, I think, is this helplessness experienced when there is no strong spirit to bring the body into submission. For if the soul is alert, I don't consider the suffering of illness and pain a problem, even though this may be a trial, for the soul is praising God and accepting this as coming from His hand. But it is a terrible thing on the one hand to be suffering and on the other not to be doing anything. This is especially true if the soul has experienced great desires not to rest interiorly or exteriorly but to occupy itself completely in the service of its great God. It has no other remedy here than patience, knowledge of its misery, and abandonment of itself to the will of God who makes use of it for what He wants and in the way He wants. This is the condition I was in then, although I was already convalescing. But, nonetheless, the weakness was so great that I lost even the confidence God usually gives me when I begin one of these foundations. Everything looked impossible to me. If I had met some person at the time to encourage me, this would have been a great help. But some only added to my fear; others, even though they gave me some hope, did not encourage me enough to help me overcome my faintheartedness.

4. It happened that a Father from the Society came there, named Maestro Ripalda, who had been my confessor some time before and was a great servant of God.[6] I told him about my situation, that I wanted to consider him to be standing in God's place, and asked him to tell me what he thought about the foundation. He began to encourage me very much. He

told me that I was growing old and that this was the reason for my cowardice. But I saw clearly that this was not the reason, for I am older now and do not experience such timidity. And he too must have understood this, but he scolded me so that I wouldn't think God was behind it. I was then considering the foundations of Palencia and Burgos together, and I had nothing for either of them. But this was not the cause of the way I felt, for I am used to beginning with less. He told me that I should by no means give them up. I had been told the same thing a little previously by a provincial from the Society, named Baltasar Alvarez,[7] but at that time I was well.

5. His words were not enough to get me to make the decision to go ahead, although they were very helpful. I did not make up my mind completely because either the devil, or as I said,[8] the illness held me bound; but I felt much better. The prioress at Valladolid assisted me as much as she could because she greatly desired the foundation of Palencia. But since she saw me so lukewarm about it, she too was afraid. Now let the true ardor come, for neither the nations nor the servants of God suffice! Therefore, it is often made clear that it is not I who do anything in these foundations, but the work is His who is all powerful in everything.

6. One day just after having received Communion and in the midst of this vacillation and indecision about making any foundation, I begged the Lord to enlighten me so that I might do His will in everything. The lukewarmness was not of the kind that could ever take away as much as one iota from this desire. Our Lord answered in a kind of reprehensive way: "What do you fear? When have I failed you? I am the same now as I was before. Do not neglect to make these

two foundations." O great God! How different are your words from those of men! I was thereby left with such determination and courage that the whole world would not have been enough to oppose me. I began at once to make arrangements for them, and our Lord began to give me the means.

7. I took two nuns with me to go and buy the house. Now even though they told me it was impossible to live on alms in Palencia, I may as well not have been told, because I already saw that it was impossible at that time to make a foundation that could have an income. I knew that since God said I should found one, His Majesty would provide. Thus, although my health had not returned entirely, I decided to go despite the harsh weather. I left Valladolid on the feast of the Holy Innocents in the year that I mentioned,[9] for a gentleman had given us a house he had rented in which we could live from the beginning of the new year until the feast of St. John the Baptist, for he had gone to live elsewhere.

8. I wrote to a canon of this city even though I did not know him.[10] But a friend of his told me that he was a servant of God, and I became convinced that he would be a great help to us. For the Lord Himself, as seen in the other foundations, chooses in each place someone to help Him. His Majesty already knows the little that I can do. I sent a message to beg this gentleman to have the house vacated as secretly as possible, for it was occupied, and not to tell the occupant who was coming. For even though some of the nobility showed their good will and the bishop was very eager for the foundation, I saw that the safest thing was to keep it from being known.

9. Canon Reinoso, for that is the name of the one to whom I wrote, did so good a job that not only did he have the house

vacated but he provided beds and a plentiful supply of things. We needed them because the weather was very cold and the previous day had been a troublesome one with fog so thick we could hardly see each other. Indeed, we had little rest until we had prepared a place to say Mass the following day, because before anyone was aware of it we had arrived. I have found that this quiet way of arriving is more fitting, for if we begin discussing opinions, the devil disturbs everything; even though he cannot gain, he stirs unrest. This is what we did, for early in the morning, almost at dawn, a priest who came with us, named Porras, a very good servant of God, said Mass. Also with us was another friend of the nuns of Valladolid, named Augustín de Victoria, who had lent me money to furnish the house and with much care had assisted me on the journey.[11]

10. There were five of us nuns who went to Palencia. With us, as well, was a lay Sister, a companion who has for some time been going about with me. She is a great and discreet servant of God who can help me more than others who are choir Sisters.[12] That night we slept little, although, as I say, the journey had been laborious because of the heavy rains.

11. I was very pleased that the foundation was made on that day since the Office was of King David to whom I am devoted. Immediately that morning I sent word to His Excellency, the bishop, who did not know yet that I was arriving that day. He came at once with the great charity he has always shown us. He told us that he would give us all the bread we needed, and he ordered his administrator to provide many things for us. There is so much that this order owes him, that whoever reads about these, its foundations, is obliged to recommend him, whether living or dead, to our Lord, and this I

ask out of charity. The joy of the people was so great and universal that there was not even one person who disapproved, which was something very unusual. Their knowing that the bishop wanted it contributed greatly to this since he was much loved in that place. The people are among the most gentle and noble that I have ever seen, and so every day I rejoice more in having made that foundation there.

12. Since the house was not ours, we immediately began to negotiate to buy another, for even though this one was up for sale, it was in a very bad place. And with the help I had from the nuns who came, it seemed that we could buy something. Although the amount was small, for that city it was a lot. But if God had not given us the good friends that He did, all would have been to no avail. For the good canon Reinoso brought a friend of his, named Canon Salinas,[13] of great charity and understanding, and they were both as concerned as if the matter were their own—even more so, I believe—and they were always concerned about that house.

13. There was in the town a shrine that inspired much devotion to our Lady called Our Lady of the Street. The devotion to her in the city and the entire region is great, and many people go there. It seemed to His Excellency and to all the people that it would be good for us to be near that church. It did not have a house attached to it, but there were two nearby which, if we bought, would be enough for us along with the church. The church had to be given to us by both the cathedral chapter and some members of the confraternity, and thus we started to try to obtain it. The cathedral chapter made us a gift of it at once, and although the negotiations with the confraternity were more difficult, the members also agreed. As I have

said,[14] if I have ever seen virtuous people in my life, they are the people of this town.

14. Since the owners of the houses saw our interest in them, they began to value them more, and rightly so. I wanted to go to see the houses, and they looked so bad to me that I didn't want them at all, nor did those who came with us. Afterward, it was clearly seen that the devil had a great role to play because it upset him that we would be there. The two canons who were negotiating about it thought that the houses were far from the cathedral, as they were, but in a more populated area of the city. We finally all decided that those houses were unsuitable for us and that we should look for another. This is what the two canons began to do those days. And they did so with such care and diligence, without failing to look at anything they thought might be suitable, that it made me praise our Lord. They became pleased with one house whose owner was named Tamayo. Some parts of the house were just right for our needs, and it was near the house of a noble gentleman, named Suero de Vega, who helps us very much.[15] He as well as other persons in the district were eager that we make the foundation there.

15. That house was not large enough, but they offered us another along with it, although this other was not the kind that could be easily adapted to the first. In sum, from the information they gave me about it, I desired that we go ahead. But the canons did not want to do so until I saw the houses first. I am so reluctant to go into the town, and I trusted so much in them that they couldn't get me to go. Finally, I went to see them and also those of our Lady of the Street, although not with the intention of buying these latter but only so that the owner of

the others would not think that we had no other choice. And they had looked so bad to me, as I have mentioned,[16] and to those who had come with me that now we are surprised that we could have thought them so bad. After that, we went to the other place, determined that those houses would be the ones for us. Although we found many difficulties, we accepted them. Yet the houses were not easy to fix up, for in order to make a church, and even then not a large one, all the good space for living quarters would have had to be taken away.

16. It is a strange thing to be resolved about something. Indeed, it was providential that I trusted little in myself, although that time I was not the only one who was mistaken. In sum, we already had it in mind to buy the houses and no other and to pay what was asked for them, which was high, and write to the owner, who was not in the city but nearby.

17. That I have gone into such detail about the buying of the houses will seem pointless until it is seen that the devil's aim was to prevent us from buying those of Our Lady of the Street. Every time I think of it, it makes me fear.

18. We were all determined, as I have said,[17] not to buy any other. One day while I was at Mass I became very worried as to whether I was doing the right thing, and a restlessness came over me that left me almost no quiet during the whole Mass. I went to receive the Blessed Sacrament, and immediately after receiving it I heard these words: "This is the one that suits you." They were such that they made me resolve definitely not to buy those I was thinking of but those of Our Lady of the Street.

I began to consider what a difficult thing it would be to do this since the business deal had been much discussed and was so dear to those who had looked after it with such care. The Lord answered me: "They do not understand how much I am offended there, and this will be a great remedy." It occurred to me that perhaps this locution might be false, although I could not believe this, for I recognized clearly from its effects that it was from the Spirit of God. The Lord said to me at once: "It is I."

19. I was left very peaceful and the disturbance I had before was taken away, although I did not know how to remedy what had been done and the many bad things that had been said about the houses, or what to say to my Sisters to whom I had stressed how bad the condition of them was and that we should in no way move there without seeing them. Yet this did not concern me so much, for I already knew that the Sisters would be agreeable to whatever I might do. But I was concerned about the others and their desire. It seemed to me they would take me to be vain and unstable since I changed my mind so quickly, something I greatly abhor doing. All these thoughts were not enough to move me either much or little to give up going to the houses of our Lady, nor did I think about their bad condition. Provided the nuns could prevent as much as one venial sin, the rest was of little importance; and in my opinion any of them knowing what I knew would have agreed with me.

20. I had recourse to the following: My confessor was Canon Reinoso, one of the two who was helping me. I was not confiding to him spiritual matters of this sort because the occasion had not arisen in which there was needed to do so. Since it has always been my custom in these matters, so as to walk along a more secure path, to do what the confessor advises

me, I decided to tell him under much secrecy, even though I could not renounce doing what I had heard without feeling much distress. But, in the end, I told him I trusted our Lord would do what I saw at other times, for His Majesty changes the mind of the confessor who is of another opinion so that what He wants is done.

21. I told him first of how the Lord was accustomed to teaching me often in this way and that up to that point many things had happened by which it was understood that these experiences were from His Spirit. I recounted what took place but told him that I would do whatever he thought, even if it would be painful for me. He is very discreet, holy, and shows good judgment in everything, even though he is young.[18] Although he saw that there would be unfavorable comment, he decided not to go against what had been heard. I told him that we should wait for the messenger,[19] and he agreed, for I trusted that God would take care of things. And so it happened, for even though we had agreed to all that the owner wanted and had requested, he asked for another three hundred ducats, which seemed foolish because we were already paying more than enough. In this we saw the hand of God because the sale was very good for the owner, and since the agreement had been made there was no sense to his asking for more.

22. What he did helped matters very much, for we said there would be no end to this. But it didn't help completely, because it was clear that if the house was suitable for conversion into a monastery, three hundred ducats wasn't reason enough to forgo the house. I told my confessor that if he thought we should buy the house of Our Lady of the Street he shouldn't worry about my reputation but tell his companion

that I was determined to buy Our Lady of the Street whether it was expensive or cheap, in miserable condition or good. Since his companion is very intelligent and alert, I believe that in seeing so quick a change he suspected something about my experience even though nothing was said to him about it, and so he did not press me any further.

23. Afterward we all saw clearly the big mistake we would have made in buying the other one. For now we are surprised to see the great advantage the one has over the other, not to mention the main advantage, for it is clearly seen that our Lord and His glorious Mother are served there and that many occasions of sin are being removed. In fact, many night vigils were held there, and since nothing more was there than the shrine, many things could be done that the devil was sad to see taken away. And we were happy to be able to serve in some way our Mother, Lady, and Patroness. And it was very wrong to have done otherwise previously, for we should not have considered any other house. Obviously, the devil was causing blindness in many matters, for there are many conveniences in Our Lady of the Street that would not have been found elsewhere. And all the townspeople were overjoyed for they had been desiring that the monastery be there, and even those who had wanted us to go to the other house were now very pleased with this one.

24. May He who enlightened me in this regard be blessed forever and ever. And He enlightens me thus in anything I manage to do well, for each day I am more amazed at the little talent I have for anything. And don't think that what I'm saying comes from humility, for each day I see it more clearly. It seems our Lord desires me and all other to know that it is

only His Majesty who does these works, and that as He gave sight with mud to the blind man, He wants someone as blind as I to do something worth more than mud.[20] Certainly, in this whole matter there were things, as I have said,[21] involving great blindness, and each time I recall it, I would like to praise our Lord again for it. But even for this I'm no good, nor do I know how He puts up with me. Blessed be His mercy, amen.

25. Well these holy canons, friends of the Virgin, immediately made haste to negotiate a contract for the houses and, in my opinion, they got them at a low price. They worked hard, for in each of these foundations God desires that those who help will merit. And I am the one who does nothing, as I have said at other times; and I would never want to stop saying this, because it is the truth. For they worked very hard in getting the house ready, and also gave money for it, because I didn't have any, and together with this they became the guarantors. In other foundations I had to undergo some anxiety before I found a guarantor, and not for so large an amount as in this instance. And that was understandable; the guarantors had to trust the Lord, for I didn't have a cent. But His Majesty has always granted me a favor which I consider very great; no one has ever lost anything by being a guarantor for me, nor was there any failure to pay back in full.

26. Since the owners of the houses were not satisfied with the two guarantors, the two went to look for the administrator of the diocese whose name was Prudencio. (I don't know if I remember correctly. They tell me this now, for since at that time we called him the administrator, I did not learn his name.)[22] He is so charitable with us, for we owed him much and still do. He asked them where they were going; they answered

they were looking for him to have him sign that guarantee. He laughed and said: "Well now, you ask for a guarantee for so much money in a way like this?" And he signed it at once while sitting on top his mule, which nowadays is something worth pondering.

27. I would not want to fail to sing the praises of the charity that I found in Palencia both in general and in particular. Truly, it seemed to me like being in the early Church, at least it is not usual now to see such a thing in the world. We had no income and they had to provide us with food, and not only were they not opposed to the foundation but they said that God was doing them the greatest favor. And if considered in the light of faith, what they said was the truth, for just to have one more church where the Blessed Sacrament is reserved is a great deal.

28. May He be blessed forever, amen. For as time goes on it is becoming clearly understood that our Lord is served by the fact that the foundation is in that place and that some inappropriate things must have been done there that are no longer done. Since many people went there for the night vigil and the shrine was in an isolated spot, not everyone went out of devotion. The situation is getting better. The statue of our Lady had been displayed with very little reverence. The bishop, Don Alvaro de Mendoza, had a chapel made in the shrine for it, and little by little things are being done for the honor and glory of this glorious Virgin and her Son. May He be praised forever, amen, amen.

29. Well, when the house was ready for occupation by the nuns, the bishop wanted this to take place with great solemnity. And so it did, one day during the octave of the feast of

the Blessed Sacrament.[23] He came himself from Valladolid, and the cathedral chapter, the religious orders, and all the people of the city joined him in the procession. There was much music. We all, with our white mantles and veils covering our faces, went in procession from the house where we were staying to a parish that was close to our Lady's house where the statue was brought to meet us, and from there we took the Blessed Sacrament and had it reserved in the church with great and well-organized solemnity. It caused much devotion. Other nuns who were on their way to the foundation in Soria came with us, all carrying candles. I believe that the Lord was very much praised that day in that city. May it please Him that He be praised forever by all creatures, amen, amen.

30. While I was in Palencia, God willed that the discalced Carmelites be separated from the calced. This was done by letting the discalced form their own province, which was all that we were desiring for the sake of our peace and tranquility. At the request of our Catholic king, Don Philip, a very long brief was obtained from Rome for this purpose.[24] And thus his majesty by obtaining this brief favored us as much as he did in the beginning. The chapter was held in Alcalá presided over by a Reverend Father named Fray Juan de las Cuevas who was then prior of Talavera. He belongs to the Dominican order and was appointed by Rome after having been nominated by his majesty. He is a very holy and prudent man, which was necessary for such a task. The king paid for their expenses, and at his orders the entire university of Alcalá helped them. With much peace and harmony the chapter was held in the College of St. Cyril, that of our discalced friars. They elected Father Maestro Gracián de la Madre de Dios as provincial.[25]

31. Because these Fathers will write elsewhere about what took place, there is no reason for me to deal with it. I have mentioned the matter because it was while I was engaged in the work of this foundation that our Lord brought to a conclusion an endeavor that was so important for the honor and glory of His glorious Mother since it concerned her order. She is our Lady and our Patroness. And this for me was one of the great joys and satisfactions of my life. It would take a long time to tell of the trials, persecutions, and afflictions that I have had to undergo during the past twenty-five years, and only our Lord can understand them. Save for anyone who knows the trials that were suffered, one cannot grasp the joy that came to my heart at seeing the matter concluded and the desire I had that everybody praise our Lord and that we pray for this our holy king, Don Philip. By means of him God brought the matter to a happy ending. Had it not been for the king, the devil was so cunning that everything would have collapsed.

32. Now we are all at peace, calced and discalced; no one can hinder us from serving our Lord. Hence, my Brothers and Sisters, since His Majesty has heard your prayers so well, let us make haste to serve Him. Let those in the present who are eye-witnesses, consider the favors He has granted us and the trials and disturbances from which He has delivered us. And those who are to come, when they find everything running smoothly, let them, for the love of our Lord, not neglect anything relating to perfection. May that which is said of some orders that praise their beginnings not be said of them. Now we are beginning, and let them strive to advance always from good to better. Let them beware, for the devil through very small things drill holes through which very large things enter.

May it not happen that those who are to come say: "These things are not important; don't go to extremes." Oh, my daughters, everything that helps us advance is important.

33. For love of our Lord I beg you to remember how soon everything comes to an end, to remember the favor our Lord has granted us in bringing us to this order and the great punishment that will befall anyone who might introduce some mitigation. Rather, fix your eyes always on the ancestry from which we come, those holy prophets. How many saints we have in heaven who have worn this habit! Let us adopt the holy presumption that with the Lord's help we will be like them. The battle will be brief, my Sisters, and the end is eternal. Let us set aside these things that in themselves are nothing, using only those that lead us to this end without end, so as to love Him and serve Him more, for He will live forever and ever, amen, amen. Thanks be to God.

PALENCIA (1580)

Summary and Background: Chapter 29

After Teresa founded Villanueva de la Jara, she began her journey back to Toledo on March 20, 1580, and arrived six days later, exhausted and seriously ill. She began to exhibit the first symptoms of the "universal cold," a strain of influenza that was ravaging Europe. In April, Teresa's emotionally unstable brother Pedro came to Toledo for a visit. He had been living with his brother Lorenzo. Pedro said that he could no longer live with Lorenzo and that he planned to go to Seville. Teresa felt both relief and concern. She knew that Pedro had been a great burden for Lorenzo and was relieved that Lorenzo would no longer have to take care of him. "My desire to see him out of your house was so great that my happiness far surpassed anything I felt on account of his trial" (LE. 2. 337. 1.). Teresa knew that "[Pedro was] crazy . . . and that he [was] a drifter" (LE. 2. 337. 1.). She also knew that he was impossible to live with. "I don't know who would be able to put up with him" (LE. 2. 338. 7.). However, Teresa feared for Pedro's life if he left Lorenzo's care. "[Pedro] has arranged . . . to go to Seville . . . and one day of sun along the way will kill him . . . and in Seville there will be nothing for him to do but spend money" (LE. 2. 337. 2.). Unexpectedly, two months later, on June 26, Lorenzo died of the influenza. Teresa was devastated.

It was at this time that Angel de Salazar ordered Teresa to go to Valladolid to prepare to make a foundation in Palencia (Valladolid is less than thirty miles from Palencia). The request had come from Bishop Alvaro de Mendoza of Palencia, the former bishop of Avila, who had assisted Teresa in founding her first monastery, St. Joseph's in Avila. Teresa was in no condition, physically or emotionally, to either travel or to make a foundation. By the time she reached Valladolid, her influenza had become so severe that it was feared that she would die. Also, Teresa had become entangled in responsibilities as a result of being the executor of Lorenzo's will, a condition of which was arranging a marriage for her nephew Francisco. "It is very hard for me now to have to get involved in arranging a marriage after taking care of so many business matters" (LE. 2. 353. 3.).

In addition to these physical and emotional sufferings, Teresa struggled to use her left arm which she had broken four years earlier. Her arm gave her such problems that Sr. Ana de San Bartolomé became Teresa's inseparable nurse on all of her journeys. It is no wonder, therefore, that Teresa had neither the energy nor desire to found another monastery at this time. "I felt so listless and so unable to think of doing anything that I could not be persuaded . . . to go ahead with [making a foundation in Palencia]" (F. 29. 1.).

Teresa was filled with "vacillation and indecision" (F. 29. 6.) about founding the monastery in Palencia and about a request to found a monastery in Burgos, so much so that she "lost even confidence in God" (F. 29. 3). In this state of heart and mind, God told Teresa not to fear to make these two foundations. This gave her the courage and energy to forge ahead.

Now that Teresa had determined to found the monastery in Palencia, she faced a familiar problem. "But neither could I find any basis for doing so because the monastery had to be founded in poverty, and they told me that it could not be sustained because the city was very poor" (F. 29. 1.). In spite of this consideration, Teresa, who was still recovering from the flu, traveled to Palencia with two nuns in order to purchase a house. There, Teresa met a gentleman who allowed her to live in his rented house for several months.

Since the community had only a limited amount of time in which they could stay in the gentleman's rented lodgings, Teresa "immediately began to negotiate" (F. 29. 12.) to buy a house. The real estate market in Palencia was in Teresa's favor. The houses were relatively cheap, and she knew it. "Although the amount [of money we had] was small, for that city it was a lot" (F. 29. 12.). Teresa had to deal with crafty businessmen, but she knew how to play the game. For example, when the owners of a couple of houses saw that Teresa was interested in them, "they began to value [the houses] more" (F. 29. 14.). However, after Teresa had looked at other houses that were up for sale, she went back to the first owners she had dealt with so that they "would not think we had no other choice" (F. 29. 15.). Teresa knew the dynamics of supply and demand and the idea behind the phrase a "buyer's market."

The original houses that Teresa looked at were located near a popular shrine dedicated to Mary under the title "Our Lady of the Street." These houses did not have adequate space for Teresa's community. However, if the shrine could be given to them as their chapel and sacristy, it would be doable. After Teresa concluded some difficult negotiations with both the cathedral chapter and the confraternity of Palencia, they decided to make a gift of the shrine to Teresa on the condition that she buy the two nearby houses. However, Teresa had second thoughts about the houses because, on closer inspection, "they looked bad to [her]" (F. 29. 14.).

In consequence, two of the canons of the cathedral spent a considerable amount of time and energy looking for another place that would be acceptable to Teresa. They found two houses owned by a man named Tamayo. Teresa decided to go ahead and make the purchase. However, one day at Mass, a "restlessness came over" (F. 29. 18.) Teresa. "I became very worried as to whether I was doing the right thing" (F. 29. 18.). However, as she was receiving communion, she heard the words, "This is the one that suits you" (F. 29. 18.). The locution was referring to the houses next to the shrine of "Our Lady of the Street."

Teresa knew what she had to do, but she dreaded doing it because negotiations for Tamayo's houses were already in progress. "The business deal [of the houses belonging to Tamayo] was much discussed and was so dear to [the canons] who had looked after it with such care" (F. 29. 18.) that Teresa was afraid of what the two canons would think of her. "It seemed to me they would take me to be vain and unstable since I changed my mind so quickly" (F. 29. 19.).

All's well that ends well. Contrary to Teresa's fears, the canons who had worked hard to find the houses that belonged to Tamayo worked tirelessly in negotiating a contract with the man who owned the houses next to the shrine of "Our Lady of the Street." They negotiated a low price and became the houses' guarantors.

The new foundation was inaugurated with great solemnity. The bishop, members of various religious orders, and the townsfolk joined in procession to the new monastery. Teresa praised the people of Palencia for their charity and hospitality. As a crowning gift, it was in Palencia that Teresa received the news that Pope Gregory XIII, through the intercession of King Philip, had allowed the Discalced friars and nuns to form a separate province.

Reflection. Life is neither neat nor tidy. It doesn't afford us the luxury of dealing with one problem at a time. We see this in Teresa's life. As Teresa was making preparations for a new foundation, she was also dealing with health issues, her mentally unstable brother Pedro, and the death of Lorenzo.

Teresa could not put her life on hold until she dealt with her personal problems. She couldn't say, "Give me a few months to myself until I'm really over the flu and I've worked through my grief regarding the death of my brother Lorenzo." No, she had a job to do; she was burdened with the hundred and one tasks of administration that had to be done.

Like Teresa, we have to go on living in spite of what we are dealing with in our personal lives. Let us say that a spouse, a parent, or sibling dies. We might be granted a week off work, but then we are expected to be back on the job the following Monday. The people whom we have to deal with will be just as nasty and petty as ever. The only difference is that we don't have the emotional resources to deal with them.

Life rarely gives us time to recuperate from an emotional or physical blow before it deals us another. Such was Teresa's life and such is ours. She never waited for things to "get back to normal" before responding to God's will. She asked God for the strength to do his will in the midst of her problems, and the strength was given to her.

Questions. Like Teresa, have you ever felt so overwhelmed by the problems of life that you began to lose "even confidence in God" (F. 29. 3.)? Have you ever considered that your ability to carry on in the midst of these feelings is an experience of God's grace?

Reflection. One of the great acts of courage that we see in this chapter is Teresa's changing her mind regarding which house to buy, in spite of the fear of what other people would think of her. "It seemed to me they would take me to be vain and unstable since I changed my mind so quickly" (F. 29. 19.). However, unlike Teresa, we can often commit ourselves to a course of action that we are not at peace with because of fear. "I can't pull out now; what would people think of me?" "I've come so far, I can't turn back." "All the preparations for the wedding are made. The hall has been rented. We signed the contract with the caterer. All our relatives are coming from a distance. My doubts and misgivings about marrying John are nothing but nerves."

We can commit ourselves to a course of action for years, be it a career, a relationship, a course of study, a vocation, etc., in which we are miserable and feel trapped. One of the great tragedies of life is that we sacrifice our peace of soul on the altar of what other people will think of us.

Questions. Have you ever committed yourself to a decision that you sensed was a mistake because you feared what other people would think? Where in your life do you sacrifice your peace of soul on the altar of what other people will think of you?

Chapter 30

Begins to treat of the foundation of the monastery of the Blessed Trinity in the city of Soria. It was founded in 1581. The first Mass was said on the feast of our Father St. Elisha.[1]

1. While I was occupied with the foundation in Palencia, which was mentioned, they brought me a letter from the bishop of Osma, named Doctor Velázquez.[2] While he was canon and professor at the cathedral in Toledo and I was still experiencing some fears, I sought to consult him because I knew he was a very learned man and a servant of God. I entreated him urgently to guide my soul and hear my confession. Although he was very busy, I asked him to do so for the love of our Lord. He saw my need and responded so willingly that I was surprised. And I consulted and confessed to him all the time that I was in Toledo, which was a long time. I spoke to him about my soul with complete openness as I usually do. This did me so much good that from then on my fears began to lessen. True, there was another reason for consulting him which I won't go into here. But, in fact, he was very helpful to me because he assured me with passages from Sacred Scripture, which is what suits me most when I am sure that one knows it well. I knew he did and that he lived a good life.

2. This letter was written from Soria where he was at that time. He told me how a lady, a penitent of his there, spoke to him about a foundation of our nuns, which she thought would be a good thing, and that he had told her he would try to convince me to go there to make the foundation. He said I should not disappoint him and that if I thought the

450

foundation was fitting I should let him know and he would send for me. I was very happy because, in addition to the fact that the place was good for a foundation I wanted to see him and tell him some things about my soul. I had grown to love him very much because of the great progress my soul made under his guidance.

3. The name of this lady who wanted the foundation was Doña Beatriz de Beamonte y Navarra because she is a descendant from the kings of Navarra and is a daughter of Don Francés de Beamonte who was of a noble and pure lineage.[3] She was married for some years and had no children, but was very wealthy and for a long time had it in mind to provide for a monastery of nuns. She spoke of this with the bishop and he informed her about the discalced nuns of this order of our Lady. What he told her pleased her so much that she greatly urged him to have the foundation made.

4. She is a mild-mannered person, generous and penitent; in sum, a very great servant of God. She owned a good house that was well-constructed and in a good location in Soria. She told us that she would give it to us along with all that was necessary for a foundation, and this she gave together with a five hundred ducat annuity at twenty-five per thousand.[4] The bishop promised to give us a very good church with a vaulted ceiling. The church was a parish church[5] but so close by that we were able to make use of it by means of a covered passageway. The bishop was easily able to make this offer—for he was poor—because there were many churches there, and so he moved the parish to another church. He gave me an account of all this in his letter. I discussed the matter with Father Provincial who was there at the time.[6] He and my friends thought

I should write through a personal messenger. The foundation in Palencia was completed, and I was very happy about the one in Soria for the reasons mentioned.[7]

5. I began to gather the nuns I was going to bring with me. There were seven, for that lady desired that there be more rather than less, in addition to a lay Sister, my companion, and myself. Somebody came for us with a stagecoach, which met our needs, for I had told the bishop that I had to bring two discalced Fathers with me.[8] And so I brought with me Father Nicolás de Jesús María, a man of great perfection and discretion, a native of Genoa. He was over forty when he received the habit, I think—at least he's forty now, and it's only a short while since he took the habit—but he has advanced so far in a short time that it seems clear our Lord chose him so he might help the order during these very troublesome times of persecution.[9] He has done a good deal. With respect to the others who could have helped, some were exiled, others imprisoned. Since he had no office, little attention was paid to him. For as I mentioned, it was only a short time that he was in the order. Or, God allowed this that there might be some help left for me.

6. He is so discreet that while he was staying in the monastery of the calced Carmelites in Madrid, as though for other business reasons, he dealt with the affairs of the discalced friars in such a disguised manner that the calced friars never knew about it, and so they didn't bother him. We corresponded frequently, for I was in the monastery of St. Joseph's in Avila, and we dealt with a suitable course of action, for this consultation gave him satisfaction. Hence it can be seen what need the order was in since so much attention was paid to me

for want, as they say, of good men.[10] It was during this time that I had experience of his perfection and discretion. Thus he is among those in this order whom I love much in the Lord and esteem highly.

7. Well, he and his lay brother companion accompanied us. He had little to do on this journey, for the one sent by the bishop conducted us in much comfort and was a help in finding good inns. When we entered the territory of the bishop of Osma, the people loved the bishop so much that when told that this was one of his projects they directed us to the good inns. The weather was fine. The daily journeys were not long. Thus, little hardship was suffered on this trip; rather, it was a happy one, for hearing the people's praise of the bishop's holiness brought me the greatest joy. We arrived in El Burgo de Osma on the Wednesday before the octave day of the feast of the Blessed Sacrament.[11] We received Communion there the following day, which was Thursday, the octave day. Since we could not reach Soria that day we stopped to eat along the way and passed that night in a church, which was not a bad place, because there was no other inn. The next day we heard Mass there and arrived in Soria around five in the afternoon. The holy bishop stood at a window in his house and blessed us from there, for we passed right by. This was no small consolation for me, since a blessing coming from a bishop and a saint is something to be highly esteemed.[12]

8. That lady, the foundress, was waiting for us at the door of her house, where the monastery was to be established. We were anxious to get inside because of the large number of people. The crowd was nothing new, for everywhere we go there is much curiosity. The world is so fond of novelty that

were it not for the veils we wear over our faces, these crowds would be a great trial. But with these veils, we can put up with them. That lady had decorated very well a large hall in which Mass was to be said, for the covered passageway leading to the church given us by the bishop had to be constructed.[13] On another day, the feast of our Father St. Elisha, Mass was said.[4]

9. That lady had prepared perfectly everything we had need of, and she let us use that hall, which was conducive to recollection, until the feast of the Transfiguration[15] when the covered passageway was completed. It was on this feast that the first Mass in the church was said with great solemnity and in the presence of a large congregation. A Father from the Society preached the sermon, for the bishop had returned to El Burgo de Osma.[16] The bishop never loses a day or an hour without working; although his health was not good, for he had lost his vision in one eye. This was my affliction in Soria, for it saddened me that the vision that was so beneficial in the service of the Lord should be lost. These are God's judgments. He must have allowed this so that His servant might gain, for the bishop did not work any less than before, and so as to test His servant's conformity with His will. The bishop told me it caused him no more distress than if it had happened to his neighbor and that sometimes he reflected that it would not grieve him if he lost sight in the other eye as well because this would allow him to live in a hermitage serving God without any other obligation. And at times he used to tell me that before becoming a bishop he had always felt called to be a hermit, and he had almost decided to give up everything and go off to become one.

10. I could not bear the thought of this since I thought he was of great benefit to the Church of God, and so I wanted him to have the office he now holds, although the day in which he was appointed bishop I felt a very great disturbance, since he sent me word immediately, as though I saw him weighed down with a heavy burden. I could neither help myself nor find peace, and I went to the choir to recommend him to the Lord. His Majesty gave me peace at once, telling me that He would be very much served by him, and this is what is really happening. Despite the illness in his eye and many other very painful illnesses and his everyday work, he fasts four days a week, and does other penances. His table consists of little that is gratifying. When he makes his visitations, he always goes on foot. His servants find this hard to put up with and complained to me about it. They must either be virtuous or not stay in his house. He has little trust in allowing important business to be handled by his administrators, and even, I think, any business; but he handles everything himself. In the beginning, for two years, he underwent the most savage persecutions there from false testimony. I was amazed because in matters of justice he is a man of integrity and rectitude. Now these persecutions are diminishing, although his persecutors had gone to the royal court and wherever they thought they could do harm. Since the good he is doing throughout the whole diocese is becoming known, these persecutions have little effect. And he has borne all of this with such perfection that he has confounded his persecutors, doing good to those he knew were doing evil to him. However much he has to do, he always finds time for prayer.

11. It seems I am becoming absorbed in praising this holy man, but I have said little. Nothing has been lost since I have mentioned this in order that it be known who is responsible for the foundation of the Blessed Trinity of Soria and also for the consolation of those who are to come, for those who are now here know the story well. Although he did not provide the income, he gave us the church and inspired this lady with the idea of the foundation, and, as I said,[17] she has a great christian spirit and is virtuous and penitential.[18]

12. Well, then, once we had taken possession of the church and prepared what was needed for the enclosure, it was necessary for me to go to the monastery of St. Joseph in Avila, and thus I departed immediately in the midst of very great heat along a road that was unfit for wagons.[19] A prebendary from Palencia, named Ribera, accompanied me.[20] He was the one who had been a great help in the work involving the covered passageway and in everything. The reason for this was that Father Nicolás de Jesús María left immediately after drawing up the contract, for there was great need of him elsewhere. This Ribera had certain business to attend to in Soria, and so he came with us. From then on, God gave him so much willingness to do good for us that he can be recommended to His Majesty as a benefactor of the order.

13. I didn't want anyone else to come with my companion and me,[21] because this Ribera is so solicitous that he was enough for me, and the less noise there is on my journeys the better I feel. On this journey I paid well for the good trip I had in going to Soria, for, although the guide knew the way to Segovia, he did not know the wagon route. Thus, he led us into places in which we often had to get down from the

wagon, and they almost had to carry it past some steep precipices. When we hired guides, they led us along the good roads and then, saying they had other things to do, abandoned us shortly before we came upon the bad roads. Prior to our arrival at an inn, about which we had not been sure, we had undergone much from the hot sun and from the many incidents in which the wagon turned over. I felt sorry for the prebendary who came with us. For now that we were told we were on the right road, we had to turn back and undo what we had done. But he was so rooted in virtue that it doesn't seem to me I ever saw him angry, which amazed me very much and made me praise our Lord, for when one is rooted in virtue, the occasions of sin are of little consequence. I praise the Lord for how He was pleased to bring us safely through that journey.

14. We arrived at St. Joseph's in Segovia on the vigil of St. Bartholomew.[22] Our nuns had been worried because of the delay, for since the roads were so bad, the delay was long. There they provided us with every comfort, for God never gives me a trial without repaying for it immediately, and I rested for eight days or more. But this foundation was made with so little hardship that there is no reason to pay any attention to the hardship of this return journey, because it was nothing. I came back pleased since it seemed to me, and I hope in His mercy, that Soria is a place where God will be served because the foundation is there, as is already becoming evident. May He be blessed and praised from age to age, amen. Thanks be to God.

SORIA (1581)

Summary and Background: Chapter 30

In March 1581, as Teresa was trying to disentangle herself from the contract with Tamayo and was arranging a new contract for the house adjacent to "Our Lady of the Street," she received a request from Alonso Velázquez, the bishop of Osma, to make a foundation in Soria. He told Teresa that Doña Beatriz de Beamonte, a rich widow, had offered half of her money to endow a convent. Teresa regretted that she could not go to Soria immediately, for Velázquez was an old friend. She wrote to Velázquez, "At present there is nothing new except a further complication about a house which makes me fear I will have to stay here this summer" (LE. 2. 383. 1.). The letter was dated March 21, 1581. To her pleasant surprise, Teresa was able to leave for Soria before she had expected (May 29, 1581).

Teresa had become acquainted with Velázquez when she lived in Toledo in 1576 and was undergoing some spiritual trials. In spite of his busy schedule as a professor of philosophy and a canon at the local cathedral, he made time every week to see Teresa in order to hear her confession and give her spiritual advice. He did so with a spirit of joy. Teresa writes, ". . . he would come every week, and was as happy as if he had been offered the archbishopric of Toledo" (LE. 1. 117. 3.).

On May 29, 1581, Teresa and nine nuns started their journey to Soria. It is believed that on this journey, Teresa said to the nuns, "Daughters, when we get to Soria, which is the end of the world, there must be no turning back; you must go on working for God." Carmelites have traditionally interpreted this story as Teresa's reference to her own "end" and her admonition that the nuns must continue the work of the reform without her. Teresa died on October 4, 1582.

There may be more fact than fiction in both this story and its interpretation, for while Teresa was in Palencia, shortly before she traveled to Osma, she wrote for Velázquez her last *Spiritual Testimony* in which we hear echoes of her *Nunc Dimittis*.

> Oh, who would be able to explain to your Excellency the quiet and calm my soul experiences! It is so certain it will enjoy God that it thinks it already enjoys the possession of Him, although not the fruition. It's as though one had given another, with heavily warranted deeds, the promise of a large revenue that the other will be able to enjoy at a certain time . . . And sometimes it even seems to it that the period from now until the end of the world would be a short time to serve the one who gave it this possession. Because, to put it truthfully, this soul is no longer in part subject to the miseries of the world as it use to be. For although it suffers more, this is only on the surface. The soul is like a lord in his castle, and so it doesn't lose its peace. (ST. 65.)

Teresa's journeys had always been herculean tasks of endurance, except the one from Palencia to Soria. Doña Beatriz de Beamonte, the benefactress of the foundation of Soria, had sent a carriage to Palencia to transport Teresa and her party to Soria. The distance was relatively short the weather was mild the land was level, and a servant was sent ahead to make accommodations for Teresa and her companions at inns along the way. It is no wonder that Teresa wrote of this journey, "That trip was recreation for me, it being a smooth journey, often with a view of rivers that provided pleasant company" (LE. 2. 406. 2.). Perhaps what added to the pleasure of the trip was Teresa's intuition that she was nearing the end of her life's labors, the relief that the housing situation in Palencia had been settled, and the knowledge that she would be seeing her old friend Velázquez once again.

The only disappointing aspect of Teresa's trip was the absence of Gracián, who had promised Teresa that he would accompany her to Soria. He had stopped briefly at Palencia, but only long enough to give his regards. He then rushed off on matters of business, without even staying for the inauguration of the new house at Palencia. Teresa felt that he could have made time if he had wanted to. "Your departure could have been excused if you had stayed at least until seeing us move into our house [in Palencia]" (LE. 2. 390. 1.). In his stead, he assigned Fr. Nicolás Doria, a Discalced Friar, to accompany Teresa to Soria.

Doria was a shrewd financier from Genoa, who later became the General of the Discalced Carmelites and had Gracián expelled from the Order. As Teresa had to deal with Doria more and more, she encountered "his stubbornness" regarding certain financial matters (LE. 2. 412. 12.). When Doria became the first counselor to the provincial and was appointed prior of Pastrana, he wrote a letter to Teresa presenting himself as a humble man questioning his own ability to govern. Teresa, sensing an ulterior motive, wrote back, "The humility of your letter made me very happy, even though I don't plan on doing what you say . . . " (LE. 2. 438. 1.).

On the journey, there occurred two events that have become a part of Teresian lore. The first is a rather humorous account of the police escort who accompanied Teresa's party. Some people upbraided the policeman, thinking that he was taking Teresa to prison on account of the Inquisition. The second event was of a more spiritual nature. Peasants, who recognized Teresa's holiness, asked her to pray that it would rain on their withered crops. Teresa, moved by their plight, prayed the Litany of the Saints, and God granted her request.

After a four-day trip (from May 29 to June 2, 1581), Teresa's company, consisting of eight nuns, her companion Ana de San Bartolomé, and Fr. Nicolás Doria, arrived in Soria. They were greeted with great hospitality by Velázquez and Doña Beatriz de Beaumont. However, this warm welcome was offset by the gawking curiosity of the townsfolk. The next day, the convent was founded. However, Teresa had to stay in Soria until August 16 to oversee "the adaptations of the house" and "the choir that still remain[ed] to be constructed" (LE. 2. 400. 2.).

During her months in Soria, Teresa cast a doubtful glance toward her next foundation—Burgos. The previous year (1580), while she was in Valladolid, Don Cristóbal Vela, the Archbishop of Burgos, passed through town. Teresa asked Don Alvaro de Mendoza, the bishop of Palencia, to approach Vela and ask him if he would give her permission to make a foundation in Burgos. The Archbishop "said that he would grant it gladly" (F. 31. 3.). However, Teresa was wise enough not to presume that what a person *says* reflects what he *will* do.

> To assume now what the archbishop will do is not wise in my judgment. For not wanting to be suspicious, we have seen clear reasons for being so. In what Canon Juan Alfonso [the canon from Palencia] writes me, the archbishop says that he always remembers the tumult that arose in Avila at the time of the first monastery. Despite the great good that came about as a result, he says that because of his experience he is obliged to prevent anything like this from happening again. What can we hope for from this? . . . He also said to a member of the Society of Jesus that the consent of the city was wanting and that without it, or without an income, he would in no way give permission. Two persons have already told me that he has a very hesitant nature. (LE. 2. 401. 4–5.)

In light of these factors, Teresa thought it would be wise not to rush into things but to enter into negotiations with the city council of Burgos beforehand. "If we have to negotiate the matter with the city, it will be better to do so from afar and slowly (LE. 2. 401. 6.). The time that it would take to negotiate with the city council of Burgos worked to Teresa's advantage, for she had to travel to Avila on business. However, her journey *from* Soria was not as pleasant as her trip *to* Soria. She traveled to Avila in great heat along treacherous roads.

> On this journey I paid well for the good trip I had in going to Soria, for although the guide knew the way, he did not know the wagon route. Thus, he led us into places in which we often had to get down from the wagon, and they almost had to carry it past some steep precipices. When we hired guides, they led us along the good roads and then, saying they had other things to do, abandoned us shortly before we came upon the bad roads . . . [Once] the wagon turned over." (F. 30. 12–13.)

On route to Avila, Teresa stopped at Segovia. She wanted to see her sister Juana and her niece Beatriz. When Teresa arrived, she discovered that a scandal had erupted. A jealous woman was spreading malicious lies that Beatriz was having an illicit love affair with her husband. In consequence, Beatriz's honor was stained. Teresa spent about a week in Segovia, never to return. Teresa would never lay eyes on her sister and niece again.

Teresa arrived in Avila on August 23, 1581, with "a slight fever" (LE. 2. 406. 2.) and felt an inconsolable loneliness. "I feel very much alone in this city where I find no one who can console me" (LE. 2. 406. 1.). The main source of Teresa's grief was the recent deaths of her brother Lorenzo and her old friend Francisco de Salcedo. "But one's human nature will not fail to feel in that place the absence of my brother and friends" (LE. 2. 402.

7.). However, there was another source of Teresa's pain. "[A]nd what is worse [than the absence of those who have been taken from me] is the presence of the ones who have remained" (LE. 2. 402. 7.).

Those who remained had brought St. Joseph's into a horrible state of affairs. The discipline had become lax. The monastery, through neglect, had fallen into disrepair, and the community had become financially insolvent. How could the first convent of her reform have degenerated so much and so rapidly? Teresa believed that the source of these problems was twofold.

First, Teresa saw that her old friend Julián of Avila, the convent's chaplain, was partly to blame. He had grown overindulgent and permissive in his old age; he too readily dispensed the nuns from the strictures of their rule. "The confessor is most to blame" (LE. 2. 377. 2.). "God deliver us from confessors who are up in years" (LE. 2. 410. 9.), groaned Teresa.

Second, María de Cristo, the prioress, lacked effective leadership skills. In writing to Gracián, Teresa said that "the prioress will suffice," but only if there is a change in chaplains. Teresa proposed Fr. Gregorio Nacianceno. But on second thought, Teresa added, "And although I say, 'will suffice,' I think I am lying because I don't think there is anyone who can handle the internal affairs of the house" (LE. 2. 402. 7.).

The community seemed to share this belief because the week after Teresa arrived in Avila, María de Cristo resigned from office and the community elected Teresa as prioress (September 10, 1581). From Teresa's perspective, the community wanted her as prioress for a very pragmatic reason. "[T]hey have made me prioress now out of sheer hunger" (LE. 2. 412. 2.).

Within a short period of time, Teresa restored monastic discipline and stabilized the community's finances. However, her time at St. Joseph's was coming to an end. Burgos lay ahead, but before leaving Avila, she had to deal with a request to establish a foundation in Granada.

Three months after Teresa came to Avila, John of the Cross arrived from Andalusia with a request to make a foundation of nuns in Granada. Teresa accepted the proposal. However, since she would soon be going to Burgos, she delegated John of the Cross and Anne of Jesus to make the foundation. They left for Granada at the end of November 1581 and made the foundation on January 20, 1582. Teresa never saw Granada or described its establishment in *The Foundations*. On January 2, 1582, Teresa left Avila, the city of her childhood, never to return. She was on her way to make her last foundation in Burgos.

Reflection. One of the most unforgettable characters of Charles Dickens' imagination is Mr. Wilkins Micawber. He is always just one step ahead of the bill collectors and, with no visible means of support, espouses an undying optimism in the belief that "something will turn up." If St. Thomas Aquinas had read *David Copperfield*, even though he probably would have enjoyed the character of Mr. Micawber immensely, he would not have been hoodwinked by

Micawber's jaunty optimism and hopefulness in future prospects. Thomas would have seen through Mr. Micawber's veneer and labeled his cheerful hope as a *falsam similitudinem* (II, II, Q. 21, a. 3), a "specious resemblance," or "false likeness" of hope. What makes Mr. Micawber's optimism hollow is that he *does nothing*. He sits back and waits for fortune to show up at his doorstep.

Teresa, like Mr. Micawber, was penniless yet optimistic. In the face of opposition from the archbishop of Burgos in making her foundation, she believed that "God will awaken other people to give [alms] and little by little he will arrange everything" (LE. 2. 401. 10.). However, her belief was not based upon the presumption that "something will turn up." Rather, Teresa said that she was at peace and trusted in God's providence because "it seems to me that I have done all that I could about this [situation] . . ." (LE. 2. 401. 7.).

Trusting in divine providence is not a substitute for action. Praying that "I put it all in the Lord's hands," without first putting one's own hand to the plow, is refusing to use the means that God provides. The *Serenity Prayer* presupposes that we accept the things that we cannot change *only after* we have courageously tried to change the things that we can.

Questions. The whole of Teresa's life is a testimony to her belief in divine providence, which was not a *falsam similitudinem* of hope or a belief that "something will turn up." As Teresa's life indicates, she did the hard work that providence requires; that is, she used the gifts that God had bestowed upon her—intelligence, common sense, and determination. Then, she trusted that God would bless her efforts to do his will. Have you ever used your "trust in divine providence" as a means of relinquishing your responsibility to act? Is your prayer "I leave it in the Lord's hands" a way of washing your hands of your obligations?

Reflection. "That lady, the foundress [of Soria] was waiting for us at the door of her house, where the monastery was to be established. We were anxious to get inside because of the large number of people. The crowd was nothing new, for everywhere we go there is much curiosity. The world is so fond of novelty that were it not for our veils we wear over our faces, these crowds would be a great trial" (F. 30. 8.).

The short journey that Teresa and her companions made from their covered ox cart to their new house is symbolic of one of the most painful experiences in life, namely, being looked at as an object of curiosity because you are different. Sometimes love demands that we place ourselves in a situation in which we feel out of place or in which we will be looked at as odd.

We have an example of this in a very poignant scene in Dickens' novel *Great Expectations*, where Joe Gargery, a simple blacksmith, who has never left his village, comes to London on an errand. He has been asked to deliver a message to an old friend named Pip. Pip had once been Joe's apprentice in the village forge but, because of a change in fortune, is now a gentleman living in London. The meeting is awkward. Joe is uncomfortably self-conscious because he feels out of place, his manners being rustic and his language unpolished.

After Joe struggles through an uneasy conversation and dinner with Pip and Pip's friend Herbert Pocket, Joe tells Pip that he has to leave. Pip protests faintly, but Joe knows the truth of the situation.

> Pip, dear old chap, life is made of ever so many partings welded together, as I may say, and one's a blacksmith, and one's a whitesmith, and one a goldsmith, and one's a coppersmith. Divisions among such must come, and must be met as they come. If there's been any fault at all today, it's mine. You and me is not two figures to be together in London; nor yet anywheres else but what is private, and beknown, and understood between friends. It ain't that I am proud, but that I want to be right, as you shall never see me no more in these clothes. I'm wrong out of the forge.[23]

Joe and Teresa had something in common. They both felt out of place. They knew that their dress and their way of life made them novelties to those about them. They both felt that they were being stared at. Joe loved Pip, and Teresa loved God. Both were willing to bear the embarrassment and the awkward moment out of love.

Questions. Life often presents us with situations that make us feel uncomfortable or self-conscious. Sometimes life demands that we place ourselves in these situations for the sake of those we love. How have you responded when these invitations to love have arisen in your life?

Chapter 31[1]

Begins to treat in this chapter of the foundation of the glorious St. Joseph of Saint Anne in the city of Burgos. The first Mass was said April 19, the octave day of Easter, in 1582.

1. For over six years some members of the Society of Jesus, very conscientious, experienced, learned, and spiritual, were telling me that our Lord would be greatly served if a house of our sacred religious order were founded in Burgos. The reasons they gave for such a foundation made me begin to desire it. On account of the many trials within the order and in the other foundations, there had been no opportunity to attempt a foundation in Burgos.

2. In the year 1580, while I was in Valladolid, the Archbishop of Burgos passed through. Having been bishop in the Canary Islands, he was afterward appointed to the diocese of Burgos and at the time was going there.[2] I asked the bishop of Palencia, Don Alvaro de Mendoza, to ask him to give us permission for a foundation, and he said he would gladly ask him. Since he thinks our Lord is served in these houses, he is very pleased when one is founded. I have already spoken of how much Don Alvaro favors this order, for while bishop of Avila he accepted the first monastery of St. Joseph and always afterward has shown us much favor and considered the affairs of this order as his own, especially those about which I consult him.[3]

3. The archbishop did not want to enter the city of Valladolid but stayed in the monastery of St. Jerome.[4] There the bishop of Palencia had a great feast prepared for him and went to dine with him and invest him with a cincture, or I don't

know what the ceremony was, that would make him an arch-bishop.[5] It was there that Don Alvaro asked of him the permission for me to found a monastery in Burgos. The archbishop said that he would grant it gladly because even when he was in the Canary Islands he had desired and tried to get one of these monasteries, for he knew me personally and came from a place where one of our monasteries was located, and thus he knew how our Lord was served in them. As a result, the bishop of Palencia told me the foundation would not fail for want of a license, for the archbishop had been very pleased about the project, and that since the Council requires the permission of the bishop but not that it be given in writing, the license could be considered as granted.[6]

4. In speaking previously of the foundation of Palencia, I mentioned the great reluctance I had to making a foundation at that time because of the serious illness from which I was suffering. They had thought I would not live, and I had still not recovered.[7] Yet illness does not usually affect me so much when I see that something is for the service of God, and thus I don't know the reason for my feeling so much repugnance as I then did. For if the reason had been scarcity of means, I had fewer in other foundations. To me, after I had seen what was to take place, the cause seemed to be the devil. And what has happened each time that there has been some trial in one of these foundations is that our Lord has always helped me with locutions and with deeds since He knows how miserable I am. I have thought, at times, how in some foundations in which there have been no trials, His Majesty didn't warn me about anything. The former is what happened here, for since He knew what I would have to undergo He immediately began

to encourage me. May He be praised for everything! Thus, in respect to this foundation, as was mentioned in regard to that of Palencia,[8] for both foundations were being discussed together, He asked, as though making a reprimand, what I was afraid of and when He had failed me: "I am the same; do not fail to make these two foundations." Since the courage these locutions have left in me has been mentioned, there is no reason for mentioning it again here. Immediately, all hesitation was taken from me. This makes it seem that the cause was not illness or old age. Thus I began to make plans for both, as was mentioned.

5. It seemed better to make the foundation in Palencia first, since it was closer, the weather was harsh, Burgos was so cold, and so as to please the good bishop of Palencia; and this is what was done, as was mentioned.[9] Since, while in Palencia, the request came for a foundation in Soria, it seemed better—for in Palencia everything was finished—to go there first and then to Burgos.[10]

The bishop of Palencia thought that an account should be given to the archbishop of what was taking place, and I begged him to do so. After I went to Soria, the bishop sent a canon, named Juan Alonso, from Palencia to the archbishop for no other purpose than that. And the archbishop wrote to me with much love of how he desired my coming, discussed the matter with the canon, and wrote to the bishop of Palencia submitting the matter to him, saying that what he did was because he knew the people of Burgos and knew that their consent was necessary in order to make the foundation.

6. In short, his conclusion was that I should go there and discuss the matter first with the city and that if the city would

not give the permission he would give it to me because he was not going to let them tie his hands; and that he had witnessed the foundation of the monastery in Avila, which was the first, and remembered the great turmoil and opposition there[11] and that he wanted to prevent this from happening in Burgos; and that it was not suitable to found a monastery unless with an income or with the consent of the city; that it would not be expedient for me and that that was why he was mentioning this.

7. The bishop considered that the deed was as good as done, and rightly so because the archbishop said I should come, and thus he sent me word that I should go. But my impression was that the archbishop lacked enthusiasm. I wrote to him thanking him for the favor he granted me but telling him that it seemed to me it would be worse to make a foundation against the will of the city than without asking them permission for it and that this would put His Excellency into more conflict (it seems I guessed the little help I would get from him if there were some opposition), and that I would try to obtain the permission from the city even though I knew this would be difficult because of the contradictory opinions usually held in matters like this. And I wrote to the bishop of Palencia begging him that since summer was almost over and my illnesses were too many for me to be living in so cold a place we should let the idea rest for the time being. I did not express my doubts about the archbishop because the bishop was already displeased with him on account of the obstacles he was setting up after having shown so much willingness, and I did not want to cause some discord between them, because they were friends. Thus I went from Soria to Avila very unconcerned about going

to Burgos so soon, and my going to the house of St. Joseph in Avila was very necessary for certain reasons.[12]

8. There lived in this of Burgos a holy widow named Catalina de Tolosa, a native of Vizcaya. I could go on at length telling about her virtues, her penance as well as her prayer, her generous almsgiving and charity, her good intelligence and courage.[13] She had given two of her daughters as nuns to our monastery of the Conception in Valladolid, I believe four years ago, and two others to Palencia, for she had been waiting that this latter foundation be made, and she brought them before I left.

9. All four turned out as one would expect of daughters brought up by such a mother, for they seemed to be no less than angels. She gave them good dowries and a full supply of other things, for she is very generous. Everything she does, she does to perfection; and she can do it because she is rich. When she came to Palencia we were so certain of the permission of the archbishop of Burgos that it didn't seem there would be any reason to delay, and thus I asked her to look for a house to rent for me so that we could make the foundation and that she provide us with some grilles and turns and charge everything to me. The thought never passed through my mind that she would spend anything of her own but only lend to me. She desired the foundation so much that she was extremely sorry to see it being set aside for awhile. And thus I returned to Avila, as I have said,[14] and was very unconcerned about dealing with the foundation at that time, but she was not so unconcerned. Thinking that all that was needed was permission from the city, she began to try to get it without telling me anything.

10. She had two neighbors, a mother and daughter, persons of high social status and very good servants of God who desired the foundation greatly. The mother, whose name was María Manrique, had a son who was a magistrate and whose name was Don Alonso de Santo Domingo Manrique. The daughter's name was Doña Catalina. Both mother and daughter discussed the matter with him so that he might seek permission from the city council. He spoke to Catalina de Tolosa asking what he should say about financial backing, for they wouldn't give the permission if there were none. She said, and this she did, that she would take on herself the obligation of giving us a house, if we had none, and also food. With this promise he presented a petition signed in his name. Don Alonso presented it with such skill that he obtained the permission from all the magistrates and from the archbishop, and he brought her the license in writing. As soon as she had begun dealing with the matter, she wrote to me that she was negotiating about the foundation. I thought she was joking because I know how reluctant people are to accept a monastery founded in poverty, and since I did not know, nor did it enter my mind, that she had obligated herself to provide for it, I thought that much more was needed.

11. Nevertheless, one day within the octave of St. Martin while I was recommending the foundation to our Lord, I thought that it could be made if the license were obtained. I couldn't bear the thought of going to a place as cold as Burgos with so many illnesses which would be aggravated by the cold. It would have been rash to make such a long journey just after finishing such a rough one, as I have said,[15] in coming from Soria; nor would Father Provincial allow me to do so. I

was reflecting that the prioress of Palencia could easily go,[16] for since everything was in order, there was now nothing to do. While I was thinking about this and very determined not to go, the Lord spoke to me in the following words in which I saw that the license was already given: "Don't pay attention to the cold weather for I am the true warmth. The devil uses all his strength to hinder that foundation; use yours with my help so that it may be realized and do not fail to go in person, for great good will be done."[17]

12. With these words I changed my mind again, for although my human nature sometimes finds these trials distasteful, my determination to suffer for this great God does not lessen. Thus I told Him not to pay any attention to my feelings of weakness when He orders me to do what would please Him, for with His help I would not fail to do it. There was cold weather and snow at the time. That which daunted me most was my lack of health, for when I have my health everything seems easy to me. This lack of health was what very often tired me out on this foundation. The cold was not bad, at least from what I felt, for in truth it seems I felt as much when I was in Toledo. The Lord had well fulfilled His words about this cold.

13. Within a few days they brought me the license, along with letters, from Catalina de Tolosa and her friend Doña Catalina,[18] urging me to hurry, for they feared lest some mishap might occur. At that time the order of the Victorines[19] came there to make a foundation; and the calced Carmelites friars were there for a long time trying to make a foundation; afterward, the Basilians came. That so many of us had come together at the same time was a great obstacle and something

to keep in mind, but also something to praise our Lord for because of the great charity of this city. For the city gave them the licenses very willingly even though it was not enjoying its usual prosperity. I have always heard the charity of this city praised, but I had never thought it was as great as it is. Some favored some orders; others favored others. But the archbishop considered all the troubles that could arise and opposed these other foundations thinking that they would be harmful to the orders founded in poverty which would then be unable to survive. Perhaps these very orders influenced him or the devil invented this so as to remove the great blessing that God brings about whenever there are many monasteries, for God has the power to sustain many as well as few.

14. For this reason, those holy women were urging me so much that I would have gone at once were it not for the business I had to attend to. I was considering how much more obligated I was to these women who were so diligent, and not to lose this opportunity through my own fault.

The locution I had heard implied that there would be much opposition. I could not understand from where it would come, for Catalina de Tolosa had already written me assuring us of the house in which she was living for our foundation and that the city was in accord and the archbishop also. I could not understand from whom this opposition to be stirred up by the devils would come, for I never doubted that the words I heard were from God.

15. In short, His Majesty gives more light to superiors, for when I wrote to Father Provincial about the foundation of which I had heard in the locution, he did not forbid me but asked if I had got permission from the archbishop in writing.[20]

I wrote about this to Burgos. They answered that they had spoken with him of how they had asked permission from the city and that he was pleased. With this and all the things he had said concerning the foundation, it didn't seem there was any reason to doubt.

16. Father Provincial wanted to accompany us on this foundation. He did so partly because he was unoccupied at the time, since he had finished preaching the Advent series, and had to visit Soria which he had not seen since its founding and which was not much out of the way; and partly because he wanted to look after my health on the journey, for the weather was harsh, and I, old and sick; and they think my life is somewhat important. Certainly this was the providence of God, for the roads were so flooded from the heavy rains that he and his companions were very necessary to guide us along the way and help pull the wagons out of the mire. This was especially so on the trip from Palencia to Burgos, which was a very daring one to make at that time. True, our Lord told me that we could go without harm, that I should not fear, that He would be with us; although I did not tell this then to Father Provincial. But these words consoled me in the great hardships and dangers that we were going through. There was special danger in a river crossing near Burgos called Paso de los Pontones. The rain had been so heavy and had lasted so long that the water flooded the bridge. As a result, the bridge could not be seen nor could we see where to pass, but all was water, and everywhere it was very deep. In sum, it was a great imprudence to cross there, especially with wagons, for just by veering a little from the course all would have been lost. In fact, one of the wagons did get into a dangerous situation.[21]

17. We had hired a guide in an inn who knew that crossing; but, certainly, it was a very dangerous one. And, oh! The inns! There was no possibility of making a full day's journey in one day because of the bad roads. The wagons usually got stuck in the mud and other mules had to be used to help pull the wagons out. The Fathers who came with us had to undergo a great deal because it happened that the muleteers we hired were young and careless. Going with Father Provincial was a great relief because he took care of everything and has such a peaceful disposition that it seems no hardship weighs him down. Thus, what was difficult he made so easy that it seemed to be a small matter—although not the crossing of the bridge, which frightened us all very much, for if seeing us enter this world of water without a road or a barge made me fear after all the strength our Lord had given me, what must have been the fear of the nuns who accompanied me? We were eight nuns: two who will return with me, and five who are to remain in Burgos, four of them choir Sisters and one lay Sister.[22] I don't think I've yet mentioned Father Provincial's name. His name is Fray Jerónimo Gracián de la Madre de Dios.[23] I have spoken of him at other times. I was making the journey with a severe sore throat, which I caught on my way to Valladolid, along with a fever that had not left me.[24] Eating was very painful. This prevented me from enjoying the good things that happened during the journey. This illness has remained with me until now, the end of June, although considerably less severe, but still very painful. All the nuns were happy on the journey; once the danger was over, they found recreation in talking about it. For those who usually practice obedience as do these nuns, it is a great thing to suffer in obeying.

18. It was through this rough journey and heavy rain that we reached Burgos. Before entering the city, our Father wanted us to go first to visit the holy crucifix[25] and recommend our foundation to the Lord and wait for nightfall, for it was early when we arrived. It was a Friday, January,[26] the day after the feast of the Conversion of St. Paul. It had been decided that the foundation be made immediately, and I had brought my letters from Canon Salinas for his relatives and friends strongly urging them to favor this foundation. (Canon Salinas, the one I mentioned in discussing the foundation in Palencia,[26] comes from this city and from an important family. He worked just as hard for this foundation as for that of Palencia.)

19. And favor it, they did. Immediately, the next day, the whole city council came in a body to see me, for they did not regret the permission they had given but rather were glad that I came and wanted me to tell them what they could do for me. If we had any fear, it was of the city. Thus we considered that now everything would go easily. Although no one knew of our coming, we thought of making it known to the archbishop so that the first Mass could be said at once as was done in almost all the other foundations. But because of the very heavy rain that was falling when we reached the house of the good Catalina de Tolosa, we did not do so.

20. That night we rested in the great comfort that this holy woman provided for us. But it proved troublesome for me. She had a large fire so as to dry us out. Although there was a chimney, the fire caused me so much harm that the next day I couldn't raise my head. So, through a window with a grate covered by a veil, I spoke with those who came to visit me.

Since it was a day in which I had to attend to business matters, I was very embarrassed.

21. Early that morning, Father Provincial went to seek the blessing of His Excellency, for we thought there would be nothing more to do. He found that the archbishop was very disturbed and angry because I had come without his permission, acting as though he had not ordered me to come or had never discussed anything about the foundation. Thus he spoke to Father Provincial extremely angry at me. When finally he conceded that he had ordered me to come, he said that he meant I should come alone to discuss the matter—but that I came with so many nuns! God delivered us from the distress it caused him! There was little use telling him that once we had the permission of the city, as he had asked of us, nothing else was left to be done than simply make the foundation and that the bishop of Palencia had told me (for I had asked him if it would be good that I come without letting the archbishop know) that there was no reason for asking the permission because the archbishop had already said how much he desired the foundation. This is the way the things happened, and they did happen in this way because God wanted the house to be founded. The archbishop himself acknowledged this afterward. If we had openly informed him, he would have told us not to come. He ended the visit with Father Provincial by telling him that if we did not have an income and our own house he would in no way grant the license; we could easily return to where we came from. And the roads were so good and the weather so beautiful!

22. O my Lord, how certain it is that anyone who renders You some service soon pays with a great trial! And what a

precious reward a trial is for those who truly love you if we could at once understand its value! But we did not then want this reward because it was making everything impossible. The archbishop made still more demands: that what would be used for income and buying the house could not be taken from what the nuns brought with them. Since a thought like this had never even entered our mind—especially in these times—everybody thought that there was no chance whatever for the foundation. But not I, for I was always certain that everything was working for the best, that the devil was setting snares so as to hinder it, and that God would accomplish his designs. Father Provincial returned, nonetheless, very happy, for he was not at that time disturbed. God so provided, and He provided also that Father Provincial would not be annoyed with me for not having obtained the archbishop's permission in writing as he had told me to do.[27]

23. Some of the friends and relatives to whom Canon Salinas had written, as I mentioned,[28] had come to see me, and some of them had come right away. They thought the archbishop should be asked for permission to have Mass in the house so that we would not have to go out into the streets, which were very muddy; and for us to go out discalced was thought to be inappropriate. There was in the house, which had been used for ten years by members of the Society of Jesus when they first came to Burgos, a suitable room that had served as a chapel. With this we thought no obstacle would stand in the way of taking possession there until we had a house. Never were we able to get the archbishop to let us have Mass there, even though two canons went to beg him for it. The most they got from him was that once we had an income, the

foundation could be made there until we bought a house. And he said that in order to buy a house we would have to have guarantors who would pay and that we would have to leave the place where we were staying. These guarantors we found at once, for the friends of Canon Salinas offered to do this, and Catalina de Tolosa provided the income for the foundation.

24. It took more than three weeks to decide on the amount of money, how and from where it would come. During this time we could not hear Mass; only very early on feast days. And I, with a fever and very ill. But Catalina de Tolosa did everything so well, because she was so generous and showed so much good will, that she provided us all, in a room where we were secluded, with food for a month, as though she were the mother of each one. Father Provincial and his companions were given lodging in a house of one of his friends, named Doctor Manso,[29] who had been a classmate and was now the canon preacher at the cathedral. Our provincial was very impatient about being detained there so long, but he did not know how he could leave us.

25. Once there was an agreement about the guarantors and the income, the archbishop ordered that the document be given to his administrator, and said that the matter would be taken care of at once. The devil could not leave off tempting the administrator. We thought there would be nothing to cause a delay and that, after we spent almost a month in trying to meet the demands of the archbishop, the administrator would be pleased with what had been done. After examining the document very carefully, the administrator sent me a memorandum saying that the license would not be given until we had a house of our own and that the archbishop did

not want the foundation to be made in the house in which we were staying because it was damp and there was too much noise in the street. And with regard to the guarantees made on the property, I don't know what complications and other things he brought up, as though we were just then beginning the whole matter. And he said that he would have no more to say about this, and that the house must satisfy the archbishop.

26. When Father Provincial saw this, he was very upset as were all the nuns. In order to buy a site for a monastery much time is obviously required, and he was annoyed at seeing us go out for Mass. Even though the church was not far[30] and we heard the Mass in a chapel without anyone seeing us, this situation was a very great hardship for His Reverence and us. By that time, I think, he had made up his mind that we should go back. I could not bear the thought of this when I remembered that our Lord told me that as His instrument I should try to make the foundation, and I was so certain that it would be made that almost nothing caused me distress. My only distress was for Father Provincial. Since I didn't know how much his friends were going to help us, as I shall mention later, I was very sorry that he had come with us. While I was experiencing this affliction (and my companions were also very afflicted, but I didn't mind theirs as much as I did Father Provincial's), but not engaged in prayer itself, our Lord spoke these words to me: "Now Teresa, hold fast." With these words, I tried with more spirit to get Father Provincial to leave and let us remain (and His Majesty must have given him the same spirit), for Lent was approaching and he had to go to preach.[31]

27. He and his friends gave orders that some rooms in the hospital of the Conception be given to us, for the Blessed

Sacrament was reserved there and Mass was said each day. This made the provincial somewhat satisfied. But there was no small struggle in getting this, for one of the rooms, which was a good one, had been rented by a widow of this city, and she did not want to let us use it even though she was not going to move there for another half year. It also upset her that one of the rooms they had given us on the top floor, which had only the bare tiles of the roof for a ceiling, had an entrance to her room. She was not satisfied with having the key to the lock on the outside but she also nailed up the entrance from the inside. Furthermore, the hospital confraternity was afraid that we were going to take over the hospital, which was something absurd, but God wanted us to merit more. They made Father Provincial and me promise before a notary that if they told us to leave we would have to do so at once. It was this promise that was the most difficult thing for me to do, for I feared the widow, who was rich and had relatives, that she would make us leave on one of her whims. But Father Provincial, who was more circumspect, wanted us to do all they asked so that we could go there immediately.

28. They gave us no more than two rooms and a kitchen. But a great servant of God, named Hernando de Matanza, was in charge of the hospital and gave us two other rooms for a parlor. He showed us great charity, and he does so to all, for he does much for the poor. Francisco de Cuevas,[32] who is the postmaster of this city, also showed us great charity, for he was much involved with this hospital. He has always helped us when there was need.

29. I have mentioned the names of those who were our first benefactors because it is right that the nuns living now, and

those who are to come after, remember them in their prayers. The founding benefactors should be remembered even more. Although at first it was not my intention to count Catalina de Tolosa among these latter, nor did it enter my mind, she has merited by her good life in the service of our Lord that He so ordain things that the title of founding benefactoress cannot be denied her. Apart from her paying for the house, for we would have had no means of doing so, she bore the indescribable cost of all these rebuffs of the archbishop. Her deepest affliction was the thought that the foundation might not be made, and she never tired of doing good for us.

30. This hospital was very far from her house. She visited us almost every day with great charity and sent us all that we needed. Because of this, the people never stopped making critical comments to her, so that if it were not for her courage, these would have been enough to make her give up the whole thing. To see what she was suffering caused me great pain. Even though she hid it most of the time, at other times she could not conceal it, especially when these comments affected her conscience. She is so conscientious that, however great were the occasions of sin that some persons provided for her, I never heard her speak a word that was offensive to God. They told her that she was on her way to hell and asked how she could do what she was doing since she had children. Everything she did was with the advice of learned men. Even if she would have wanted to do otherwise, I would not have consented for anything in the world to her doing something she should not do, even if it would have meant my giving up a thousand monasteries, to say nothing of just one. But since the business matters concerning the foundation were kept secret, I

am not surprised at what was in the minds of the people. She answered with prudence, for she has a great deal of it, and suffered the remarks in such a way that it truly seemed God was teaching her and gave her the ability to please some and bear with others. And He gave her the courage to put up with everything. How much more courage for doing great things do the servants of God have than do those of high nobility if they are not His servants; although she, being of noble descent, is not without much nobility in her background.

31. Well to return to what I was dealing with,[33] once Father Provincial had us in a place where we could hear Mass and observe enclosure, he had the heart to go to Valladolid where he was to preach. Yet he was distressed at not seeing in the archbishop any hopeful sign that the license would be granted. Although I always insisted that it would be given, he could not believe this. And, certainly, there were many reasons for his not believing this which need not be mentioned here. If he had little hope, his friends had less, and they made him more discouraged.

I was more relieved to see him gone because, as I have said,[34] the greatest suffering I had was to see his. He left us the instructions to find a house that we could own, which was something very difficult because until then not even one house was found that was for sale. Our friends, especially those of Father Provincial's,[35] were given greater charge over us, and all agreed not to speak a word to the archbishop until we had a house. The archbishop always said that he desired this foundation more than anyone. And I believe it, because he is such a good Christian that he wouldn't speak anything but the truth; but in his deeds it didn't appear that he desired this since he demanded things that seemed impossible for us to comply with. This was the devil's scheme to prevent the foundation. But, O Lord, how obvious it is that You are powerful, for the very scheme the devil used to prevent it, You used to do something better. May You be blessed forever.

32. From the vigil of St. Matthias, when we began living in the hospital, until the vigil of St. Joseph[36] we were conferring about this and that house. There were so many obstacles that we could not buy any of those that were for sale. I was told of one house owned by a gentleman, which had been up for sale for many days, and even though so many religious were looking for a house, God was pleased that none of them found it suitable. Now, they are all surprised, and some really sorry about this. Two persons had spoken to me about the house. But there were so many who spoke badly of it, that I paid no attention to it, thinking it would be unsuitable.

33. One day I was speaking with Doctor Aguiar, who I said was a friend of our Father Provincial's.[37] He was looking very carefully for a house for us. He said that he had looked at some but that nothing appropriate could be found in the whole city and that it didn't seem possible to find any, as others were telling me. I then remembered the one I mentioned that we had disregarded. I thought, even though it's as bad as they say we can take care of our present need and later on sell it. I told Doctor Aguiar about it and asked him if he would do me the favor of looking at it.

34. To him, this didn't seem to be a bad plan. He had not seen the house, and even though it was a stormy and rough day, he wanted to go there at once. There was an occupant in it who had little interest in its being sold and did not want

to show it to him, but its location and the little he could see pleased him greatly, and thus we decided to try to buy it. The gentleman who owned it was not here but the power to sell it had been given to a priest, a servant of God whom His Majesty inspired with a desire to sell it to us and deal with us very honestly.[38]

35. It was arranged that I go to see it. It pleased me to such an extreme that if they had asked for twice as much as they did, it would have seemed cheap to me. I am not exaggerating, because two years before they were offering the owner that much, and he did not want to sell it. The next day a priest[39] and Doctor Aguiar went there, and when the latter learned of the amount of money that would be acceptable, he wanted to sign the contract at once. I had informed some of my friends, and they had told me that if I gave this amount I was giving five hundred ducats too much. I told Doctor Aguiar, but he thought the price was cheap if I gave what was asked for. I was of the same mind. I myself would not have hesitated because it seemed to me like a gift, but since the money belonged to the order, I had some scruple. We met about this before Mass on the vigil of the feast of our glorious Father St. Joseph. I told them that after Mass we should meet again and come to a decision.

36. Doctor Aguiar is a very intelligent man and saw clearly that if our desire were made public we would either have to pay much more for the house or not buy it. Thus he was very careful and made the priest promise to come back there after Mass. We nuns went to recommend the matter to God, who said to me, "Do you hesitate over money?" letting me know that the house was suitable for us. The Sisters had prayed

very much to St. Joseph that they might have a house by this feastday, and although there was no thought of having it so soon, he heard their prayers. Everyone urged me to conclude the contract. And thus it was done, for Doctor Aguiar found a notary at the door,[40] which seemed ordained by the Lord, and came with him and a witness and told me it was opportune to sign the contract. Having closed the door of the room so that nothing would be known (for this was Doctor Aguiar's fear), we concluded the sale, in accord with all the legal demands, on the vigil of the glorious St. Joseph,[41] as I have said. It came about through the careful diligence and intelligence of this good friend.

37. No one thought the house would be sold for so little.[42] Thus, as the news spread, the buyers began to appear and say that the priest who sold it gave it away practically and that the sale should be nullified because of the great fraud. The good priest suffered very much. They immediately informed the owners, a gentleman, as I said,[43] and his wife, both from the nobility. They were so happy that their house was being made into a monastery that they approved, although there was nothing else they could now do. Immediately, the next day, the deed was drawn up, and a third of the price was paid. Everything was done according to the requests of the priest. Although some things in the agreement were onerous to us, we accepted everything for his sake.

38. It may seem pointless that I spent so much time in telling about the buying of this house, but indeed those who considered the things in detail thought it was no less than a miracle, both in the price, which made the house seem like a gift, and in the fact that many from religious orders were so

blinded that after looking at it did not want to buy it, as though it had never been in Burgos. Those who saw it were amazed and blamed the religious and called them fools. And a monastery of nuns (even two monasteries—one had been recently founded; the other had moved here from elsewhere after their former house had burned down) had looked at it a little while ago. So too did a wealthy person who is trying to found a monastery. They all let it go, and now they are very sorry.

39. Such was the outcry in the city that we saw clearly how right the good Doctor Aguiar was to keep the whole matter secret and in being so diligent about this. Indeed, we can say that, after God, it was he who gave us the house. Good intelligence is a great help in everything. And since he has so much, God moved him and brought this work to completion through him. For more than a month he helped and advised us on how to adapt the house well and with little cost. It seemed as though our Lord had kept it for Himself, for almost everything seemed to be already done. Indeed, as soon as I saw it and how everything was as though made to order for us and done so quickly, it seemed like a dream. By bringing us to such a paradise, our Lord repaid us generously for what we had suffered. Because of the garden, the view, and the water, the property is nothing else but that. May He be blessed forever, amen.

40. The archbishop learned of it immediately and rejoiced in our success, thinking that his obstinacy had been the reason, and he was very right. I wrote to him that I was happy he was pleased and that I would hurry to adapt the house so that he could give us his final permission. Once I told him this, I made haste to move in because I was told that they wanted to keep

us where we were until the deed or I don't know what was signed. Thus we moved into one room even though an occupant was still living in the house,[44] for there was also some trouble in getting rid of him. They told me that the archbishop was very angry about our moving in. I tried to appease him as much as I could, for, because he is good, even though he does get angry, he soon gets over it. He was also angry when he learned that we had the grates and the turn, for he thought that I wanted to go ahead at all costs. I wrote to him that this was not the case, but that in a house for persons living a life of recollection these are customary, that I hadn't even dared to put up a cross so as not to appear to be going ahead before having permission, and this was true. Notwithstanding all the good will I showed, there was no way of getting him to grant the license.

41. He came to see the house and was very pleased with it and showed us much kindness but did not give us the permission, although he offered more hope. There was still I don't know what contracts to be made with Catalina de Tolosa. Everyone was very afraid that he would not give it. But Doctor Manso, whom I mentioned,[45] as the other friend of Father Provincial's, was too good a friend of the archbishop's to be waiting for the proper time before reminding him and urging him. It was very distressing to Doctor Manso to see us going about as we were. For even though there was a chapel in this house, which was never used except for saying Mass for the owners, the archbishop never allowed Mass to be said for us in the house. On feastdays and Sundays we had to go out to a church in order to hear Mass.[46] Fortunately it was nearby, although between the time we moved and the time

the foundation was made, a month more or less passed by. All the learned men said there was sufficient reason for allowing Mass in the chapel. The archbishop who is a very learned man understood this too. So it seems there is no other explanation than that our Lord wanted us to suffer. Although I bore it better, there was a nun who in seeing herself out on the street trembled from the distress she felt.

42. In drawing up the contracts there was no little trouble, because one minute they were satisfied with the guarantors, the next minute they wanted the money; and they made many other vexing demands. In this, the archbishop was not so much to blame but one administrator who was very hostile to us. If in God's providence it had not been necessary for this administrator to go on a trip and another take his place, it seems we would never have obtained the license. Oh, what Catalina de Tolosa had to suffer in all this is impossible to say! She bore everything with a patience that amazed me, and she did not tire of providing for us. She gave all the furnishings we needed to set up the house, such as beds and many other things, for she had a well supplied house. It seemed that we were lacking no necessity, even if she lacked it in her own house. Other founding benefactors of our monasteries have given much more in property and wealth, but for none of them was the cost as much as one-tenth of what she went through. And if she had had no children, she would have given all that she could. She desired so much to see the work completed that everything she did toward this end seemed to her little.

43. Seeing so much delay, I wrote to the bishop of Palencia begging him to write again to the archbishop. The bishop was disgusted with him, for everything the archbishop did to us the

bishop took as done to him. And what amazed us was that the archbishop never thought he was offensive to us in anything. I begged the bishop to write again to the archbishop saying that since we had the house and had done what he had wanted that he should bring the matter to a close. The bishop sent me an open letter for the archbishop written in such a way that if I had given it to him we would have ruined everything. Thus Doctor Manso, my confessor and adviser, did not want me to give it to him. Although it was very courteous, it spoke some truths that, given the temperament of the archbishop, were enough to annoy him, for he was already annoyed by some of the messages the bishop had sent to him, and they were close friends. The bishop used to tell me that just as through the death of our Lord enemies had become friends so though me friends had become enemies. I told him that from this he could see what I was. I had taken special care, in my opinion, so that they would not become angry with each other.

44. I begged the bishop again, with the best reasons I could think of, that he write another very friendly letter to the arch-bishop and remind him of the service the monastery would render to God. He did what I asked him, which was no trifle. But since he saw that writing the letter was for the service of God and a favor to me, which he has always been ready to grant, he finally forced himself. He wrote to me afterward that of all the things he had done for the order nothing compared with his having had to write this letter. In short, this letter was so effective, together with the diligence of Doctor Manso, that the archbishop gave us the license.[47] He sent it with the good Hernando de Matanza, who arrived with no little joy. On this day the Sisters had been more distressed than ever, and the

good Catalina de Tolosa so much so that she could not be consoled. It seems that the Lord at the time when he was about to give us the joy wanted to afflict us more. Even I, who had not been lacking in confidence, was lacking in it the night before. May His name be blessed without end and praised forever and ever, amen.

45. The archbishop gave Doctor Manso permission to say the first Mass the next day and to reserve the Blessed Sacrament. And the Father Prior of San Pablo, who belongs to the Dominican order (to which our order owes so much as well as to the Society of Jesus), said the high Mass with much solemnity provided by musicians who came unrequested with their wind instruments.

All our friends were very pleased and so too was almost the whole city, for they had felt very sorry to see us in such a situation. They were so critical of what the archbishop was doing that I sometimes felt more sorry at what I heard people were saying about him than I was about what we ourselves were going through. The joy of the good Catalina de Tolosa and of the Sisters was so great that it inspired me with devotion and I said to God: "Lord, what do these your servants seek other than to serve you and see themselves enclosed for You in a place they will never leave?"

46. No one but those who experience it will believe the joy that is felt in these foundations once we are enclosed where no secular person can enter, for however much we love them it is not enough to take away this great consolation in finding ourselves alone. It seems to me comparable to taking many fish from the river with a net; they cannot live until they are in the water again. So it is with souls accustomed to living in the

running streams of their Spouse. When taken out of them and caught up in the net of worldly things, they do not truly live until they find themselves back in those waters. This I always observed in each of these Sisters; this I know from my own experience. Nuns who see in themselves the desire to go out among seculars and converse with them a great deal should fear that they have not discovered the living water of which the Lord spoke to the Samaritan woman[48] and that their Spouse has hid it from them, and rightly so since they are not satisfied in being with Him. I am afraid that this latter stems from two causes: either they did not embrace the religious state for Him alone; or, after having embraced it, they do not recognize the great favor God has granted them in choosing them for Himself and freeing them from being subject to a man who is often the death of them and who could also be, God forbid, the death of their souls.

47. Oh, my Spouse, true God and true man! Should this favor be taken so lightly? Let us praise Him, my Sisters, because He has granted it to us and let us not tire of praising so great a King and Lord, who has prepared for us a kingdom without end in exchange for some little troubles which will end tomorrow and which come wrapped in a thousand joys. May He be blessed forever, amen, amen.

48. A few days after the house was founded, it seemed to Father Provincial[49] and me that in the endowment Catalina de Tolosa had provided for this house there were certain difficulties that could have given rise to a lawsuit and cause her some worry. And we wanted more to trust in God than to be the occasion for giving her any suffering. For this and some other reasons, with the permission of Father Provincial, we nullified

in the presence of a notary the contracts concerning the money she had given us and returned all the documents. This was done in great secrecy so that the archbishop wouldn't know of it, for he would have been hurt. But doing this also hurt the house. When it is known that a monastery is founded in poverty, there is nothing to fear because everyone helps. But when people think it has an income, to be without one is dangerous and the monastery will be left temporarily without means. Catalina de Tolosa has provided for a remedy that will become possible after her death. She has arranged that her two daughters, who were to make profession in our monastery of Palencia that year, would transfer to this house their inheritance that would have been promised to Palencia at their profession. And to another daughter, who desired to receive the habit here, she has left the family estate which amounts to as much as the income she wanted to provide.[50] The only drawback is that these goods cannot be used at once, but I have always held that we will not be in want. The Lord who provides that alms be given to our other monasteries founded in poverty will awaken some to give them here, or will provide the means by which nuns can support themselves. Since no monastery had been founded under such conditions, I sometimes begged the Lord that since He had desired that this foundation be made He ordain that it be helped and have what is necessary, and I had no desire to leave here until I saw whether someone wanting to be a nun would enter.

49. While I was thinking about this one day after Communion, the Lord said to me: "Why do you doubt? Everything is now finished; you are free to go." He thereby let me know that they would not lack what was necessary. These words so

impressed me that I had no more worry than I would have if I had left the nuns with a very good income. I immediately began to plan my departure, for it seemed to me I was no longer doing anything else here than enjoy myself in this house, for it suited me perfectly, and I could have been a greater help, although with much more hardship, in other monasteries.

The archbishop and the bishop of Palencia remained good friends. Soon the archbishop began to show us much kindness and gave the habit to Catalina de Tolosa's daughter[51] and to another nun who within a short time entered here. Up to the present, there are some persons who have been looking after us. Nor will our Lord allow his brides to suffer if they serve Him as they are obliged. May His Majesty give them the grace for this through His great mercy and goodness.

BURGOS (1582)

Summary and Background: Chapter 31

Teresa had a deep aversion to traveling to Burgos, especially in the winter. "I couldn't bear the thought of going to a place as cold as Burgos with so many illnesses which would be aggravated by the cold" (F. 31. 11.). Yet, God, through a locution, provided her the strength to go forward. "Don't pay attention to the cold weather for I am the true warmth" (F. 31. 11.).

Teresa began her journey to Burgos on January 2, 1582. She was in bad health; the weather was wretched and the roads were full of mud and snow. On the way, Teresa developed a large sore in her throat that prevented her from talking and eating "anything that had to be chewed" (LE. 2. 432. 5.). By the time she arrived in Palencia, the road to Burgos had become trackless and impassable; nevertheless, Teresa forged ahead on what was one of the most harrowing journeys of her life. Along the way "[t]he wagons usually got stuck in the mud" (F. 31. 17.), and several times they almost overturned.

The most treacherous leg of the journey was reserved for the last. "There was a special danger in a river crossing near Burgos . . . The rain had been so heavy and had lasted so long that the water flooded the bridge. As a result, the bridge could not be seen nor could we see where to pass" (F. 31. 15.). Though the wagons, carrying eight nuns, made the crossing, Teresa's wagon was almost carried away by the current of a river.

It was this event that gave rise to the story that as Teresa began to complain to God, she heard a voice from heaven saying, "My daughter, don't you know that this is how I treat my friends." And Teresa responded, " Yes, my Lord, I know. That is why you have so few!"

Once Teresa arrived in Burgos, she and the nuns were taken into the home of their benefactress Doña Catalina de Tolosa, a rich noblewoman. Catalina had written to Teresa assuring her that a house would be provided for a convent and that the city council and the archbishop were in favor of the foundation. However, by the time Teresa arrived, the archbishop had had a change of heart.

Gracián spoke to the archbishop and reminded him that *he* had invited Teresa to come to Burgos. The archbishop retorted that Gracián had misunderstood his meaning. The archbishop meant that he had invited Teresa to come to Burgos in order to *discuss* the *feasibility* of a foundation. He told Gracián that Teresa would have to have both a house and an income before he would even think of giving his consent. As far as the archbishop was concerned, Teresa could "return to where she came from" (F. 31. 21.). "[He] was extremely angry with [her] (F. 31. 21.).

It seems that the underlying reason for the archbishop's opposition was financial. At the time, many other religious orders were in the process of establishing themselves in Burgos. These houses would attract benefactors, which meant that a source of revenue for the diocese would diminish. The last thing that the archbishop needed was a convent founded in poverty.

At first, it looked as if the archbishop's demands would be met almost immediately when Doña Catalina offered Teresa both an endowment and the use of her house as a convent. However, the archbishop put the matter in the hands of a faultfinding administrator. He reported to the archbishop that Doña Catalina's house was too damp to live in and unsuitable for a life of contemplation because it was located in a noisy part of town.

In consequence, Teresa and her nuns had to move out of Doña Catalina's house. For the next two months they lived in a "very crowded" (LE. 2. 436. 1.) rat-infested attic of a hospital until they found a house that was acceptable to the archbishop. By the time Teresa had moved to the hospital, she was no longer bedridden, through far from well.

When Teresa was not engaged in house hunting, she was occupied with her usual load of correspondence. In one of her letters, Teresa mentions that she had brought with her from Avila her niece Teresita, Lorenzo's daughter, who was a novice at St. Joseph's in Avila. Teresa whisked Teresita out of town because Teresita's brother Francisco and his mother-in-law were putting undue pressure on Teresita to give them her share of their father's inheritance.

As Teresa was taking care of Teresita and the community in Burgos, she was also scurrying around trying to find a suitable house for her foundation. She questioned whether or not she would be able find one because "so many religious were [also] looking for a house" (F. 31. 32.). Fortunately, there was one house that many religious communities found unsuitable but that exceeded Teresa's expectations. They purchased the house on March 12, 1582, and moved in six days later. Teresa informed the archbishop. He "rejoiced in our success" (F. 31. 40.). However, when Teresa began to make necessary adaptations (installing the convent turns and grilles), the archbishop became furious and refused to grant Teresa the necessary license to officially establish the monastery. His opposition was so vehement that he even refused to allow Mass to be celebrated in their house. This meant that the nuns had to leave their home every day in order to attend Mass.

At this point, Teresa asked her friend, the bishop of Palencia, to intercede for her. "He was disgusted with [the archbishop]" (F. 31. 43.) and wrote him an angry letter. He showed the letter to Teresa before he sent it. When Teresa read it, she knew that it would make the situation worse, so she asked him to write another one in its stead. He consented, though he bristled. "[The bishop] wrote to me afterward that of all the things he had done for the order nothing compared to his having had to write this letter" (F. 31. 44.). The revised letter must have been effective because shortly after the archbishop received it, he then granted the license.

Mr. Hyde had once again turned back into Dr. Jekyll. The archbishop graciously preached at the dedication of the new foundation and, in a true spirit of humility, asked pardon from the community for all the grief he had caused it.

However, Teresa had the last word. She was so grateful to Catalina de Tolosa for all her help that when Teresa realized that Catalina's endowment might give rise to a lawsuit from the Jesuits, to whom Catalina had promised to bequeath much of her wealth, Teresa nullified the contracts that would guarantee an income for her community. "This was done in great secrecy so that the archbishop wouldn't know of it" (F. 31. 48.). In short, Teresa was able to found her last community according to her ideal, *in poverty*, the very condition that the archbishop had so adamantly opposed. The poor guy had no idea whom he was dealing with.

Reflection. Despite the disgust that he felt toward the archbishop of Burgos, the bishop of Palencia restrained his indignation and wrote a letter of supplication on behalf of Teresa. Yet, he told Teresa that "of all the things he had done for the order nothing compared to his having had to write this letter" (F. 31. 44.). There is an important consideration in the bishop's choice to restrain his rage rather than to vent his spleen.

If the bishop of Palencia had sent his original letter, though he would have experienced temporary relief from his rage, he would have jeopardized Teresa's enterprise. Before the archbishop had received the letter, he was already "extremely angry" (F. 31. 21.) with Teresa and his administrator was "very hostile" (F. 31. 42.) toward her.

An angry letter at this juncture, criticizing the archbishop's action, not only would have enraged the archbishop, but it would have given him an excuse to deny Teresa permission to make a foundation in his diocese. If the bishop of Palencia had sent his original letter, Teresa's foundation in Burgos may have never become a reality.

However, because the bishop of Palencia exercised self-restraint by writing a second letter, Teresa's foundation was established. Furthermore, the bishop's act of self-control allowed him to lay aside his rage and grow in the virtue of true meekness.

Every time we control our temper, we grow in the virtue of meekness. And meekness, writes St. John Climacus, makes us "impervious to insults."[52] True meekness is like a suit of armor. It so blunts the sting of the snubs and rudeness of daily life that we are less likely to go on the attack.

Questions. Has rage ever blinded you to the consequences of venting your anger? Have you ever considered that the self-restraint of meekness is a form of strength?

Reflection. As Teresa comes to the end of her chronicle of the foundations, she alludes to one of the great sacrifices that they demanded of her: to live a life that deprived her of the very things she sought by leaving the Incarnation—silence and solitude. Except for the first five years when she lived at St. Joseph's in Avila, this desire never materialized. From 1567, when she founded Medina del Campo to the end of her life (she died less than six months after the foundation of Burgos), Teresa tells us that she felt like a fish out of water.

> No one but those who experience it will believe the joy that is felt in these foundations once we are enclosed where no secular person can enter, for however much we love them it is not enough to take away this great consolation in finding ourselves alone. It seems to me comparable to taking many fish from the river with a net; they cannot live until they are in the water again. So it is with souls accustomed to living in the running streams of their Spouse. When taken out of them and caught up in the net of worldly things, they do not truly live until they find themselves back in those waters. (F. 31. 46.)

St. John of the Cross writes, "As regards this road to union, entering on the road means leaving one's own road."[53] These words are a summary of Teresa's life. She was willing to leave the path that she wanted to travel to God and journey by a path that God had marked out for her.

Letting go of the dreams and the designs that we have for our lives in order to follow God's call is one of the most painful decisions that we can make. Sometimes this will involve making the choice to modify or curtail our plans. At other times, it will mean accepting the harsh reality that our dreams will never be fulfilled. On a daily basis, it will mean allowing our schedule to be shattered by the demands of charity. In short, walking the path of faith is the willingness to relinquish control.

Questions. All of us are like Teresa, in the sense that the reality of our lives does not always correspond to our plans and dreams. Sometimes our dreams do not materialize as a result of circumstances beyond our control. However, as we have seen in Teresa's life, sometimes God asks us to sacrifice our dreams for the sake of doing his will. How have you responded when God has asked you to relinquish your dreams in order to follow his call?

Epilogue
JHS

1. It has occurred to me to record here how the nuns of the first monastery that was founded, St. Jospeh's in Avila, about which I wrote in another work and not in this book,[1] transferred their obedience to the order after having first professed it to the bishop.

2. When the monastery was founded, Don Alvaro de Mendoza was bishop, the one who is now bishop of Palencia. All the time that he was in Avila he was extremely helpful to the nuns. And with regard to our giving obedience to the bishop, I heard from our Lord that it would be expedient to give it to him.[2] This was borne out afterward, for in all the disagreements with the order and in many other things that happened we clearly found great support in him. Never did he allow any priest to make a visitation nor did he do anything more in that monastery than what I asked him. This arrangement lasted seventeen years, a little more or less, for I don't remember,[3] nor did I ever intend that this jurisdiction be changed.

3. When those years were over, the bishop of Avila was transferred to the diocese of Palencia.[4] At that time I was in the monastery of Toledo, and our Lord told me that it was fitting for the nuns of St. Joseph's to give their obedience to the order, that I should try to bring this about because in not doing this there would soon be a relaxation of observance in that house. Since I had heard in a former locution that it was good to give it to the bishop, it seemed the Lord was contradicting

Himself.[5] I didn't know what to do. I told my confessor who is now bishop of Osma and who is a very learned man.[6] He told me there was no contradiction, that formerly the one way was necessary and that now another was and that he thought it would be better if the monastery in Avila were united with these others than alone; and that this was true has been clearly seen in many ways.

4. He made me go to Avila to discuss the matter. I found the bishop of a completely different opinion, for in no way would he agree to this. But since I told him some of the reasons for the harm that could come to the nuns, and he loved them very much and has very good intelligence, and God helped, he thought of some other weightier reasons than the ones I had given him and decided to allow the transfer of jurisdiction. Even though some priests told him that this was not a good thing to do, he did not change his mind.

5. It was necessary to submit the matter to the vote of the nuns. For some of them the change was a very painful one to make. But since they respected me, they accepted my reasons, especially when they realized that now that the bishop, to whom the order owed so much and whom I loved, was gone, they could no longer have me with them. This made a strong impression on them, and thus this important matter was concluded. All the friars and nuns have seen clearly how lost that house would have been in doing the contrary. Blessed be the Lord who so carefully looks after the affairs of His servants! May He be blessed forever, amen.

CONCLUSION

On April 19, 1582, the community of Burgos was established. Teresa remained there until July 27. During this time, even though the archbishop had approved the foundation, the Jesuits were opposing its existence. Teresa had to combat their "serious calumnies" and "despicable interests" (LE. 2. 450. 2.), most of which were financial. To dissuade Doña Catalina de Tolosa from being a benefactor of Teresa's convent and to woo her into their camp, the Jesuits told Catalina "that they didn't want her to have anything to do with the discalced nuns lest she be contaminated by [their] manner of prayer" (LE. 2. 450. 3.).

Teresa was planning to leave Burgos shortly after she dealt with this problem but stayed on until July 27 to oversee necessary repairs to the convent. On May 23, Ascension Thursday, the Arlanzón river had risen and overflowed its banks, flooding the new convent. The community was forced to live on the second floor. The flood was so severe that it was necessary for workmen to break the windows and doors on the first floor of the convent in order to let the water out.

When Teresa was finally able to leave, she planned to go back to Avila where she was still prioress. She was accompanied by Ana de San Bartolomé, her faithful nurse, and her niece Teresita, who was due to make her profession in Avila. Their first stop was in Palencia. While there, Teresa wrote a letter to Doña Teresa de Layz, the founding benefactor of the Carmel of Alba (see F. 20.). Doña Teresa had tried to exercise so much control over the nuns in Alba that they had "begun to fear her" (LE 2. 372. 1.). Doña Teresa even tried to force the convent to accept postulants whom the community considered to be unsuitable candidates. In addition, Doña Teresa wanted Teresa to transfer Tomasina Bautista, the prioress of Burgos, to Alba because she disapproved of the current prioress Juana del Espiritu Santo. Teresa flatly refused Doña Teresa's request.

On August 25, Teresa and her two companions traveled on to Valladolid. There, Teresa was once again confronted with Teresita's brother Francisco and his mother-in-law. They came armed with lawyers claiming that Lorenzo's will was invalid. Teresa was used to lawsuits and the threat of lawsuits. However, what she didn't expect was that María Bautista (her cousin), the prioress of Valladolid, had taken sides with Francisco's mother-in-law. María even tried to convince some of the other nuns to align themselves with the lawyers. Over the years, María Bautista had become authoritarian and quarrelsome and had grown resentful of Teresa's preeminence. Teresa was stung to the heart. "I was eaten up with sadness over this" (LE. 2. 465. 3.).

On September 15, Teresa and her companions left Valladolid and traveled to Medina del Campo. She arrived exhausted and suffering from a fever and sore throat. Alberta Bautista, the prioress, received Teresa coldly, for she held a grudge against Teresa. Many years before, Teresa had reprimanded Alberta for boycotting recreation.

Alberta believed that the nuns should be concerned only about prayer.

Just before Teresa left Burgos to return to Avila, she heard God tell her. "Go! You still have to suffer greater things." On her journey, former friends turned against her; she was treated with ingratitude and disrespect, and she witnessed the growing laxity of her communities. These were her final sufferings and purifications. Yet, she had one small prospect of joy in sight, to arrive home in Avila and celebrate Teresita's profession. But Teresa was even deprived of this consolation.

Fr. Antonio, who was the temporary Vicar of Castille, ordered Teresa to go to Alba de Tormes to oversee the election of the new prioress and to give support to the daughter of the Duchess of Alba, who was near the end of her pregnancy. The Duchess of Alba wanted to see Teresa again. And since she was a very generous benefactor of the Reform, Antonio did not want to disappoint her. When Antonio ordered Teresa to go to Alba, he thwarted her plans to attend Teresita's profession. "Never have I seen her suffer from a command given by a superior so much as she did from this one," said Ana de San Bartolomé.[7]

Teresa never made it home to Avila. She arrived at Alba de Tormes on September 20, 1582. She died a daughter of the Church in the arms of her beloved nurse Ana on October 4, 1582, less than six months after making her last foundation.

Notes

Prologue

1 Teresa wrote the history of the first foundation, St. Joseph's in Avila, in her *Life*, chs. 32–36. Fr. García de Toledo was the confessor for whom Teresa wrote the *Life*, especially the account of the foundation of St. Joseph's. See introduction to the *Life*, vol. I, {A Report in Writing}; also *Life*, ch. 34, no. 6, no. 5.

2 Fr. Jerónimo Ripalda (1535–1618) joined the Society of Jesus in 1551. While rector of the Jesuit college in Salamanca in 1573, he became Teresa's confessor. He was rector also of Villagarcia, Burgos, and Valladolid. He died in Toledo. See *Spir. Test.*, 58, no. 3, no. 8.

3 The other seven monasteries were: Medina del Campo (1567); Malagón (1568); Valladolid (1568); Toledo (1569); Pastrana (1569); Salamanca (1570); and Alba de Tormes (1571).

4 The foundation in Duruelo (1568), which transferred to Mancera in 1570.

5 The monastery in Salamanca.

6 The date, in fact, was August 25.

Chapter 1

1 The foundation was made August 24, 1562.

2 In regard to the number of nuns in each monastery, Teresa later allowed for an increase to twenty. See *Way of Perfection*, ch. 2, no. 9, no. 5; Life, ch. 32, no. 13; ch. 36, no. 19.

3 This Sister, María Bautista (de Ocampo) (1543–1603), later became prioress of Valladolid. She was one of Teresa's most frequent correspondents. See ch. 29, no. 5; *Life*, ch. 32, no. 10.

4 This well still exists. The Sister alluded to is again María Bautista. Teresa called the well "the Samaritan woman's well."

5 Alonso Maldonado (c.1510–c.1600) had been a Franciscan missionary in Mexico (1551–1561). He became a defender of the rights of the indigenous people and pleaded their cause in Madrid and Rome before the king and the pope. A man of extreme zeal, he was at the end of his life tried by the Inquisition.

6 One of the hermitages she arranged to have constructed in the garden of St. Joseph's in Avila.

7 St. Thérèse of Lisieux, *Story of a Soul*, trans. John Clarke, O.C.D. (Washington, D.C.: ICS Publications, 1975), 192.

Chapter 2

1 No general had ever been to Castile. A general, Fr. John Alerio, had presided at the general chapter held in Barcelona in 1324.

2 See *Life*, ch. 32, nos. 13–15; ch. 33, no. 16. In the final chapter of this book of *Foundations*, she tells how her monastery at Avila returned to the jurisdiction of the Carmelite order.

3 The historian of the monastery of the Incarnation, María Pinel, wrote that the number reached 180 nuns. See *Biblioteca Mística Carmelitana*, 2:140. (Henceforth cited as BMC.)

4 The general, Fr. John Baptist Rossi (1507–1578), whose last name was Latinized in Spain to Rubeo, was elected general in 1564 and visited Avila, February 16–18, 1567.

5 Don Alvaro de Mendoza (d. 1586) was appointed bishop of Avila in 1560, and under his jurisdiction St. Joseph's was placed when Teresa's provincial refused to accept it. Always a staunch supporter of Teresa's work, he was buried, at his request, in the monastery church of St. Joseph in Avila.

6 This is true of Spain. In Italy, the primitive rule was being observed at Monte Oliveto, near Genoa. In regard to the primitive rule, see *Life*, ch. 36, no. 26, no. 27.

7 For these patent letters of Rubeo to Teresa, one dated April 27, 1567, and the other May 16, 1567, see *Monumenta Historica Carmeli Teresiani*, ed., Institutum Historicum Teresianum (Rome: Teresianum, 1973–), 1:67–71. (Henceforth cited as MHCT.)

8 See ch. 1, no. 8.

9 The patent letter granting permission for the foundation in Castile of two monasteries of the Teresian Carmel for friars was signed by Rubeo in Barcelona, not Valencia, August 10, 1567. See MHCT 1:67–71.

10 The provincial at the time, as of April 12, 1567, was Alonso Gonzáles, and the former provincial was Angel de Salazar.

11 John Greenleaf Whittier, "Maud Muller" in *The Poetical Works of Whittier* (Boston: Houghton Mifflin Company, 1975), 48.

Chapter 3

1 See, for example, *Life*, ch. 23, nos. 3, 9; ch. 33, no. 7.

2 Fr. Baltasar Alvarez (1533–1580) was not provincial at that time, 1573, but was substituting for the provincial, Gonzalo Dávila, who was in Rome.

3 Don Pedro González, bishop of Salamanca, to which diocese Medina belonged.

4 Julián de Avila (1527–1605) was ordained in 1558 and appointed chaplain of St. Joseph's in 1563, remaining so until the year before his death. His sister, María de San José (Dávila) was among the first four nuns to take the habit at St. Joseph's.

5 This young lady was Isabel Fontecha. She received the habit in Medina in 1567 and took the name Isabel de Jesús.

6 From St. Joseph's she took María Bautista and Ana de los Angeles. From the Incarnation came: Inés de Jesús, Ana de la Encarnación (Tapia), Teresa de la Columna (Quesada), and Isabel de la Cruz (Arias).

7 Antonio de Heredia (1510–1601) made the first foundation of Teresian Carmelites in 1568 with St. John of the Cross. He changed his name to Antonio de Jesús, held important offices in the order, and assisted at the deaths of both Teresa and John of the Cross. See nos. 16–17.

8 Doña María Suárez.

9 The monastery was Our Lady of Grace; the priest friend, Alonso Esteban.

10 These two out of the four from the Incarnation were Isabel Arias, the subprioress, and Teresa de Quesada.

11 Domingo Báñez (1528–1604) was one of the most distinguished theologians of the sixteenth century. See *Life*, ch. 36, no. 15; see also ch. 34, no. 14; ch. 39, no. 3.

12 Teresa thought that a foundation could not exist without the reservation of the Blessed Sacrament. She discovered her error later. See ch. 19, no. 3.

13 For clarification on Teresa's understanding of "Lutherans" see the introduction to *The Way of Perfection* in *The Collected Works of St. Teresa of Avila*, vol. 2 (ICS Publications: Washington, D.C., 1980) pp. 19–20 {Historical Context}.

14 This merchant was Blas de Medina.

15 She was a niece of Cardinal Quiroga, the general inquisitor. In 1581 she entered the Carmel in Medina, taking the name Elena de Jesús. Her daughter, Jerónima de la Encarnación, was already a member of that community.

16 In ch. 2, nos. 5–6.

17 See no. 3.

18 This was St. John of the Cross (1542–1591), then a Carmelite with the name Juan de Santo Matía.

19 Thomas Alvarez, Fernando Domingo, *Saint Teresa of Avila: A Spiritual Adventure*, trans. Christopher O'Mahony (Washington, D.C.: ICS Publications, 1981), 22.

20 William Thomas Walsh, *St. Teresa of Avila: A Biography* (Milwaukee: Bruce Publishing Company, 1943), 315.

Chapter 4

1 In chs. 4–8 Teresa inserts a short treatise concerning the life of prayer in her communities, useful not only for her daughters but for confessors and spiritual directors as well.

2 The story of the foundation of St. Joseph's in Avila (*Life*, chs. 32–36) was written in 1565. Teresa wrote this chapter of the *Foundations* in the later months of 1573 at Salamanca. The reason she had not founded more was that the apostolic visitator Pedro Fernández, O.P., had appointed her prioress at the Incarnation (1571–1573). For the seven monasteries, in addition to Avila, see prol., no. 3.

3 See for example *Way of Perfection*, ch. 21, no. 7.

4 See *Way of Perfection*, ch. 21, no. 7; Life, ch. 20, no. 16.

5 Teresa wrote carefully in the margin: "I am not dealing here with founders of Religious orders, for since God chose them for a great work, He gave them more grace." This annotation may have been motivated by the same scruple that occasioned a cancellation in the previous number for which she substituted "and this is true." In the autograph, paragraph no. 7 is highlighted by vertical lines in the margin. See parallel passage in *Interior Castle*, V, ch. 4, no. 6.

6 In no. 5.

7 Sr. Geneviève of the Holy Face (Céline Martin) A Memoir of my sister *St. Thérèse*, trans. Carmelite Sisters of New York (New York: P. J. Kenedy & Sons, 1959), 99.

8 Ibid., 99–100.

Chapter 5

1 For example, see *Life*, ch. 17, nos. 5–7; *Way of Perfection*, ch. 31, no. 8; *Interior Castle*, IV, ch. 1, no. 8.
2 Mt 25:40.
3 Ph 2:8 "obedient unto death."
4 For the second reason, see no. 14.
5 Allusion to Ps 34:9.
6 In no. 1.
7 Lk 10:16.
8 1 K. 18:38 {3 K. 18:38}.
9 The first reason is stated in no. 4.
10 For the Teresian proverb in this respect, see *Interior Castle*, VII, ch. 4, no. 7, no. 8.
11 Allusion to Mt 26:31–35, 67–75.
12 On this subject, see *Interior Castle*, VII, ch. 4, no. 5, no. 6.
13 Thomas Green, S.J., *Darkness in the Marketplace: The Christian at Prayer in the World* (Notre Dame: Ave Maria Press, 1981), 48.
14 Pierre Descouvemont, *Thérèse of Lisieux and Marie of the Trinity*, trans. Alexandra Plettenberg-Serban (New York: Alba House, 1997), 84–85.

Chapter 6

1 In this chapter Teresa exposes a kind of psychological anomaly that only appears to be mystical in nature. She creates her own terminology, a number of expressions, in order to speak of it: *embebecimiento* (nos. 1, 2, 6, 7): absorption; *embobamiento* (no. 3): stupefaction; *pasmos* (no. 5): states of daze; *pausada* (no. 5): listless; *amortecimientos* (no. 6): swoons.
2 See *Life*, ch. 20.
3 This kind of self-abandonment (*dejarse*) to these absorptions was practiced by the group within the illuminist movement known as dejados. Their spirituality developed along unorthodox lines. See *Collected Works of St. Teresa*, 1:7 {*Life*–Introduction}.
4 In ch. 7.
5 In no. 2.
6 In ch. 5, nos. 2, 10–11.
7 In no. 6.

8   Teresa is purposely vague about their identities, and it is not easy
    to pinpoint either the place or the names. Fr. Silverio believed
    she was referring to Alberta Bautista who died a saintly death at
    the age of 35, and to Inés de la Concepción, the lay Sister, both of
    the monastery in Medino del Campo. See BMC 6:51.
9   Inés de Jesús (Tapia).
10 In no. 4.
11 She is speaking of herself; see *Life*, ch. 25, no. 14.
12 Allusion to 1 Sm 15:22 {1 Kgs 15:22}.
13 Allusion to what was said in chs. 4 and 5.
14 Allusion to Mt 16:19.

Chapter 7

1   Under the term "melancholy," Teresa includes a whole series of
    emotional and mental disorders difficult to reduce to a definite
    category. The humor called melancholy (black bile) was in the
    past looked upon as one of the four chief bodily fluids. Mental
    disorder was supposed to be caused by an excess of this humor.
2   See *Way of Perfection*, ch. 24, nos. 4–5.
3   In nos. 2–3.
4   In no. 3.
5   The danger to one's salvation; see nos. 3–4.
6   In no. 5.
7   In nos. 3–4.
8   Here Teresa is suggesting that these nuns, lest they suffer physi-
    cal weakness, be dispensed from the perpetual abstinence from
    meat (see *Constitutions*, no. 11); fish was a customary substitute
    for meat in her Carmels.
9   In nos. 8–9.
10 *The Collected Works of St. Teresa*, vol. 3, 419.
11 St. Augustine, *The Monastic Rules*, trans. Sr. Agatha Mary, S.P.B.,
    and Gerald Bonner. Commentary by Gerald Bonner (Hyde Park:
    New City Press, 2004), 112–113.

Chapter 8

1   This statement is a marginal gloss in Teresa's hand.
2   Teresa is referring to herself. See *Life*, ch. 29, nos. 5–7; *Interior
    Castle*, VI, ch. 9, nos. 12–13.

3 Teresa noted in the margin: "Fray Maestro Domingo Báñez."
4 In no. 3.
5 Allusion to Mt 15:27.
6 Teresa is referring to her own experience. As for the man of whom she speaks, some think it was Juan Manteca, a peasant from Avila famous for his extraordinary mystical experiences. After speaking with him, Teresa was left dissatisfied with his spirit. He was later brought to justice for his fraud. See BMC 19:81.
7 St. Francis de Sales, *Introduction to the Devout Life*, trans. John K. Ryan (Garden City: Image Books, 1966), 131.

Chapter 9

1 Doña Luisa de la Cerda. See *Life*, ch. 34, no. 1.
2 Malagón is a small town, still today, in the province of Ciudad Real. In feudal times it belonged to the duchy of Medinaceli.
3 Her confessor at the time was Domingo Báñez, O.P. See ch. 3, no. 11; *Spiritual Testimonies*, 58, no. 17. Báñez was opposed to Teresa's desires for absolute poverty (see Life, ch. 36, no. 15). His opposition was based on the mind of the Council of Trent (1545–1563), Session 25, *De reformatione regularium*, ch. 3.
4 April 11. Teresa urged Doña Luisa to build her nuns in Malagón a new monastery, the construction of which she supervised carefully. Inaugurated December 8, 1579, this building remains today, an exceptional relic still housing Teresa's daughters.

Chapter 10

1 Because of the kind of life this young man lived, Teresa does not give his name. He was, in fact, Don Bernardino de Mendoza, brother of the bishop of Avila, Don Alvaro de Mendoza, and of Doña María de Mendoza, who is also spoken of in this chapter.
2 The estate was called Rio de Olmos and was close to the river Pisuerga toward the south of the city. It had been previously occupied by a community of Carmelite friars who moved into the city February 1, 1563. Besides being unhealthy, the place was impractically located in view of the nuns' dependence on alms, for Teresa had founded the monastery in poverty.
3 He died in Ubeda in February of 1568 while Teresa was in Alcalá de Henares.

4 She arrived in Valladolid August 10, 1568, and on August 15 inaugurated the foundation at Rio de Olmos.

5 The monastery of the Carmelite friars. See no. 2.

6 They were Isabel de la Cruz, Antonia del Espíritu Santo, and María de la Cruz.

7 See ch. 3, no. 2.

8 St. John of the Cross who in Valladolid underwent a kind of apprenticeship in the new form of Carmelite life under the guidance of Teresa. See ch. 3, nos. 16–17.

9 See no. 2.

10 The priest was Julián de Avila who later wrote of this event: ". . . and when I gave the Blessed Sacrament to the Mother, I saw her in a great rapture, which she often experienced before or after receiving Communion" (BMC 18:221). The painter Rubens immortalized this scene.

11 From August 15 until October of the same year when they moved to a temporary location.

12 Don Francisco de los Cobos had been a secretary and confidant of Charles V and a counselor of Philip II. He died in 1547.

13 The bishop of Avila was Don Alvaro de Mendoza. See *Life*, ch. 36, nos. 1–2.

14 February 3, 1569, they moved to the place inside Valladolid known today as the *Rondilla de Santa Teresa*.

15 She speaks of the third, youngest daughter in no. 13.

16 Antonio Manrique de Padilla entered the Jesuits March 8, 1572, and was a novice under the direction of Baltasar Alvarez, the former confessor of Teresa's.

17 This confessor was Fr. Jerónimo de Ripalda, S.J.

Chapter 11

1 She was Estefanía de los Apóstoles who received the habit in Valladolid July 2, 1572. The fame of her simple and saintly life spread even to the king, Philip II, and many edifying stories were told about her. A manuscript biography of her was written by María de San José. Despite this mention, Teresa then neglects to tell us about her.

2 Doña Luisa de Padilla, widow of Don Antonio Manrique and mother of Don Martín de Padilla.
3 Ch. 10, no. 15.
4 The prioress of Valladolid was María Bautista.
5 Domingo Báñez. See ch. 3, no. 5, no. 11.
6 At the time (July 1573), Teresa was probably in Salamanca.
7 That is, December 8–28, 1573.
8 A monastery of Dominican nuns in Valladolid.
9 Doña Casilda was professed a week after her fifteenth birthday, January 13, 1577. But this story has a further ending, a surprise and disappointing one for Teresa. In a letter to Gracián, September 17, 1581, she speaks of the news, "shocking" to her, that Doña Casilda, then about twenty, had left the Carmelite monastery in Valladolid. It seems both Casilda's mother and the Jesuit confessor, neither of whom got along with the subprioress, had some influence on the decision. Casilda joined the Franciscan nuns of Santa Gadea del Cid, where she became abbess.
10 Flannery O'Connor, "Parker's Back" in *The Complete Stories of Flannery O'Connor* (New York: The Noonday Press, 1971), 513.
11 Ibid., 514.
12 Flannery O'Connor, *Letters of Flannery O'Connor: The Habit of Being*, ed. Sally Fitzgerald (New York: Farrar, Straus, Giroux, 1979), 275.
13 E. E. Cummings, "A Poet's Advice to Students," quoted from A Miscellany, ed. George J. Firmage (New York: October House, 1965), 335.

Chapter 12

1 This chapter heading is not in Teresa's hand. The account of this nun's life and virtues is an example of the kind of necrological literature later imitated by Teresa's friars and nuns alike. The monastery referred to is Valladolid (see ch. 10).
2 Beatriz de la Encarnación (Oñez) (d. 1573) was born in Arroyo, in the province of Valladolid, received the habit of Carmel September 8, 1569, and made profession in 1570.
3 See *Constitutions*, nos. 29, 30, 39, and 43.
4 In nos. 4–9.

Chapter 13

1 In ch. 3, nos. 16–17.

2 In fact, she was satisfied only with Fray John of the Cross. See ch. 3, nos. 16–17.

3 To distinguish the two groups in Carmel, Teresa uses the terms "calced" and "discalced," which stem from a difference in footwear. In these *Foundations* and in her *Letters* she refers to them as well by the stuff of their habits: cloth or frieze (rough wool).

4 Don Rafael Mejía Velázquez. See MHCT 1:74–75.

5 The official name was and still is today Duruelo. But the place looks more like a small farm or pastureland than a town and gives the impression of being even more insignificant than it was formerly.

6 The Sister companion was Antonia del Espíritu Santo, one of the four first nuns who formed the little community of St. Joseph's in Avila. The priest was Julián de Avila, the first chaplain of that monastery in Avila.

7 The foundations were: Duruelo (1568), which was transferred to Mancera (1570), Pastrana (1569), Alcalá (1570), Altomira (1571), La Roda (1572), Granada (1573), La Peñuela (1573), Los Remedios in Seville (1574), Almodóvar del Campo (1575). Since Duruelo had been abandoned, there were only nine.

8 See ch. 2, no. 5. The previous provincial was Angel de Salazar and the present one was Alonso González.

9 See *Litterae Patentes P. Joannis Baptista Rossi* in MHCT 1:68–71.

10 In ch. 10.

11 This important paragraph shows how St. John of the Cross received special, personal instructions from St. Teresa about the spirit and way of life of the new Carmels she was founding.

Chapter 14

1 It was the First Sunday of Advent, November 28, 1568. See MHCT 1:74–75.

2 In 1569, the First Sunday of Lent fell on February 27. Teresa had written "the first week of" the following Lent, but later crossed out "the first week of." Nonetheless, the visit did occur around the first week of Lent. She left Valladolid February 22 for Toledo passing through Medina, Duruelo, and Avila.

3   These two were Father Lucas de Celis and Brother José de Cristo, a deacon. Neither of them persevered for long. See Silverio de Santa Teresa, *Historia del Carmen Descalzo en España, Portugal y América*, 15 vols. (Burgos: El Monte Carmelo), 3:206–07. (Henceforth cited HCD).

4   Don Luis de Toledo was both a relative of the Duke of Alba and lord of Mancera, the town to which the foundation of Duruelo was transferred, as well as of five other towns. See HCD, 3:234.

5   Its full name is Mancera de Abajo to distinguish it from Mancera de Arriba. The first foundation in Duruelo was transferred to Mancera June 11, 1570, and remained there until 1600 when it was transferred to Avila. See HCD, 3:234–40.

6   After the digression on Mancera, Teresa returns to her account of Duruelo.

7   Walsh, Ibid., 346.

8   St. Augustine, "On The Catechising of the Uninstructed" in *St. Augustine: On the Holy Trinity, Doctrinal Treatises, Moral Treatises*, trans. S. D. F. Salmond, D.D., in *Nicene and Post-Nicene Fathers of the Christian Church*, ed. Philip Schaff (Grand Rapids: Wm. B. Eerdmans Publishing Company, 1956), 311.

Chapter 15

1   Martín Ramírez (d. 1568), a wealthy merchant from Toledo, provided for the foundation in Toledo.

2   A Galician, from Santiago de Compostela, Pablo Hernández (b. 1528) was one of the many Jesuits who helped Teresa in carrying out her mission. Her letters reveal her trust in him, and at this time she responded by giving him power to proceed in her name.

3   The chaplaincy is a fund established for the celebration of daily Mass in a particular church by chosen chaplains.

4   Today this feast is known as the Annunciation. Teresa left Valladolid Feb. 21, 1569, stayed in Avila for about two weeks and arrived in Toledo March 24, 1569.

5   They were Isabel de San Pablo (1547–82) and Isabel de Santo Domingo (1537–1623). The latter was a nun in whom Teresa placed special trust. She was made prioress in Toledo and later sent as prioress to Pastrana where she had to deal tactfully with the difficult situations caused by the Princess of Eboli (see ch. 17, no. 17).

6 The archbishop of Toledo was the noted Bartolomé de Carranza (1503–76), who was then involved in a struggle because of the proceedings instituted against him by the Spanish Inquisition. The diocese was being governed by an administrator.

7 Pedro Manrique de Padilla (d. 1577) was the uncle of Casilda de Padilla, whose vocation is described in chs. 10–11.

8 These are still preserved and venerated by the Carmelite nuns in Toledo. One represents Jesus having fallen with the cross, and the other represents Him seated during His Passion in deep suffering and meditation.

9 Alonso de Avila (d. 1586) was one of the many merchants of judeoconverso origin from Toledo. A short biography of him in manuscript form exists in the conventual archives of the Carmelite nuns in Toledo and was written by P. Hernando Dávila.

10 Alonso de Andrada was a young twenty-two year old student.

11 In no. 6.

12 From May 14, 1569, to the end of May 1570.

13 In nos. 4 and 11.

14 Doña Luisa de la Cerda.

15 In nos. 1–2.

Chapter 16

1 Ana de la Madre de Dios (Palma) (1529–1610) was married and became a widow at age 21. She met Teresa in the palace of Doña Luisa de la Cerda and generously offered her wealth for the foundation in Toledo. She made her profession there November 15, 1570, and governed as prioress several times. She died in the Carmel of Cuerva.

2 At first Teresa wrote: "I had to be careful about what I said." She then added between the lines, "the prioress . . . what she said," so as to make the account sound more impersonal.

3 Teresa had first written, "she came to speak to me. I asked her, etc." She obviously wanted to withhold the part she played in these incidents, as is indicated at the end of this number.

4 She is speaking of Petronila de San Andrés (Robles del Aguila) (1545–1576) born in Toledo and professed there in 1571. See BMC 5:444–446.

5   J. H. Elliott, *Imperial Spain 1469–1716* (New York: New American
    Library, 1963), 224–228.
6   H. G. Wells, "The Country of the Blind," in *The Door in the Wall
    and Other Stories* (Doylestown: Wildside Press, 2004), 133.
7   St. Thérèse of Lisieux, *Story of a Soul*, Ibid., 179.

Chapter 17

1   In 1569, the months of May, June, and July kept Teresa busy with
    activities and travels, which may be summarized as follows:
    May 14, the foundation day of the Carmel in Toledo; May 30,
    leaves for Pastrana and arrives the same day in Madrid; June 8,
    arrives in Pastrana; June 23, foundation day for the Carmel of
    nuns in Pastrana; July 13, foundation for the friars in Pastrana;
    July 21, returns to Toledo.
2   They were six in all, four from the Incarnation and two from the
    Carmel in Malagón.
3   Ruy Gómez de Silva, a Portuguese by birth, was brought up
    with Philip II, who liked and favored him. His wife, Doña Ana
    de Mendoza, better known by her title, the Princess of Eboli, was
    a capricious, willful woman who later became a source of much
    trouble for Teresa and her nuns.
4   Her confessor at that time was Father Vicente Barrón. See *Life*,
    ch. 7, no. 16–17; *Spir. Test.*, 58, no. 16.
5   Doña Leonor de Mascareñas (1503–1584), Portuguese by birth,
    had become Philip II's governess and was later dissuaded by
    him from entering a monastery. In 1564 she founded in Madrid a
    monastery of Franciscan nuns called "Descalzas Reales," which
    was close to her mansion where Teresa occasionally stayed.
6   Mariano Azzaro (Fr. Ambrosio Mariano de San Benito) (1510-
    1594), was born in Bitonto, Italy, in the province of Bari. Hav-
    ing studied theology and law to such effect that he attended
    the Council of Trent, he was also skilled in mathematics and
    engineering. As an engineer in the service of Philip II, he was
    examining the possibility of making the Guadalquivir navigable
    from Seville to Córdoba and of using it for irrigation purposes
    when he experienced the call to become a hermit. Later, as a
    Carmelite friar, he continued to be esteemed by the king and

consulted on various engineering projects. Hasty and impulsive, he was at times difficult to deal with as is evident in Teresa's correspondence.

7   Juan de la Miseria (Giovanni Narduch) (c. 1526–1616) was born in Boggiano, Italy, in the province of Naples. A painter, disciple of Sánchez Coello, he is remembered especially for the portrait he did of Teresa in Seville in 1576. After joining Teresa's friars, he later transferred to the Carmelites of the observance and then to the Franciscans, but finally returned to the Teresian Carmelites and went on the foundation to Genoa. In his old age he suffered from paralysis and blindness. He died in Madrid where his body is preserved incorrupt.

8   In Dn. 13.

9   Mateo de la Fuente (1524–1575), born in Alminuete, near Toledo, later placed his hermits under the rule of St. Basil because of the demands of the Council of Trent.

10 When she speaks of the Council as coming, she is referring to the introduction of the decrees of the Council of Trent into Spain. In the constitution *Lubricum genus*, November 17, 1568, Pius V granted a year within which to comply. See Council of Trent, Sess. 25, ch. 5, *De reformation religiosorum.*

11 See no. 3.

12 At the time she was writing this chapter (1574–1576), the opposition to her had begun.

13 Duruelo, which at the time of this writing had been transferred to Mancera, as is indicated further on in no. 14.

14 Alonso González and Angel de Salazar, respectively.

15 In fact, about two months. She left Toledo May 30 and returned July 21.

16 In no. 6.

17 Baltasar de Jesús (Nieto) (1524–1589), a restless and inglorious figure in the history of Carmel, became the first superior of Pastrana. Omitting her customary accolade about the person being a great servant of God, Teresa refers to him as neither young nor old and a very good preacher. Nor did Teresa want the foundation established until Fr. Antonio arrived July 13.

18 During Lent 1574.

19 Ruy Gómez died July 29, 1573. His widow, the princess, thirty-three at the time, distressed over her loss, insisted on becoming a nun in the Carmel at once.
20 In ch. 21.
21 In no. 16.
22 Jean H. Mariéjol, *Philip II: The First Modern King*, trans. Warren B. Wells (New York: Harper & Brothers, 1933), 308.

Chapter 18

1 The two foundations were those in Pastrana, one for the nuns and one for the friars. Teresa returned to Toledo July 22, 1569, where she bought the house mentioned in ch. 15, no. 17.
2 The rector was Martín Gutiérrez (1504–1573). On a trip to Rome for the election of a general to succeed St. Francis Borgia, he was taken prisoner by the Huguenots and died in captivity.
3 Teresa's monasteries were now of two kinds: those founded in poverty, dependent on alms, and those founded with the endowment of a fixed income. See ch. 9, nos. 2–4.
4 Probably not remembering the name of the bishop, Teresa left the space blank; she never did remember to fill it in. The bishop's name was Don Pedro González de Mendoza.
5 This lady was probably Doña Beatriz Yáñez de Ovalle, a relative of Teresa's brother-in-law.
6 This chapter was being written sometime between 1574–1576.
7 María del Sacramento (Suárez) (d. 1589), originally from the monastery of the Incarnation and later the prioress of Alba de Tormes.
8 See ch. 3, nos. 11–14.
9 October 31, 1570.
10 The chapter is a community meeting at which faults in the observance of the constitutions are corrected. See *Constitutions*, no. 43 in no. 24.
11 Teresa is here referring to the legend in the Roman Martyrology (October 21) concerning the eleven thousand virgins martyred near Cologne by the Huns; one of them named Cordula fled at first and hid, but later, moved by the grace of God, offered herself to the persecutors and was beheaded.

Chapter 19

1   See ch. 18, no. 3.
2   Nicolás Gutiérrez, a Salamancan businessman, had six daughters in the monastery of the Incarnation, all of whom later entered the Teresian Carmel.
3   In ch. 18, no. 2.
4   In fact, two nuns came from Medina and one from Valladolid; later three others joined them from Avila.
5   See ch. 18, no. 3.
6   They were Poor Clare Franciscan nuns.
7   It was the custom to toll the church bells on the vigil and the day itself of All Souls. See no. 2.
8   She was appointed prioress of the monastery of the Incarnation in Avila by the apostolic visitator, Pedro Fernández, O.P., in July of 1571 and took possession of the office in October. Fernández had been named to the office by Pius V, August 20, 1569.
9   The apostolic visitator, Pedro Fernández.
10 The gentleman's name was Pedro de la Banda.
11 See ch. 3, no. 2; ch. 10, no. 4.
12 September 28, 1573. The sermon was preached by the noted Diego de Estella.
13 Doña María Pimentel was a daughter of the fifth Count of Benevente and wife of Don Alonso Zúñiga, the third Count of Monterrey.
14 In fact, in 1579, Teresa had to obtain permission from the bishop to move the community to another house, and after her death in 1582, the nuns moved.
15 St. Francis de Sales, *Introduction to the Devout Life*, trans. Michael Day (Anthony Clarke: Wheatampstead, Hertfordshire, 1954), 115.

Chapter 20

1   Domingo Báñez, the noted Dominican theologian, had been Teresa's confessor during the years 1561–1567. For other instances of his opinion in this regard, see ch. 9, no. 3; Life, ch. 36, no. 15. In regard to the Council of Trent, see ch. 9, no. 3.
2   Teresa de Layz was a daughter of Don Diego Layz and Doña Beatriz de Aponte. "Pure blood" was the term used to exclude

Jewish or Moorish background and illustrates a prejudice of the time.

3   He was, in fact, administrator of the University of Salamanca from May 17, 1541, to February 1, 1566.

4   It was the office of administrator for the duke. See no. 1.

5   See Jon 1–2.

6   January 25.

7   She feared giving this impression if she had a part to play in the account she was giving. See ch. 16, no. 3.

8   Teresa's difficulties in remembering the dates are manifest in the titles of the following three chapters.

9   Charles Dickens, *Dombey and Son* (New York: Penguin Books, 1985), 84.

10 Ibid., 312.

Chapter 21

1   See chapter 19, no. 6. Pedro Fernández (d. 1580) was a great help to Teresa and her foundations especially during the years 1571–1574.

2   She arrived in Salamanca July 31, 1573.

3   They were received into the order by Teresa. The mother took the name Ana de Jesús and the daughter, María de la Encarnación. They made their profession July 2, 1575. Both of them later exercised the office of prioress.

4   The apostolic commissary and visitator, Fr. Pedro Fernández, invested with pontifical authority.

5   The discalced friar was St. John of the Cross, though it seems the first Mass was said by Julián de Avila. Antonio Gaytán from Alba de Tormes was converted, through Teresa's influence, to a more spiritual life. Assisting the Saint on her foundations of Segovia, Beas, Caravaca, and Seville, he became the recipient of her great confidence, especially in the foundation of Caravaca in which Teresa authorized him to act in her name. His daughter Mariana de Jesús (1570–1615) was admitted by Teresa into the monastery of Alba de Tormes at the exceptional age of seven as an act of gratitude for the services rendered by her father.

6 Isabel de Jesús, sister of Andrés Jimena (see no. 5), best known
   for the incident at Salamanca (Easter 1571) when, as a novice,
   she sang a song that sent Teresa into a rapture. She was later a
   prioress both in Palencia and Salamanca.
7 That is, from March 19 to September 24 when Teresa took possession of the houses for the new monastery.
8 Don Juan de Orozco y Covarrubias de Leiva, prior of the cathedral chapter and later bishop of Guadix and Baza.
9 They moved on September 24, 1574.
10 See no. 1. Teresa left Segovia September 30, 1574. She concluded
   her three year office of prioress October 6. It might be remembered that shortly after she took possession of the house in
   Segovia, Teresa sent Fr. Julián de Avila and Gaytán to bring the
   fourteen nuns in Pastrana to Segovia where they would be free
   of the disturbances caused by the Princess of Eboli. They arrived
   in Segovia in five wagons April 7, 1574. See chapter 17, no. 17.

Chapter 22

1 February 24. Teresa had written 1574. She erred on the date
   also in nos. 4 and 19. But in the three instances the final 4 was
   corrected to 5.
2 In ch. 21, no. 1.
3 In ch. 21, no. 1.
4 See ch. 2, nos. 3–4.
5 She is referring to one of the military orders of knights of that
   time called the Order of Santiago (St. James). In a military order,
   the knights combined the principles of monasticism and chiv-
   alry, pledging themselves to the practice of asceticism and the
   recitation of the canonical hours as well as to the defense of
   Christendom against the infidel. Certain territories were governed by the order and were under its jurisdiction rather than
   the ecclesiastical. See no. 13.
6 Here she begins an account of the conversion and vocation of
   Catalina Sandoval y Godínez (de Jesús) (1540–1586) which led
   to the foundation in Beas. Catalina succeeded Ana de Jesús as
   prioress in 1582. St. John of the Cross was her spiritual director
   until her death.

7 Allusion to Jn 9:2.
8 In no. 5.
9 March 19, 1558.
10 In 1560; her mother (see no. 13), in 1565.
11 January 19, 1574.
12 Allusion to what was referred to in no. 14.
13 February 24. Accompanying Teresa on the journey were Fr. Julián de Avila, Antonio Gaytán, and Fr. Gregorio Martínez (1548–1599), who received the habit of the discalced Carmelites in Beas from Fr. Gracián and the name Gregorio Nacianceno. Venerable Ana de Jesús (1545–1621), at whose request St. John of the Cross wrote his commentary on the Spiritual Canticle, was appointed the first prioress.
14 They took the names Catalina de Jesús and María de Jesús. Like her sister, María de Jesús (1549–1604) also had St. John of the Cross as her spiritual director, and three of his letters to her have come down to us. In 1589 she went to Córdoba as Prioress.
15 What follows is a kind of appendix to the chapter.
16 Cf. ch. 17, nos. 7, 14, 15.
17 Bartolomé Bustamente. Before entering the Society, he had been a secretary to Cardinal Pardo de Tavera and was acquainted with the cardinal's nephew, the husband of Doña Luisa de la Cerda.
18 In no. 1.
19 In no. 6.
20 Her provincial at that time was Jerónimo Gracián.
21 St. John of the Cross, "Letter 21" in *The Collected Works of St. John of the Cross*, trans. Kieran Kavanaugh, O.C.D., and Otilio Rodriguez, O.C.D. (Washington, D.C.: ICS Publications, 1991), 756–757.
22 Aelred Squire, *Asking the Fathers: The Art of Meditation and Prayer* (New York: Paulist Press, 1973), 129.

Chapter 23

1 Here too she wrote 1574; the date was corrected to read 1575.
2 She deals with the Caravaca foundation in ch. 27. Fr. Jerónimo Gracián (1545–1614), an important figure in Teresian history, was born in Valladolid, studied at the university of Alcalá, and was ordained a priest in 1570. Exceptionally gifted, he entered

the novitiate in Pastrana in 1572. After meeting Teresa in 1575, he worked closely with her until her death. Later, falling into disfavor with Doria, he was expelled from the order. He died in Brussels.

3 Gracián's father, Diego Gracián, was a secretary in one of the offices of Philip II.

4 Juan de Jesús (Roca) (c. 1540–1614) was born in Sanahuja in Catalonia. A fellow student with Gracián at Alcalá, he entered the novitiate in Pastrana a few months before his companion.

5 The prioress was Isabel de Santo Domingo (1537–1623), one of Teresa's outstanding daughters, who went with the foundress from St. Joseph's in Avila to Toledo, became prioress there, and after a few months was sent to Pastrana as prioress, where she had to deal with many difficult situations because of the Princess of Eboli's meddling in community affairs. The nun about whom Gracián spoke to the prioress was Bárbara del Espíritu Santo.

6 See Gracián's, *Historia Fundationum* in MHCT 3:539–541.

7 The words, "or almost none like him," were added between the lines and strengthen Teresa's glowing evaluation of Gracián.

8 They had twenty children, thirteen reaching adulthood.

9 The friar to whom she is referring was Angel de San Gabriel. Going to extremes in austerities and ascetical testings, he had to be corrected by Domingo Báñez, O.P., and replaced by St. John of the Cross; cf. MHCT 1:128–131. The absent prior was Baltasar de Jesús (Nieto); cf. ch. 17, no. 15, no. 17.

10 She began to write "was about to regret," but then changed.

11 Cf. ch. 3, nos. 16–17; ch. 13, no. 1.

12 Teresa seems to deny that the discalced had constitutions from the Father General, Rubeo, and she seems to do so again in no. 13. Nonetheless, around 1568 he did approve constitutions for the friars which were an adaptation of those written by Teresa for her daughters, but apparently they were not used for long. Cf. B. Zimmerman, *Regesta Rubei* (Rome, 1936), pp. 58–65; BMC 6:399–406; PP. Tomás–Simeón, *La Reforma Teresiana* (Rome, 1962), pp. 97–100.

13 The apostolic visitator, Fr. Francisco Vargas, appointed Gracián a delegate apostolic visitator in September of 1573. In 1574, Gracián

was appointed vicar provincial of the Carmelites of the Observance in Andalusia, and in 1575 his authority was extended to the Teresian Carmel. Cf. MHCT 1:184–185.

14 P. Marie-Eugene, O.C.D. *I Want to See God: I am a Daughter of the Church*, trans. Sr. M. Verda Clare, C.S.C. (Westminster: Christian Classics, Inc., 1986), 262.

Chapter 24

1 In ch. 23, no. 1.

2 The meeting between Gracián and Teresa took place in April 1575. Not until August 3 did the nuncio Ormaneto extend Gracián's authority to all the discalced Carmelites. See MHCT 1:221–223.

3 See ch. 27, no. 6.

4 This should read Andalusia and not Castile. In no. 2 she states that Gracián was apostolic commissary in Andalusia. Beas was in the ecclesiastical province of Andalusia; see no. 4.

5 Don Cristóbal de Rojas y Sandoval (1502–1580), son of the marquis of Denia, had been bishop of Oviedo, Badajoz, and Córdoba, as well as an active member of the Council of Trent.

6 In the division of Spain into provinces, Beas came under the civil jurisdiction of Castile; but ecclesiastically it belonged to the diocese of Cartagena in Andalusia.

7 Cf. no. 2.

8 Fr. Gregorio Nacianceno who had already accompanied Teresa on the foundation to Beas. See ch. 22, no. 19, no. 13.

9 May 26, 1575.

10 Their names were: María de San José; Isabel de San Francisco; Leonor de San Gabriel; Ana de San Alberto; María del Espíritu Santo; and Isabel de San Jerónimo.

11 She mentioned only one discalced friar in the group; the other men mentioned were Julián de Avila and Antonio Gaytán. See no. 5.

12 See no. 4.

13 See Council of Trent, Session 25, *De Refonnatione regularium*, ch. 3.

14 According to María de San José, the archbishop's opposition came from his desire that Teresa and her daughters reform the

existing monasteries of nuns in Seville rather than found a new one. See her *Libro de Recreaciones* (Burgos: El Monte Carmelo, 1913), *Recr.* 9.

15   May 29, 1575. The "said Father" was Fr. Mariano.

16   She had two patent letters from Fr. Rubeo, the general of the Carmelites: one of April 27, 1567; another of April 6, 1571. See MHCT 1:62–65; 110–112.

17   Walsh, Ibid., 446.

18   *Saint Teresa of Avila: A Spiritual Adventure*, Text by Tomas Alvarez O.C.D., and Fernando Domingo, O.C.D., trans. Chistopher O'Mahony (Washington, D.C.: ICS Publications, 1981), 105.

19   Shirley du Boulay, *Teresa of Avila: an Extraordinary Life* (New York: BlueBridge, 2004), 201.

20   *Saint Teresa of Avila A Spiritual Adventure*, Ibid., 109.

21   Walsh is rather emphatic on this question. He writes: "Then [Teresa] decided to take the nuns back to Beas and make the foundation at Caravaca." Ibid., 456. However, Walsh doesn't present any evidence to substantiate this claim.

Chapter 25

1   That is, from May 26, 1575, until February of the next year, a period of nine months.

2   Fr. Gracián.

3   Beatriz de la Madre de Dios. See ch. 26, nos. 2–16.

4   See ch. 27, no. 20.

5   Lorenzo de Cepeda (1519–1580) had departed for America in 1540, and now returned to Spain, a widower, accompanied by three of his children (Francisco, Lorenzo, and Teresita) and his brother Don Pedro. A wealthy man, he disembarked in Sanlúcar de Barrameda and began to help Teresa with her foundation in Seville. Soon, he turned to Teresa for direction in his own spiritual life, and a number of her letters of spiritual direction to him have come down to us. See *Spiritual Testimonies*, no. 41.

6   Garciálvarez (or García Alvarez) continued to help the nuns afterward in the capacity of confessor to the community. From the letters of Teresa to María de San José, one deduces that he was a generous man but lacking in learning and discretion. His

interference in community affairs led to his dismissal as confessor of the community.

7 This took place April 5, 1576. The house cost 6,000 ducats, but in a letter to Fr. Mariano, May 9, 1576, Teresa speaks of the great bargain they got and of how the house could not be bought now for 20,000.

8 María de San José (Salazar) (1548–1603). Born in Toledo, she became a servant in the household of Doña Luisa de la Cerda where in 1562 she met Teresa. In 1570 she took the habit in Malagón and in 1575 accompanied Teresa to Beas and then Seville becoming prioress there. Through correspondence she kept up a warm friendship with Teresa. In 1584 she founded the Carmel in Lisbon. But later, falling into disfavor with Doria, she was imprisoned there. In 1603 she was sent to Cuerva where she died.

9 An irregularity in the contract which had apparently gone unnoticed made the purchaser liable for a sales tax called the *alcabala*. Since the community could not pay the tax, the guarantor was held responsible. To avoid arrest, Don Lorenzo went into sanctuary.

10 Fernando de Pantoja (d. 1582) was prior of the Carthusian monastery of Santa María de las Cuevas in Seville from 1567 to 1580. He was as well a native of Avila. See BMC 6:250–251.

11 This took place June 3, 1576. When the procession was over Teresa knelt before the archbishop and received his blessing, but then, to her embarrassment, the archbishop knelt before her and asked for her blessing in the presence of all the people. See BMC 18:469.

Chapter 26

1 June 4, 1576, at 2 a.m.

2 To temper the sadness of the nuns in Seville over Teresa's approaching departure, Fr. Gracián ordered Teresa to pose for a portrait which was painted by Fray Juan de la Miseria. Still preserved by the nuns in Seville, it is the only definitely authentic portrait we possess of the Saint. When Teresa saw the finished product, she remarked in good humor, "May God forgive you,

Fray Juan, for now that you have painted me, you have made me look ugly and bleary-eyed." See J. Gracián, *Peregrinación de Anastasio* in BMC 17:201–202.

3   In ch. 18, nos. 4–5; 24, no. 6.

4   Beatriz de la Madre de Dios (Chaves) (1538–1624), this daughter of Alfonso Gómez Ibero and Juana Gómez de Chaves, made her profession September 29, 1576. In the next year her mother was professed as Juana de la Cruz (see no. 15). Her unfortunate childhood may account for the malice she later showed toward the prioress, María de San José, who as a result was deposed. Beatriz then was appointed prioress by Cardenas, the Carmelite provincial of the observance. In less than a year, new superiors, appointed through the intervention of the king, deprived her of office because of both her imprudent leadership and the debts the monastery had accumulated. María de San José was once again elected. Beatriz eventually repented and lived a long and useful life.

5   In nos. 3–5.

6   In no. 9.

7   This monastery was founded January 6, 1574.

8   Gracián was twenty-nine. But Teresa was mistaken about the age of Beatriz who at the time was not twenty-seven but thirty-six.

9   May 29, 1575, the same day on which the first Mass was said. Cf. ch. 24, no. 18.

10 She made her profession Sept. 29, 1576. See Teresa's letter to María de San José, June 18, 1576.

11 She made her profession Nov. 10, 1577.

12 Edwin Arlington Robinson, "Isaac and Archibald," in *Selected Poems of Edwin Arlington Robinson*, ed. Morton Dauwen Zabel (New York: Collier Books, 1965), 25.

13 St. Augustine, *Expositions of the Psalms, Vol. 5,* trans. Maria Boulding, O.S.B. (Hyde Park, New York: New City Press, 2003), 20.

Chapter 27

1   In ch. 22.

2   After Catalina, she left a blank space with the intention of filling in the surname which was de Otalora. Doña Catalina was the

widow of Alonso Muñoz, a wealthy and influential gentleman of Caravaca, who had been a member of the councils of Castile and of the Indies.

3 The Jesuit was Father Leiva. The three young ladies were: Francisca de Saojosa, Francisca de Cuéllar, and Francisca de Tauste.

4 Rodrigo de Moya, widower of Doña Luisa de Avila, was the father of Francisca de Cuéllar.

5 In making the foundation in Beas, Teresa brought with her enough nuns for two foundations (see ch. 24, no. 4). But since Caravaca was under the jurisdiction of the Order of the Knights of Santiago, the license for the foundation had the condition that the foundation render obedience to the council of the Order of Knights, which was something unacceptable to Teresa (see ch. 23, no. 1; ch. 24, no. 3). For this and other reasons the nuns destined for Caravaca were brought to the Seville foundation.

6 On March 10, 1575.

7 In no. 1.

8 Teresa's letter to Philip II has been lost, but the royal dispatch bearing the date June 9, 1575, is still conserved (see BMC 6: 257–262), as is also Teresa's grateful reply in a letter dated July 19, 1575.

9 In ch. 24, nos. 3–4. She left on May 18.

10 Ana de Alberto (Salcedo) (d. 1624), a native of Malagón, who was one of the first to be professed there. She accompanied Teresa from Malagón to Beas and Seville and from the latter went to Caravaca. At Caravaca she met St. John of the Cross and became one of his spiritual daughters.

11 Ambrosio de San Pedro (d.c. 1593), a native of Pastrana who was at the time vicar of Almodóvar del Campo, and Miguel de la Columna, not a Father but a lay Brother who was later to cause some trouble by signing a slanderous statement claiming that Gracián was living a depraved life. He later declared that he had not read a word of the statement and had been pressured into signing it by Fray Baltasar de Jesús (Nieto), Jerónimo Tostado, and others.

12 They arrived in Caravaca December 18, 1575. The Blessed Sacrament was reserved January 1, 1576 (see chapter heading).

13 This was Francisca de Saojosa, who later, though, was accepted through the intervention of Fr. Gracián and made profession June 1, 1578.

14 Lorenzo de Cepeda (see ch. 25, no. 3).

15 Thinking this would be the end of her book, Teresa left some blank spaces as though what was to follow would serve as an epilogue to what she had written.

16 1 K. 19:2–5 {3 K. 19:2–5}.

17 Gregorio Martínez y López who took the name Gregorio Nacianceno (see ch. 24, no.5).

18 See ch. 21, no. 2; ch. 22, no. 2, and ch. 24, no. 20. She is referring probably to the patent of April 6, 1571 (See MHCT 1:110–112).

19 She is referring to the general chapter at Piacenza in Italy, celebrated under the presidency of Father Rubeo in May and June of 1575. The definitory of the chapter imposed on Teresa the command to retire definitively to a monastery in Castile and not go out to make any new foundations. Teresa wanted to submit to this order immediately, but Father Gracián prevented this. As apostolic visitator, he held jurisdiction independent of the superior general. In the acts of the chapter there is no record of this order imposed on the Saint.

20 Teresa uses this term "accidental joy" in the theological sense of her time, but with a very original application. Accidental joy was that joy experienced by the blessed in heaven that did not flow directly from their vision of God.

21 Allusion to 2 Sm 6, 14–15 {2 K. 6, 14–15}.

22 She leaves another space of one or two lines and then concludes with the following colophon.

23 In the prologue, no. 2.

24 In view of the circumstances, Teresa thought that her work of founding new monasteries had come to an end.

Chapter 28

1 Neither this chapter nor those that follow were numbered by Teresa. At the close of the preceding chapter she inserted the four counsels given her by the Lord for her Carmelite Fathers. Editors usually omit them because they are not a part of this work. See *Spiritual Testimonies*, 64.

2   The foundation in Seville was made in 1575–1576; the present foundation was made in 1580.

3   The word "almost" was inserted by Teresa between the lines.

4   Father Juan Bautisa Rubeo; see ch. 2.

5   She is alluding to Frs. Pedro Fernández and Francisco Vargas, O. P., named visitators by Pius V in 1569, and to Fr. Gracián, delegate of the latter (1573) and confirmed in his office by the nuncio Ormaneto (1574).

6   The "holy nuncio" was Nicolás Ormaneto who died in Madrid June 18, 1577. His successor, Felipe Sega (c. 1537–1596) came to Spain (Aug. 30, 1577) badly disposed toward Teresa and her work because of misinformation he had received in Rome prior to his departure. He was in fact a relative of Cardinal Filippo Buoncompagni, Cardinal protector of the Carmelites and nephew of Pope Gregory XIII. Thus, Teresa says the new nuncio was a distant relative of the pope.

7   One of Teresa's ways of referring to the Carmelites of the Observance; cf. ch. 13, no. 1.

8   In a brief dated October 18, 1578, Sega placed the discalced friars and nuns under the authority of the Carmelite provincials of Castile and Andalusia.

9   Allusion to Jon 1:4–15.

10 The four counselors were: Don Luis Manrique, the king's chaplain and major almoner; Fray Lorenzo de Villavicencio, an Augustinian; and the Dominicans, Hernando del Castillo and Pedro Fernández. On April 1, 1579, they nullified the authority of the provincials over the discalced friars and nuns and appointed in their place as vicar general Teresa's former provincial, Fr. Angel de Salazar.

11 Agustín de Ervías was a learned canon of Cuenco, who exchanged his office for parish priest of Villanueva de la Jara because of his desire for the care of souls.

12 Alonso Velázquez (d. 1587), after spending some years as professor at the University of Alcalá, was made a canon of Toledo, where he became Teresa's confessor and advisor. He was later appointed bishop of Osma, and then, archbishop of Santiago. See *Spir. Test.*, 65.

13 She is alluding to the punishment imposed by Sega; see no. 4. This monastery near La Roda was founded in 1572.

14 Gabriel de la Asunción (1544–1584) was a native of Pastrana and much esteemed by the prince and Princess of Eboli. As prior he governed the monastery at la Roda from 1576–1580 and there acted as spiritual director of Catalina de Cardona.

15 She arrived in Malagón Nov. 25, 1579.

16 From Toledo she chose María de los Mártires (for prioress) and Constanza de la Cruz; from Malagón, Elvira de San Angelo (for subprioress) and Ana de San Agustín.

17 In no. 11.

18 Allusion to 1 K. 19:9–13 {3 K. 19:9–13}.

19 Catalina de Cardona (1519–1577) who arranged for the foundation of this monastery died May 11, 1577.

20 Catalina de Cardona had been governess to Don Juan de Austria, son of Charles V, and to Don Carlos, son of Philip II. In 1563 she withdrew to the solitude of La Roda, and in 1571 began to wear the Carmelite habit, but with the friar's cowl.

21 The hermit's name was Fr. Piña, and he had his hermitage on the mount of La Vera Cruz.

22 "or other things" was added between the lines by Teresa.

23 "a woman" was added in the margin by Teresa.

24 The Carmelite nuns in Toledo; see no. 26.

25 Teresa wrote "Mercenarians." They were, in fact, the Trinitarians at Fuensanta.

26 The part about the tunic was added between the lines by Teresa.

27 This took place May 6, 1571. The habit was given by the prior, Fr. Baltasar de Jesús, in the presence of the prince and Princess of Eboli.

28 In ch. 17, nos. 6–15.

29 The tomb (sepulcher) included a carved representation of the dead Christ surrounded by His Mother and others.

30 Gracián crossed out the "Fray" and wrote "Don."

31 In no. 20.

32 Gabriel de la Asunción; see no. 11.

33 February 21.

34 See no. 8.

35 A *beata* was a woman who wore a religious habit and lived a pious Christian life without belonging to any religious order.

36 The origin of this group of *beatas* was a hermitess named Catalina de Cardona, who lived in a cave only a few miles from Villanueva de la Jara. She was attracted to Carmelite spirituality. She "received the habit of our Lady of Mt. Carmel" (F. 28. 30.) at the hands of the Discalced Carmelite friars in Pastrana, and her spiritual directors were Discalced Friars from the nearby monastery in La Roda. Her holy life inspired these nine women to band together and live a holy life, which they did by living in a small house abutting St. Anne's shrine in Villanueva de la Jara. When Catalina de Cardona died in 1577, these nine women needed guidance. Since Catalina was a Carmelite in spirit, they decided to appeal to Teresa to become Carmelite nuns.

Chapter 29

1 The monogram IHS precedes the chapter title. The chapter number was omitted. The feast of King David was celebrated December 29.

2 The major superior (vicar general) was Fr. Angel de Salazar. See ch. 28, no. 6.

3 See *Life*, ch. 36, no. 2. Don Alvaro de Mendoza had been appointed bishop of Palencia June 28, 1577.

4 August 8, 1580. The previous March, Teresa became a victim of what was called the "universal influenza," a virus that swept through and leveled Spain that year.

5 The prioress was María Bautista de Ocampo (see ch. 1, no. 3). A native of Toledo, she was the daughter of Teresa's cousin. At the age of eighteen, she was taken by Teresa to live at the Incarnation and was the first to suggest the founding of a new monastery (see *Life*, ch. 32, no. 10). She became a discalced nun at St. Joseph's and was one of the two from St. Joseph's to accompany Teresa on the second foundation of Medina. In 1568, she transferred to Valladolid and in 1571 became prioress there. She was one of Teresa's most frequent correspondents. But in her last days she sided with the mother-in-law of Teresa's nephew Don Francisco de Cepeda who was contesting the inheritance left to St. Joseph's

in Avila by Teresa's brother Lorenzo. According to Blessed Anne of St. Bartholomew, Teresa in her last visit to Valladolid shortly before her death was treated rudely by the prioress María Bautista on account of this family dispute over the inheritance.

6   It was he who encouraged Teresa to write about her foundations; see prologue, no. 2.

7   See ch. 3, no. 1 and no. 3.

8   In no. 1.

9   December 28, 1580.

10   Jerónimo Reinoso (1546–1600), from then on a close friend of Teresa's.

11   The first, Porras, was confessor to the Carmelite nuns in Valladolid. The second, Agustín de Victoria, was a benefactor of the nuns in Valladolid and had a daughter who was a member of the community, María de San Agustín. Also accompanying Teresa from Valladolid to Palencia was Fr. Gracián.

12   This lay Sister was Blessed Anne of St. Bartholomew (1549–1626). Having entered St. Joseph's in Avila, she learned to write in order to serve as secretary to Teresa. After Teresa broke her arm on Christmas Eve, 1577, Blessed Anne accompanied her on her journeys, nursed her in her illnesses and was with her when she died. Eventually Blessed Anne went to France with a group of Sisters to make foundations there. She became a choir Sister and later prioress. She founded convents at Tours (1608) and at Antwerp (1612) where she remained till her death. Her autobiography and numerous letters have been published. The other four nuns were: Inés de Jesús (Tapia), a cousin of Teresa's; Catalina del Espíritu Santo; María de San Bernardo; and Juana de San Francisco.

13   Martín Alonso Salinas (d. 1592).

14   In no. 11.

15   Suero de Vega was the son of Juan de Vega, who had been viceroy of Navarra and Sicily and president of the royal council. One of his sons became a discalced Carmelite, Juan de la Madre de Dios.

16   In no. 14.

17   In nos. 15–16.

18 He was thirty-five at the time.

19 The messenger who would be sent by the owner to negotiate the contract (see no. 16).

20 Allusion to Jn 9:6–7.

21 In nos. 14, 15, 23.

22 The administrator for the bishop was Don Prudencio Armentia; he was also a canon of the Palencia cathedral.

23 May 26, 1581.

24 The brief, *Pia consideratione*, given by Gregory XIII on June 22, 1580. See MHCT 2:191–207.

25 This chapter took place in March of 1581. St. John of the Cross was elected a provincial counselor. For the full documents, see MHCT 2:236–316.

Chapter 30

1 June 14, 1581. In Teresa's time it was generally believed among Carmelites that the prophets Elijah and Elisha often dwelt on Mt. Carmel and that saintly men continued to live there in solitude. These hermits, living in the spirit of the prophets, were later converted by the preaching of the apostles. On one side of the mountain, they then built a church or oratory in honor of our Lady. Thus, according to this tradition, they were the first among all religious orders to be called children of the Blessed Mary of Mount Carmel. Following this version of the order's beginnings which was the accepted one in her time, Teresa as with Elijah refers to Elisha as our Father St. Elisha. Cf. ch. 27, no. 17; ch. 28, no. 20.

2 See ch. 28, no. 10.

3 Beatriz de Beamonte y Navarra (d. 1600) also contributed generously to the foundation of a Carmel in Pamplona in 1583. There she entered as a nun and took the name Beatriz de Cristo.

4 This endowment was a generous one. Twenty-five per thousand would be the equivalent of 2.5% since sums were expressed in proportions of one thousand rather than one hundred (per cent) so as to avoid decimal percentages.

5 The church was originally named Our Lady of the Villas, but Doña Beatriz had the name changed to Blessed Trinity.

6   Fr. Gracián who was then in the city of Palencia.

7   In no. 2.

8   The seven nuns were: Catalina de Cristo (elected prioress on June 15), Beatriz de Jesús, María de Cristo, Juana Bautista, María de Jesús, María de San José, and Catalina del Espíritu Santo. The lay Sister was María Bautista. Teresa's companion was her nurse and secretary, Blessed Anne of St. Bartholomew. Accompanying this group of nuns were: Fr. Nicolás Doria and Brother Eliseo de la Madre de Dios; Pedro de Ribera (of whom Teresa speaks in nos. 12–13) sent by Don Alvaro de Mendoza; a chaplain by the name of Chacón and a police officer for security, both provided by the bishop of Burgo de Osma; and finally Francisco de Cetina, a chaplain sent by Doña Beatriz.

9   Nicolás de Jesús María (Doria) (1539–1594), born in Genoa, spent his early life as a banker. Arriving in Spain in 1570, he settled in Seville, but then sacrificed his future in finance for the religious life, taking the discalced Carmelite habit in 1577. In 1585, he was elected provincial at the chapter in Lisbon. His interference in the governing of the discalced nuns put him in opposition with Fr. Gracián and St. John of the Cross. He secured the expulsion of Gracián from the order in 1592. In 1593 he attended the general chapter in Cremona in which the separation of the two branches of Carmelites was approved. He died in Alcalá de Henares while holding the office of General.

10 She is alluding to the adage, "For want of good men, my husband was mayor."

11 May 31, 1581.

12 Not only did he give her his blessing, but, as did the archbishop of Seville, he afterward made the Saint give him her blessing.

13 Teresa herself supervised this work.

14 See no. 1.

15 August 6.

16 The Jesuit Father was Francisco de la Carrera.

17 In no. 2.

18 In the autograph the word "penitential" is followed by the word "and" and then a long, blank space is left as though Teresa had intended to add something.

19 She left Soria on August 16.

20 See no. 8.

21 Blessed Anne of St. Bartholomew.

22 August 23.

23 Charles Dickens, *Great Expectations* (New York: Penguin Books, 1996), 224.

Chapter 31

1 This chapter (without a number in the orginal manuscript) was written in Burgos the last days of June (cf. no. 17) at a time in which Teresa's health was very poor. The more than average number of misspellings, repetitions, and obscure or ambiguous constructions point to Teresa's weakened and exhausted condition, although the account itself is a very lively one.

2 An Avilan, his name was Don Cristóbal Vela (d. 1599). His father Blasco Nuñez Vela, was the viceroy of Peru under whose orders two of Teresa's brothers fought against Pizarro. Both the viceroy and Teresa's brother Antonio died in the battle of Iñaquito in 1546. Francisco Nuñez Vela, the viceroy's brother, was Teresa's godfather. Don Cristobal was bishop in the Canary Islands from 1575 to 1580 when he was appointed archbishop of Burgos. There he remained until his death.

3 See ch. 29, nos. 1, 11, 27; ch. 2, no. 5; cf. ch. 10, no. 6; 13, no. 6; 17, no. 11.

4 The monastery, today in ruins, was better known as Our Lady del Prado and located outside the city.

5 He received the pallium, which is worn at certain times by archbishops.

6 She is referring to the Council of Trent. See Session 25, *De reformatione regularium*, ch. 3.

7 See ch. 29, no. 1. She is referring to the influenza she contracted in Toledo and from which she suffered a relapse in Valladolid.

8 In ch. 29, no. 6.

9 In ch. 29, no. 6.

10 In the orginal she mistakenly wrote Soria instead of Burgos.

11 See *Life*, ch. 36, nos. 15–17.

12 Teresa had to return to Avila because of some difficulties in the community with regard to certain minor abuses in the

observance of poverty and abstinence and also because of the community's financial problems. The prioress, María de Cristo, renounced her office, and Teresa was elected prioress. In her letter of Nov. 8, 1581, she wrote to María de San José, "they have now made me prioress out of pure hunger."

13 Catalina de Tolosa (1538–1608), the widow of Sebastián Muncharez, had seven children who entered Teresa's Carmel. Two daughters were professed in Valladolid, Catalina de la Asunción and Casilda de San Angelo; two in Palencia, María de San José and Isabel de la Trinidad; and one in Burgos, Elena de Jesús. Her two sons became discalced Carmelite priests, Sebastián de Jesús, provincial of Castile 1603–1606, and Juan Crisóstomo, later a professor at Salamanca college. In her fiftieth year, Catalina herself entered the Carmel in Palencia.

14 In no. 7.

15 In ch. 30, nos. 13–14.

16 Inés de Jesús (d. 1601), a cousin of Teresa's, had been professed at the Incarnation in Avila and became the first prioress at Medina del Campo. In 1580, she went with Teresa to the new foundation in Palencia where she became prioress.

17 The words of our Lord in the autograph are enclosed within variously shaped strokes of the pen and thereby highlighted.

18 Catalina Manrique (see no. 10). These letters were received by Teresa in Avila on November 29.

19 The Minims of St. Francis de Paula.

20 In Alcalá on April 9, 1581, Fr. Gracián had already given the license for the foundation.

21 This wagon was the one in which Teresa was riding.

22 They were: Tomasina Bautista (prioress), Inés de la Cruz, Catalina de Jesús, Catalina de la Asunción (daughter of Doña Catalina de Tolosa), and María Bautista, a white veiled nun. The two who were to return with Teresa were Blessed Anne of St. Bartholomew and Teresa's niece Teresita.

23 She mentioned this in ch. 29, no. 30.

24 Cf. ch. 29, no. 1.

25 The holy crucifix was venerated at the time in the monastery of the Augustinians and is now in the Cathedral of Burgos.

26 In ch. 29, no. 12.
27 Cf. no. 15.
28 In nos. 18–19.
29 Pedro Manso had been a classmate of Gracián's at the University of Alcalá. He served as Teresa's confessor when Gracián left Burgos. He was later appointed bishop of Calahorra (1594) where he brought the discalced Carmelite nuns (1598) and friars (1603).
30 The church of San Gil.
31 To Valladolid; see no. 31.
32 Hernando de Matanza was the city magistrate and the mayor's brother. Francisco de Cuevas had been a member of the court of Charles V and was married to the Toledan writer Luisa Sigea de Valasco.
33 In nos. 26–27.
34 In no. 26.
35 Pedro Manso (cf. no. 24) and Antonio Aguiar (cf. no. 33).
36 That is, from Feb. 23 to March 18.
37 Doctor Antonio Aguiar, a physician, had been a classmate of Gracián's at the University of Alcalá. Teresa had not yet mentioned him specifically (cf. nos. 23, 25, 33).
38 The owner was Dori Manuel Franco. There were two priests given the authorization to sell: Diego Ruiz de Ayala and Martín Pérez de Rozas.
39 That is, one of those authorized to sell.
40 Juan Ortega de la Torre y Frias.
41 The sale was finalized March 16, 1582. The nuns moved in March 18.
42 The price was 1,290 ducats.
43 In nos. 32 and 34.
44 Jerónimo del Pino and his wife Magdalena Solórzano.
45 In no. 24.
46 The church and hospital of San Lucas, a few yards from the houses bought by Teresa.
47 The license is dated April 18, 1582.
48 See Jn 4:7–15.
49 Fr. Gracián had returned from Valladolid.
50 Elena de Jesús who because of her young age did not make profession until June 5, 1586 (cf. no. 12).

51 Elena de Jesús received the habit from him April 20. Not only did the archbishop preside at the ceremony but he also preached and publicly accused himself for not having given the license earlier and asked pardon for what he had made Teresa and her nuns go through. See BMC 2:328.

52 St. John Climacus, *The Ladder of Divine Ascent*, trans. Colm Luibheid and Norman Russell (New York: Paulist Press, 1982), 146.

53 St. John of the Cross, "The Ascent of Mount Carmel" in *The Collected Works of St. John of the Cross*, trans. Kieran Kavanaugh, O.C.D., and Otilio Rodriguez, O.C.D. (Washington, D.C.: ICS Publications, 1991), 161.

Epilogue

1 In *Life*, chs. 32–36.

2 See *Life*, ch. 33, no. 16.

3 Actually, it lasted fifteen years, from 1562 to 1577.

4 He was appointed bishop of Palencia June 28, 1577. Before mid-July, Teresa had left Toledo for Avila. On August 2, Don Alvaro made the transfer of jurisdiction legal. See MHCT 1:365.

5 Cf. *Life*, ch. 33, no. 16.

6 Alonso Velázquez. Cf. ch. 28, no. 10 and no. 12.

7 Quoted from *St. Teresa of Avila* by Stephen Clissold (Westminster: Christian Classics, 1979), 247.

Biblical Index

The Institute of Carmelite Studies promotes research and publication in the field of Carmelite spirituality. Its members are Discalced Carmelites, part of a Roman Catholic community—friars, nuns, and laity—who are heirs to the teaching and way of life of Teresa of Jesus and John of the Cross, men and women dedicated to contemplation and to ministry in the Church and the world. Information concerning their way of life is available through local diocesan Vocation Offices or from the Vocation Directors' Offices:

1233 S. 45th Street, Milwaukee, WI 53214

1 Fallons Lane 1628 London, ON, Canada N6A 4C1

P.O. Box 3420, San Jose, CA 95156-3420

5151 Marylake Drive, Little Rock, AR 72206